Confronting Vietnam

INTERNATIONAL HISTORY
PROJECT SERIES

James G. Hershberg
series editor

Brothers in Arms
The Rise and Fall of the Sino-Soviet Alliance, 1945–1963
edited by Odd Arne Westad

Economic Cold War
America's Embargo against China and the Sino-Soviet Alliance, 1949–1963
By Shu Guang Zhang

WOODROW WILSON CENTER PRESS
STANFORD UNIVERSITY PRESS

CONFRONTING VIETNAM

Soviet Policy toward the Indochina Conflict,
1954–1963

Ilya V. Gaiduk

Woodrow Wilson Center Press
Washington, D.C.

Stanford University Press
Stanford, California

EDITORIAL OFFICES:
The Woodrow Wilson Center Press
One Woodrow Wilson Plaza
1300 Pennsylvania Avenue, N.W.
Washington, D.C. 20004-3027
Telephone 202-691-4029
www.wilsoncenter.org

ORDER FROM:
Stanford University Press
Chicago Distribution Center
11030 South Langley Avenue
Chicago, Ill. 60628
Telephone 1-800-621-2736; 773-568-1550

Library of Congress Cataloging-in-Publication Data

Gaiduk, I. V. (Il'ia V.), 1961-
    Confronting Vietnam: Soviet policy toward the Indochina Conflict,
1954–1963 / Ilya V. Gaiduk.
        p. cm.—(Cold War International History Project series)
Includes bibliographical references and index.
    ISBN 0-8047-4712-1 (alk. paper)
    1. Indochina—Foreign relations—Soviet Union. 2. Soviet
Union—Foreign relations—Indochina. 3. Soviet Union—Foreign
relations—1953–1975. 4. Vietnamese Conflict, 1961–1975—Soviet Union.
I. Title. II. Series.
    DS546.5.S65 G35 2003
    959.704'3347—dc21
                                2002155618

For my mother

ABOUT THE CENTER

The Center is the living memorial of the United States of America to the nation's twenty-eighth president, Woodrow Wilson. Congress established the Woodrow Wilson Center in 1968 as an international institute for advanced study, "symbolizing and strengthening the fruitful relationship between the world of learning and the world of public affairs." The Center opened in 1970 under its own board of trustees.

In all its activities the Woodrow Wilson Center is a nonprofit, nonpartisan organization, supported financially by annual appropriations from the Congress, and by the contributions of foundations, corporations, and individuals. Conclusions or opinions expressed in Center publications and programs are those of the authors and speakers and do not necessarily reflect the views of the Center staff, fellows, trustees, advisory groups, or any individual or organizations that provide financial support to the center.

The Cold War International History Project

The Cold War International History Project was established by the Woodrow Wilson International Center for Scholars in 1991. The project supports the full and prompt release of historical materials by governments on all sides of the Cold War and seeks to disseminate new information and perspectives on Cold War history emerging from previously inaccessible sources on "the other side"—the former Communist bloc—through publications, fellowships, and scholarly meetings and conferences. The project publishes the *Cold War International History Project Bulletin* and a working paper series and maintains a website, cwihp.si.edu.

In collaboration with the National Security Archive, a nongovernmental research institute and document repository located at George Washington University, the project has created a Russian and East-bloc Archival Documents Database at Gelman Library, George Washington University. The database makes available to scholars photocopies from Russian and other former Communist archives donated by the project, the National Security Archive, and various scholars. The database may be explored through a computer-searchable English-language inventory. For further information, contact the National Security Archive, Gelman Library, George Washington University, Washington, D.C. 20037.

At the Woodrow Wilson Center, the project is part of the Division of International Studies, headed by Robert S. Litwak. The director of the project is Christian F. Ostermann. The project is overseen by an advisory committee that is chaired by William Taubman, Amherst College, and includes Michael Beschloss; James H. Billington, librarian of Congress; Warren I. Cohen, University of Maryland at Baltimore; John Lewis Gaddis, Yale University; James G. Hershberg, George Washington University; Samuel F. Wells, Jr., associate director of the Woodrow Wilson Center; and Sharon Wolchik, George Washington University.

The Cold War International History Project was created with the help of the John D. and Catherine T. MacArthur Foundation.

Contents

AVPRF	Archive of Foreign Policy of the Russian Federation
CC	Central Committee
CCP	Chinese Communist Party
CDNI	Committee for the Defense of National Interests, Laos
CIA	Central Intelligence Agency
CPSU	Communist Party of the Soviet Union
DMZ	Demilitarized zone
DRV	Democratic Republic of Vietnam
FO	Foreign Office (Great Britain)
FRUS	Foreign Relations of the United States
ICC	International Commission for Supervision and Control, sometimes called International Control Commission
KGB	Committee on State Security (Russian acronym)
MAAG	Military Assistance Advisory Group
NATO	North Atlantic Treaty Organization
NLHX	Neo Lao Hak Xat, Lao Patriotic Front
NLFSV	National Liberation Front of South Vietnam
Pathet Lao	Movement "Lao Nation"
PAV	People's Army of Vietnam
PRC	People's Republic of China
PRO	Public Record Office (Great Britain)
RLG	Royal Lao Government
RGANI	Russian State Archive of Contemporary History
RGASPI	Russian State Archive of Social-Political History
SEATO	Southeast Asia Treaty Organization
USSR	Union of Soviet Socialist Republics
Vietcong	Viet Nam Cong San (Vietnamese Communists), People's Liberation Army in South Vietnam
Vietminh	Viet Nam Doc Lap Dong Minh, League for Independence of Vietnam
WPV	Workers' Party of Vietnam, also called the Lao Dong Party

Series Preface

James G. Hershberg

Few, if any, Cold War events convulsed U.S. politics and society, or wreaked greater devastation and inflicted greater suffering on a region of the world, more than the Vietnam War and related conflicts in Southeast Asia. There, in the decades after World War II, the twin dramas of decolonization and East-West hostility intersected violently. In their public pronouncements, successive American presidents, from Truman to Eisenhower, Kennedy, Johnson, and Nixon, justified American involvement (first in support of the French and then in replacing them), military engagement, and the ensuing sacrifice of lives and treasure, on the grounds that the struggle represented a crucial battleground in the global confrontation with world communism led by the Soviet Union. And yet, behind the scenes, experts puzzled at the true nature of the Kremlin's relationship with Ho Chi Minh's Vietnamese communist regime and argued over Moscow's motives, objectives, and capabilities to influence the course of events, especially in the context of its evolving relationship with its communist ally-turned rival, the People's Republic of China.

In his first book, *The Soviet Union and the Vietnam War* (1996),[1] Russian scholar Ilya V. Gaiduk drew upon previously unavailable Moscow archives to offer a fresh account of the communist superpower's involvement at the height of what Vietnamese call the "American" or "Second Indochinese" war, from 1964, when the Tonkin Gulf incident heralded the deepening of direct U.S. military engagement, through the years of blood leading to Washington's departure and defeat a decade later. Together with equally groundbreaking works on China's policies and actions in relation to the Vietnam War,[2] Gaiduk's book marked a breakthrough in clarifying the murky tale of how intra-communist politics and relations affected, and were affected by, the evolution of the war.

Gaiduk's current volume, *Confronting Vietnam: Soviet Policy toward the Indochina Conflict, 1954–1963,* both constitutes an essential prequel to his earlier work—and therefore to an understanding of the origins of America's full-scale military entry into the Vietnam "quagmire" and the validity, or lack of

James G. Hershberg is associate professor of history and international affairs at George Washington University and editor of the Cold War International History Project Series. From 1991 to 1997 he was the first director of the Cold War International History Project at the Woodrow Wilson International Center for Scholars.

same, of Washington's perceptions of the Soviet role there—and a comparably trail-blazing contribution to understanding the tangled history of the Cold War in Southeast Asia during earlier crises. These range from the latter stages of the French colonial war to the world crisis over Laos (which, few remember, aroused President Kennedy's fears regarding the region far more than Vietnam when he first took office) and include the high-stakes Geneva conferences to deal with both (in 1954 and 1961–62, respectively). Not only has Gaiduk gone where no analyst has gone before in tackling this story in a historically rigorous fashion, but he has, if anything, been even more successful than in his prior work in excavating crucial materials from the Soviet archives, despite considerable practical obstacles, and combining these sources with the results of prior historiography and of extensive work in U.S. and British repositories, among other materials.

The result is a tremendously exciting and original work that brings to light fresh information and insights to area specialists and general Cold War historians alike, gathering a vast amount of hard-earned data in well-organized and engaging narrative. Anyone interested in the conflicts in Southeast Asia or in Soviet foreign policy, Sino-Soviet relations, or U.S.-Soviet relations during the Stalin and Khrushchev eras will find *Confronting Vietnam* must reading. Moreover, it also serves as a useful case study in several broader contexts: the history of the international communist movement and of nationalist-revolutionary movements; the difficulties and vicissitudes of Soviet "alliance management" (which frequently seems to be as much of a misnomer as "crisis management" sometimes was when that term was fashionable); international diplomacy, particularly in the revelations on the communist sides of the Geneva gatherings and often difficult ties between Moscow and Hanoi; and as a test case for "pericentrism," the argument that, in the new Cold War international history, historians must pay increased attention to the actions of smaller countries in explaining the outcomes and dynamics of vital international events rather than simply presuming that they were determined by decisions made in superpower capitals.[3] Also, in the lamentable absence of access to crucial Vietnamese foreign policy archives for this period, one may hope that this work as well as others exploiting communist archives will contribute to the efforts of scholars, both Vietnamese and foreign, to persuade Hanoi authorities to open further their historical repositories so that their country's international relations are not reconstructed solely on the basis of other nation's sources.[4]

As editor of the Cold War International History Project Series, and as former director of the project, I consider it is a special pleasure to publish Ilya Gaiduk's work. When the project first organized a conference on Soviet foreign policy during the Cold War, which took place in a frigid Moscow in January 1993, one of the highlights was Gaiduk's paper on the Vietnam War, based on materials from the archives of the Central Committee of the Communist Party of the Soviet Union in the old CC headquarters in Staraya Ploschad (Old Square) and co-written with an archivist who had helped gather the materials. Then a young scholar at the Institute of General History of the Russian (former Soviet) Academy of Sciences specializing on the history of Soviet-American relations, Gaiduk had taken on the task of preparing the report despite lacking any prior experience working on the Vietnam War. (All other Russian historians lacked such experience, too, since the topic had previously been considered too sensitive for serious research.) All of the papers at the conference were unprecedented in their use of Soviet archival materials—past conferences, even during Gorbachev's glasnost, had featured the absurd situation of Russian historians using Western sources and archives, combined with public Soviet sources, on Moscow's foreign policy—but Gaiduk's paper was especially eyebrow-raising for its revelations of tensions between Moscow and Hanoi even at the height of cooperation during the war against Washington.[5] Following the conference, Gaiduk joined the first group of Cold War International History Project fellows, young scholars from former communist countries, to spend the first half of 1993 in Washington, D.C., which gave him an opportunity to expand his research on the topic to American collections such as the Harriman Papers at the Library of Congress and the Lyndon B. Johnson Library in Texas, and to establish fraternal ties with U.S.-based Vietnam specialists.

In the succeeding years Gaiduk's career and work have put him at the forefront of the "next generation" of Cold War scholars to emerge from the communist bloc, epitomizing the multi-archival, multi-national, multi-lingual research and writing that the end of the superpower rivalry has made possible. Striving tenaciously to overcome the frustrations of archival research in Moscow, presenting his work at international conferences, utilizing archives in the United States and Britain and establishing ties with Vietnamese colleagues, obtaining and taking advantage of prestigious fellowships in at the Norwegian Nobel Institute in Oslo and the Wilson Center and its Kennan Institute in Washington, all the while dealing personally with the travails of an ongoing economic and political crisis in Russia, he has, in effect, single-handedly created a Russian field of scholarly studies on the Indochina conflict, and in so doing brought to an international audience long-hidden chapters of that tragic history. Though, as he would be the first to acknowledge, important materials remain elusive, particularly in closed files in Hanoi and in the Presidential Archives in Moscow, Gaiduk's work now offers a unique and compelling window on the Soviet and communist dimension of one of the Cold War's most fateful—and fatal—stories, and provides a new point of departure for further investigations.

Notes

1. Ilya V. Gaiduk, *The Soviet Union and the Vietnam War* (Chicago: Ivan R. Dee, 1996).

2. See, for example, Zhai Qiang, *China and the Vietnam Wars, 1950–1975* (Chapel Hill, N.C.: University of North Carolina Press, 2000); Zhai Qiang, "Beijing and the Vietnam Peace Talks, 1965–1968: New Evidence from Chinese Sources," CWIHP Working Paper no. 18 (Washington, D.C.: Wilson Center, 1997); Chen Jian, *Mao's China and the Cold War* (Chapel Hill, N.C.: University of North Carolina Press, 2001), chaps. 5, 8; Odd Arne Westad, Chen Jian, Stein Tonnesson, Nguyen Vu Tung, and James G. Hershberg, eds., "77 Conversations between Chinese and Foreign Leaders on the Wars in Indochina, 1964–1977," CWIHP Working Paper no. 22 (Washington, D.C.: Wilson Center, 1998); and Yang Kuisong, "Changes in Mao Zedong's Attitude towards the Indochina War, 1949–1973," CWIHP Working Paper no. 34 (Washington, D.C.: Wilson Center, 2001).

3. Tony Smith, "New Bottles for New Wine: A Pericentric Framework for the Study of the Cold War," *Diplomatic History,* vol. 24, no. 4 (Fall 2000), pp. 567–591.

4. A limited number of scholars, such as David Marr, Robert Brigham, Nguyen Vu Tung, and Mark Bradley, have begun to tap Vietnamese archives and sources on the post-World War II period and the conflicts with France and the United States, and a number of oral history conferences on the war have taken place, but there has been a lack of extensive access to Foreign Ministry or Vietnamese Workers' Party (Lao Dong) archives or secret materials related to international relations. See, e.g., Frederik Logevall, "Bringing in the 'Other Side': New Scholarship on the Vietnam Wars," *Journal of Cold War Studies,* vol. 3, no. 3 (Fall 2001), pp. 77–93, and, on the oral history conferences, Robert S. McNamara, James G. Blight, and Robert K. Brigham, with Thomas J. Biersteker and Col. Herbert Y. Schlander (ret.), *Argument without End: In Search of Answers to the Vietnam Tragedy* (New York: Public Affairs, 1999).

5. For a revised version of this conference paper, see Ilya V. Gaiduk, "The Vietnam War and Soviet-American Relations, 1964–1973," in *CWIHP Bulletin* 6–7 (Winter 1995/1996).

Preface

Wann? Wie? und Wo? das ist die leidige Frage.

J. W. Goethe
Faust, II, 5

Arnold Toynbee pointed to curiosity as a driving force of a historian's activity.[1] Curiosity leads people who devote their lives to the study of the past to penetrate the time and understand origins of events, consequences of upheavals, and implications of the processes that took place many years ago. Historians very often purposefully move backwards, deeper and deeper into the past, from the event to its precursor, trying to find an explanation for what happened later and why.

After I completed my book on Soviet policy toward the Vietnam War,[2] I understandably decided to begin studying what preceded the war, the U.S. military involvement, the Soviet attitude toward the processes that led to the war's outcome, and the reason that the Soviet Union—which always expressed its apprehension about the danger of war in Southeast Asia—and other countries were not able to avert it. My interest in the period before 1964 was also stimulated by some reviews of my earlier book, reviews that said the book lacked coverage of the events that took place in the earlier period and questioned the conception of the book on the grounds that it was impossible to understand the rationale for Soviet policy toward the war in Vietnam without an analysis of the earlier period.[3] Although I maintain the view that the period after 1964 represents a totally new phase of the Vietnamese conflict and should be studied in its own right, I felt that without an exploration into the background of the Vietnam War my study of Soviet policy toward the conflict in Indochina that took place after the French had exited would be incomplete.

Thus, curiosity together with a desire to answer my critics became the two factors that led me to feel the need to write a second book on the Soviet Union and Vietnam. It is fortunate that, unlike for the post-1964 period, archival sources on the earlier years were much better. Most of the Russian archival documents that deal with the events of the Vietnamese crisis in the 1950s and early 1960s have been declassified and made available to scholars. Although documents located in the archive of the Russian foreign ministry are being declassified in Russia more slowly than scholars prefer, by the time I started work on this book, a large collection of Soviet diplomatic documents on the conflict in Indochina had been opened in the Archive of Foreign Policy of the Russian Federation. Among those documents are memoranda of conversations between Soviet and foreign leaders and diplomats in various countries, analytical information and reports from USSR diplomatic missions abroad addressed to Moscow, letters and reviews prepared by various foreign ministry departments for the minister and his deputies, as well as the ministry's correspondence with the Central Committee of the Communist Party of the Soviet Union and other bodies of the government.

An important supplement to Soviet foreign policy documents is located in the former CPSU Central Committee archive, which was recently renamed in the Russian State Archive of Contemporary History. In addition to information and memoranda prepared by the Soviet embassies in Vietnam and Laos, the archive provides access to annual embassy reports. I also found in this archive some of the documents that were missing from the Foreign Ministry's archive.

Unfortunately the doors of the presidential archive remain tightly closed for the overwhelming majority of scholars, and therefore the Soviet Politburo's decisions and records of conversations of the Soviet leaders mainly with their Communist colleagues are still inaccessible to historians. An exception has been made only for the part of the so-called Stalin collection that was moved to another former Communist Party archive that is now known as the Russian State Archive of Social Political History. It is in this archive that I was able to find several important documents on Soviet-Vietminh relations from the early 1950s and Stalin's attitude toward revolutionary movements in Asia and, in particular, in Vietnam. The lack of documents from the highest levels of Soviet decision making has been more or less covered by the findings in other Russian archives where the collections contain evidence on the Kremlin's decisions, as well as in other countries' archival collections and publications of documents that are valuable mainly as sources on Soviet leaders' meetings and conversations with their Western counterparts. For this book, I found such sources in the United States, Great Britain, and France (in France, mainly in published collections).

After the 1996 publication of my earlier book on the Vietnam War, a large number of studies of this war came to light, primarily in the United States. Unlike the works that were published before, with their emphasis on the U.S. role in the conflict, the newer studies concentrated on the involvement of other countries in that region. The recent studies have marked the birth of the truly international history of the Vietnam War, the foundation of which was laid down by the books of British scholar R. B. Smith.[4] In 1998, a volume on the Vietnam War was published by Macmillan that comprised articles written by U.S., British, Vietnamese, Russian, and Chinese historians, analyzing the participation of various countries, the Soviet Union and China among them, in the Indochina conflict.[5] Two years later a collection of articles edited by Lloyd C. Gardner and Ted Gittinger added Korea, Japan, and U.S. European allies to this list.[6] A book on China and both wars in Vietnam written by Zhai Qiang provides, perhaps for the first time, a most comprehensive account of Beijing's role in the conflict on the basis of documents from Chinese archives.[7]

Not only have these and other works[8] confirmed and enlarged the conception formulated by this author in *The Soviet Union and the Vietnam War,* they also served as important sources for my research of the earlier period. I have also benefited from the publication of memoirs of Soviet leaders and diplomats that have come out in recent years in Russia as well as in other countries.[9] As a result, this new book benefits from my ability to define a more ambitious task for myself and base my assessments and conclusions on a much broader body of sources than was the case with my earlier book.

The task of this book, as I formulated it from the outset, is to analyze the foundations of Soviet policy toward the Indochina conflict and find an answer to the question of whether Soviet policy had undergone any significant changes of direction in the period leading up to the Vietnam War, which began in 1965. It was necessary to discover the motives that were behind the Soviet leaders' actions, the factors that influenced their attitude toward the conflict, and the relation of Moscow's policy toward Vietnam with other foreign policy objectives and priorities.

This book concentrates on the period after the 1954 Geneva conference on Indochina, which ended the French phase of the war. The reasons for such a focus seem obvious. First, the first Indochina war represented quite a different phenomenon, with its own origins and history. Second, it is hardly possible to describe a consistent Soviet policy toward Indochina before 1954. At that time Moscow's attention in Asia was mostly consumed by the processes in China and their implications for Cold War confrontation. Nevertheless, events relating to the 1954 Geneva conference, as well as the conference itself and its decisions, are put under close scrutiny in this book because without them it is impossible to understand later developments in Indochina and the Soviet approach to them. The same considerations dictated the need to devote one of the first chapters to the origins of Soviet-Vietnamese relations and Stalin's views of them. Because inter-action between Moscow and Hanoi played an important role in Moscow's policy toward the region in the 1950s and early 1960s, an analysis of these relations oc-cupies a substantial part of this book. Some questions and problems can be more easily approached if our knowledge includes what had transpired between the So-viet Union and the Vietminh and between Stalin and Ho Chi Minh in the earlier years. Furthermore, the issue of the continuity of Soviet policy beginning in the early 1950s, through the events of the conflict with the French, and then through the war in Southeast Asia becomes clearer with this knowledge.

The study ends with the two fateful and tragic incidents that, in my view, marked a watershed in the Vietnam conflict: the coup d'état against President Ngo Dinh Diem in South Vietnam and the assassination of President John F. Kennedy in the United States.

Vietnam is the almost exclusive focus of this book because of its central po-sition in the region and its dominant role in the Indochina conflict. The failure to find a lasting solution to the Vietnamese problem and the division of the coun-try into two halves with hostile regimes in each part transformed Vietnam into kindling for international tension and war. The conflict there smoldered throughout the period after the Geneva conference, threatening to develop into a serious crisis and spread to other countries of the region. Events in Laos in the late 1950s and early 1960s proved the conflict could spread and, being closely linked to developments in Vietnam, drew attention of the world community. Therefore, the Laos crisis also became one of the subjects of the present study.

The third country of Indochina—Cambodia—was for a time able to remain apart from the developing conflict. The situation in Cambodia benefited from the flexible policy of the Cambodian leader, Prince Norodom Sihanouk, who was balancing between the West and the East. He achieved relative stability dur-ing the period under consideration in this book. Only years later did the flame of the war in Vietnam engulf Cambodia. For this reason, Cambodia receives only marginal attention in this book, and then only Cambodia's policy connected with the Geneva accords and Sihanouk's peace initiatives.

The order of priorities of this study was determined mainly by what impor-tance Moscow attached to various events in Southeast Asia. Events in In-dochina, however, were not the only ones that drew the attention of the Soviet leaders, especially at the highest levels. At the time when the conflict in In-dochina presented the Kremlin with difficult options, Soviet leaders were pre-occupied with their relations with the West, had to pay attention to the tension and contradictions within the socialist camp, and strove to strengthen their po-sitions in the world communist movement. By the end of the 1950s, the dispute with the People's Republic of China demanded more and more attention from the USSR. Therefore, Soviet policy toward Indochina cannot be analyzed in isolation from other problems and pressures Moscow had to deal with in the outside world. Cold War polarization strongly influenced the Kremlin's approach toward developments in Vietnam and its neighboring countries.

While working on this book, I had to explore a mostly unknown land. True, some scholars in their books on the Vietnamese conflict had touched upon the Soviet Union's role and involvement in it.[10] A deep and comprehensive study on the history of Soviet–North Vietnamese relations has been written by Douglas Pike,[11] but his book concentrates on the years after the U.S. intervention in the Vietnam War, with only first chapters devoted to the preceding period. Relations between the USSR and North Vietnam in the 1950s became the subject of a brochure written by a student from Norway, Mari Olsen, on the basis of her findings in the Russian Foreign Ministry archive.[12] Some aspects of Soviet policy in Indochina were touched upon in the book written by Ang Cheng Guan on Sino–North Vietnamese relations in 1956–1962[13] and in the book by Zhai Qiang. Earlier, P. J. Honey provided a detailed account of the DRV's attitude and policy toward the Sino-Soviet dispute; the book was based partly on his own personal experience as a witness.[14] But no one had undertaken a complex approach to Soviet policy toward the Indochina conflict in the 1950s and early 1960s, analyzing it from the broader perspective of international relations in the Cold War years and basing it on documents and materials from Russian archives. With this book I try to fill the gap while clearly recognizing all the shortcomings of this first attempt; however, I am fully conscious that this will not free my work from subsequent critical evaluation by other historians and interested readers.

Arduum videtur res gestas scribere. It seems difficult to write a history. I more than once recalled these words of Roman historian Sallustius while in the process of writing this book. Yet my difficulties might have been even more painful were it not for the help, support, and encouragement of many individuals and institutions. Much of the basic research for the book was done in the Archive of Foreign Policy of the Russian Federation and the Russian State Archive of Contemporary History, both in Moscow. The collections of these two archives contain valuable materials for students of Soviet diplomacy. I am grateful to the people who work in those archives for their cooperation and assistance in locating the documents I needed and making them available for me. I also wish to thank the archivists of the Russian State Archive of Social Political History for providing me with documents from the Stalin collection, which had just opened for scholars at that time.

My archival findings would not be complete without the archives of other countries. My research fellowship from the Nobel Institute in 1995 enabled me to perform research in the Public Record Office, Kew Gardens, Great Britain. I am also indebted to Lloyd Gardner and Ted Gittinger, who included me in the list of participants in the series of conferences on the Vietnam War at the Lyndon B. Johnson Library in Austin, Texas, in 1993–2001 and thus gave me the opportunity to not only take part in these symposia but also look for appropriate documents in the library's collection. Finally, my research for this book was supported by a grant from the Bureau of Educational and Cultural Affairs of the U.S. Department of State, administered by the Kennan Institute for Advanced Russian Studies of the Woodrow Wilson International Center for Scholars, with funds provided by the Bureau of Educational and Cultural Affairs of the U.S. Department of State through the Regional Scholar Exchange Program. This grant allowed me, at the final stage of the work, to supplement the book's documentary basis with important materials from the U.S. National Archives and the Manuscript Division of the Library of Congress.

I owe thanks to my colleagues and friends, both in Russia and in other countries, whose interest in and enthusiasm about my book buttressed my sense of responsibility and determination to complete this study. Among this large group, I especially want to thank Christian Ostermann, director of the Cold War International History Project at the Woodrow Wilson Center, whose friendship and encouragement helped me complete the manuscript and prepare it for publication. I also want to express my deep gratitude to Jim Hershberg, the Woodrow Wilson Center's Cold War series editor, who not only was an attentive and astute reader of the manuscript but has also been, since the early days, an enthusiastic supporter of my project on the Vietnam War. The manuscript was read in its entirety by George Herring and Larry Berman, and I am grateful to these leading U.S. experts of Vietnam War history for their comments and suggestions. I wish to acknowledge my gratitude to Mary Marik for her critical skill and her efforts in editing this manuscript and improving my English and to Yamile Kahn, production editor, and Joseph Brinley, director of the Woodrow Wilson Center Press, who professionally guided the manuscript through the publication process. I also wish to express my thanks to Robert Litwak, Blair Ruble, and many others at the Woodrow Wilson Center with whom I shared six months as a Kennan Institute research fellow. I am immensely grateful to all these individuals, whose help and cooperation are important in whatever virtues this book may have, although they have no part in its faults. I also wish to thank the Kennan Moscow Project and the U.S.-Russian Joint Commission on Prisoners of War/Missing in Action for their assistance and cooperation.

My special thanks are reserved for the people who were around me during the long course of this project: for my colleagues and friends at the Institute of World History of the Russian Academy of Sciences, Vladimir and Tatiana Pozniakov among them; and to my relatives, who are always eager to provide their support, sympathy, and encouragement. Finally, I am most indebted to my mother, Lidiya, whose love and patience helped me survive all the disappointments and setbacks of this life. The book is dedicated to her.

1. The Origins

Dear and Beloved Comrade. I am awaiting
your order so as to come, to kiss you, and to present
a report on the question of Vietnam.

Ho Chi Minh to Stalin
October 17, 1952

Those who are searching for the origins of Soviet involvement in the Indochina conflict must pay attention to what happened in Moscow in late 1949 and early 1950.

In December 1949, Moscow witnessed two important events: the seventieth birthday of Iosif Vissarionovich Stalin and the visit of the leader of the victorious Chinese Communists, Mao Zedong. Although Mao sat next to Stalin at the official birthday reception at the Bolshoi Theater, Mao was only one among many other Communist leaders who came to Moscow to take part in Stalin's birthday celebrations, and his visit was not a formal tribute to the *Vozhd'* (great leader) of the world proletariat. Rather, Mao wanted to establish close relations with the Soviet Union and lay a foundation of the alliance between the two countries.

This is not the place to discuss the Soviet-Chinese negotiations that led to the Treaty of Friendship, Alliance, and Mutual Assistance between the Soviet Union and the People's Republic of China (PRC) signed in February 1950. These negotiations and the resulting documents have been thoroughly analyzed by other scholars.[1] Yet during the negotiations Mao raised the issue of Vietnam. In one of his conversations with Stalin, in January 1950, the Chinese leader informed his counterpart that Ho Chi Minh, then leading the struggle against the French colonialists in Indochina, was eager to come to Moscow and negotiate the prospects of Soviet-Vietnamese cooperation.[2]

By early 1950, according to Chinese sources, the subject of Vietnam had been discussed by the Soviet and Chinese leaders several times, first when Liu

Shaoqi, Mao's closest subordinate in the Chinese Communist Party, came to Moscow in late June 1949 and then during the Stalin-Mao meetings. The Soviet and Chinese leaders agreed that it was primarily the Chinese responsibility to support Ho Chi Minh and the Vietminh, a broad association of the Vietnamese political organizations dominated by communists.[3] At first glance, Stalin should have been impressed by the success of the Vietnamese communists in the war against the French. In 1949 and early 1950 the French expeditionary corps lost more than ten thousand dead, two hundred fortified points were destroyed, and the Vietminh maintained control over more than forty-two thousand square kilometers in the mountainous areas of the country.[4] On the liberated territory the communists established "free zones" in which they set up local administration, built factories, and organized agrarian communes. In 1950 there were thirty-six state enterprises with four thousand workers in those zones.[5] At the same time the Vietnamese communists waged guerrilla warfare in areas occupied by the French and their Vietnamese allies.

Nevertheless, the Soviet leader's attitude toward developments in Indochina was ambivalent at best. He apparently was influenced by his experience dealing with national liberation movements in Asia that went back to the 1920s. Stalin always viewed these movements through the prism of communist revolution in European countries. For example, in March 1925, he concluded that, because of the temporary stabilization in the West, revolutionary prospects seemed more promising in the East. Therefore he deemed it necessary for the Western Communist parties to find ways to coordinate the struggle of the working class in advanced countries with the revolutionary movements in the colonies and dependent countries.[6]

Stalin's enthusiasm about developments in Asia proved to be fatal for the Chinese Communists who followed instructions from Moscow in their relationship with the Guomindang, or Nationalists. The Chinese Communists failed to secure leadership positions in the alliance with the Nationalists and were unable to accelerate the revolutionary process in China.[7] The outcome of the events in China in 1926–1927 discouraged Stalin from maintaining his overly optimistic approach to the idea of revolution in Asia. Moreover, his failure to estimate correctly the developments in China made him suspicious whenever it was necessary for him to deal with local communists.

It is therefore not surprising that in the following years Stalin never paid much attention to the East. His attitude was conditioned mainly by the general orientation of Soviet foreign policy toward Europe, where the danger of the new war was becoming more evident in the 1930s. It is understandable also that during World War II Moscow could not afford to be occupied with events in Asia if they were not directly related to the Soviet struggle against Germany and Japan.

Yet the end of the war did not change this situation significantly. Even China, at first, was no exception; and in 1945 Moscow took no immediate notice of Vietnam's August Revolution and took no steps to recognize the Democratic Republic of Vietnam (DRV) proclaimed by Ho Chi Minh on September 2, 1945, although Moscow's overall reaction might have been sympathetic.[8]

After World War II, as before it, Stalin subordinated the Eastern direction of Soviet foreign policy to the problems of the West. Accordingly, his policy toward Vietnam was determined by processes that were under way in France, where communists occupied ministerial posts in the government. Stalin did not want to undermine prospects of the French Communist Party in its bid for power by supporting the struggle for independence in Indochina, which was a part of France's colonial empire. As a result, all contacts with Ho Chi Minh at that time went through the French Communists who did not block the first Indochina war budget and emergency measures related to the prosecution of the war. It is not surprising, then, that the conservative deputies in the France's National Assembly applauded "their own Communist colleagues *and* the Soviet Union for leaving France to fight its war in Indochina without outside disturbance." The French Socialist premier, Paul Ramadier, praised the "correct attitude of the Soviet Government" on the Indochina question.[9]

Although objective factors were influential in directing Soviet attention away from the East, in the case of Vietnam Stalin's personal prejudices still played an important role. The leader of the French Communists, Maurice Thorez, once confided to his Hungarian comrades that "Stalin was somewhat distrustful of Ho and his group." Thorez said Stalin thought that Ho Chi Minh had gone too far in his contacts with U.S. and British intelligence. Furthermore, Stalin was annoyed by Ho's unwillingness to seek his advice and consent prior to taking action. As an example, Thorez mentioned the dissolution of the Indochinese Communist Party in 1945 and complained that he had had a hard time convincing Stalin that it was just a tactical step in order to win support of Vietnamese nationalists.[10]

It is clear from Thorez's testimony that Stalin suspected Ho Chi Minh of being too independent and nationalist oriented to be a loyal follower of Moscow's political line. Stalin's suspicion was not unfounded. The Soviet leader was apparently informed that, in 1945, the United States assisted the Vietminh in establishing an intelligence network and guerrilla army against Japanese troops in Indochina. Moreover, Ho Chi Minh tried to win U.S. recognition. Secret direct contacts took place between representatives of the Vietminh and the United States in 1946 and 1947.[11] This information added substance to Stalin's generally cautious attitude toward supporting Asian communists, an attitude based on the conviction that the prize of Communist parties in France and Italy—disciplined, solidly aligned with Moscow's political line, and well equipped to gain power in local governments—far outweighed the advantages of any successes in Indochina.

Even the overall deterioration of the situation in Europe in 1947 and the failure of all attempts to consolidate Communist power beyond the limits reached by the Soviet army did not change significantly Stalin's policy toward Indochina. Although Andrei Zhdanov, the principal Soviet ideologist, emphasized Vietnam along with Indonesia in his speech commemorating the foundation of the Cominform in 1947,[12] his words were followed by only propaganda, not practical steps. Moscow's sporadic and sometimes spontaneous attempts to establish contacts with the Vietminh in 1947 and 1948 came to nothing, to the obvious disappointment of Soviet officials who were irritated by the Vietnamese Communist leadership's vacillations over its relations with the USSR.[13] Moscow continued its policy of a successful "divorce" of its interest in the colonial question from its goals in the West.[14] The process of Soviet reappraisal began after the Communist victory in China in 1949.

Soviet policy toward China bore all the characteristic features of Moscow's strategy in Asia. Stalin's distrust of the Chinese Communists and Mao Zedong personally was founded on the same ideology and rooted in the same personal prejudices that characterized his views of the Vietminh and Ho Chi Minh. In addition, Stalin's approach to the China issue was undoubtedly influenced by his bitter experience of 1926–1927.[15] As early as autumn 1940, Stalin discussed his views of the Chinese Communist Party (CCP) with General Chuikov, who was on his way to China. The Soviet leader said that the CCP consisted largely of peasants and tended to underestimate the strength of the working class.[16] This alone made the CCP unreliable in Stalin's eyes, an opinion he did not change after the end of the war. Nikita Khrushchev confirmed in his memoirs that Stalin was critical with regard to the leader of the Chinese Communists. He even called Mao a "cave-dweller-like Marxist,"[17] which meant that Stalin considered Mao's views primitive and outdated. Such an attitude led to the underestimation by Moscow of the ability of the Chinese Communists to achieve success in their contest for power with the Guomindang. As a result, after the war Stalin repeatedly requested the CCP to compromise with the Guomindang.

Chinese Communist military gains during the civil war caused Stalin to reconsider his approach to relations with the CCP, and the Communist victories in 1949 put an end to Moscow's hesitation about which side—the Guomindang or the Chinese Communist Party—it should deal with. During the Sino-Soviet negotiations in Moscow, Stalin praised the victory of the Chinese revolution, called Mao "a Marxist leader," and even apologized for interfering with the CCP's policymaking in the post–World War II period.[18] Moreover, after a period of uncertainty, Stalin agreed to rescind the treaty the Soviet Union had concluded with Chiang Kaishek's government and sign a new treaty with Communist China.

Mao Zedong at this point suggested to Stalin that he invite Ho Chi Minh to Moscow to discuss questions of Soviet-Vietnamese cooperation. Since Beijing had already decided to recognize the Vietminh,[19] the Kremlin decided to follow the Chinese lead and respond favorably to the Vietnamese overtures. It was difficult for Stalin to reject Mao's proposal of an invitation to Ho because a rejection would inevitably lead to Chinese bewilderment and to uncomfortable questions, especially because on January 16 the Vietnamese leader was already in China waiting for news from Moscow.

Stalin, however, was not at all enthusiastic about meeting with Ho Chi Minh and regarded a formal recognition of the Democratic Republic of Vietnam granted by the Soviet Union on January 30, 1950, as sufficient under those circumstances.[20] Stalin's telegram to the Soviet ambassador in Beijing contained a message from Philippov (Stalin's pseudonym) to Ho, in which Stalin told the Vietnamese leader about Mao's suggestion and said he had no objections to Ho's visit to the Soviet Union. Stalin then stated: "If you have not changed your plan concerning your coming to Moscow after [the publication of] the Soviet note on the recognition of Vietnam, I will be glad to see you in Moscow."[21] Thus Stalin clearly hinted to Ho Chi Minh that the diplomatic recognition of the DRV by the Soviet Union would be a good enough start and the Soviet leadership could offer the Vietnamese Communists nothing else at that stage.

Ho Chi Minh (intentionally or not) overlooked Stalin's hint. In his response from Chita, a town on the territory of the Soviet Union, he informed Stalin that he would like to keep his trip secret mainly because if the French learned about his absence from Vietnam, "they could undertake political and military actions." Ho Chi Minh deferred to Stalin about the secrecy of his visit and emphasized that the Central Committee of the Vietnamese Communist Party would agree if Stalin wanted his arrival to be official. "Upon arrival," Ho wrote to the Soviet leader, "I would like you to permit me to come directly to you."[22]

Ho Chi Minh's visit to Moscow[23] did not change Stalin's reluctance to provide all-out support to the communist struggle in Indochina and therefore was not a success for the Vietnamese. The Soviet leader turned Ho over to the Chinese, as was agreed during the negotiations with Liu Shaoqi and later with Mao Zedong, and Liu and Mao promised that the CCP was ready "to offer every assistance needed by Vietnam in its struggle against France."[24] The Vietnamese leaders undoubtedly attempted to persuade Stalin to agree on something comparable to the Sino-Soviet treaty of alliance. At the reception honoring the Sino-Soviet treaty, Ho Chi Minh—feigning humor—confronted the Soviet leader with the question of why Moscow could not sign a similar agreement with the

DRV. In response, Stalin referred to the secret character of Ho's visit and to the unavoidable disclosure of his presence in the Soviet Union if such an agreement were to be concluded. Ho then put forward the bizarre suggestion that Stalin provide a plane to Ho for a brief flight over Moscow and then stage an official airport welcoming reception. This would resolve the problem. Stalin laughed, acting as if the whole exchange was not more than a joke.[25]

Nikita Khrushchev, who either had been a witness to the Stalin-Ho conversation or had had a first-hand account of it, included this episode in his memoirs. He strongly criticized Stalin for his behavior during the negotiations with the Vietnamese leader. Khrushchev believed Stalin insulted and condescended to Ho during their meetings. With his colleagues in the Politburo, Stalin could not conceal his distrust of Ho Chi Minh. Stalin later often spoke of Ho's visit and complained that the decision to recognize Vietnam had been premature. Khrushchev concluded that Stalin did not believe in the possibility of the Vietminh's victory.[26]

The situation changed somewhat with the outbreak of the Korean War in June 1950. The open confrontation between the Soviet allies—North Korea and China—and the West led by the United States opened Stalin's eyes to the importance of the war in Indochina, which had now become a part of the common struggle against U.S. imperialism and U.S. satellites. Moscow regarded the U.S. attack on North Korea as the realization of the plan of a three-pronged invasion of mainland China, with the other two prongs directed from Taiwan and Vietnam.[27] In these circumstances Moscow more readily displayed enthusiasm over Ho Chi Minh's successes, which were in fact rather impressive by the fall of 1950.

On September 16 the Vietminh forces with the support of their Chinese advisers began the so-called Border Campaign against French troops. This campaign was probably conceived during Ho's negotiations in Moscow and Beijing, although Chinese scholars attributed it wholly to the PRC leaders.[28] It seems possible that both Ho Chi Minh and Mao Zedong had preliminary discussions about such a campaign with Stalin, especially since a similar strategy was used, on Stalin's advice, by the Chinese Communists in 1945.[29] Following Stalin's proposal to Mao that the CCP send some of its troops to the border between Mongolia and northeast China in order to receive Soviet weapons and divert the Japanese forces, in September 1945 the Chinese Politburo decided to move its forces to the North and with Soviet support create in the Northeast large revolutionary bases.[30]

The Border Campaign in Vietnam was thus similar to the Chinese maneuver five years earlier. The goal of the campaign was the capture by the Vietminh of territories in the North of Vietnam on the border with China in order to create base areas directly backed by the PRC. The campaign ended with a decisive Vietminh victory. Ho Chi Minh himself was eager to report to "beloved comrade Stalin" on the success of the operation. He began his letter with information on the results of the Vietminh's offensive. According to Ho, the Vietminh forces, which included more than twenty-five thousand regulars, about one thousand guerrillas, and eighteen thousand civilians, fought against six thousand French troops.[31] During this campaign the Vietnamese Communists eliminated about twenty-three hundred French officers and captured another twenty-five hundred.[32] But a more important result of the offensive was the occupation by the Vietminh of a number of provinces in the North of Vietnam on the border with China (Cao Bang, Dong Khe, That Khe). This provided the Vietnamese Communists with direct communications with their Chinese ally, whose vast territory became the strategic rear of the Vietminh.

In his letter to Stalin, Ho Chi Minh emphasized the important role played in the campaign by the Chinese advisers. "I must inform you," he wrote to Moscow, "that the C[hinese] C[ommunists] from the C.C.P. have sent some of their best people to us as advisers, and they rendered valuable services to us."[33] In contrast, Ho did not mention any substantial aid from the Soviet Union, which had obviously been limited to what Stalin had advised during the Moscow negotiations. This limitation was the obvious implication of the Vietnamese leader's words at the beginning of his letter, when he wrote about the "big help rendered by you [apparently by Stalin personally] *and the Chinese Communist Party*."[34] Nevertheless, Din (as Ho Chi Minh called himself in his correspondence with Stalin) hurried to balance his praise of the Chinese with the acknowledgement of the leading roles of the Soviet Union and Stalin, in particular. "Dear Comrade Stalin," wrote Ho, "Am I right in regarding our success, though relatively minor, as a part of great victory of revolutionary internationalism whose the most heroic and beloved leader you are[?]"[35]

The success of the Communist forces in Vietnam bolstered Soviet expectations of developments favorable for Moscow in the situation of sharp confrontation with the West. Having failed to outbid the United States in Europe, Stalin was eager to compensate for this failure with success in the Far East. At the same time, he tried to avoid the danger of global war and rely in most cases on local liberation movements to weaken the West and to acquire new allies. U.S. analysts predicted that South Asia and Southeast Asia were the regions where the Soviets were most likely to apply their plans to achieve objectives "through measures short of armed aggression across frontier."[36]

U.S. predictions were only partly correct, however. Indochina remained the only region where Stalin was prepared to encourage the militant course. His attitude was influenced by the growing prospects of the Communist victory in

Vietnam. As years passed and the U.S. involvement in the Vietnamese conflict deepened, another factor could play an important role—the fact that the Vietminh struggle inflicted damage to the prestige of the U.S. administration in the eyes of the peoples of the Third World who condemned U.S. help to French colonialism, and in the eyes of Washington's allies who witnessed the U.S. inability to suppress Communist insurgency in a relatively small country. Thus, Vietnam was a special case.

With respect to the other countries of the region, Moscow was more circumspect and limited its action to advice and moral support. Moreover, when advising Asian Communist leaders, Stalin tried to discourage them from exclusive reliance on the armed struggle. For example, in his letter to the Indonesian Communists, Stalin from the outset rejected the necessity of the "military revolution," emphasizing instead the task of agrarian reform. He criticized the "spirit of leftism" among members of the Communist Party and praised practical, "molecular," "dirty" work in the sphere of everyday needs of workers, peasants, and intelligentsia.[37]

To convince Asian communists of the correctness of such a reformist course, Stalin often referred to the experience of China tested by developments in Vietnam. He pointed out that a successful guerrilla war needed not only a large country "which has a number of forestry and mountainous areas far from railways and cities," but also a "solid rear" provided by a powerful ally. This would guarantee liberated zones established by Communist insurgents from encirclement by rival forces.[38] The example of the Chinese Communists who "moved to Manchuria and found there a solid rear in the friendly Soviet state" confirmed such a requirement. "It is noteworthy," Stalin reasoned, "that only after the Chinese comrades had obtained the solid rear and only after they leaned against the USSR as against their own rear, the enemy lost a possibility to encircle them, while the Chinese Communists got an opportunity to wage planned offensive against the Chiang Kaishek army from North to South."[39] The implication of these instructions to the Indonesians is very clear: Moscow did not want to encourage armed struggle of those Communists whose chances for success, because of the absence of the necessary conditions outlined by Stalin in his letter, were minimal. On the other hand, the situation in a very few countries might be regarded as satisfying the requirements set forth by the Soviet leader.

One may argue that the letter to the Indonesians only confirms the domino theory put forward by the U.S. administration in those years as a justification for its policy in Indochina. In fact, if one country becomes controlled by Communists, in a few years it could serve as a strategic rear for a communist insurgency in neighboring country, and the chain reaction might be limitless. But the theory did not take into account many other factors, not least of them the unwillingness and, in some cases, the inability of the powerful allies, primarily the Soviet Union and China, to support new Communist regimes and render them the necessary material aid upon which they as underdeveloped economies would unavoidably be dependent. Even in Vietnam, where the prospects of Communist victory were promising, the local insurgents waited in vain for substantial assistance from the Soviets for their struggle.

Moscow's reluctance to be involved in conflicts in Asia was heightened by the difficulties the Soviet allies encountered in Korea. It is possible to agree (with some reservations) with Charles McLane, who wrote in 1966 that "[h]ad the Korean effort succeeded, the strategy of armed struggle, we may imagine, would have been vindicated in Soviet eyes and would have been more widely urged throughout the East than heretofore. The ensuing chapter in Moscow's Eastern policy would have been different. The Korean venture did not, however, succeed."[40]

In fact, the Korean War worsened the international environment of the Soviet Union. Out of fear of Communist attack elsewhere in the world, the Truman administration tripled the U.S. defense budget. Washington also decided to station U.S. troops permanently in Europe. And it also took the action "Stalin may have feared most of all," that is, to rearm the West Germans.[41] In Asia the Soviet Union perceived increased determination on the part of the United States to counter the Communists in Vietnam, Burma, Malaya, Thailand, and other countries when the United States provided direct aid to local regimes and rendered assistance to the European countries that had colonies in the region.

In this situation Stalin had to abandon any militant aspirations and seek a less turbulent course in Asia. The victims of Stalin's reorientation of Soviet policy were primarily the Vietnamese Communists who had to relinquish any hopes for substantial Soviet help. In addition, the failure of the Vietminh offensive in the Tonkin delta area in 1951 buried its plans of a "general counteroffensive" aimed at seizing the delta. The Vietminh shifted its operation to upper Laos and northwestern Vietnam.[42] It became apparent to Ho Chi Minh and his brothers in arms that their final victory was still years away.

In 1952, the Communist Party of the Soviet Union (CPSU) was preparing for its nineteenth congress, the first in more than ten years. The congress must have become a significant event not only in the life of Soviet Communists but also of their comrades abroad. As usual, invitations were sent to representatives of foreign Communist parties to come to Moscow to attend the forum, but Ho Chi Minh himself, unlike other Communist leaders, had to write to Stalin to ask permission to come.

On September 30, 1952, a ciphered telegram was received in Moscow addressed to Comrade Philippov. In it Ho Chi Minh informed the Soviet leader that he had arrived in Beijing and wanted very much to come to Moscow to participate in the CPSU congress. Again, Ho expressed his desire to visit Moscow incognito or under a false name because "if I would go to Moscow openly, first, this would provide enemies with a pretext for political attacks against me and, second, [my] open trip would cause many inconveniences related to my reception."[43]

This excessive preoccupation with secrecy on the part of Ho Chi Minh seems strange, considering the recognition of the DRV by the Soviet Union and the presence in Moscow of the DRV embassy, which had opened in March 1952. Yet as he wrote to Stalin in September 1952, Ho Chi Minh may have kept in mind the deteriorated situation in international relations as a result of the Korean War and the Soviet leader's resulting unwillingness to make public the contacts of his country with representatives of national liberation movements in Asia. In any case, Ho's principal goal was not so much participation in the party congress as a meeting with Stalin, for in the last paragraph of his letter he stated that his purpose was "to inform you and to discuss with you some issues of the struggle of Vietnam and questions of the activity of the labor [sic] party."[44] On October 2, he received a telegram from Moscow in which Stalin consented to the Vietnamese leader's arrival to Moscow "unofficially."[45]

Stalin's positive response did not mean that Ho Chi Minh's visit was welcome. The Soviet leader obviously intended to devote only as much time as necessary not to alienate a representative of a national liberation movement. Thus when Ho on October 17 sent the Kremlin a request about the meeting, during which he was planning to inform his powerful ally about the situation in Vietnam,[46] Stalin in all probability decided to grant such an opportunity to the Vietnamese leader. But this was the most that the *Vozhd'* was prepared to do. One month later, on the eve of Ho Chi Minh's departure from the Soviet capital, Ho sent a request for an additional meeting with Stalin. On the basis of available documents, it seems Stalin ignored this request.

On November 15, V. Grigorian, head of the CPSU Central Committee commission responsible for relationships with foreign communist parties, sent Stalin a message in which he informed the *Vozhd'* that Ho Chi Minh "orally" let him know that he was planning to leave for Vietnam shortly and would like to meet with "Comrade Stalin for several minutes." If Stalin could not receive the Vietnamese leader, Ho was going to write a message to him.[47] This message, finally sent to Stalin on November 19, said:

> Very much beloved and respected Comrade. Today I am leaving for my country. I thank you very much for what you have done for me. I promise you to work diligently in the realization of the agrarian program and in waging our patriotic war. I hope I will be able to

come back in two or three years so as to submit to you a report on the results of our work. I wish you very good health and very long life. I embrace you heartily. Din.[48]

Thus in 1952, as earlier, Soviet policy toward Vietnam remained uncertain. Throughout the first post–World War II decade, the discrepancy between Moscow's words and deeds vis-à-vis Vietnam was striking. On the one hand, Soviet leaders hailed the struggle for national liberation that had developed in a number of Asian countries, expressed Soviet support for the aspirations of oppressed peoples for independence and national sovereignty, and condemned plans of European imperialists to restore their colonial empires. At the same time, Moscow did almost nothing to help in any material way the struggle of those peoples, indicating that, in general, Stalin as well as his successors assigned a low priority to operations in the colonial world compared with European policy. The Korean War further discouraged Moscow from risking a further involvement in a war in the remote regions of Indochina or Southeast Asia. An early expert conclusion that "Soviet efforts in the colonies, despite repeated reminders to the international movement that more vigorous activity was needed there, were on the whole parsimonious,"[49] was accurate.

Vietnam was not an exception to typical Soviet strategies in Asia. Although the prospect of success of the national liberation struggle in Vietnam was more promising than in other Asian countries, the most the Kremlin was prepared to do was give its blessing to China for rendering assistance to the Vietminh. Such assistance might have included Soviet weapons and equipment channeled to Beijing in the framework of the two countries' cooperation in the Korean War. In addition, Stalin could not overcome his distrust of Ho Chi Minh, whom he probably suspected of being more a nationalist than a communist.

After it failed to achieve its goals in Korea, the Soviet Union decided to turn to a more conciliatory policy with the West, and after Stalin's death in March 1953 it announced its desire for peaceful coexistence. The new collective leadership in the Soviet Union did not hesitate to sacrifice a total victory of the Vietminh in favor of better relations with Western countries. Soviet leaders regarded the war in Indochina as an obstacle to this new policy, and they were prepared to search for compromise in order to settle the conflict, which threatened global war. They had decided to counter this risk with a much lesser risk— negotiations.

2. To Divide or Not to Divide

The Russians, and perhaps the Chinese,
are thinking in terms of a partition of Indo-China.

John Tahourdin
Head of South East Asia Department, British Foreign Office, London
March 19, 1954[1]

It was a sunny day in July 1954. In front of the Palais des Nations in Geneva a stocky man wearing pince-nez stood looking at the impressive Mont Blanc, which towered with its snowy top over the city. The man addressed the accompanying people: "What an impressive mountain! But we are standing too close to it. The more we move away, the better we can see its grandeur. The same is true with the Geneva Accords. We have just approved them and do not yet realize their significance. It will reveal itself more and more with the passage of time."[2]

The stocky gentleman was Vyacheslav Molotov, the Soviet foreign minister and head of the Soviet delegation at the Geneva conference, which for almost three months dealt with the problems of peace in Asia. Now the harsh declarations, heated debates, and secret talks were left behind, and the Soviet minister could express his satisfaction with the results of the conference that settled a conflict in Southeast Asia and removed the danger of war in that region.

The road that led to this day and place was long and precarious, and it is not easy to find the beginning of this journey. Did it begin with an exchange of diplomatic notes in the summer and early fall of 1953? Or did its origin lie in France's fateful decision to restore its power over its colonies in Indochina just after the end of World War II? In any case, only after almost seven years of unsuccessful struggle against the Vietnamese resistance movement led by the Communist-dominated Vietminh, did French authorities begin thinking about a diplomatic resolution of a war that had become an unbearable burden for the country.

Therefore the hint contained in the Soviet note of September 28, 1953, that a "number of important questions concerning the situation in the countries of Southeast Asia and of the Pacific"[3] could be a subject of discussion at a projected international conference was received in Paris with hope. It indicated that the Soviet Union—with its great influence over Asian communists, including Ho Chi Minh—was prepared to assist Paris in finding an honorable way out of the "dirty war." This hope grew even stronger when the Chinese prime minister, Zhou Enlai, repeated in his declaration of October 8 his country's readiness to contribute to the "consolidation of peace in the Far East and in the world."[4]

By putting forward the possibility of settling the war in Indochina, Moscow of course pursued its own goals. The Soviets regarded the war in Indochina with apprehension for they saw it as a conflict that could become an international crisis. Their view strengthened as U.S. involvement in the war deepened. The Soviet leaders were well informed about financial and military aid provided by the United States to France. The situation was even more delicate in Soviet eyes because of the fact that on the other side of the barricades in Vietnam were Communists who claimed the Democratic Republic of Vietnam had been recognized by the Soviet Union in 1950.[5] The Soviet interest in developments in faraway Southeast Asia was slight, however, compared with European problems.

European problems were actually closely related to what was going on in Southeast Asia, with France being a focal point of this relationship. The Soviets were preoccupied with Western plans to establish the European Defense Community (EDC) that envisaged the participation of the Federal Republic of Germany. Moscow regarded the EDC as a revival of German militarism and, because France was vacillating about endorsing the new organization, tried to influence French public opinion by evoking the ghost of the German threat. In his speech before the Supreme Soviet in August 1953, Soviet leader Georgii Malenkov used strong words: "A militarist Germany, regardless of whether it would appear in its former clothes or under the cover of the 'European Defence Community,' is a mortal enemy of France and all other neighboring countries. Therefore, any attempt to tie France to the 'European Defence Community' would mean the giving out France to German revanchists."[6] Therefore, it seems credible that the Kremlin hoped to induce Paris to reject the EDC by offering Soviet assistance in extricating France from the quagmire of the Indochinese war.

An additional factor in the calculations of Soviet decision makers was China. Ever since the proclamation of the People's Republic of China in 1949, Moscow undertook efforts to facilitate Beijing's entry into the world community and its recognition by other countries. The Korean War did not help this process. But Stalin's death and the end of the hostilities in Korea opened new opportunities for achieving this goal. In fact, recognition of China seemed even more attainable within the framework of the new Soviet policy of relaxation of international tensions and rapprochement with the West.

One element of this policy was a Soviet proposal to organize an international conference with the participation of great powers, whose task it would be to find a solution to the most urgent problems of international relations and thus contribute to detente. The PRC was repeatedly included by the Kremlin in the list of the main participants. In the September 28 note to the governments of France, Great Britain, and the United States, Moscow substantiated this claim. After it stated that there were important international problems that demanded "urgent consideration" by France, Great Britain, the United States, the People's Republic of China, and the Soviet Union, the note emphasized that "according to the UN Charter, it is first of all with these countries that the responsibility for guaranteeing peace and international security lies."[7]

The idea of a peaceful resolution to the Indochina conflict at an international conference became even more attractive to the war-weary French public after an exchange of telegrams between the leader of the Vietnamese Communists, Ho Chi Minh, and the managing editor of a Swedish newspaper, the *Stockholm Expressen,* on November 29, 1953. In the telegrams the Vietminh leader, after stressing the determination of the Vietnamese people to carry the war to the victorious end, declared that if the French government wished "to bring about an armistice and solve the Vietnam problem through negotiations, the people and government of the Democratic Republic of Vietnam will be prepared to discuss the French proposal."[8]

Paris did not remain aloof from these peace feelers. The French prime minister, Joseph Laniel, in a number of presentations in the National Assembly asserted the readiness of his government to begin negotiations with the adversary.[9] In spite of these peaceful pronunciations, by 1954 neither side in the conflict was prepared to abandon its military course and sit down at the negotiating table. The French leaders hoped for the success of the war plans put forward in July 1953 by General Henri Navarre. The Vietminh likewise was striving for victories in order to achieve new battlefield successes that would bring advantages in future negotiations.[10]

The first days of 1954 saw progress on the way to realization of the Soviet idea of a great-power conference. In identical notes sent to Moscow by the United States, Great Britain, and France, the Western powers informed the Soviet leaders that they agreed to hold a conference of foreign ministers of the four states in Berlin on January 25.[11] Although it was expected in the West that this conference would deal predominantly with German and Austrian issues, the French were not ready to reject outright the evident Soviet intention to discuss in Berlin the prospects of a future conference with the participation of all five great powers, including the PRC. Foreign Minister Georges Bidault of France made this plain during the conference of the three Western powers in Bermuda in December 1953. Bidault's advocacy of the Soviet idea, which was shared by his English colleagues, was the result of the expectation that cooperation with China would facilitate the search for a peaceful settlement in Southeast Asia.[12]

Vyacheslav Molotov, the Soviet foreign minister, was eager to use every opportunity during the Berlin conference to keep the hopes of his French colleague alive, to the great displeasure of the U.S. secretary of state, John Foster Dulles. Dulles informed Washington on January 27, 1954, that during dinner with the French delegation Molotov "made an offer of Soviet good offices in regard to Indo-China if the French Government would indicate exactly what were its views in regard to a settlement. This was preceded by an obvious hint that in return France should give at the conference here some evidence of a favorable attitude towards the ideas of a Five-Power Conference."[13] In another conversation with Bidault, Molotov was even more outspoken. When the French foreign minister expressed his government's preoccupation with finding an "appropriate solution of the Indochina question which would not assail national honor," Molotov immediately responded that "in resolution of the Indochina question the best assistance could be rendered to France by China." As if to emphasize this thesis, Molotov stated, "Without China it will be difficult to resolve this problem."[14]

Molotov did not attempt to keep secret his approaches to the French. During one of his conversations with Dulles, he confided to his U.S. counterpart that he had suggested to Bidault the mediation of the Soviet Union and China toward a solution of the Indochina problem. Not very much surprised, Dulles responded with his readiness to assist with the problem of a conference on Asia, adding that an agreement reached on this point of the agenda "would be of great significance."[15]

The Soviet foreign minister's efforts were not fruitless. Although the Western powers refused to discuss the issue of the five-power conference in the form suggested by Molotov at the beginning of the conference in Berlin—a conference dealing with general problems of international relations such as disarmament, prohibition of the atomic weapon, and other global issues—they had to accede to a meeting of the five foreign ministers with the purpose of considering a peaceful settlement of the Korean and Indochinese questions.[16] They also agreed on China's participation in the conference. In light of Washington's strong refusal to abandon its policy of nonrecognition of the Chinese Communist regime, British foreign minister Anthony Eden sought to avoid the controversial issue of Beijing's status. Eden suggested that the communiqué of the

Berlin conference simply list the countries in alphabetical order. It was specified, therefore, in the part of the document that dealt with Indochina, that representatives of the United States, France, Great Britain, the Soviet Union, China, and other concerned states would be invited to the conference in Geneva to discuss the problem of restoring peace in the region.[17]

The Soviets expressed their satisfaction with the results of the Berlin conference, but it appears they were more satisfied with the prospect of Beijing playing a greater role in the international arena than with the prospect of the settlement of the conflict in Indochina. In Molotov's report to the plenary session of the Central Committee of the CPSU on March 2, Molotov analyzed the results of the Berlin conference primarily from the viewpoint of the admission of China to the club of great powers: "We tried to use an obvious interest of the French government in extricating itself somehow from the situation which arose in Indochina so that the People's Republic of China got the opportunity, at last, to occupy its place at a great-power meeting on international questions. *Now the first step was made.*"[18]

But was the Chinese reaction to the results of the Berlin conference as optimistic as Molotov's? Even without appropriate documents from Chinese archives, it is known that Molotov, before agreeing on the text of the final communiqué of the conference, requested approval not only of his colleagues in Moscow but also of the comrades in Beijing. The Soviet ambassador to China, Pavel Yudin, on orders from Moscow, visited Zhou Enlai on February 16 and informed him of the draft of the decision proposed by Eden at the restricted session the day before. The ambassador asked for the opinion of the Chinese leadership and insisted on an urgent reply because the next session was scheduled for February 17.[19] Zhou promised to consult with Liu Shaoqi and then report on it to Mao Zedong. At four o'clock in the morning of February 17, Zhou called Yudin and asked him to inform Moscow that the Chinese leaders "entirely agree with the opinion of the Soviet government with respect to Eden's project."[20]

In light of this exchange, the assertions of some scholars about Beijing's dissatisfaction or even animosity toward the Soviets, who allegedly had not defended the status of China sufficiently at the Berlin conference, seem questionable.[21] Although the Chinese might have felt some disappointment over the wording of the Berlin conference communiqué, they were realists who could not but realize that Molotov had done all that was possible in promoting China in the great-power club. He had set the door ajar, and it was now up to China to squeeze its way through—with Soviet help, of course.

Proof that the Chinese shared this view can be found in Molotov's conversation with the Chinese ambassador in Moscow, Zhang Wentien, soon after the Berlin conference. After expressing the PRC government's support of the decisions of the Berlin conference, the ambassador emphasized that "the PRC is going to take an active part in the Geneva conference and it holds the view that if there will not be great successes at the conference, any success would be important, since for the PRC the way for active participation in international affairs is opening."[22]

Even Secretary of State Dulles, who could hardly be suspected of being a Molotov sympathizer, gave credit to the Soviet foreign minister's ability to get concessions. Reporting on the Berlin conference at a meeting of the U.S. National Security Council, Dulles described Molotov's behavior at the conference as very smart.[23] At the same time, the secretary of state evidently tried to justify his concessions to the Soviets. He put the blame on Bidault and Eden for their softness vis-à-vis Molotov's intrigues and substantiated his own position through his concern over the fate of the EDC. "Secretary Dulles said he believed it to be apparent that if Bidault had not gone back to Paris with something to show on Indochina, the Laniel Government would have fallen at once and would have been replaced by a government which would not only have a mandate to end the war in Indochina on any terms, but also to oppose French ratification of EDC." In other words, Dulles was sure that "if we had vetoed the resolution regarding Indochina, it would have probably cost us French membership in EDC as well as Indochina itself."[24]

The other two U.S. allies, France and Great Britain, expressed a reserved optimism with regard to the prospects of a settlement of the Indochina war. In his speech at the National Assembly on March 5, 1954, Prime Minister Laniel declared: "Until 1953 there were two opposite tendencies in French public opinion. Some hoped to resolve the conflict by the way of negotiations, while others believed it was possible to win by means of war. Today these debates should be terminated. We are unanimous, in fact, in the hope to settle the conflict by means of negotiations."[25]

In Moscow, officials of the Ministry of Foreign Affairs began to consider prospects of success at the forthcoming conference in Geneva. As soon as the Berlin conference was over, the inhabitants of the building at the Smolenskaya Square began preparations to assure Soviet success. They wrote memoranda and policy papers, weighed various options for the settlement of the Indochina conflict, and met with Chinese and Vietnamese colleagues to coordinate their work.

As early as February 26, the DRV ambassador in Moscow, Nguyen Long Bang, met with Kirill Novikov, the head of the Foreign Ministry's Southeast Asia Department and, on behalf of the Central Committee of the Workers' Party of Vietnam, requested instructions about "what should be the line of behavior of the DRV government in connection with the forthcoming Geneva conference of 26 April 1954."[26] Later, on March 26, the Vietnamese ambassador asked to provide the DRV delegation with various analytical materials concerning the situation in Indochina.[27] The Chinese, seen from the record of Molotov's conversation with Beijing's ambassador, were more independent. Nevertheless, they also asked for their Soviet comrades to share their experience on preparing for an international conference.[28]

Before they advised their allies, the Soviets had to work out their own attitude on many questions relating to the Geneva conference: the composition of the conference at the Indochina phase, procedural problems like those of the chairmanship, tactics during the course of the conference, and, most important, a possible solution to the conflict in Indochina.

Moscow seems to have harbored certain views about a possible solution as early as the conference in Berlin. On January 29, U.S. intelligence reported to the State Department that it had received information that "the Soviet Union had ordered its Ambassador in France to test the French reaction to a possible settlement in Indochina based on the following provisions: there would be a provisional armistice line drawn at the 16th parallel . . .; the French would evacuate Hanoi and Tonkin Delta. . . ."[29]

The French were not alone in being approached by Soviet diplomats on the issue of the division of Vietnam as a possible resolution of the Indochina conflict. At the beginning of March, an official of the U.S. embassy in London informed the head of the Southeast Asia Department of the British Foreign Office, John Tahourdin, that a diplomat from the Soviet embassy, Rodionov, during a meeting had suggested that "if it was not possible to reach a settlement on the basis of Ho Chi Minh's joining a Vietminh/Vietnam coalition government, the solution might be a partition of the country on the sixteenth parallel." "Such an arrangement," Rodionov argued, "might help to guarantee China's southern frontiers."[30] Two days before this conversation took place, a Soviet representative in London, Nikolai Belokhvostikov, approached H. A. F. Hohler of the Foreign Office with a similar suggestion.[31]

Soviet diplomats would not have probed the position of the Western powers with regard to a possible division of Vietnam without being sure that such a solution would be met with approval by Moscow's allies. The Chinese agreed with their Soviet comrades on the subject of partition. In a conversation with Molotov on March 6, Chinese ambassador Zhang Wentien himself raised the issue of partition along the sixteenth parallel and stated that "this is a very advantageous proposal for Ho Chi Minh and it should be accepted if it is put forward officially."[32] The Vietminh's attitude toward a possible settlement of the conflict did not quite coincide with the opinion of their powerful allies. In a March 5 conversation between Pavel Yudin, the Soviet ambassador to China, and Hoan Van Hoang, the DRV ambassador to China, the Vietnamese envoy boasted about the successes of the People's Army on the battlefield and mentioned "great difficulties" that could arise during negotiations on a cease-fire with the French. "There is no definite front line in Vietnam," reasoned the ambassador, "and, as a result, it would be extremely difficult to determine a demarcation line and a demilitarized zone. . . ."[33]

The Vietnamese ambassador's arguments obviously ran against the idea of partition.[34] But Moscow seems to have been more sensitive to the needs of its Chinese ally than to the interests of the so far ephemeral Democratic Republic of Vietnam. By mid-March, Soviet diplomats in foreign capitals were presenting partition as the most expedient solution. For example, M. Zhivotovsky of the Soviet embassy in London in a conversation with Tahourdin "suggested that there was a similarity between the Korean and Indo-China problems." When the British diplomat asked him what this similarity was, Zhivotovsky replied that "if partition was to be the solution for Korea, such an arrangement might also be suitable for Indo-China." Furthermore, Zhivotovsky hinted that the Chinese were also interested in such a solution since "the Chinese were 'definitely sensitive' (he repeated this twice) to what went on on their southern frontier."[35]

While the British looked favorably upon Soviet suggestions for the solution to the Vietnam problem and the French were not hostile,[36] Moscow also had to account for the U.S. position in the course of preparation for the Geneva conference. U.S. and Soviet positions were opposite on almost all issues. Although the U.S. secretary of state agreed on the convocation of a conference to deal with the Korean and Indochina questions, he did this, as we have seen, out of concern not to alienate his French allies. But, as compensation for this concession, he insisted on the insertion in the text of the final communiqué in Berlin a provision aimed against Communist China that specified that "neither the invitation to, nor the holding of" the conference with the participation of the PRC would imply diplomatic recognition "in any case where it has not already been accorded."

In the period after the Berlin conference, Dulles—the mainspring of U.S. foreign policy—did his utmost to eliminate the very reasons for such a forum. Lloyd C. Gardner wrote, "The best thing from Washington's viewpoint, of course, would be if by the time of the Geneva Conference there was nothing to negotiate. So he [Dulles] discouraged serious preparations for serious negotiations."[37] However, Dulles had to consider the desperate situation on the battlefields in Vietnam where the best units of the French Expeditionary Corps were being assaulted by the Vietminh at Dienbienphu, a fortress created by General Navarre to defend the delta and regarded by French public opinion as a symbol of the war in Indochina.

The French occupied this fortress in November 1953, a move that most likely prevented a Vietminh thrust into Laos and provided support for indigenous forces opposing the Vietminh in this area. General Navarre hoped that a show-down with the Vietnamese Communist forces over the possession of the fortress would cause the defeat of the Vietminh and turn the tide of the war. By March 1954, however, Vietminh troops had encircled Dienbienphu, which had been subjected to their constant assaults since March 13. Despite massive French air bombardment, the French area of defense was constantly shrinking, and it became obvious that the situation was grave.[38]

Unable to prevent the convocation of the Geneva conference while Dienbienphu was threatened, the U.S. secretary of state hoped to neutralize any gains by Communist countries that might result from the conference. Dulles as well as President Dwight D. Eisenhower and many other officials in Washington regarded the prospect of Ho Chi Minh's victory as the beginning of the process that would lead to Communist dominance in the region and the loss of Southeast Asia for the free world. This was the so-called domino theory formulated by Eisenhower at his press conference on April 7, 1954: "Indochina was the first in a row of dominoes. If it fell its neighbors would shortly thereafter fall with it . . . ."[39] To prevent such an outcome or, if that would not be possible, to lessen its scope, Dulles suggested "united actions" of free nations. In his address before the Overseas Press Club of America in New York one week earlier, on March 29, Dulles declared that the threat of communism in Asia should be met by "united action."[40] Immediately after this declaration, Dulles began to build up a military alliance in Southeast Asia.

Moscow watched with apprehension the U.S. activities to create a new and aggressive bloc in Asia. But if the Soviets did not possess necessary instruments—except propaganda—to prevent this process, they could counter it by supporting China in its claim for "membership in the great-power game."[41]

Since the Berlin conference, Soviet officials in conversations with foreign colleagues insisted on the equal status of China among other great powers at Geneva. On March 17, during a conversation between Deputy Foreign Minister Vasilii Kuznetsov and Ambassador Charles Bohlen of the United States, Kuznetsov handed Bohlen an aide-mémoire about procedural questions relating to the Geneva conference. (The aide-mémoire would have been a formal exchange of diplomatic notes if the Soviets in their document had not mentioned that they had consulted the Chinese on the issues touched upon in it and that the latter had given their consent.) Bohlen immediately called attention to the fact of the consultation with the Chinese and noted that it had been agreed at the Berlin conference that the inviting states were the Soviet Union, the United States, Great Britain, and France; he implied that it was not at all necessary to request China's preliminary agreement on the questions relating to the convocation of the conference in Geneva.[42] In response, Kuznetsov stated that in the official communiqué the PRC was mentioned as an equal participant in the conference in Geneva along with the other four powers. "In addition," Kuznetzov reasonably noted, "we consider it expedient to discuss organizational questions preliminarily so as not to divert the conference to technical problems later, thus making its work more fruitful."[43]

The Bohlen-Kuznetzov conversation marked the beginning of the real war of diplomatic notes that continued throughout the period that preceded the Geneva conference. Each side, basing its position on differing interpretations of the wording of the Berlin communiqué (which was, in fact, rather vague on this point), defended its position with respect to China's status at the forthcoming conference. This wrangle displeased the other participants in the conference, particularly the British. In his memorandum of March 20, Assistant Under Secretary of State Denis Allen, quite an influential figure in the British Foreign Office, wrote that the U.S. position on this issue, "although formally correct, appears to be unrealistically rigid." He drew attention to the fact that only in consultation with the Chinese would it be possible to settle the participation of other countries. Therefore, ipso facto, China's status was different from that of "other interested states" not listed in the communiqué. And, in Allen's opinion, "to insist formally and rigidly that this procedural question is a matter for decision by the four powers might merely compel the Communists to press the thesis that it is a matter for the five."[44] This was exactly what happened.

While clashing with the United States over the issue of China's role as a great power and criticizing U.S. attempts to drive its allies into a military pact, Soviet Foreign Ministry bureaucrats worked out various plans for Geneva.[45] On orders from Molotov, the Southeast Asia Department compiled a list of questions pertaining to the Geneva conference. Soviet leaders wanted to know the Western countries' attitude toward the composition of the Indochina phase of the conference, particularly their view on a possible invitation for representatives of the DRV government. Moscow worried that the West intended to settle the Indochina question by depending on the agreement about Korea. The Soviets were also eager to find out how the French military viewed prospects of the war in Indochina and what plans the United States had with respect to that region. Of course, the Soviet leaders would have liked information about the Western powers' approach to the terms of a peaceful settlement in Indochina, in particular, their views on the fate of the "puppet regimes" in Indochina, on elections, and on the future relationship between the Associated States (Vietnam, Laos, and Cambodia) and France.[46]

Moscow needed this information not only to work out its posture at the forthcoming conference in Geneva but also to formulate positions for discussions with China and the Vietminh so as to have an agreed position on all issues. The

Soviets wanted to counterbalance Dulles's "united action" in Southeast Asia with Molotov's "united front" in Geneva.

The Soviets therefore invited Zhou Enlai and Ho Chi Minh to Moscow in early April. The Chinese had in fact been talking since the beginning of March about the necessity of a preliminary tripartite negotiation. In his conversation with Molotov on March 6, 1954, the Chinese ambassador to the Soviet Union, Zhang Wentien, touched upon Beijing's intention to invite Ho Chi Minh to China toward the end of the month. He also asked the Soviet foreign minister about the possibility of a trip to Moscow for Ho Chi Minh "for discussing the positions at the Geneva conference." Molotov understood the need for such a trip but added that this issue would be considered by the CPSU Central Committee.[47] Apparently the Central Committee found it useful to have preliminary discussions with the Soviet allies, and on March 31, Molotov informed the Chinese ambassador that Zhou Enlai and Ho Chi Minh were expected to come to Moscow on April 2.[48]

The first meeting between the Soviets and their Asian allies took place on April 3. Although the records of the negotiations in Moscow in early April are still classified, recommendations prepared by the Foreign Ministry for one of Molotov's conversations with Zhou Enlai and Ho Chi Minh are available. During this conversation Molotov was expected to discuss "not only the question of conditions for ending hostilities in Indochina acceptable to the USSR, the PRC, and the DRV, but also the question of what platform for maintaining peace in Indochina and complete settlement of the Indochinese problem should be put forward" by the three delegations.[49]

Moscow decided to advocate the following positions at the Geneva conference vis-à-vis Indochina's participation:

- Insist on the participation of the Democratic Republic of Vietnam in the conference;
- "[N]ot to raise objections to the participation of representatives of Laos, Cambodia, and Baodaist Vietnam";
- Support the invitation of "democratic Laos and Cambodia" to the conference but "not to make their participation as a necessary condition."[50]

Moscow conditioned acceptance of a proposal for an end of hostilities on the fulfillment of such steps as France's recognition of the sovereignty and independence of the DRV and the withdrawal of all French troops from the territory of Vietnam, Laos, and Cambodia. At the same time Moscow suggested that the DRV recognize economic and cultural interests of France in the region. The Soviets were going to discuss with their Chinese and Vietnamese allies the issues of free all-Vietnam elections and the formation of a coalition government.

The partition of Vietnam was the most sensitive issue that Moscow raised during negotiations with Zhou Enlai and Ho Chi Minh. Moscow's recommendations included the following carefully formulated point:

> To exchange opinions with Ho Chi Minh and Zhou Enlai about the position which is to be occupied in case a question of the division of Vietnam in two parts will arise at the conference in any form (for example, on the sixteenth parallel). To ask them also whether it is not expedient, on our part, to work out an acceptable version of such a division of Vietnam on the condition that all other terms acceptable to the DRV are met (recognition of the DRV sovereignty, withdrawal of French troops, etc.).[51]

These recommendations show once again that the Soviet Union was prepared for a compromise and regarded partition as the best solution to the Indochina problem. The Chinese shared this view with their northern neighbor. We do not know Ho Chi Minh's attitude toward this suggestion although it can be assumed that such a solution would be unsatisfactory to the Vietnamese leader whose armies were winning on the battlefield. Perhaps he even argued against such a settlement. But he encountered the firm position of China, which was the Vietminh's principal supplier for its war against the French.

Mikhail Kapitsa, who attended the negotiations in Moscow, wrote later that Zhou Enlai expressed concern about the growth of U.S. involvement in the conflict in Indochina if the war would continue. "In case the Americans did not interfere substantially in developments in Vietnam, the People's Army of the DRV will be able to liberate all the northern part of the country, including Hanoi and Haiphong, in the course of two years," reasoned Zhou Enlai. "However, it is difficult to count on winning two more years, since the USA is accelerating its involvement." Zhou did not conceal his skepticism about the prospect of China's open support of the Vietminh struggle. "The question arises," Zhou argued, "whether China steps in, if the Americans will invade the territory of Vietnam. This question troubles the Americans, remains a mystery for them. The Vietnamese comrades believe China will be able to take part openly in hostilities on the Vietnamese territory. The Central Committee of the Chinese Communist Party thinks, however, that it is impossible for the Chinese army to take part in operations on the territory of Vietnam, because this counterpoises China to other peoples of Southeast Asia. The United States would use this participation for establishing a bloc extended from India to Indonesia."[52] Zhou Enlai repeated his arguments at the next meeting, adding that on the issue of China's involvement in the war in Vietnam there was disagreement between the Chinese and Vietnamese comrades. Thus Zhou demonstrated that the Chinese were interested in a peaceful resolution of the conflict in Southeast Asia, and he excluded the possibility of undermining the process of negotiations.[53] In this situation Ho Chi Minh obviously had no other choice but to acquiesce to his allies' point of view.

It is safe to suggest that during the negotiations in early April all principal questions relating to the Communist position at the forthcoming conference in Geneva were settled. Tactics were to be worked out later that month during negotiations at the conference with the Vietminh delegation headed by Vice Premier Pham Van Dong. Moscow could now complete work, which had started in March, on the directives to the Soviet delegation.

The principal task of the Soviet delegation at the conference would be the agreement on an armistice in Indochina on conditions acceptable to Ho Chi Minh's government as well as the start of negotiations between the DRV and France about further steps aimed at restoring peace in the region. Yet, while "[m]aintaining and defending at the conference legitimate interests of the Democratic Republic of Vietnam, the Soviet delegation should at the same time pursue the objective of strengthening Soviet relations with France."[54]

Directives envisaged three possible positions for the Soviets at the conference, the first of which was labeled, in the Bolshevist tradition, the maximum program. Moscow's maximal demands included the withdrawal of French troops from the territory of Vietnam and recognition of the sovereignty and independence of the DRV. This position carried with it the implication that the whole of Vietnam would be under the rule of the Vietminh. Moscow's second position was based on the principle of partition. The Soviets were prepared to agree on the withdrawal of French troops from the "territory north of the sixteenth parallel" with a subsequent withdrawal from South Vietnam during the agreed period. After French withdrawal there should be a referendum in the South about unification of the country. If this position was found unacceptable to the Western countries and their allies, the Soviets had a fallback third position that envisaged a cessation of hostilities on the condition of French troops regrouping at specially determined points in Vietnam and subsequent direct negotiations between France and the Vietminh about terms for the restoration of peace in Indochina. All three positions included points about the establishment of joint supervisory commissions, recognition by the DRV of the economic and cultural interests of France, and the end of U.S. involvement in Indochina.[55]

Although the second position seems to have been most attractive to Soviet policymakers, Moscow possessed information that the Eisenhower administration was against any settlement in Indochina based on recognition of the Democratic Republic of Vietnam.[56] The Kremlin, however, nourished hopes that it would be possible to use disagreements between the United States, on the one hand, and Britain and France, on the other, to reach a favorable solution. For this, the British position showed the most promise.

Throughout the period after the Berlin conference, London firmly and consistently spoke in defense of a peaceful solution to the Indochina problem. The British foreign minister, Anthony Eden, had played an important—perhaps even crucial—role in facilitating the agreement on a meeting at Geneva. His position reflected the Churchill government's general policy, which was based on the necessity of negotiations with Communist countries. After Berlin, in March and April of 1954, the British resisted U.S. pressure for military action in Southeast Asia. They occupied a cautious position with respect to U.S. plans for a bloc in Southeast Asia because they feared that such plans would undermine any positive results obtained at the Geneva conference.

Eden and other British diplomats pondered possible ways to resolve the Indochina conflict peacefully. The British emphasized geopolitical considerations. They "wanted a settlement in Indochina that would provide a non-Communist buffer zone north of Malaya, where British were already involved in fighting a Communist-led insurrection. They also wanted guarantees for Laos, Cambodia, and Thailand, which, together with a buffer state in southern Vietnam, would form a Southeast Asian cordon sanitaire for the Commonwealth nations of Burma, India, and Malaya."[57] Partition was therefore the most acceptable solution to the Indochina problem for London as well.

Eden began to think about such a solution in early 1954.[58] It is not surprising that Foreign Office bureaucrats soon included this option in their recommendations for the Geneva conference. Soviet hints in favor of partition only stimulated this process. In early March John Tahourdin, head of the Southeast Asia Department at the Foreign Office, informed the British ambassador to Saigon, Hubert Graves, that his department was endeavoring to consider various settlement options that could be put forward before Geneva. Tahourdin referred to the information received from the Chinese and the Soviets and concluded that although the Foreign Office had thus far considered a cease-fire pending negotiations and a settlement based on the Vietminh's admission to a coalition government, the time had come to consider a third option, that is, partition. This option, however, involved many questions that needed to be answered before partition was accepted as the solution to the Indochina problem. Although it was necessary to find a form of partition that was acceptable to both the French and the Vietnamese, the Foreign Office was more preoccupied with the problem of "how a solution in Indo-China based on partition would affect Siam and Burma and our own position and that of Americans in Southeast Asia."[59]

After weighing all other choices, the Foreign Office Southeast Asia Department reported to Eden in April that there might be no favorable solution to the Indochina problem and the most the British could strive for was the adoption of the least disadvantageous course. In this light the department had concluded that "a solution based on the partition of Vietnam and the safeguarding of the independence of Laos and Cambodia might be best as a *pis aller.*"[60]

Therefore, Moscow could expect that at the conference the British would not oppose Soviet efforts aimed at reaching the settlement of the Indochina problem based on partition. If so, the chances of a favorable outcome from the Geneva conference seemed good. Of the nine probable participants of the conference, at least three—the Soviet Union, China, and Great Britain—regarded partition the least undesirable of all options. France was not against such a solution on the same grounds. The Vietminh had no choice other than to agree with its powerful allies while it hoped for unification of Vietnam after elections. Laos and Cambodia were not counted as countries that could resist the division of Vietnam if the conference guaranteed their independence and sovereignty while it applied pressure on the Vietminh to withdraw its armed units from those countries' territory. As a result, only the United States and the Vietnamese government of Bao Dai might oppose partition and, therefore, jeopardize the process of peaceful settlement.

The U.S. position had evolved during April. At the beginning of the month, in a conversation with the British ambassador in Washington, Sir Roger Makins, Under Secretary of State W. Bedell Smith dismissed partition as an idea the United States had already examined and rejected,[61] but on the eve of the conference Washington indicated that the division of Vietnam might be acceptable.[62]

In the meantime, in Moscow the Foreign Ministry was compiling lists of members of the Soviet delegation, arranging lodging in Geneva, and establishing communications between Geneva and the Soviet capital. The USSR delegation of about 200 persons included Vyacheslav Molotov, head of the delegation; his deputies Vasilii Kuznetsov and Andrei Gromyko; Sergei Vinogradov, the Soviet ambassador in France; Kirill Novikov, the head of the Southeast Asia Department; and Alexander Lavrishchev, the future first Soviet ambassador to the Democratic Republic of Vietnam. In addition to diplomats and Foreign Ministry officials, the delegation included people from the Ministry of Defense and the KGB.[63] The delegation was headquartered at the Hotel Metropol although Molotov occupied the Villa Blanche with its vast, pretentious armchairs and garish decoration.[64]

Moscow had also taken care to guarantee good press coverage of Soviet activities in Geneva. Eighteen correspondents of the main Soviet newspapers and radio stations were sent to Geneva to follow every twist and turn during the course of the conference and to uphold the Soviet people's vigilance against "intrigues of American imperialists."[65] Among the journalists was Yuri Zhukov, a correspondent of *Pravda* who, then and later, sometimes assumed responsibilities of an unofficial messenger to Western diplomats.

The Kremlin had to think about its allies as well. The primary Soviet concern was the Chinese. Moscow arranged for an aircraft to bring the PRC delegation to Geneva and for a car—a Zis-110—for Zhou Enlai and a driver for that car. In response to a Chinese request, Soviet security personnel searched the villa Grand Mont-Fleuri where Zhou Enlai was going to stay, in an attempt to discover eavesdropping devices; Soviets were also involved in checking food prepared for the Chinese premier.[66]

With their Vietnamese allies, the Soviet Foreign Ministry officials finalized the last details of the coordinated tactics for the conference.[67] The Soviets and the Vietnamese discussed such issues as possible terms of a settlement of the conflict, the Vietminh's declarations at the conference, the composition of the DRV delegation, and prospects for participation in the conference by representatives of insurgent movements in Laos and Cambodia.[68] Pham Van Dong, who headed the DRV delegation, asked his Soviet colleagues to think over questions such as an armistice in Vietnam, DRV membership in the French Union, France's economic and cultural interests in Vietnam, and the withdrawal of French troops from Indochina. He pointed out that the Vietnamese would like to consult with the Soviets about these issues so as "to avoid mistakes and deviations from the agreed course" in Geneva.[69]

For the Vietminh, the best solution to the Indochina conflict was the complete withdrawal of the French troops and immediate elections in Vietnam, which would certainly have brought victory to the Communists and their allies among the nationalists. As a result, Ho Chi Minh would be able to maintain his authority over the whole of Vietnam. But it was clear to the Soviets, who had retained withdrawal as part of their maximum program, as well as to the Chinese that the West, especially the United States, would hardly agree to such a conference outcome. It was therefore necessary to find a compromise acceptable to each party in the conflict and to their allies or, as President Eisenhower put it, to find a middle course between the unattainable and the unacceptable. Moscow saw the middle course as the partition of Vietnam; Beijing and London agreed. Paris acquiesced. Washington grudgingly conceded to partition. All that remained was to work out forms of a compromise and guarantee the result against possible violations. This became the task of the conference that opened on April 26, 1954, at the Palais des Nations in Geneva.

3. Making Peace at Geneva

The primary task that is laid upon the parties
to a peace conference is to make peace,
and to make it quickly, even at the price
of not making it well.

A. J. Toynbee[1]

Geneva is well suited for a peace conference. As the site of the League of Nations, this city represents the spirit of compromise and peaceful intentions. "Who could remain unaffected by this pervasive climate of tolerance, by the calm that seemed to soften the very air?" exclaimed chroniclers of the 1954 conference.[2]

For some participants, however, Geneva was a controversial symbol. The United States was inclined to associate it with appeasement before the Second World War. The Soviets remembered their failure to create a collective security system in Europe and their expulsion from the League of Nations. It would not be surprising if both the U.S. secretary of state and the Soviet foreign minister came to Geneva full of determination to prevent a repetition of his country's experience.

The first delegations arrived in Geneva on April 24, 1954. *Pravda* correspondents reported that it was particularly crowded at the airport that day. "[R]epresentatives of Swiss authorities, journalists, cameramen, photo correspondents were waiting for the delegations of the three great powers, the USSR, the USA, and the People's Republic of China."[3] The Chinese and Soviet delegations came in succession. Zhou Enlai's plane landed first at 3:30 in the afternoon. Vyacheslav Molotov, the Soviet foreign minister, arrived two hours later, but his arrival was quiet compared with the arrival of his Chinese counterpart. Everybody at the airport was anxious to see the Chinese foreign minister and Mao Zedong's right-hand man, the legendary Zhou.[4] The U.S. secretary of state, John Foster Dulles, arrived that evening and received less attention than his Communist rivals.

The heads of delegations made their statements at the airfield. Molotov, as always, read words prepared and approved in Moscow. He noted that for the first time since World War II all the great powers would take part in an international conference, and he mentioned all of them by name, starting with France. The Soviet foreign minister pointed out that his delegation regarded as "the most important task of the Geneva conference" the restoration, as soon as possible, of peace in Indochina. He expressed his conviction that conference participants should want to lessen international tension and strengthen peace in the world. If this happens, Molotov stressed, the conference "will achieve its positive results."[5]

The conference opened on Monday, April 26, with a discussion of how to end the Korean War. While undoubtedly important, this question was not the main concern of the Big Five, and at the conclusion of the conference Molotov confided to Eden: "on the Korean question from the very beginning he [Molotov] did not hope for much."[6] Molotov's counterparts seemed to share this opinion, particularly the French, whose main preoccupation was not Korea but Indochina. As a result, while the participants in the Korean phase of the conference exchanged diatribes, others made an effort to resolve issues concerning Indochina.

Most important was the issue of the composition of the conference. The Communist side long before had made it clear that the Vietminh's participation was indispensable to its success. The French objected, referring to Bao Dai's opposition and to the fact that it was impossible to negotiate with an adversary while hostilities continue. Foreign Minister Georges Bidault of France put forward these arguments during his conversation with Molotov on April 27. Bidault suggested, instead, that participants should include the five great powers and the three Associated States—the French-supported regimes in Vietnam, Laos, and Cambodia.[7] Molotov was not against the participation of the Associated States, but he remained adamant about inviting the Vietminh to the conference. Molotov stated that "he could not imagine how it is possible to discuss the issue of the restoration of peace in Indochina if the participation of the directly interested sides is not expected."[8] The Soviet foreign minister repeated this argument to Bidault at least twice.

Bidault reported on his exchange with Molotov to Dulles and Eden the same day. They concluded that "it opened distinct possibilities for negotiation."[9] The Western ministers were encouraged that Molotov, while insisting on the Vietminh's participation, did not mention the Communist "governments" of Laos and Cambodia, and he had agreed to limiting the conference to as small a number of powers as possible. The only difference was whether the number would be eight (the Big Five plus the three Associated States) or nine (those eight countries plus the Vietminh).

Eden reported that Dulles "strongly urged M. Bidault to agree to the participation of Vietminh." Eden advised his French colleague to demand a price for what he considered a concession to the Soviets and, in exchange, settle the problem of the evacuation of the wounded from Dienbienphu. "M. Bidault," Eden reported, "seemed much attracted by this idea."[10]

But Eden's advice turned out to be counterproductive. When Bidault next spoke with the Soviet foreign minister, he touched on this subject by saying that it was very difficult for the French government to agree on the participation of the Vietminh because the Vietminh did not consent to the evacuation of the wounded. Molotov immediately interpreted Bidault's comment as preliminary conditions, and he discarded Bidault's arguments that the Vietminh was not the state, which Bidault had raised because the Berlin communiqué had stated that only states could take part in the conference. Molotov accused Bidault of creating artificial obstacles "aimed at the postponement of the opening of the conference on the question of the restoration of peace in Indochina."[11]

For Dulles the issue of the composition of the conference appeared to be of secondary importance. Since he had agreed on the participation of Communist China, the invitation to the Vietminh mattered little to him. Furthermore, Dulles might have understood Molotov's logic that it was impossible to negotiate about peace and the wounded without the opposing party.[12] Dulles was more interested in Soviet views on how to resolve the Indochina problem, and he used Molotov's visit to him on April 27 to question the Soviet foreign minister about this.

Dulles opened the conversation on Indochina by expressing his fear that the Indochina conflict could be the beginning of a chain of events with far-reaching consequences. He said that developments since the Berlin conference had not allayed his concern. Dulles concluded his introductory remarks with the hint that although he himself did not see any solution to this problem, Molotov might have had some in mind.[13] In response, Molotov assured his U.S. counterpart that "no country, including the faraway Soviet Union, wished enlargement of Indochinese war" and added, apparently referring to U.S. efforts to aid France and to form a military alliance in Southeast Asia, that "a great deal depends on United States policy."[14] Dulles deliberately ignored the hint. Instead, after discussing the issue of the composition of the conference on Indochina, he again pressed Molotov to reveal his views on a possible solution to the conflict. He even suggested continuing the discussion of this subject at a later meeting. But, to Dulles's disappointment, the Soviet foreign minister remained evasive. "After some inconclusive discussion of subject," Dulles reported to Washington, "Molotov took his leave having failed to rise any of the flies I had cast."[15]

Why was Molotov silent about a settlement of the Indochina question? Dulles suspected (and it was probably true) that the Soviet delegate had come to find out the suggestions the Americans were prepared to make concerning Indochina. Another reason for Molotov's reticence might have been his unwillingness to deprive the Communist side of room for maneuver by laying out their cards before the actual play had even started. Molotov's primary goal at this stage was to obtain the Western powers' consent to the participation of the Vietminh in the conference. Only after both sides of the conflict had occupied their places at the negotiating table would it be possible to discuss further steps toward the settlement.

The firm position of the Soviets on the issue of the Vietminh's participation bore quick results. As early as April 29, Douglas Dillon, the U.S. ambassador to France, reported to his superiors that Bao Dai, the former Vietnamese emperor who at that time occupied the position of the chief of state of Vietnam, "received arguments that Viet Minh be present at Geneva with less objection than had been feared."[16] Marc Jacquet, the French minister responsible for relations with the Associated States in the Laniel cabinet, was sent to Bao Dai's residence in Cannes and used strong language to convince him that no other solution would be in the interest of his government. Three days later, the Vietnamese foreign minister, Nguyen Quoc Dinh, informed Dulles of Bao Dai's final agreement to his representatives' participation in the conference as well as to the Vietminh's invitation to Geneva.[17] Jean Chauvel, a member of the French delegation and France's ambassador in Switzerland, advised Andrei Gromyko of Bao Dai's decision on the day it was made. It was agreed that the Soviets would invite the Vietminh and the French would invite the governments of the three Associated States to attend the conference.[18] On May 4, the delegation from North Vietnam headed by Pham Van Dong arrived in Geneva.

As soon as the problem of conference participation had been resolved, the great powers turned to the question of the chairmanship. At the meeting of the heads of the Western delegations that took place at Bidault's residence, villa Joli-Port in Versoix, on May 1, it was agreed that Bidault would suggest to Molotov that the rotation of the three chairmen of the Korean phase of the conference—Molotov, Eden, and Prince Wan Waithayakon of Thailand—should be continued. If the Soviets refused, the three Western foreign ministers decided to suggest a single chairman, Prince Wan.[19]

The Soviets were not satisfied with this Western proposal, however. On May 5, in a conversation with Chauvel, Gromyko proposed instead a rotation among the five (or four, since France was a participant in the fighting).[20] This suggestion was absolutely unacceptable to the United States because of its opposition to the PRC, but the latter proposal was obviously designed by the Soviets as a bargaining chip only, since they had already decided who should preside at the sessions devoted to Indochina. The same day that Gromyko conversed with

Chauvel, Molotov dined with Eden. Their conversation of course turned to the problem of the chairmanship. "M. Molotov," Eden reported to London, "at once suggested that he and I should alternate." In response to Eden's reference to the French and U.S. opposition to this arrangement, the Soviet foreign minister said that the only alternative would be for the head of each delegation to preside in turn, which was clearly impracticable. In his attempt to persuade his counterpart, Molotov throughout the evening "seemed to be developing the theme that the success of this conference largely depended upon him and me, and *it was our task to bring in his case the Chinese, and in mine the Americans, into line,*" Eden telegraphed the Foreign Office.[21]

Molotov's implicit reference to China's possible intransigence during the negotiations seems strange since the Soviets had had preliminary discussions with Zhou Enlai in Moscow and had apparently worked out a common position on this issue well before Geneva. During the conference Molotov often hinted at China's more rigid attitude. These hints were interpreted by diplomats and journalists and later by scholars as proof of serious disagreements between the Soviets and the Chinese.[22] The Soviets successfully created an image of the intransigent Chinese compared to the flexible Soviets and convinced the Westerners that they had no option except to come to an agreement with the Soviets. Otherwise they risked an encounter with the uncompromising stance of the Chinese.

China's implied intransigence did not prevent Molotov from promoting his Asian ally's interests; Molotov played the role of a lady who introduces her young provincial protégé to high society. Dulles reported to Washington that at the luncheon on April 30, to which Molotov had invited both Eden and Zhou Enlai, the "host raised no question of substance but seemed interested rather in encouraging cordiality between his guests."[23] Eden found Zhou "inaccessible and rough, hard, cold and bitterly anti-American."[24] Zhou's behavior notwithstanding, this encounter led to other meetings during which many problems of Sino-British relations were settled.

The Americans disapproved of the overtures their allies made toward the Chinese. Such a rapprochement with the Communist regime in China contrasted to the multiple disagreements between Dulles and Eden at the conference. Dulles was so annoyed with the British foreign secretary's behavior (for example, Eden's silence in the face of Russian and Chinese attacks on U.S. policy in Korea) that he almost lost control of himself when he expressed his disappointment in a conversation with Eden. He even warned his British colleague that the "consequences could be disastrous for the close U.S.-U.K. relations he wanted to maintain."[25] But the U.S. secretary of state was not able to stop the processes initiated at the conference. Bitterly disappointed, Dulles left Geneva on May 3 after he had assigned the duty of negotiating the peace in Indochina to Under Secretary of State Walter Bedell Smith.

The situation on the battlefields of Indochina had meanwhile become desperate for the French. Starting on March 30 and throughout April, the Vietminh's fierce attacks against the French fortress at Dienbienphu continued day after day and night after night. Soon the territory controlled by the French was reduced to a circle with a diameter of a little more than one kilometer. With the capture by the Vietminh of the northern part of the airport, it became almost impossible for the French to support the defenders with parachuted supplies.[26]

On the evening on May 1, the Communist troops of General Vo Nguyen Giap launched their final offensive. On May 6, a violent and massive Vietminh attack supported by heavy artillery fire resulted in the French capitulation the next day. On May 8, the news of the French loss arrived in Geneva just as the Indochina phase of the conference convened for its first session. For the Communist delegates it was "literally a miracle," Nikita Khrushchev remembered.[27] It was a miracle because the fall of Dienbienphu suddenly changed the overall context of the negotiations. The Americans tried to convince their French allies it was not a military disaster,[28] yet the loss of the fortress created a heavy psychological effect in France and was perceived negatively by French public opinion. More than that, it demonstrated the futility of French efforts to achieve victory over the Vietminh on the battlefield. Negotiations appeared to be the only solution.

The U.S. president was correct, however, when he said that the French had inflicted "great losses on the enemy." The Communist forces were almost exhausted as a result of their victory at Dienbienphu. Ho Chi Minh made it clear in early April during the negotiations with his Soviet and Chinese allies in Moscow that the Vietminh had mobilized all their resources in order to win the battle at Dienbienphu, and they could not sustain the continuation of another military operation of a similar scale. The Vietnamese leader even pondered the possibility of a retreat to the Chinese border in case of failure at Dienbienphu.[29] The fall of Dienbienphu confirmed to the Vietnamese Communists that they needed a respite. At a meeting of the Soviet, Chinese, and Vietnamese military experts in Geneva, the Vietnamese representative, Ha Van Lau, pointed out that the DRV was interested in ending hostilities because, first, "the Government policy [is] to maintain peace and, second, a breathing-space is necessary for the army and the country and it is necessary to use a present favorable political and military situation for concluding an advantageous agreement on the settlement of the Indochina question."[30]

Moscow was eager to jump at the opportunity and promote negotiations when both sides were exhausted and striving for peace. The Soviets could count on the support of the British delegation and its head, Foreign Secretary Anthony Eden. Meetings between representatives of the two delegations on the eve of the Indochina phase of the conference showed that, as before, both delegations were inclined to consider partition as the most acceptable solution.[31]

Scenarios worked out in Moscow had prepared the Soviets for much bargaining. These scenarios left the initiative for putting forward proposals to the Vietnamese and the Chinese delegations, thus allowing the Soviets to play the role of arbiter.[32] It is not surprising, therefore, that Molotov postponed his conference address until after Pham Van Dong and Zhou Enlai had had an opportunity to speak.

Molotov waited to speak until May 14, at the fourth plenary session. The major part of his speech contained standard Soviet accusations about France and the United States waging a colonial war in Indochina, and he criticized the French proposals for not dealing with political problems. At the same time, Molotov accepted the French proposal about the conference guaranteeing the eventual settlement and suggested the establishment of a supervisory commission composed of neutral countries.[33]

The first days of the Indochina conference thus set a pattern of Soviet negotiating behavior. In their public declarations at plenary and at restricted sessions beginning on May 17, Molotov and his deputies consistently supported their Vietnamese allies who put forward maximal demands concerning various aspects of the settlement of the conflict. The Soviets combined these expressions of support with denunciations of the intransigence of the Western powers and their aggressive designs in Indochina. At the same time, Soviet diplomats formulated their own proposals that, though close to the position of the Vietminh, took into account the interests of the Westerners and thus created a basis for a compromise. In private conversations with members of the French, British, and U.S. delegations, the Soviets made further attempts to persuade their counterparts of the soundness of their proposals while they tried to find out what the Western delegations were ready to suggest. Many times during the conference Molotov left this task to Zhou Enlai who, through his exchanges with the British and the French, was eager to play a role of mediator between the warring parties.

It would be an oversimplification to state that there were no disagreements among the Communists. But disagreements were being overcome during consultations among the three delegations at various levels. And soon after the opening of the negotiations on Indochina, Molotov suggested arranging discussions among the military experts of China, the Soviet Union, and the DRV in addition to the meetings of the diplomats.[34]

Soviet tactics soon brought positive results. After early prolonged and heated debates, the participants agreed on such issues as the evacuation of the wounded from Dienbienphu; the separation of the political and military questions, with priority given to the latter; and the beginning of military staff talks to study conditions for a cease-fire. All this was presented by the Soviet press as the "first success on the way to the restoration of peace in Indochina."[35] Molotov, particularly in private conversations during this period, played the role of a detached and objective negotiator who was eager to find a solution to the minor problems so that negotiators could approach the principal ones as soon as possible. Walter Bedell Smith, who replaced Dulles as the head of the U.S. delegation, after a meeting with his Soviet colleague, observed that "it was as though he [Molotov] were looking at the whole situation through a magnifying glass and analyzing its various aspects."[36]

The situation changed in early June when the Soviet foreign minister returned to Geneva from Moscow where he had spent a few days. His position became more rigid and uncompromising compared with his previous attitude. At the plenary session on June 8, in his address to the conference, Molotov proposed that the conference participants examine political problems and suggested that they consider military and political questions on alternate days.[37] Zhou Enlai and Pham Van Dong supported this proposal, which altered the May agreement that priority be given to a military solution.

The Soviet delegation also stalled on the issue of the composition and competence of an international commission whose task was the supervision of an armistice in Indochina. At a restricted session on May 31, Molotov's deputy, Andrei Gromyko, suggested that the commission be composed of officials from Poland, Czechoslovakia, India, and Pakistan.[38] The Western delegates questioned the ability of such a commission to perform its functions effectively on the grounds that socialist countries could not be regarded as truly neutral. A discussion about the meaning of neutrality ensued. Delegates also disagreed about the relationship between the international commission and joint commissions composed of representatives of the belligerents. Deadlock was evident as well in the negotiations concerning Laos and Cambodia.[39]

Why had the Soviet position changed? Was Moscow dissatisfied with the concessions made by Molotov in May? Did Molotov have new instructions from the Kremlin to defend more vigorously the interests of the Vietnamese friends? Or was it only a tactical maneuver to probe the positions of the Western powers and to demonstrate to the Soviet allies that Moscow supported their interests above all else? Could Moscow have wanted to influence the outcome of debates in the French National Assembly that started on June 1?

In any case, when Molotov met with Bidault on the eve of his uncompromising June 8 speech, he was reasonable and polite. Most of their conversation was devoted to the composition of an international supervisory commission. Molotov listened while Bidault explained why France could not agree on the composition proposed by Gromyko: the character of Soviet relations with Poland and Czechoslovakia was different from relations France had with Pakistan and, especially, India, which Paris did not regard as a truly neutral country because of existing problems in bilateral relations. Nevertheless, Bidault was not opposed to India's membership in the international commission. In response, Molotov did not exclude other candidates from the commission; he added that, while considering the composition of the commission, it was necessary to take into account the existence of its members' political relations with both warring parties. To substantiate his desire to resolve this problem, Molotov stressed that the Soviet delegation was eager to facilitate the settlement of the conflict and it was "not going to give up in searching for appropriate ways to this end."[40] He assured Bidault that there was a basis for a solution of the issue although such a solution might not be ideal.

Molotov was likewise in good humor when he met the same day with Walter Bedell Smith. Again touching on the issue of the membership of the supervisory commission, he admitted that he was ready to reexamine Czechoslovakia and Poland as candidates. Yet he stated openly that "he could not agree to any membership not on 50-50 basis, that is 50% Communist and 50% non-Communist." He also underlined that at least two of the members of the commission were required to have diplomatic relations with the DRV. "He was absolutely adamant on this question."[41]

Molotov, contrary to expectation, did not become angry over Smith's warning about a possible U.S. intervention in case the Vietminh had "too great appetites" and "over-reached themselves." He also did not react to the U.S. diplomat's hint that bordered on the threat that if the question of the composition of the commission could not be resolved, "there were great risks inherent in the situation in Southeast Asia." Molotov remained unimpressed even by Smith's final remark to the effect that it was futile to try to reach agreement with the Communists on anything else when even such a matter as the composition of the supervisory commission could not be settled.[42]

The Soviet foreign minister's flexible behavior during conversations with Bidault and Smith made his uncompromising address on June 8 inexplicable. But two days later, on June 10, four military experts—two from the French delegation, Colonel de Brébisson and General Delteil, and two from the Vietminh delegation, Ha Van Lau and Ta Quang Buu—met secretly between 10:00 p.m. and midnight on the outskirts of Geneva in an isolated villa that had been hastily rented for the purpose.[43] The Vietnamese openly demanded a northern part of Vietnam where the Vietminh would establish their own state. When the seemingly astounded French delegates asked whether the Vietminh delegates agreed to splitting the country, Buu admitted that it would be only a temporary partition that would come to an end as a result of all-Vietnam elections.[44]

The proposals made at this late-night meeting represented a significant step forward from Pham Van Dong's position on May 25, when he agreed to regrouping regular military forces into zones established by the conference, thus tacitly accepting a temporary de facto partition.[45] The Soviets and the Chinese not only knew about the secret meeting between the French and the Vietminh delegates, they had been closely involved in its preparation, which had been concentrated in the hands of military advisers and experts of the three delegations who, at Molotov's initiative, got together for regular meetings soon after the opening of the Indochina phase of the Geneva conference. The aim of these meetings was to work out recommendations for the Communist delegations concerning forms of the settlement. For example, during the meeting on May 19, the military experts discussed the situation in Vietnam and the zones for regrouping troops. Ha Van Lau, who represented the DRV delegation, informed his colleagues that the Vietminh occupied the most secure positions in the North of Vietnam. In the South the situation was quite opposite, with Central Vietnam being between these two extremes. The Vietnamese delegate went on to present three alternatives for troop regroupment. He almost repeated the previous opinion of the DRV government, which had rejected the idea of a division of Vietnam along any parallel as "politically disadvantageous" and instead supported regroupment on the basis of the situation in the country after the fall of Dienbienphu.[46]

The Chinese experts of course regarded this plan without enthusiasm. At the meeting of May 27, a Chinese representative put forward arguments in support of partition. He suggested a division of Vietnam along the fourteenth, fifteenth, or sixteenth parallel and argued, paradoxically, that partition would make it possible to create a "political and economic unity of the country."[47]

The Soviets played the role of arbiters in this dispute and, at a meeting that took place on May 28, they observed that there were, in fact, two plans for regroupment, the Vietnamese plan and the Chinese plan. Because the Vietminh experts were ready to consider the Chinese proposal, the Soviets suggested that the two delegations meet and discuss their points of view because they were very familiar with the situation. "If you need our help," assured the Soviet comrades, "we will render it with pleasure."[48] The Chinese readily agreed and promised they would be able to bring the positions of the two delegations closer together.

We do not yet know what methods the Chinese used to persuade their Vietnamese friends that the partition of Vietnam was the best solution to the Indochina problem. But at a military experts meeting on June 9, on the eve of the secret gathering at the villa, Pham Van Dong discussed a scenario based on the idea of partition. Two Soviet military advisers, F. A. Fedenko and N. P. Tzygichko, recommended that the Vietminh representatives talk with the French and open their situation map and put forward proposals about zones of regroupment. "With all lucidity it is necessary to raise the issue of the liberation of the Red River Delta," dictated the Soviet experts, "by motivating this that the Delta is connected with the remaining part of North Vietnam economically and politically and that it could not be isolated from this territory."[49] Thus, not only did the Soviets know about secret discussions between the military representatives of France and the Vietminh, they, in cooperation with their Chinese allies, had prepared "the most productive stage of the Geneva conference."[50]

To make the Western delegations recognize fully the significance of the concession made by the Vietminh on the issue of partition and, at the same time, to create a smokescreen around the relationship of the Communist delegations so that suspicions were not raised about pressure exerted on the DRV delegation, Communist delegations might well have decided to accompany this important leap forward with diatribes by Molotov and Zhou Enlai on June 8 and 9. At the same time, the revival of the proposal to discuss political as well as military issues was probably designed to placate the Vietnamese Communists who had agreed on partition with the hope that eventual all-Vietnam elections would put an end to the division of their country.

If this was an intention of the Soviet and Chinese delegates, it was successful. A depressed and downcast mood had reigned at the conference since the plenary sessions of June 8 and 9, when even Eden, who was always striving for a compromise, experienced a failure of nerve and concluded that an agreement at Geneva was most unlikely.[51] However, a light at the end of this tunnel suddenly glimmered once again.

That the new proposals had been made by the Vietminh delegation became public very soon thanks to Edouard Frédéric-Dupont, the French minister responsible for the Associated States who tried to prevent the fall of the Laniel government by presenting to the National Assembly in France the news about favorable developments in Geneva.[52] Although he failed and the Laniel government fell on June 12, his information indicated that the Communists did not want the conference to break down and were ready to take steps to prevent its collapse. Soviet journalist Yuri Zhukov, who dined with a U.S. journalist, Kingsbury Smith, on June 9, confirmed this. Zhukov assured his counterpart that "Molotov was confident that agreement could be reached at the Conference" but warned that "it would take time."[53] To reinforce W. Bedell Smith's opinion of Zhukov as "sometimes rather reliable,"[54] at the thirteenth restricted session on June 14, Molotov made concessions on the mode of voting in the international supervisory commission and proposed that India be made its permanent chairman.[55] Molotov continued his search for a compromise at the meeting with Eden the next day.[56]

On June 16, it was Zhou Enlai's turn to suggest concessions. During his conversation with Eden, the Chinese foreign minister recognized the necessity for separate discussions of the situation in Laos and Cambodia, which the Chinese and Vietminh delegations had refused to acknowledge since the beginning of the conference, and Zhou promised that "there would be no difficulty in getting an agreement from the Viet Minh to the withdrawal of their troops from Laos and Cambodia as part of the withdrawal of all foreign bases." Eden remained convinced that Zhou wanted a settlement of the conflict and therefore feared that the conference might fail.[57] The same day, at the restricted session, Molotov proposed that Indonesia join the international supervisory commission along with India, Pakistan, Czechoslovakia, and Poland. He also put forth the possibility of a three-member commission composed of representatives from India, Indonesia, and Poland, and he returned to his previous view about the priority of a military solution over political questions.[58]

Although some observers and scholars interpreted these Communist concessions as being influenced by their concern over forthcoming Anglo-American negotiations in Washington and U.S. intentions to depart from the Geneva conference,[59] these concessions were instead a continuation of the line approved in Moscow in April that was aimed at the settlement of the Indochina conflict on the basis of the division of Vietnam. Nevertheless, the Soviets seemed to be concerned about the departure of the leading delegates of the United States and Great Britain and the announced negotiations in the United States. Molotov revealed this concern in the course of the meetings with his Western counterparts. Bidault assured Molotov that the negotiations in Washington were not of primary importance because France would not participate in them. He also said that Paris intended to prevent the breakdown of the conference and expressed his personal desire that the negotiations at Geneva continue at the highest possible level.[60] The same assurances were made to the Soviet foreign minister by W. Bedell Smith, who said that the conference "should be kept going while there was hope of reaching reasonable settlement."[61] Eden shared his colleagues' opinion and, in response to Molotov's question of whether he thought that the ministers had already completed all their work and further negotiations should be held between the warring parties, he stressed that the "ministers had done everything they could at the present stage of the conference. Yet, in his opinion, they will have to meet with each other once again" to settle such problems as supervision and guarantees.[62]

During these conversations Molotov tried to persuade his counterparts that agreement at the conference was still possible and the Communist delegations were ready to occupy realistic positions. In the Soviet view, however, this could not be said of the U.S. position. Molotov frankly told the head of the U.S. delegation that the Americans could veto the actions of their allies, all their public assurances to the contrary notwithstanding.[63] In a conversation with Eden Molotov was even more outspoken on this issue. "The Americans," he said, "seem to be worried, lest the French would agree on too big concessions, though this [concern] was based on nothing, and the U.S. Government's position, apparently, is aimed at keeping the French from finding an exit from the existing situation."[64] Molotov repeated this twice.

The Soviet minister was not far from the truth. Although Washington emphasized at every opportunity that the United States was only an interested nation "which, however, is neither a belligerent nor a principal in the negotiation,"[65] the actions of the U.S. administration before and during the conference demonstrated that Washington tried to influence the positions of its allies and the Associated States of Vietnam, Cambodia, and Laos regarding the conditions of peace in Indochina.[66] The seven points worked out by the U.S. and British leaders at the negotiations in Washington at the end of June were specifically designed, in Dulles's words, to "stiffen French position *so that they would not accept terms which we would be unwilling to respect.*"[67] These points determined the limits of the French bargaining position and the conditions of the U.S. support of any future settlement. The essence of the seven points came down to two demands: independence of Laos and Cambodia; and the division of Vietnam along the eighteenth parallel, with the southern part remaining non-Communist.

Dulles, the initiator of the seven points, was skeptical about prospects for their realization. In a memorandum to be sent to President Dwight D. Eisenhower, the U.S. secretary of state expressed his doubts that the French would succeed in getting peace on the U.S. terms. The only factor that could induce Moscow and Beijing to accept these terms, Dulles believed, was the threat of U.S. intervention.[68]

Soviet leaders harbored no illusions about Washington's possible intentions in Southeast Asia. In his report about the Geneva conference to the plenum of the CPSU Central Committee, Molotov referred to the U.S. attempts to create a military pact in Southeast Asia and concluded that the "U.S. government's agreement to participate in the Geneva conference was just a forced concession to the position of England and France on this question. Its calculations with respect to Indochina have not been based at all on the desirability of reaching an agreement on the Indochina question at the Geneva conference."[69]

The Soviet foreign minister informed his Communist Party comrades that the conference had entered its most important phase. He emphasized that during this phase it was necessary to approach political issues that were even more significant because of plans to divide the territory of Vietnam into two parts. Molotov justified the partition because it "would eliminate numerous pretexts for mutual encounters . . . of military units." At the same time Molotov warned of negative consequences of partition if the Geneva conference avoided decisions about political issues that included, first, the prompt organization of all-Vietnam elections and the establishment of a united and democratic Vietnamese government.[70]

Molotov touched on the political situation in France as well. During his conversation with Eden on the eve of his departure from Geneva, the Soviet foreign minister wondered if new opportunities would occur as a result of the fall of the Laniel government and the accession of Pierre Mendès France as the new premier in France. Eden warned Molotov that the new French cabinet would not agree to France's surrender, and Eden doubted that Mendès France's conditions differed from those of his predecessor. Eden did not expect the new premier to be more pliable.[71] In Moscow Molotov was accordingly cautious in his estimate of the new French government. "It would be risky now to make any conclusions on the issue whether changes in the government of France will influence the course of the Geneva agreement," he declared at the plenum. "Yet it is known that the new government of France regards the acceleration of the resolution of the problem of the restoration of peace in Indochina as one of its principal tasks."[72]

The new French premier had promised to reach agreement on Indochina within four weeks from the moment of his accession to power.[73] This deadline caused much controversy among observers at the time of the conference and among scholars later. Some regarded the public deadline as a courageous step aimed at a prompt settlement of the conflict. *Pravda* journalists hailed Mendès France's promise because it, in their words, indicated "not an ordinary change of the Cabinets who have the same policy, as it often happened thus far in France, but a certain political shift which is conditioned by the failure of the foreign policy course." The journalists drew attention to the fact that for the first time since World War II the government had to resign because of a foreign policy issue, and they advised readers to see to "what degree the new French government will take into account the mood of the majority of the people."[74] Others, especially the representatives of the non-Communist Vietnamese, accused Mendès France of easing the way for a settlement favorable to the Vietminh.[75]

In other words, according to Devillers and Lacouture, "the diplomats considered 'a month to make peace' somewhat too little, although the soldiers thought it rather too long."[76]

Despite the deadline imposed by the new French premier, the last weeks of June and first days of July did not show substantial movement toward the settlement. However, Zhou Enlai, who left Geneva later than other heads of the great-power delegations, arranged a June 21 reception at his villa for the Laotian and Cambodian delegations, and two days later he met with Mendès France. Both events reflected the Chinese desire to keep the negotiations going. At a reception organized by the Chinese in honor of the Vietminh delegation, Zhou provided the Laotians and Cambodians an opportunity to meet and discuss with Pham Van Dong issues of mutual interest. This created conditions for further meetings, the venue of which often became the headquarters of the Chinese delegation.[77]

The meeting between Zhou and Mendès France took place at the French embassy in Bern. The Chinese premier was rather reserved and official in his conversation with his French counterpart. Zhou had undoubtedly been informed that during the National Assembly vote for Mendès France to become premier, Mendès France had rejected Communist votes of support, a situation that did not help soften Zhou's watchful attitude toward the French. But he used this meeting with Mendès France to expound on the Chinese position with respect to Indochina.

From the outset Zhou declared that his country was opposed to the extension and internationalization of the Indochina conflict. He agreed that, although the military and political aspects of the negotiations were closely linked, for the moment military issues had a priority. His greatest concern was that U.S. bases could appear in the Associated States. Zhou probably felt relief when Mendès France assured him that the "French Government had not the slightest intention of allowing them to be established."[78]

Turning to the issue of Vietnam, Zhou Enlai assured his counterpart that the "Chinese delegation were doing their best to urge the Vietminh Government to bring together not only the Vietminh Government and the French Government, but also the Vietminh Government and the Vietnam Government of Bao Dai." In conclusion Zhou urged the French premier to meet with the representatives of the Vietminh.[79] When Mendès France asked Zhou's opinion about the way in which troops should be regrouped, Zhou supported the idea of large regrouping areas for the two parties of the conflict.

Although nothing decisive resulted from this meeting of the two premiers, the conversation helped clarify views of the French and Chinese governments and facilitated future direct negotiations between Mendès France and Pham Van

Dong. The basis of such negotiations had already been prepared by the meetings of the two delegations' military representatives, who continued to discuss possible ways to settle the conflict. On June 28, Ta Quang Buu proposed that the provisional frontier between the two parts of Vietnam be drawn slightly to the north of the thirteenth parallel.[80] This proposal was, of course, unacceptable to Paris; Mendès France adhered to the eighteenth parallel as his ultimate demand. Despite the differing approaches, the talks continued. Soon they were supplemented by military talks in the Tonkin delta, which began on July 4, and by the establishment of the military commissions on Laos and Cambodia.

These developments in Geneva and in Indochina apparently made Moscow anxious to resume high-level negotiations in Geneva. On July 4, Molotov asked the British ambassador when Eden was going to come back to Geneva. William Hayter assured the Soviet foreign minister that Eden had declared his intention to return to Geneva but had not specified the date.[81] Moscow asked Beijing the same question on the following day. On the order of the Center (in other words, the Kremlin), Moscow's chargé d'affaires in China, V. Vas'kov, met with Mao Zedong and informed him that the CPSU Central Committee considered it necessary to use the favorable situation in France for resolving the Indochina question. According to Vas'kov, Molotov was planning to go to Geneva on July 7 and meet with Mendès France before official sessions of the conference resumed. The Soviet diplomat hinted that "it would be good if comrade Zhou Enlai could arrive in Geneva before 10 July." Mao replied that Zhou was at that time in Kwangsi Province where he met with Ho Chi Minh and Vo Nguyen Giap. He could return to Beijing not earlier than on July 6 or 7, then go to Moscow on July 9 or 10, and arrive in Geneva at the earliest on July 12 or 13.[82] This was apparently acceptable to Moscow since, as it turned out, Eden came to Geneva on July 12 as well, and Molotov had time to meet with Pierre Mendès France and probe the new French government on issues of the negotiations.

Molotov arrived in Geneva on July 8 as planned, and the next day he received Jean Chauvel, who headed the French delegation in the absence of Mendès France. Chauvel began the conversation with the information that the French premier was coming to Geneva on July 10 and he would like to meet with Molotov.[83] Chauvel also used this opportunity to complain to the head of the Soviet delegation about the intransigence of the Vietminh representatives, and he asked for a meeting between French and Russian military experts to explain the difficulties that had arisen in the talks with the DRV. Molotov admitted that there were obstacles that should be overcome on the way to peace. In spite of the obstacles, Molotov assured Chauvel, the general tendency of the conference was favorable to its successful outcome and the Soviet delegation was ready to help in finding "concrete" solutions.[84]

Following the Molotov-Chauvel conversation, Colonel Brébisson met with the Soviet military experts Fedenko and Tzygichko on July 10. The French delegate informed his Soviet colleagues about three problems discussed at the negotiations with the Vietminh: the demarcation line, regroupment zones in Laos, and the evacuation of French troops from the Tonkin delta. The first issue caused the greatest controversy because the Vietminh insisted on the thirteenth or fourteenth parallel as the location of the demarcation line, contrary to the eighteenth parallel proposed by the French. Brébisson explained to the Soviets that Paris was interested only in providing Laos with access to the sea. Therefore it was essential to retain French control of colonial route no. 9 that ran from Laos to the seacoast. The coast itself, Brébisson assured his counterparts, including the port of Tourane (Danang), was not important. The French were not interested in the airfield at Tourane either. Keeping this in mind, Brébisson suggested, "it would be possible to find other narrow places in Vietnam for drawing the demarcation line," not only the eighteenth parallel.[85]

Emphasizing the impartiality of the French demand, the French colonel brought up the interest of the Bao Dai government of Vietnam in the port and airfield at Tourane as well as its interest in Hue, the ancient capital of the country. Clearly nodding at the United States, he even hinted that some third countries were interested in this part of central Vietnam. The French, Brébisson reiterated, were interested only in route no. 9 to provide Laos with access to the seacoast.[86]

The content of this meeting was reported to Molotov and could have been used by the Soviet foreign minister during his conversation with Mendès France, which took place the same day. However, the Soviet minister remained a supporter of the demands of his Vietnamese friends, at least on the surface. When the conversation turned to the problem of the demarcation line, Molotov and Mendès France each repeated their positions, which had been evoked many times by each side during the negotiations. Neither seemed prepared to make concessions.[87] Moreover, Molotov used the issue of the demarcation line to speak again of the need to discuss political problems at the conference. He pointed out that political questions had not been touched on by the conference although they were of importance. The French premier agreed with Molotov, perhaps to the surprise of the Soviets who recalled the constant refusal by Mendès France's predecessors to discuss political issues. Mendès France informed Molotov that the French delegation was trying to prepare an appropriate declaration that should be acceptable to all participants in the conference.[88]

Although Molotov and Mendès France did not budge in their views on the location of the demarcation line and on other issues, their first conversation was not inconclusive. They decided that from then on the main activity at the conference should take place during private meetings of the participants. Mendès France admitted that "unofficial conversations and personal contacts between representatives could be more useful at the present stage of the negotiations than plenary sessions." Molotov concurred by saying that the Geneva conference had "already passed over the period of making speeches." Molotov stated that the time had come to move from a general discussion to concrete decisions.[89] As a result, the Molotov–Mendès France conversation initiated a number of private talks, meetings, and discussions that marked the final ten days of the conference in Geneva.

On July 11, the French premier met with the head of the Vietminh delegation, Pham Van Dong, for the first time. This meeting symbolized the abandonment of the previous French policy of denying the utility of direct contacts with the adversary, and the DRV representative tried to underline the turnabout. Although his villa was next door to the villa where Mendès France was living, Pham Van Dong used his black Zis limousine provided by the Soviets to come to the meeting with the head of the French delegation.[90]

After Anthony Eden and Zhou Enlai arrived in Geneva on July 12, unofficial talks reached their full tempo. Only the U.S. representative, W. Bedell Smith, was absent initially. But after repeated urging from Eden and, especially, Mendès France and negotiations in Paris on July 13 and 14, Dulles agreed to Smith's return to Geneva on July 17.[91]

Private talks and secret contacts were not very fruitful in the beginning. As before, there were three principal issues over which debate developed: the demarcation line, all-Vietnam elections, and the organization of international control. The situation in Laos and Cambodia was closely related.

The most recent concession made by Pham Van Dong about the demarcation line was in a conversation with Mendès France on July 13; they had talked about the sixteenth parallel.[92] This was the line considered by Moscow as acceptable long before the Geneva conference. Not surprisingly, Molotov tried to capitalize on such a concession on the part of the Vietminh. Talking to Mendès France on July 15, Molotov commented that Pham Van Dong had made a substantial step forward by abandoning the territory between the thirteenth and the sixteenth parallels. It was necessary to take into account, the Soviet minister hinted, that a "strong force of persuasion was required" to make the DRV abandon the captured territory. Now it was up to the French to compensate this Vietminh concession in finding an appropriate demarcation line.[93]

Molotov also insisted on fixing a deadline for all-Vietnam elections and substantiated his demand by reminding Mendès France of the partition of Vietnam. Because the country would be divided, Molotov reasoned, the Vietnamese expected that the Geneva conference would set the date for Vietnam's reunification.[94] He remained unmoved by Mendès France's arguments about insufficient conditions in Vietnam for holding early elections.

Failing to convince Molotov of the validity of the French positions on the major questions that separated France and the DRV, Mendès France suggested they be resolved at tripartite meetings with participation by Molotov, Eden, and himself. Such meetings, the French minister said, could help come to compromise on controversial issues, "to make concessions on some questions while compensating them on others." Molotov would have to inform the Chinese and the Vietminh about the contents of such meetings, and Eden would inform the U.S. delegation.[95]

Molotov agreed, and the first tripartite meeting took place on July 16. Molotov, however, continued to insist that, first, the date of all-Vietnam elections should be fixed by the conference and, second, the sixteenth parallel should be the demarcation line between North Vietnam and South Vietnam.[96] Moreover, at the meeting of July 17, he unexpectedly called on his Western counterparts to join in holding a restricted session of the conference the next day. Eden, who was annoyed, told W. Bedell Smith that "Molotov had now become the most difficult and intransigent member of Communist delegation."[97]

While appearing intransigent to the Western delegations, at his meetings with Zhou Enlai and Pham Van Dong, the Soviet foreign minister was preparing a basis for future compromise. On July 16, Molotov informed his allies about his conversations with the British and the French and shared his impression that the French might agree to a demarcation line only somewhere to the north of the sixteenth parallel. He also asked his allies whether it was worthwhile to insist that the elections in Vietnam be held in 1955 or to recommend a more flexible formula that would allow both sides to decide, not later than June 1955, on the date of the elections. Zhou proposed three options: the elections should be held not later than June 1955, the elections should be held during 1955, or not later than June 1955 both sides would decide on the date of the elections. He said that he had discussed this issue with Ho Chi Minh, and the Vietminh leader had agreed on third option as a compromise.[98] However, at the conclusion of their meeting, they agreed that in Pham Van Dong's forthcoming conversation with the French premier, he would insist on the sixteenth parallel and a specific date for the elections.[99]

At their meeting the next day, the Communist delegates again discussed the issues of the demarcation line and the elections. Pham Van Dong acceded to a demarcation line drawn slightly to the north of route no. 9, but he demanded in exchange concessions from the French on the timing of the all-Vietnam elections. Zhou Enlai supported Dong's position. But Molotov again suggested they determine only the period of time during which the elections should be held. The exact date of the elections, the Soviet foreign minister said, could be determined by representatives of both sides in Vietnam later on.[100] The Communists were also prepared to assent to the French proposal concerning the composition of the International Control Commission (ICC), which would include India, as chair, along with Canada and Poland.[101]

Molotov immediately informed Mendès France of the results of his discussions with his allies, a significant step forward compared with the Vietminh's earlier demands. But the French premier, according to his agreement with Dulles in Paris, continued insisting on the demands as they appeared in the seven points of the Anglo-American communiqué and refused to concede on any of the principal issues. The Soviets began to suspect that the Western powers' objective was to prolong the negotiations until July 20 and then confront the Soviets with an alternative to either agree on the French proposals or accept responsibility for the failure of the negotiations. It was Molotov's suspicion that caused him to insist on holding the restricted session on July 18.[102] He shared his concern with his allies and received their full support.

At the restricted session, Molotov drew participants' attention to the possibility that a basis for peace in Indochina had been established. He appealed to the delegations to recognize the accomplishment and praised the private conversations that had made it possible. The U.S. delegation reported to the State Department that "Molotov said that all this shows recent private talks have had success and he expressed belief that such success would continue."[103] For W. Bedell Smith and his Western allies, this restricted session was the "strangest performance to date."[104] They tried in vain to receive clarification of Molotov's intentions from Zhou Enlai, who pretended to know nothing about the purpose of the Soviet action. It is apparent, however, that the Soviets wanted to demonstrate that they regarded the negotiations optimistically and it would not be their fault if the conference failed.

Yet the possibility of failure was quite real on July 18, when only three days remained until the deadline imposed by Mendès France. On that day Eden reported to London that, in his view, the conference had "no more than fifty-fifty chance of reaching agreement."[105] The delegations continued to discuss various options, trying to reach a compromise. At this stage the Chinese, apparently with Soviet consent, had moved to the front line in pushing for settlement.

After the restricted session of July 18 was over, Zhou Enlai approached Eden and informed the British foreign secretary that he agreed that the ICC could consist of India, Poland, and Canada.[106] The Western delegations received this news with satisfaction.[107] On the next day, Wang Bingnan, secretary general of the Chinese delegation, met with a French delegate, Colonel Guillermaz, and confided to him that Zhou Enlai agreed that the elections in Vietnam could be postponed for two years, until 1956, with the provision that during this period representatives of the North and the South would meet to agree on the precise date.[108] And, finally, on July 19, Wang Bingnan informed Guillermaz that his delegation and the Vietminh delegation agreed that the demarcation line should be drawn ten kilometers to the north of route no. 9, that is, somewhere near the seventeenth parallel.[109] This agreement was confirmed during a meeting of Eden, Mendès France, Molotov, Zhou, and Pham Van Dong at the headquarters of the French delegation on July 20. Zhou Enlai and his subordinates put to use the decisions that had been made at the meetings of the three Communist delegations several days earlier.

Thus the last obstacles on the way to peace in Indochina seemed to have been removed and the delegations were ready to gather at the plenary sessions to sign and publicize the final documents of the conference. But the démarche of the Cambodian delegation, which refused to sign any document that allegedly infringed on the sovereignty of Cambodia, delayed the outcome. The Cambodians objected to the conferees' decision to deny Cambodia's right to join an alliance and request military assistance from the United States or any other country. Sam Sary, the head of the Cambodian delegation, expressed concern about the danger of Communist expansionism and wanted to reserve the right to ask the United States to establish bases on Cambodian territory.[110]

Cambodia's protest perturbed the Chinese, who continued to insist on guarantees against the establishment of military bases in Laos and Cambodia. During his conversation with Eden on July 17, Zhou Enlai repeated the Chinese point of view on the issue of military alliances and bases on its southern borders. "China's policy in regard to South East Asia is quite simple," stated the Chinese premier. "They approved of a Locarno-type arrangement which as many States as possible would join, so that a large area of peaceful co-existence in Asia should be created. But the proposed South-East Asia Alliance would split the area just as N.A.T.O. had split Europe, and would make peaceful co-existence very difficult. . . . As regards the three Associated States in particular they should be independent, sovereign and neutral."[111]

At his meetings with Molotov and Pham Van Dong, Zhou Enlai again voiced Chinese concern over military alliances and bases. On July 16, he noted that the United States, England, and France had probably agreed on the establishment of a military bloc in Southeast Asia. "If the Americans will be able to draw Bao Dai's Vietnam, Laos, and Cambodia into a military bloc," warned Zhou, "the agreement proposed by us that prohibits the establishment of foreign military bases on the territory of the mentioned states would lose the significance we attach to it."[112]

Therefore, the refusal of the Cambodians to sign an agreement that would deny them the right to join alliances and invite foreign military personnel on their territory threatened to undermine the results of the conference. Molotov suspected that the Cambodian demands were a consequence of U.S. intrigues. He was partly right. The U.S. conference delegation was dealing with the Cambodian and Laotian delegations according to Dulles's instructions, which stated: "Continue encourage Laotians and Cambodians to proclaim their peaceful intentions but warn them against making any commitments to Communist bloc which might compromise their present defenses or hinder their participation in defense arrangements which may be made hereafter."[113] In any case, the Soviet minister understood that it would be necessary to find an acceptable formula that would reconcile the Cambodian demands with the interests of the Soviet Union's Chinese allies and, at the same time, prevent the failure of the conference.

The entire world was waiting for the final act at Geneva. The hall of the Palais des Nations was illuminated. Journalists, experts, and curiosity seekers gathered to witness this historic event. But the debates with the Cambodians lasted longer than the limit set by Mendès France in June. A very plausible legend describes how, in order to prevent the fall of the Mendès France government, someone thought of stopping the clock at the Palais des Nations. It stood at midnight all night.[114]

The solution was found at 2:00 a.m. on July 21. Molotov conceded that the Cambodians might appeal for foreign military aid if it was under external threat. Under pressure from Mendès France, delegates extended the same right to Laos as well.[115] Later that day, the conference participants gathered for the final plenary session. They discussed ten documents prepared for their consideration: the three agreements on the cessation of hostilities, each of which was accompanied by two unilateral declarations, and the final declaration of the Geneva conference. To these documents were added a unilateral declaration by the head of the U.S. delegation, an amendment to the final declaration from the state of Vietnam, and an oral statement of Cambodian claims on part of the territory of Vietnam. The last two were not accepted by the conference.[116]

Molotov in his speech at the plenary session summed up the results of the conference and their significance, noted the Vietminh's contribution to the success of the delegation, drew attention to the importance of the PRC's participation in the conference, and stressed that the Geneva agreements that divided Vietnam into two halves created the new task of reunification of the country "in accordance with national interests of all the Vietnamese people."[117]

Many scholars have analyzed the significance of the Geneva conference and its agreements.[118] Western estimates of course differed from the approaches of representatives of Communist countries. But most analysts have regarded these agreements as a compromise, however imperfect, among the clashing interests of the countries involved. Although the conference dealt with the Indochina problem, Indochina itself was not the preoccupation of the conference; the representatives of the five great powers were more concerned with the general situation in international relations, European and national security, and the normalization of bilateral relations. They were ready to sacrifice the interests of the countries of Indochina if that would help them achieve their desired aims. As often happens in diplomacy, the small countries—in this case the Southeast Asian countries—were but pawns in the game of the great powers.

The controversy over the European Defense Community is an example of this great-power negligence. Although allegations of a deal between Mendès France and Molotov on the EDC are almost certainly false,[119] the fact remains that both the United States and the Soviet Union tried to use the conference to influence the French decision on the EDC. Unlike Washington, Moscow had to approach this problem more carefully and indirectly so as to avoid accusations of interference in France's internal affairs. Therefore Molotov had to drop the subject of European security from a June 10 conversation with Mendès France, when the French minister refused until after the Geneva conference to discuss any issues other than the settlement in Indochina. Nevertheless, the Soviet foreign minister hinted to the French premier that the Soviet Union was ready to assist France in achieving "honorable and just conditions" of peace, implying that in response Paris should take into account the Soviet interests in Europe. Molotov tried to make this implication clearer when he stated that "the position of Mendès France as Prime Minister of France, inspires the Soviet delegation's respect. *This position aimed at the establishment of peace in Indochina will promote the strengthening of peace all over the world.*"[120]

Further proof that there was no global bargaining (*marchandage planetaire,* in Georges Bidault's words) between the Soviets and the French was Molotov's conversation with Mendès France on July 21, immediately after the end of the Geneva conference. During their conversation, which lasted about two hours, the Soviet minister tried to convince the French premier that the European Defense Community could not guarantee security on the continent and should be rejected in favor of other forms of cooperation between countries in Europe, including those proposed by Moscow. In his argument, Molotov emphasized the interests of both France and the Soviet Union and prospects for Soviet-French relations that did not always conform to the objectives of the United States. "America," Molotov argued, "was far from Germany and perhaps she was more prepared to pursue a more risky policy. France and the Soviet Union are interested in more cautious policy in the question of the rearmament of Germany."[121] These anti-EDC arguments addressed to the French premier would have been unnecessary if a secret deal had been struck between Moscow and Paris.

Mendès France drew Molotov's attention to the difficulties his government encountered on the issue of the EDC. He referred to external pressures on France in favor of the ratification by Paris of the EDC treaty and suggested that the Soviet Union work out a proposal that would be acceptable for the West. At the same time he warned Molotov that he could not guarantee that the various French opinions on the issue would be reconciled in a way acceptable to the Soviets.[122] The conversation ended with mutual assurances of peaceful intentions in both countries.

Although the Soviet leaders were preoccupied with issues of general peace and European security, it would be an exaggeration to claim that Moscow was indifferent about the Geneva conference's decisions that concerned the situation in Indochina. First, the Soviets were apprehensive that the crisis in Southeast Asia could grow into a world conflict with unpredictable consequences. The Geneva Accords removed this danger, at least for the time being. Moscow had supported its Vietnamese allies and secured for Ho Chi Minh a territory that could become a nucleus of a new Communist state in Asia closely allied with the socialist community. The USSR had also brought in from isolation another ally, Communist China, and introduced Beijing to the great-power club, thus enlarging the PRC's possibilities in international politics.

Soviet leaders appeared to be less concerned that, as a result of the decisions made in Geneva, Vietnam became divided. Moscow did not regard the division as a fatal outcome. Other divided countries in the world (Germany and Korea before the Korean War) had demonstrated that such an international solution could guarantee peace and stability for a prolonged period of time. Therefore Moscow from the outset considered partition an acceptable compromise and viewed it optimistically. The Soviet leaders of course did not exclude eventual reunification but regarded it as possible in another international situation, in their parlance, a "correlation of forces." In other words, if Moscow had not been able to reach its maximum program objectives, it certainly exceeded the minimum in good Soviet tradition.

The Geneva conference occurred just as Molotov's role was about to undergo a change. James Cable wrote in his book that the conference was Britain's swan song as a great power.[123] For Molotov also the Geneva conference was his swan song as a powerful Soviet foreign minister. One year later, at another Geneva conference, Molotov did not possess the same power and authority in the Kremlin that he had enjoyed during these Indochina negotiations. Khrushchev, who was playing an increasingly dominant role in Soviet foreign policy, was beginning to undercut Molotov. He was still influential in 1954, and Molotov's behavior contrasted starkly with the time when he was only a mouthpiece for the ruthless Soviet dictator, Stalin, in the international arena. All participants in the conference who had known Molotov from those days, especially Smith and Eden, noted the change.

W. Bedell Smith, who had met Molotov when he was the U.S. ambassador in Moscow soon after the end of World War II, was impressed by Molotov's transformation. In his report from Geneva on one of his meetings with the head of the Soviet delegation, Smith noted that at the conference Molotov "went further, was much more frank, made no charges, by implication or otherwise, no recriminations. . . . There is apparent much greater self-confidence and authority."[124]

Eden's reports praised Molotov's reasonableness and desire to find a compromise. In a telegram to the Foreign Office on his dinner with the Soviet delegation, the British minister wrote:

> M. Molotov was in unusually relaxed mood, and talked freely on a number of subjects unconnected with the present conference. . . . On matters concerning the conference itself he was also most amenable. I do not think that throughout the evening he disagreed with anything that I said in the course of frank discussion of our problems here, nor did he even seek to make a merely debating point. His whole attitude was in contrast to our experience of him in Berlin [at the January–February 1954 four-power conference]. He seemed genuinely anxious that the conference should succeed, and also considerably worried over the situation in Indochina.[125]

Molotov's attitude did not change during the course of the negotiations and, on July 12, Eden wrote: "Molotov gave the same impression as in the earlier part of the Conference that he wished to do what he could as a joint chairman on procedural matters."[126]

The foreigners' image of Molotov does not correspond with the estimates of his Soviet superiors and subordinates. Khrushchev wrote of his colleague's rigidity, outdated views on developments in the world, the lack of "elasticity."[127] Oleg Troyanovsky, aide to Molotov and his interpreter at the Geneva conference, found many similarities in the characters of his chief and Secretary of State Dulles:

> [B]oth were dogmatists to their very marrow, both considered the [social] systems they represented incompatible with one another, both regarded the possibility of any prolonged agreements between the United States and the USSR with skepticism, both feared that their leaders, Eisenhower and Khrushchev, could agree on unjustifiable concessions and compromises.[128]

In spite of the similarities in the characters of the two foreign ministers, Molotov, unlike Dulles, remained in Geneva and tried to obtain a compromise that would eliminate the danger of war in Indochina. He was often rigid in his demands concerning, for example, the composition of the ICC or the question of elections in Vietnam, but he was ready to make concessions on these and other issues. The softening of Molotov grew from the change in Soviet priorities after Stalin's death. The new party leaders wanted a relaxation of their relations with the outside world, and Molotov, as one of them, also recognized that such a change was necessary. He had always been a disciplined Communist who had obediently followed instructions approved in Moscow, however much he disagreed with them. But in the case of Indochina, it seems that he supported the decisions made by the Kremlin; hence the flexibility, readiness for compromise, relaxed mood, and good humor that were noted by Molotov's Western colleagues at the Geneva conference. He was apparently satisfied with the outcome of the conference, and he was convinced that its significance would be more appreciated with the passage of time.

4. From Support to Cooperation

The negotiations have revealed the complete unity
of views of the governments of the Soviet Union
and the Democratic Republic of Vietnam on the issues
of the international situation, as well as in the
sphere of the further development of political,
economic, and cultural cooperation between the USSR
and the Democratic Republic of Vietnam.

Excerpt from Joint Communiqué
Soviet–North Vietnam negotiations
July 18, 1955[1]

The Geneva conference was over, and the clock at the Palais des Nations—stopped to meet the deadline imposed by Mendès France—started counting out the hours of the new period in Indochina. The Soviets displayed cautious enthusiasm about prospects for developments in the region; their declaration on the conference results emphasized that "the cease-fire in Indochina opens to the peoples of Vietnam, Laos, and Cambodia opportunities for economic and cultural progress under peaceful conditions which, at the same time, will create a basis for the development of friendly cooperation between those peoples and France." Moscow drew attention to the importance of the Geneva provisions that prohibited the establishment of foreign military bases on the territory of the Indochinese states, as well as their membership in military alliances. The declaration referred to the free general elections envisaged by the Geneva Accords for July 1956 that would create conditions for the unification of Vietnam, "in accordance with national interests and aspirations of all the Vietnamese people." This provision, according to the Soviet declaration, "means the defeat of those aggressive forces who strove for dismemberment of Vietnam with the purpose to convert South Vietnam in one of the springboards of a projected new aggressive bloc in Southeast Asia."[2]

Moscow evidently was satisfied with the outcome of the Geneva conference, its satisfaction related not only to the end of the war in Indochina but also to the elimination of the danger that the Indochina war could develop into a global conflict. Because the Soviets expected new opportunities to be created in the sphere of international relations, the Kremlin inserted into the text of its declaration the following paragraph:

> The Soviet Government believes that the agreements on the cease-fire and the restoration of peace in Indochina, while contributing to the relaxation of international tension, create favorable conditions for the settlement of other unresolved important international issues concerning not only Asia, but also Europe, and first of all, such issues as the stoppage of arms race and prohibition of the nuclear weapon, the safeguarding of collective security in Europe and the settlement of the German question on peaceful and democratic basis.[3]

Thus the Soviet declaration demonstrated once more that at Geneva Moscow was concerned not only with the war in Indochina. It was, however, ironic that Moscow expressed hope at finding a solution of the German question: after settling the issue of Vietnam by splitting this country in two, Moscow called for the opposite outcome for divided Germany.

Despite their optimism, the Soviets could not but realize the shortcomings of the Geneva settlement. The vague wording of the conference documents, especially the final declaration, could result in grave consequences during implementation. Furthermore, the final declaration containing the most important provisions for determining the future political structure of Vietnam was not signed by conference participants; because of this, it remained only a compendium of good intentions, not the obligations assumed by the powers for fulfillment. Moscow was particularly concerned about the attitude of the U.S. delegation for it publicly acknowledged the terms of the Geneva Accords but did not sign or verbally endorse them. The Soviet government expressed its concern in its declaration, which noted that U.S. representatives had tried to prevent a successful outcome of the conference: "The U.S. did not want to participate in the joint work along with France, England, the USSR, the PRC, and other states in order to guarantee the restoration of peace in Indochina."[4] With these words, Moscow seems to be pointing out the country responsible for any future violations of the Geneva settlement.

These misgivings notwithstanding, for Moscow "the Geneva Accords signif[ied] an important victory of forces of peace and a serious defeat of forces of war" and meant "an international recognition of the national liberation struggle and great heroism of the peoples of Indochina displayed in this struggle."[5]

The Vietminh's reaction to the Geneva agreements was less sanguine than Moscow's. Ho Chi Minh's statement that a "diplomatic victory" had been achieved at Geneva did not conceal the fact that the Vietnamese Communists received less than they had expected. It was to those disillusioned with the decisions made at Geneva that Ho Chi Minh attempted to justify the results of the conference. He assured them that the demarcation line that split the country into two halves was a "temporary and transitional measure" necessary for the restoration of peace as a condition for national unification through general elections. He rejected the notion that this line meant a "political or territorial border." A special paragraph in his statement was devoted to the Communist compatriots in the South toward whom the Vietminh leadership must have felt the greatest remorse. Ho Chi Minh expressed his conviction that the Vietminh had "put the interests of the whole country above local interests, permanent interests above present interests" and would struggle for "unity, independence and democracy" in Vietnam hand in hand with other people.[6]

Whatever disappointment the Vietnamese Communist leaders felt about the outcome of the Geneva conference was apparently alleviated by the hope that their powerful allies in Moscow and Beijing would assist them in the implementation of the agreements, which the Vietminh believed depended on strengthening the Democratic Republic of Vietnam. In his response to Moscow's congratulatory telegram, Ho Chi Minh, after promising to struggle for the maintenance of peace in Indochina and unification of the country, openly stated that he and his comrades-in-arms expected that "in the struggle for the realization of these objectives we will enjoy your help."[7]

Pham Van Dong was the first to approach Moscow for help. On his way back from Geneva, he and Zhou Enlai stopped in Moscow, and during his first conversation with a Soviet foreign ministry official, Kirill Novikov, head of the Southeast Asia Department, Dong asked the Soviet government to "render the DRV assistance in working out a plan of friendly countries' help to the DRV. He stated that with the end of hostilities the DRV will have to actively deal with economic buildup. The DRV government would be grateful if we [Soviets] assist them in determining where and what it is possible to buy at the cheapest prices."[8]

Not expecting a resolute response from a bureaucrat of the Soviet Foreign Ministry and wanting to discuss more strategic issues of cooperation between the Soviet Union and the Democratic Republic of Vietnam, the DRV vice premier requested through Zhou Enlai a meeting with the highest Soviet leaders.[9] His subsequent meeting with Soviet premier Georgii Malenkov was discouraging, however. Mikhail Kapitsa, who was closely involved in everything that concerned the Geneva conference and its aftermath, wrote that Malenkov, although taking a positive attitude toward Dong's requests for Soviet help, explained at length that it was beyond the capacity of the Soviet Union to support all the people's democracies that existed in the world. Therefore, the Soviet leader reasoned, it would be expedient to divide functions between Moscow and Beijing. The Soviet Union would concern itself with socialism and democracy in Europe, and China would be concerned with Southeast Asia. Kapitsa noted that "Pham Van Dong reacted coldly to this idea."[10] Such a reaction was quite understandable. What could China, itself in desperate need of assistance from developed countries, give the DRV? Beijing would pass to Vietnam only what remained of the help it received from other socialist allies.

Malenkov's words to Dong should not be taken literally. The Soviets did not refuse to render assistance to the DRV. A division of responsibilities rather than a division of labor was the Soviet conception, at least in the early period after the Geneva conference. The new Soviet leaders, rhetoric notwithstanding, were retaining the policy of their predecessor, Stalin, and were adhering to the view that because of geographic proximity and a common past and traditions, China would better understand the problems of the Vietnamese Communists. Moscow planned for China to become a Soviet agent in Southeast Asia rather than an independent player. That this was the case is proved by the first steps that Moscow and Hanoi took on the path to bilateral relations.

As soon as the Geneva conference was over and the ephemeral state of the Democratic Republic of Vietnam had acquired its territory, full-fledged diplomatic relations became prominent on the agendas of the two countries. Although the Soviet Union had recognized the DRV in 1950, the Kremlin had not appointed a diplomatic representative to Vietnam. The Vietminh, however, had sent to Moscow an ambassador, Nguyen Long Bang, who served as a liaison officer between the Soviet leaders and Ho Chi Minh. Now the time had come to repair this imbalance. On August 4, 1954, Deputy Foreign Minister Valerian Zorin met with the North Vietnamese ambassador and informed him that the Soviet government officially asked for the DRV government's consent to the nomination of Alexander Lavrishchev as Soviet ambassador to Vietnam. Zorin let his counterpart know that his superiors were prepared to send the ambassador even before the liberation of Hanoi, "if the DRV government finds it expedient." If the ambassador arrived in those uncertain circumstances, Moscow wished only to know where in North Vietnam the ambassador should arrive and what the conditions were in that location.[11] In the same conversation the Soviet official informed Nguyen Long Bang that Moscow was assembling the staff for the Soviet military attaché in Vietnam. He asked the North Vietnamese official's opinion about when it was desirable for the military attaché to leave for Vietnam, in other words, before or after the arrival of the ambassador.[12]

After several days the Vietminh envoy forwarded his government's response to Kirill Novikov. He said that the DRV accepted Lavrishchev's designation "with great delight" and would like the Soviet embassy to "arrive to Vietnam the earlier the better." As to the military attaché, Bang stated that it would be good if he left for Vietnam at the same time as the embassy, or even earlier.[13]

North Vietnam was eager to receive the Soviet diplomatic mission, and the Soviet Union was eager to demonstrate its support of its new allies in Southeast Asia, but the Kremlin's choice of ambassador to the DRV seems strange. Alexander Andreevich Lavrishchev had served in the USSR Foreign Ministry since 1939 and could be considered a career diplomat because he had occupied some important positions in the Soviet diplomatic hierarchy. But he was not an Asia expert, least of all an expert on Indochina. Lavrishchev's prior posts included minister in the Soviet embassy in Bulgaria and ambassador to Turkey. He served as the head of the Fourth European Department and then became the head of the department responsible for the Balkan countries. Just before his assignment to Vietnam he was the head of the First European Department, which supervised relations with the West European countries, including France.[14] In this capacity Lavrishchev was included in the Soviet delegation to the Geneva conference as an adviser.[15] Thus the Soviet choice for ambassador to Vietnam could have been due to the Soviet interest in developing relations with France and Moscow's awareness that it was France that would remain the principal Soviet counterpart in Indochina.

The Vietminh kept insisting on the arrival of the Soviet embassy's staff in Vietnam at the earliest possible date. Nguyen Long Bang repeated this request during his meeting with Lavrishchev on August 10. Since the Vietminh had not yet occupied Hanoi, they suggested that the Soviet embassy staff should go to Thai Nguyen, about eighty kilometers north of Hanoi, where the temporary Vietnamese Communist government had been established. Because conditions in Thai Nguyen were poor (in Bang's words: "in the area of the temporary residence of the [Vietminh] government there are enormous difficulties with lodging and even difficulties with provisions are possible"), the DRV ambassador recommended that Soviet diplomats not bring families and bulky luggage with them.[16]

While insisting on the expeditious arrival of the Soviet diplomats, the DRV leaders were even more interested in the presence in North Vietnam of the Soviet military mission. The Vietnamese ambassador said they "urgently needed advice of the Soviet military representatives" for the implementation of the cease-fire agreements.[17] But the designation of the Soviet military attaché required more time than the selection of the Soviet ambassador. Finally on October 14, 1954, Novikov sought North Vietnamese consent for the assignment of General Pavel Bunyashin as military attaché to the DRV.[18]

The delay in appointing a military attaché actually had not retarded Soviet military assistance to the DRV. During his meeting in Moscow with Kirill Novikov, Pham Van Dong asked the Soviets to provide ships to the Vietnamese for transporting Vietminh troops from the South to the North of Vietnam.[19] In his memorandum to Vyacheslav Molotov, the head of the Southeast Asia Department recommended against such assistance, advising instead that ships from India, France, England, and Poland be borrowed.[20] However, the Central Committee of the Soviet Communist Party evidently decided that assistance to the DRV in regrouping its troops would facilitate the fulfillment of the Geneva Accords. Soviet ships along with vessels from Poland were provided to the DRV.[21]

Soviet aid to the Ho Chi Minh regime to help implement the cease-fire agreements was not the only Soviet–North Vietnamese cooperation in the first months after the Geneva conference. The situation in Vietnam made Soviet economic help no less vital for the fledgling Communist state. Splitting Vietnam into two parts was not beneficial for the country, which had been ravaged by war for more than eight years. The two parts of Vietnam—the North and the South—complemented each other economically. The northern zone possessed rich reserves of mineral resources (coal, anthracite, iron ore, vast apatite deposits, wolfram, tin, uranium phosphate deposits, tungsten, and chromium),[22] and the southern part produced agricultural products (rice, rubber, spices, and textiles). Thus the division of Vietnam created an economic imbalance that made both sections dependent on external aid.

The DRV possessed territory that was more developed industrially than the South. The textile plants of Nam Dinh, the cement plants of Haiphong, the coal mines of Hon Gay and Dong Trieu, dozens of power plants and power stations, locomotive and streetcar workshops, and flood control and irrigation systems required only proper management to serve the new Communist regime. But management was the very thing the DRV lacked. It had no educated cadres of Vietnamese engineers and technicians, and the new leaders did not trust the French engineers remaining in Vietnam and were reluctant to exploit their knowledge and abilities. The situation for the Vietnamese was complicated by the fact that the departing French had dismantled all the equipment that was possible to remove: dock cranes, railroad repair equipment, and even radium for the X-ray machines in the hospitals in Hanoi.[23]

The situation led the DRV authorities to ask for help from their powerful allies. This issue became urgent in the fall of 1954. On October 28, Nguyen Long Bang visited the Soviet Foreign Ministry and informed officials there about the desperate situation in the DRV, which was on the brink of famine because of the loss of the May and October rice harvests. The Chinese had agreed to send the DRV rice, Ambassador Bang said, but the PRC did not have ships. The Vietnamese asked for Moscow's consent to transport rice from China in some of the ships that had been provided by the Soviet Union for the transport of Vietminh troops.[24]

The threat of famine in the northern zone had made it clear to Moscow that the DRV could not survive without sufficient economic assistance. In January 1955, the Foreign Ministry's Southeast Asia Department sent Molotov a memorandum that drew his attention to Ambassador Lavrishchev's conversations with DRV representatives in which they consistently brought up the subject of economic and technical assistance to North Vietnam from friendly countries and, in particular, the Soviet Union. The Vietnamese had prepared and handed to the ambassador a "draft of directives on general postwar reconstruction of the DRV economy," which assumed friendly economic help from allies as a precondition for the plan's success. The memorandum emphasized that the restoration of the North Vietnamese economy was crucial as a factor in the struggle for the unification of the country and that unification could not be achieved without help from friendly countries. Ambassador Lavrishchev suggested that the Soviet Union promise Ho Chi Minh economic aid but only after the final reconstruction plan was worked out.[25]

The ministry in Moscow thought that Lavrishchev's suggested response was unsatisfactory on the grounds that the issue of forms and amount of help was as yet unclear. But the Foreign Ministry officials were also eager to find out the Chinese attitude toward the problem of aid to the DRV and, in particular, toward dispatching to the DRV advisers from countries other than China. The memorandum eventually prepared by the Southeast Asia Department recommended coordination with the Chinese comrades to reach a common position on this issue.[26]

The Chinese apparently did not object to Soviet involvement in assisting North Vietnam economically, and on January 19, 1955, the USSR Council of Ministers decreed that, in order to evaluate the scope of Soviet aid, Moscow would send to Hanoi a group of experts who would be assigned to prepare for the Soviet government "materials and documents necessary for working out respective agreements on the procedure and forms of the use of the gratuitous help in the amount of three hundred million rubles provided by the Soviet Union to the Democratic Republic of Vietnam for the restoration of its economy in 1955–1956."[27] During their trip the experts were to pay special attention to the situation in the mining industry and to sea and river transportation, including conditions in the ports. They were requested to analyze the financial and trade policy of the new regime. The directives to the Soviet specialists did not recommend that they demonstrate an "excessive interest" in the questions that were the subject of the DRV-China aid agreement, but they were advised to maintain "necessary and friendly contact with PRC advisers on the issues relating to the study of economy of the DRV."[28]

The Soviet delegation's visit to the North of Vietnam produced a draft agreement on Soviet aid for the restoration of North Vietnamese economy.[29] The draft envisaged Soviet assistance to the DRV for the repair and building up of industrial and communal enterprises, for the organization of a meteorological service, geological exploration works, and medical services. The Soviet Union promised to deliver goods necessary to the economy and the population of the DRV. The amount remained at three hundred million rubles. The draft prepared by the Soviet experts became the basis of the agreement signed during the July 1955 visit to the Soviet Union of the DRV government delegation headed by Ho Chi Minh.

The first official visit of Ho Chi Minh as head of a sovereign state was a triumph for the leader of the Vietnamese Communists after the humiliations he had suffered during his 1950 and 1952 visits to Moscow and his meetings with Stalin. Regardless of his changed circumstances, Ho Chi Minh had no illusions about the obstacles that existed on the way to cooperation between the two countries. The principal obstacle was the Soviet fear lest the Soviet-DRV alliance undermine the process of détente inaugurated by the Soviet collective leadership in its relations with the West. As a result, Moscow was extremely sensitive to any steps that could shatter the fragile peace in Indochina established by the Geneva conference. Therefore the fulfillment of the provisions of the cease-fire agreements by May 1955 made a good basis for the talks between the two allies. The Central Committee of the Workers' Party of Vietnam (WPV) had confirmed to Moscow in advance by telegram from Hanoi that the last units of French troops had been evacuated from Haiphong; at the same time the Vietminh troops had been successfully transferred from South Vietnam to the North.[30] In its response, the Kremlin heartily congratulated its Vietnamese comrades and expressed its awareness that they would be able to complete the "tense struggle" for a unified democratic Vietnam.[31]

Another factor that might have helped overcome Soviet reluctance to align closely with Hanoi was the growing U.S. presence in Indochina. Soon after the Geneva conference the Eisenhower administration made its "most crucial Vietnam decisions."[32] On August 12, 1954, the U.S. National Security Council approved a new policy statement for Southeast Asia (NSC 5429). The document recounted the damage inflicted to U.S. prestige by the recent French reverses in Indochina and declared that it was imperative that the United States "protect its position and restore its prestige in the Far East by a new initiative in Southeast Asia, where the situation must be stabilized as soon as possible to prevent further losses to Communism through (1) creeping expansion and subversion, or

(2) overt aggression."[33] Washington was going to achieve this goal by means of a new military alliance, a Southeast Asia Treaty Organization (SEATO). The U.S. administration also decided to exclude the French as the intermediary in its contacts with South Vietnam and assumed an obligation to train South Vietnamese military forces. On August 18, the State Department notified the French government that Washington would authorize its military mission in Vietnam to train the Vietnamese.[34]

In early September, eight powers—the United States, United Kingdom, France, Australia, New Zealand, Pakistan, Thailand, and the Philippines—adopted in Manila the Pacific Charter "that affirmed the right of self-determination and expressed the intent of the signatories to resist all Communist attempts in the treaty area to subvert freedom."[35] The so-called Manila Pact led to the establishment of SEATO on February 19, 1955. By May 1955, it had already become clear that U.S. influence in Indochina "was rapidly superseding that of France." During the talks in May between France and the United States in Washington, Dulles indicated that the U.S. administration would no longer adhere to a joint Franco-American policy toward Vietnam.[36] Thus the prospects for any future collaboration between the former colonial power and the new patrons of "free Asia" appeared bleak.

These developments had not escaped the attention of Soviet policymakers who, during meetings with foreign representatives as well as in analytical documents, expressed their concern over U.S. penetration into Indochina. Because India was one of the countries responsible for supervising the implementation of the Geneva Accords, Indian leaders were most receptive to these Soviet comments. In an April 1955 conversation with the Indian ambassador to Moscow, Kumar Menon, Soviet premier Nikolai Bulganin revealed the Kremlin's irritation over Washington's policy in Southeast Asia:

> It is annoying that the large tasks completed by the countries that want détente in international relations were practically undermined by other countries. Last year India, the Soviet Union, and China made great efforts to achieve the Geneva agreements, and this was done not only to stop the war in Indochina, but also to reach détente in international relations as a whole. . . . Now when an agreement on the Indochina question concluded, intrigues continue along the southeast borders of China, in which the initiator is the United States. The same can be said about the situation in the region of Indochina. *The Americans have kicked or are kicking the French out there at the expense of blood and sufferings of the peoples of Indochina.*[37]

At a meeting between Bulganin and Indian premier Jawaharlal Nehru, they also discussed the issue of U.S. policy and strongarm tactics. The Soviet leader spoke again about Moscow's desire to ameliorate the world situation and its contribution to the settlement of the Austrian question, to the end of the conflict with Yugoslavia, and to the Soviet invitation issued to Konrad Adenauer to visit Moscow. "However," Bulganin complained, "the Soviet government could do nothing with those men from the United States who want to prove, by any means, that they could achieve something by their policy of strength. . . . [S]uch a policy could bring nothing good to the United States itself." Nehru agreed with his counterpart's point and added that he did "not understand why a man with strong muscles should publicly demonstrate his muscles all the time."[38] Although they did not raise the issue of Indochina and Vietnam openly this time, the Soviet and Indian premiers most likely had it in mind.

Soviet anxiety over developments in Indochina was also evident in the opening passage of a memorandum that Foreign Minister Molotov sent the CPSU Central Committee on May 19:

> At the present time the activity of the Americans has increased in South Vietnam; it is aimed at ousting the French from Vietnam. The Americans are trying to undermine the economic position of France. They are working actively to oust the French from the army, trying to assign their advisers to the most important posts. They strengthen their political influence by bribing not only political leaders but whole organizations.[39]

Moscow's concern was understandable because one of the premises of peace in the region, the French presence, began disappearing. The growing U.S. influence would demand a Soviet response and its deeper involvement in a conflict in a remote region. But North Vietnam welcomed this situation that the Kremlin wanted to avoid. Ho Chi Minh undoubtedly factored in the growing U.S. influence when he was planning his visit to the Soviet Union.

Counting on Soviet apprehension about the increasingly active U.S. role in the region, the North Vietnamese leader decided to probe Moscow's attitude toward military cooperation with the DRV. In a conversation with the Soviet ambassador in Hanoi, Ho raised the question of Vo Nguyen Giap's inclusion in the delegation to Moscow. Ho Chi Minh characteristically expressed his opinion that the DRV minister of defense should not visit Beijing and Moscow. He also told the ambassador he was going to bring up before the Central Committees of Soviet and Chinese Communist parties the question of agreeing to a plan for the DRV's defense. He continued that it would therefore be expedient to convene in Beijing a meeting of responsible military officials from the USSR, the PRC, and

63

the DRV with Giap's participation.[40] Thus, while he made a concession on Giap's trip to Moscow, he also put forward a demand for some form of military cooperation.

Moscow's response was evasive. Apparently, the question of close cooperation in the military sphere had been discussed with the Vietnamese several times before. Therefore the Soviet Foreign Ministry found it wise to ask the military's advice. The military's response was unequivocal. In a letter, the general staff drew the attention of the Foreign Ministry to the fact that Chinese military advisers to the People's Army of Vietnam (PAV) "know specifics of that country and its army quite well. They have many years of experience in assisting the Vietnamese comrades on the questions of the buildup of armed forces, the training and education of soldiers." As to help from the Soviet Union, the letter received from the general staff continues, "the Vietnamese comrades could at any time receive necessary consultation from us through the command of the People's Liberation Army of China as it is practicing in the present time."[41] The Soviet Foreign Ministry then cabled the Soviet ambassador in Hanoi; the ministry's response avoided any clear-cut promises or obligations on Moscow's part. After agreeing with Ho Chi Minh that it would be inexpedient for Vo Nguyen Giap to come to the Soviet capital, the Foreign Ministry went on: "As to the question of convoking in Beijing a meeting of Soviet and Chinese military officials together with Vo Nguyen Giap, inform Com. Ho Chi Minh that this question, in your opinion, could be considered during his visit to Moscow after having taken into account the Chinese comrades' views on this issue."[42]

While the North Vietnamese government delegation was visiting China, the Soviets worked out their positions for the negotiations with Ho Chi Minh. The Foreign Ministry together with the Ministry of Foreign Trade and the Ministry of Defense prepared directives for the Soviet–North Vietnam talks that were sent to the CPSU Central Committee for approval. The principal objective of the negotiations, as formulated in the directives, was:

> [F]urther development of friendly political, economic, and cultural cooperation between the USSR and the Democratic Republic of Vietnam with the purpose of all possible strengthening of the Democratic Republic of Vietnam and its international status, the unification of Vietnam on the basis of democracy, the complete implementation of the Geneva Accords on Indochina, and the earliest possible restoration of the people's economy of the Republic.[43]

The Soviet Union was planning to render necessary assistance to support the DRV's struggle for the unification of the country. Moscow approved of Hanoi's intentions to cooperate with the French on this matter and advised the Vietnamese to agree on the existence in South Vietnam for the time being of a "political regime different from the regime in the DRV (a republican regime with the participation of the French capital in the sphere of economy and a slower tempo of democratic reforms)."[44] North Vietnamese cooperation with the French was necessary as a counterweight to the U.S. influence in South Vietnam.[45]

On the question of the DRV's cooperation with China and the Soviet Union, the directives contain the following passage, which reflects the essence of the Kremlin's policy in Indochina: "Give Ho Chi Minh to understand that on practical questions relating to rendering aid to the Democratic Republic of Vietnam, it is expedient for the Vietnamese comrades to consult and ask for the advice of the Chinese friends more often, taking into account that the latter are familiar with the situation in Vietnam and that the DRV government has to solve at this time the problems that have been recently resolved or are being solved in China."[46] The Soviet leadership decided to reject the idea of joint Sino-Soviet economic and military missions to North Vietnam on the grounds that "practice of cooperation between the Chinese and Vietnamese friends has already been established and has proved its value, which does not exclude, of course, rendering technical assistance to the DRV on the part of the Soviet Union."[47]

Thus Moscow did not want to abandon the division-of-responsibilities principle in its relations with the DRV. This was also evident in the instructions concerning concrete issues of bilateral relations. Although the Soviet Union was ready to allocate three hundred million rubles for the restoration of the North Vietnamese economy (in the final communiqué this amount was increased to four hundred million rubles[48]), help the DRV in the construction of industry and the training of Vietnamese youth in Soviet colleges and universities, and send its advisers to North Vietnam, nothing like the Soviet-Chinese Treaty of Friendship, Alliance, and Mutual Assistance was on the agenda of the Soviet leaders. On all questions relating to political and military cooperation with the DRV, Moscow was prepared to act only through the Chinese allies.

To compensate for their reluctant relations with the "Vietnamese friends," the Soviet leadership planned to organize an impressive reception ceremony for the DRV delegation from the moment it landed in the USSR. At Ho Chi Minh's stopovers in Irkutsk, Novosibirsk, and Sverdlovsk, he was to be greeted by the highest local officials and hundreds of Soviet citizens. All the members of the CPSU Central Committee Presidium had to meet the delegation at the capital's central airport, with Nikita Khrushchev, Nikolai Bulganin, and Kliment Voroshilov, the chairman of the Presidium of the Supreme Soviet of the USSR (analogous to the position of president in a Western country) among them. In the group greeting Ho Chi Minh were the heads of almost all leading ministries and all deputies of the foreign minister. Three to four thousand Muscovites were gathered at the airport to hail the leading representatives of the "heroic people of Vietnam."[49]

The program for the visit was likewise impressive. On the second day after his arrival, Ho Chi Minh was to talk to Voroshilov and Bulganin as well as negotiate with the Soviet leadership and ministers. Another meeting with the Soviet leaders was planned for the fifth day of the visit. A reception for five hundred to six hundred guests was to be organized in the Kremlin in honor of the delegation. The Vietnamese were invited to see the All-Union Agricultural Exhibition and an atomic power station.[50]

The splendid reception for the North Vietnamese delegation was designed not only to conceal Soviet reluctance to develop full-scale cooperation with the DRV but also to use the Hanoi regime to put obstacles in the way of U.S. penetration in the region. Although determined to avoid military obligations to Hanoi, Molotov in May suggested that the Workers' Party of Vietnam "pay more attention to the work in South Vietnam with the purpose of the intensification and rallying of patriotic and anti-imperialist forces in that part of Vietnam."[51] The Soviet foreign minister prepared a draft of a telegram to Ho advising him "to use the situation in South Vietnam for the strengthening of public forces there who are for the unification of the country on the democratic basis and who are for national independence of the country."[52] In other words, the Soviets found it useful to work with the South Vietnamese population and even act through religious sects in the South in order to instigate anti-American feelings in the country.

When he arrived in Moscow, Ho Chi Minh submitted to his hosts a list of questions on a broad range of problems relating to DRV internal and external policy. To Ho's question of who was the "principal enemy of the Vietnamese people,"[53] the Foreign Ministry responded: "Tell Com. Ho Chi Minh that, in our opinion, at the present time the principal and most dangerous enemy of the Vietnamese people is American imperialism, which undertakes active actions aimed at the wrecking of the Geneva agreements and the transformation of Vietnam into an American colony." The ministry emphasized that, "in the Soviet government's opinion, it would be necessary to direct the efforts of the Vietnamese comrades toward the intensification of work among all strata of the population of South Vietnam in order to counter the American influence."[54]

Although these Soviet instructions, had they been known to the West, would certainly have been treated as instigators of the subversive activities in South Vietnam that led to the Vietnam War, they fell far short of Hanoi's strategy in the South in later years and within the customs of international politics, which include manipulation of public opinion in other states.[55] Moscow wanted to limit North Vietnamese activity toward South Vietnam to a secret propaganda war against the Saigon regime, while not excluding some sort of cooperation between the North and the South. Consequently the Soviets could not approve public demonstrations of hostility by the North Vietnamese regime vis-à-vis its southern counterpart.

As early as December 1954, the head of the Southeast Asia Department, Kirill Novikov, addressed a memorandum to Molotov, in which he expressed his concern that information agencies in the DRV always characterized the Ngo Dinh Diem regime as a "puppet clique," "lackey of American imperialism," or a similar epithet. Novikov suggested that because, according to the Geneva agreements, the two Vietnamese governments would consult in July 1955 and hold general elections in 1956, the Soviet Union should "recommend carefully to the government of the Democratic Republic of Vietnam not to resort to epithets of various kinds in relation to both Ngo Dinh Diem and his government."[56]

In sum, the Soviet–North Vietnamese negotiations in Moscow demonstrated that the most that the Soviet leaders were prepared to do for the DRV was provide political and moral support in the struggle for implementation of the provisions of the final declaration of the Geneva conference, especially the general elections and the assistance toward the restoration and development of the DRV economy. The joint communiqué signed upon the completion of Ho Chi Minh's visit to the USSR in the summer of 1955 contained the usual formal words about the unity of views of the leaders of both countries, the international situation and prospects of bilateral cooperation, their unanimity of opinion on the execution of the Geneva Accords, and their hopes for further strengthening of peace in the world and a relaxation of international tensions. The communiqué also stressed the importance of consultations between North and South Vietnam and condemned "attempts to include South Vietnam, Laos, and Cambodia in the zone covered by the aggressive military bloc in Southeast Asia (SEATO) which was in contradiction to the Geneva Accords."[57]

The United States was not mentioned by name in the communiqué; however, the Soviet and North Vietnamese governments "drew attention" to the "attempts" on the part of "some foreign countries" to interfere in the affairs of South Vietnam, Laos, and Cambodia and to "thrust on those countries" military agreements incompatible with the Geneva Accords.[58] The Soviets promised to raise the issue of political settlement in Vietnam at the upcoming summit of the four great powers that was scheduled for late July in Geneva.[59]

The Moscow negotiations in 1955 apparently did not satisfy Hanoi's expectation for a full-fledged alliance with the Soviet Union. Moscow was unwilling to jeopardize its process of détente with the West and undermine the Geneva settlement by any display of an open alignment with the Communist regime in the

North of Vietnam. Yet it could not disregard the needs of a friendly regime in Southeast Asia either. The Kremlin tried to solve this dilemma by developing its cooperation with the DRV in the economic sphere and encouraging the struggle for the implementation of the Geneva Accords. But by declaring the Soviet Union's adherence to the agreements reached in Geneva, Soviet leaders were actually signaling their satisfaction with the preservation of the status quo in Indochina as established in July 1954.

5. Neither Peace nor War

*. . . Since the Government in South Viet-Nam adhered
unflinchingly to the position that it was not a
party to the Geneva Agreement or Final Declaration
and therefore under no obligation to discuss
elections and to the view that in any case it was
unrealistic to think that any elections held in
Communist North Viet-Nam could be free, there was
nothing that could be done.*

**Documents relating to British Involvement in
the Indo-China Conflict, 1945–1956[1]**

Ho Chi Minh was still in Moscow when, on July 16, 1955, South Vietnamese premier Ngo Dinh Diem broadcast his rejection of elections in Vietnam. Diem's rebuff was a response to Pham Van Dong's June statement about the DRV's willingness to hold a consultative conference on elections. Referring to the fact that his government did not sign the Geneva agreements that were concluded "against the will of the Vietnamese people," Diem declared that he was not bound in any way by them. Although he did not reject the principle of free elections as a means of achieving the unification of Vietnam, he considered free elections impossible as long as there was a Communist regime in the North.[2]

Diem's broadcast occurred four days before the deadline imposed by the final declaration of the Geneva conference, which prescribed in paragraph seven that consultations on future elections in Vietnam were to be held "between the competent representative authorities of the two zones from 20 July, 1955, onwards."[3]

South Vietnam's rejection was hardly a surprise to the Hanoi leadership and its Soviet and Chinese allies. Although hope always existed that the South Vietnamese regime—to preserve the appearance of compliance with the Geneva Accords—would at least agree to consultations about general elections in Vietnam, nobody believed that the elections themselves would ever take place. Victor Bator, an author who analyzed the Geneva Accords and their implementation, asks:

> Would Ho Chi Minh let his country slide into the area controlled by America? Would Diem be willing to disappear behind the bamboo curtain? Would Communist China allow Ho Chi Minh—even if Hanoi wanted—to align himself with the Free World? Or, for that matter, would the United States look with indifference on Diem making a deal with Ho Chi Minh, [Mao Zedong], or [Zhou Enlai]?[4]

Bator concludes: "The answers to all these questions could only be *no.*"

Several reasons account for such an outcome. First, the Geneva documents were "extremely vague in their references to a political settlement and to nation-wide elections."[5] The final declaration that contained provisions about the eventual political settlement in Vietnam was not signed by any of the conference participants. Moreover, South Vietnamese officials protested from the outset that they had not been consulted about the cease-fire agreement and the declaration insofar as they covered Vietnam. The United States only took note of the Geneva documents, promising not to upset the settlement by threats or use of force. In addition, the Geneva conference had not worked out effective machinery for implementation of the accords. The cease-fire agreement envisaged the establishment of international commissions on supervision and control (the International Control Commissions, or ICCs) composed of representatives of India, Canada, and Poland, with India occupying the chair. The main task of the ICC for Vietnam would be to supervise the fulfillment of the cease-fire, the regrouping of troops, the nonviolation of the demarcation line as well as prevent the introduction of arms and war matériel into both zones of Vietnam.[6] In addition to these principal obligations, the commission members were to be responsible for arranging for the supervision of the all-Vietnam elections.

To ensure the effectiveness of the commission's activities, the Geneva conference had specified in paragraph thirteen of the final declaration that participants "agree to consult one another on any question which may be referred to them by the International Supervisory Commission. . . ."[7] But it was unclear what form such consultations would take. In fact, the historical introduction to the documents relating to British involvement in the Indochina conflict stated, "the Conference devised no standing machinery through which member States might discharge their responsibility."[8] Eventually such machinery was devised, and the foreign ministers of Great Britain and the Soviet Union—both countries were responsible for financing the commissions in Indochina—became the channel for the transmission of reports from the ICCs to the other conference participants and to the referees, to whom complaints of violations of the Geneva agreements were addressed.

The role of the cochairs was as ambiguous as the wording of the conference documents, however. "[T]heir authority rested on no clear foundation. Indeed, the Agreements and the Final Declaration are oblivious of their very existence; and though they became virtually the executive arm of the conference, there was no sanction for their authorities except the practical needs of the situation."[9]

This ambiguity of their position notwithstanding, neither the Soviets nor British opposed their continuing leading role in the implementation of the Geneva agreements. Both Vyacheslav Molotov and Anthony Eden were determined not to allow the settlement in Indochina be undermined, which would push the world back to the situation fraught with the danger of war. For Eden, "more than other statesmen present, Geneva came close to being the model Cold War solution. He had a big stake in its success. . . ."[10] As for Molotov, the Geneva conference was the last gleam in the coming twilight of his power in the Kremlin, and he might have been anxious to remove any shadow from it. The risk of failure for Moscow and London was negligible, for no one could reproach the cochairs for poor fulfillment of their obligations because no such obligations had been fixed by the Geneva documents. As a result, when these "fathers" of the settlement in Indochina left office—Eden to become prime minister and Molotov to sink into obscurity—the cochairs lost the personal aspect and became only routine duties of the serving foreign ministers.

Yet neither the ICC, which was responsible for supervision of the general elections, nor the cochairs, who served mainly as go-betweens for the conference participants, possessed the instruments necessary to enforce the political provisions of the Geneva agreements. Who would pressure Ngo Dinh Diem? The Soviet Union did not have diplomatic relations with South Vietnam. The British, although they had recognized the Saigon regime, did not enjoy any influence over its leaders. The only country that could impose its will on the South Vietnamese leaders was the United States, but its leaders were least enthusiastic about the outcome of the Geneva conference, and the Eisenhower administration refused to be directly associated with its agreements. It regarded the allocation of even part of the territory of Vietnam to the Communists as a betrayal of the principles of the policy of containment, and it was determined to prevent Ho Chi Minh from extending his power farther south than the seventeenth parallel. The United States intended to use any means necessary to create in the South a bastion against Communist penetration of the region. And for Washington the political provisions of the Geneva agreements had become an obstacle to its plans.

Although the United States always tried to present itself as a champion of free elections—compared with Soviet tyranny—no one doubted that, if such elections were to take place in Vietnam, a Vietminh victory would have been the outcome.[11] Although the British advocated holding the elections and risking a Vietminh victory,[12] the Eisenhower administration, especially Secretary of State John Foster Dulles, found this unacceptable. The best solution for the United States was to neither oppose the elections nor risk them. Most U.S. officials wanted to manipulate the election issue: "Saigon could seize the propaganda advantage by announcing its willingness to begin talks on July 20, in preparation for a 1956 vote. If Diem insisted on numerous safeguards to guarantee a free election, the DRV would probably balk and thus appear to be the obstacle to the election process."[13] Diem in fact chose a more straightforward way. On July 16, because he considered fair elections in Vietnam impossible, he simply spoke out against negotiations with the Communist regime of Ho Chi Minh on the elections issue.

To prove it was serious about its stand against elections, the South Vietnamese government went even further. On July 20, the anniversary of the Geneva agreements, it proclaimed a day of national shame. That morning a crowd of several hundred young men armed with sticks, knives, and other weapons that could easily be found in their backyards attacked the hotels where the members of the ICC were staying. The crowd broke open rooms, cut telephone connections, and destroyed and stole personal belongings of the ICC staff. An Indian member of the ICC for Laos who was visiting Saigon was attacked and injured. The demonstrators also burned the commission's cars, which were parked outside the hotels. Similar demonstrations occurred at several places in South Vietnam. In no case did the South Vietnamese authorities take measures to bring the rioters under control.[14]

The timing of Diem's statement on the elections and of the demonstrations against the Geneva agreements could not have been worse. On July 18, the heads of the governments of the four great powers—France, Great Britain, the Soviet Union, and the United States—gathered in Geneva for their first summit meeting since the end of the Second World War. An outright violation, such as Diem's, of international agreements was regarded by those who wanted a more favorable atmosphere in international relations as a threat to their plans. Summit participants issued strong messages condemning the South Vietnamese government and demanding that it take all necessary action for the proper functioning of the ICC. But their declarations in favor of all-Vietnam elections seemed to be just a formality. None was prepared at that time to move farther. Even the Soviets were reluctant to spoil "the spirit of Geneva," the only result of the 1955 summit.

The draft of the directives to the Soviet delegation showed that the issue of Vietnamese elections was not on the list of Soviet priorities at the 1955 summit. Before the directives were drafted, the Soviets started receiving indications from the West that the elections in Vietnam were hardly possible in Vietnam's existing situation. For example, a Polish representative to the ICC, R. Melkhior, visited the Soviet embassy in Hanoi in January 1955 and confided that a prominent member of the British Labour party doubted that the elections were possible since a proper political climate for them did not exist in Vietnam. Ngo Dinh Diem could not come to Hanoi, while Ho Chi Minh had no opportunity to go to Saigon. If Ho Chi Minh won the election, Diem would not be able to form an opposition, and in the opposite circumstances Ho Chi Minh could be repressed. The Labourite believed that Diem was ready to start negotiations with the DRV in July and that he had the support of the U.S. ambassador in Saigon, J. Lawton Collins, because Diem intended to accuse the Hanoi regime of suppressing freedom and sabotaging further talks. Regarding British policy, the Labour Party member confirmed that, although England was supporting anti-Communist regimes in Asia, it would not oppose regime change as a result of internal processes and would not resort to military intervention.[15] This British politician's opinions, relayed to the Soviets, were close to reality, and it was not the only confirmation of Western plans regarding Vietnam to reach Moscow.

With this knowledge and unwilling to overemphasize the issue of Vietnam at the Geneva summit of 1955, which was to be devoted to more global and urgent problems of East-West relations, Moscow took a passive attitude toward the question of the Vietnam elections. Directives from Moscow confined the Soviet delegation at Geneva to registering the fact that the fulfillment of the military clauses of the Geneva agreements of 1954 had created a favorable situation for political settlement in Indochina. The Soviet delegation had to "draw attention of the conference participants to the political and economic chaos that existed in South Vietnam as a result of foreign interference and that Ngo Dinh Diem's government pursues a policy aimed at the disruption of the general elections in Vietnam in 1956." The Soviets planned to state their support for holding a consultative conference between representatives of both parts of Vietnam with the help of the ICC, in case such necessity would arise.[16] It is noteworthy that, in the course of the work on the draft, all accusations against the United States were eliminated from the text of the directives, additional confirmation that Moscow did not want to allow the issue of Vietnam to destroy whatever prospects there were for normalization of relations with the West. The only problem that was resolved at the conference of four great powers in Geneva in 1955 was the transfer of the duties of the chairman of the 1954 Geneva conference from Anthony Eden to Harold Macmillan, who had succeeded Eden at the Foreign Office.[17]

Although the Soviets displayed passivity at the summit and did not press the Vietnam question, they were determined not to abandon it entirely. At Geneva in 1955 Eden assured Molotov that Britain, France, and the United States would recommend to Diem that he communicate his position on elections directly to the DRV.[18] Molotov, reassured, recommended that Hanoi request that the cochairs urge the Saigon government to agree to a consultative conference with the DRV even after Diem's refusal on August 9 to engage the Hanoi regime in direct correspondence.[19] The result was a letter from Pham Van Dong to the cochairs requesting their intervention in securing the implementation of the political terms of the Geneva agreements.

But Diem remained adamant. He had Washington's tacit approval, and he did not react to public pronouncements by his masters in the United States. A British official assessed Diem: "So long as Mr. Diem believes he can rely on American support whether or not he takes American advice, I doubt whether he will be deflected from his obstinate purpose."[20] What Washington did not expect was the DRV's behavior in these circumstances. "From the north came reasonable-sounding statements and an underlying moderate position that made it increasingly difficult to show 'that the failure to secure free elections is the fault of the Communists.'"[21]

This reasonable attitude remained the characteristic feature of Hanoi's stance until after all hopes for a peaceful solution of the problem of unification had disappeared. In the fall of 1955, the Vietnamese Communists had not yet abandoned plans to achieve unity of the country under their rule through elections. In a conversation with a Soviet diplomat, a member of the Politburo of the WPV, Truong Chinh, shared his own and his colleagues' views on the prospects of unification. To achieve this goal, he said, there were "two forms and two methods of the struggle": those of peaceful struggle, and those of force and violence. "In the present political situation," said Truong Chinh, "the most profitable for the Vietnamese people are the method and the form of peaceful struggle." Hanoi's use of peaceful struggle was conditioned, said the WPV leader, "by our adherence to the spirit and letter of the Geneva agreements." Truong Chinh warned, however, that this did not mean they were incapable of using violence. But the use of peaceful means, he repeated, in the existing political situation was more profitable.

Then Truong Chinh touched upon how to achieve the unity of the country peacefully. "Vietnam was temporarily divided in two zones," he argued. "Each zone has its own political system. . . . Each zone has its own government and armed forces. *Under such conditions neither zone can force the other and gain the upper hand.* Any such attempt would lead to war. . . . But we have to choose what kind of unification it will be: an immediate and complete unification or an incomplete, partial unification. *We are not demanding an immediate and complete unification. We even agree to a pro forma unification, and this is still better than the division of the country."*[22]

Truong Chinh further elaborated on the methods of such a unification. There must be general elections, after which a national assembly of the whole of Vietnam would be created. This assembly would elect the central government and would adopt a constitution accepted in both zones. Both the National Assembly and the government would include representatives of both zones. Armed forces of each zone would have their own rules and internal regulations but they would represent two parts of the one army. Internal policy would be organized in each zone. They would together, Chinh said, guarantee political freedoms and agrarian reform, but reform in the South would be different from in the North. Such a unification, Truong Chinh concluded, would not lead to complete unity, and the governing circles in South Vietnam would see that they still retained their positions and advantages.[23]

Even after the failure of their attempts to begin consultations with the Diem regime, the North Vietnamese leaders clearly did not abandon their intentions to unify the country peacefully. Moreover, they were prepared to be flexible during the process. Their behavior did not support the image of intransigent and militant Communists that was created by U.S. and South Vietnamese propaganda.

Quite to the contrary, it was Diem who proved his intransigence and rigidity throughout the period leading up to the failure of general elections in Vietnam. On October 23, 1955, the Diem government held a referendum in South Vietnam that approved of the removal of Bao Dai as chief of state and his replacement by Ngo Dinh Diem. Three days later, South Vietnam was proclaimed a republic with Diem as its president. Diem announced his plans to hold a unilateral election of a national assembly on March 4, 1956. This assembly was to draw up a constitution for the new republic. These unilateral steps by Diem undermined what remained of the political provisions of the Geneva Accords.

States that had approved these accords did not act decisively to take issue with Diem. Western countries led by the United States recognized the new republic by the end of 1955. Great Britain was among the countries that did not risk its alliance with Washington by openly protesting violations of the Geneva agreements. Arthur Combs wrote, "As the year drew to a close, Anthony Eden and his government, finally resigned to the failure of the accords, abandoned their last trench line. . . . The British were now merely casting about for some way to forestall public admission of Geneva's death."[24] In November 1955, Denis

Allen, a senior Foreign Office official, advised the British government to distance itself from its duties as a sponsor of the Geneva accords.[25] As a result, when he was asked on December 21 about Diem's statement on unilateral elections, the British foreign secretary stated that this was the internal affair of Vietnam. Britain was also inclined to regard its role and responsibility as cochair as "neither more nor less than those of the other Powers adhering to the Final Declaration of the Geneva Conference."[26] France, also, ignored the South Vietnamese defiance.

Moscow could do little to prevent the peace built up at Geneva from falling apart. Although the Soviets possessed enough weapons in their diplomatic arsenal to insist on more decisive actions against violations of the international agreement, the question was whether they wanted to draw down their stores to achieve goals not on their list of priorities. Because the possibility of peaceful unification had not disappeared completely, it was necessary for the Kremlin to act in support of the aspirations of its Vietnamese friends. The Soviet Union therefore successfully played the role of a faithful ally at the meetings of cochairs and at other international forums.

After the July 1955 summit, the two cochairs of the 1954 Geneva conference met in November 1955. By that time the Soviet and British foreign ministers had received a number of appeals and declarations supporting the idea of elections and condemning the policy of South Vietnam. Among this material was Pham Van Dong's August 17 letter to the cochairs and a letter from Zhou Enlai in support of the DRV position. In addition, Molotov and Macmillan possessed the fourth interim report prepared by the Vietnamese ICC, in which the Polish and Indian delegations warned of their inability to carry on the ICC activities "in the face of the declared opposition of the government of the State of Vietnam to the Geneva Agreements."[27] The cochairs decided to issue a letter on the Vietnam question; in it they would express their concern over the fulfillment of the Geneva agreements.

A draft of a letter proposed by Macmillan drew attention to the unsatisfactory implementation of some provisions of the agreements. It referred to the ICC's fourth interim report and pointed out the lack of cooperation between civil and military authorities of the northern and southern zones in their observation of articles 14(c) and 14(d) of the Vietnam cease-fire agreement.[28]

Articles 14(c) and 14(d) had been a battleground and a basis for accusations and counteraccusations for the North and the South since the first days after the Geneva conference. Article 14(c) required each party "to refrain from any reprisals or discrimination against persons or organizations on account of their activities during the hostilities and to guarantee their democratic liberties." Article 14(d) contained the provision that if "any civilians residing in a district controlled by one party" wanted to go and live in the zone assigned to the other party, they should have an opportunity to do so without any obstacle being created by the authority in that district.[29] Hanoi accused Diem of violating the cease-fire agreements because, in order to consolidate his power, he clearly tried to rid South Vietnam of real or assumed supporters of the Vietminh and he organized repressions against them. Diem, in turn, condemned Hanoi for violating the freedom of movement of its own people because of the North Vietnamese regime's earlier attempts to prevent the emigration to the South of 860,000 Red River delta inhabitants who decided to flee from the Communists after the victory of the Vietminh.[30]

Moscow objected to Macmillan's emphasis on articles 14(c) and 14(d). Molotov, in a letter to the CPSU Central Committee, said that the British foreign minister avoided "the main question of the unsatisfactory implementation of the provisions of the Geneva agreements concerning the preparation to the all-Vietnamese elections" while putting forward questions of the fulfillment of articles 14(c) and 14(d). Furthermore, Macmillan claimed that both the North and South Vietnamese were responsible for the violation of these articles. Because of this, in Molotov's opinion, Macmillan's draft could not be considered satisfactory. The following passage in the Soviet foreign minister's letter to his superiors is noteworthy: "However, *taking into account the English desire to drag out the solution of this question* [the question of the election], as well as taking into consideration an indisputable advantage for us that a joint message of the two chairmen will be sent to the participants of the Geneva conference and to the members of the International Commission on supervision in Vietnam, which draws attention to the unsatisfactory situation of the implementation of the Geneva agreements, the USSR Foreign Ministry finds it expedient to agree with Macmillan's draft of the message."[31] Instead of the paragraph in the British draft that stressed the failure of both sides to comply with articles 14(c) and 14(d), Molotov proposed a suggestion to the other conference participants and the ICC members that they send the cochairs their proposals for the improvement of the implementation of the Geneva agreements.

Molotov's letter shows that for Moscow the postponement of the solution to the elections problem was clearly preferable to the British decision to drop it entirely. If the British position on elections prevailed, Moscow could remain the only country, except perhaps for India, that continued to support the issue of elections. The battle would then be lost even before hope was abandoned that the elections would be held at the time specified at Geneva.

The message of the cochairs was not made public until December 21. It is unclear why such a delay took place. Possibly the Soviets decided to consult the Indians before the publication of the message; Nikita Khrushchev and Nikolai

Bulganin were on an official visit to India in November–December 1955. Nehru did discuss the political impasse in the implementation of the Geneva agreements with the Soviet leaders. And the joint Soviet-Indian communiqué of December 13, 1955, regretted the obstacles raised to the implementation of the Geneva agreements and urged all signatories to the Geneva settlement to eliminate these obstacles.[32]

In reply to the cochair's message of December 21, 1955, China, the DRV, Cambodia, Poland, and the Soviet Union proposed to reconvene the Geneva conference in order to settle all the problems relating to the settlement in Indochina. This idea had already been suggested by Pham Van Dong in September, but now it was supported by North Vietnamese allies as well as by Cambodia. China, on January 25, 1956, and North Vietnam on February 14, 1956, reiterated their appeals about reconvening the conference. Both countries wanted to invite the ICC powers to take part in it as well, on the grounds that "they understand the conditions in Vietnam and can make a useful contribution."[33] On February 18, the Soviet Union issued a note that supported this and declared that since "the measures previously taken by the two Chairmen to improve" the situation in Indochina had not "yielded positive results," Moscow shared "the opinion of the Governments of the Chinese People's Republic and the Democratic Republic of Viet-Nam about the expediency of summoning a new conference on Viet-Nam."[34] Hanoi's demand for a new Geneva conference was designed mainly as propaganda, however. Truong Chinh, who was in Moscow on the occasion of the twentieth CPSU congress at the time the diplomatic note was issued, informed his counterpart, Deputy Foreign Minister Vasilii Kuznetzov, that the central committee of his party had discussed the question of 1956 general elections in Vietnam several times and came to the conclusion that sufficient conditions for holding these elections did not exist. Yet the Vietnamese people hoped they would take place in July 1956. But because the consultative conference had not yet begun there would obviously be no elections during July. "If we were to inform the people about this," reasoned Chinh, "the result would be a sharp change for the worse in the mood of the people." How would it be possible to avoid such an outcome? Hanoi believed that "the best form would be the convening of the conference of nine states, participants of the Geneva conference on Indochina, plus three member states of the International Control Commission who will make a decision on this question."[35] Thus the DRV believed that the elections would be unsuccessful in any case and was searching only for a plausible way to explain this fact to its own people.

Kuznetzov referred to the Indian proposal to arrange a meeting of the two cochairs instead of a whole conference and warned Truong Chinh that the new conference might not be convened. The Soviets asked the opinion of their Vietnamese comrade on what to do in such a case. Truong Chinh repeated the North Vietnamese leadership's desire to convene a new conference; however, he thought it would be possible to agree on the meeting of the two cochairs, during which it would be necessary "to insist on the convening of a new conference on Vietnam."[36]

Armed with the consent of the Vietnamese allies, Moscow in March 1956 agreed to a meeting of the cochairs. In their note to the British government on March 30, the Soviets confirmed their support of the Chinese and North Vietnamese proposal for a new conference: "The summoning of such a conference would in the opinion of the Soviet Government, be the most expedient and effective means of settling the position in Vietnam." However, Moscow nodded toward Britain's opinion as well as toward the Indian proposal and said it "[did] not object to the preliminary discussion by the Chairmen of the Geneva Conference on Indo-China of the question of possible measures to guarantee the implementation of the Geneva Agreements in Viet-Nam, *including the question of summoning a new conference,* bearing in mind that this will help to more quickly reach agreement concerning the summoning of the above-mentioned conference."[37] By one stroke the Kremlin reconciled the opposing opinions of its allies and the West while it kept uppermost its own interests, which were based on its unwillingness to change the status quo in Vietnam. Moscow even seemed to be ready to close its eyes to the recent developments in Indochina although these developments threatened the whole edifice of the peace settlement created at Geneva.

On January 19, 1956, the South Vietnamese government requested the withdrawal of French troops by April 29, 1956, saying that the troops' presence in the South "was incompatible with Viet-Nam's concept of full independence."[38] Such a right was provided to the states of Indochina by the Geneva agreements. At Geneva, the Vietminh as well as its Communist allies considered the French the other party of the agreement, and their plans with respect to the future of the peace in the region were based on this assumption. It was expected that the French troops would remain in South Vietnam at least until the July 1956 elections. The withdrawal of French troops, although logical in the process of eliminating the French presence in the region, had started soon after the Geneva conference. This meant, however, that the French army ceased to be a guarantor of the cease-fire provisions and its responsibility would have to be assumed by the South Vietnamese government, the very government that refused more than once to be bound by the Geneva agreements.

Diem continued to take unilateral steps aimed at making South Vietnam an independent entity and the demarcation line its international boundary. On March 4, 1956, the election of the South Vietnamese constituent assembly took place. Later that year this assembly "debated" and approved a constitution for the Republic of Vietnam. Not only did the referendum of 1955 and the elections of 1956 create a formal basis for a new state in South Vietnam, they also solidified the Saigon regime and promoted Diem in the eyes of his U.S. partners. With these developments in the South, the peace in Vietnam started to resemble a house of cards ready to collapse. The first casualty was to be the International Control Commission.

The Indians first sounded the alarm. In a February 19, 1956, letter to the two cochairs, Nehru suggested that a review of the situation was necessary and could take place at a meeting of the cochairs. On March 26, the ICC chairman in Vietnam, G. Parthasarathi, warned the South Vietnamese about the serious situation in case a decision was not taken on the succession to the French high command.[39] In spite of this warning, on March 30, Saigon concluded an agreement with France for the complete evacuation of French troops and the dissolution of the French high command by April 28, 1956. On April 3, France informed the cochairs of the agreement. One week later, almost one hundred years after the first French soldiers had arrived in South Vietnam's capital, the last parade of French troops took place in Saigon.[40]

Much now depended on the outcome of negotiations that opened in London on April 11 between Lord Reading and Andrei Gromyko, representatives of the cochairs of the Geneva conference. Before these conversations took place, the new Soviet ambassador to the DRV, Mikhail Zimyanin, met with Vietnamese officials, discussed the subject of the forthcoming talks, and tried to explore Hanoi's views on the prospects of the situation in Vietnam. In one conversation, Pham Hung, a prominent member of the Central Committee of the Lao Dong Party (also known as the Workers' Party of Vietnam [WPV]), informed the Soviet diplomat about a preliminary Central Committee discussion of the situation created in Indochina as a result of the French withdrawal. The North Vietnamese leadership believed the situation was very precarious, for "the French have left and can no more bear responsibility for the implementation of the [Geneva] Agreements, while Diem does not recognize these Agreements and refuses to become a French successor in the fulfillment of their obligations assumed at Geneva." Therefore, the North Vietnamese believed that the struggle for the implementation of the Geneva agreements would be "prolonged and difficult," making it necessary to strengthen North Vietnam and emphasize the necessity of observance of the Geneva agreements. Hanoi did not reject the possibility of negotiations with the South; in fact, it stressed that it would be useful to arrange a "direct meeting with Diem as France's successor."[41] The North Vietnamese also advocated the continuation of the activity of the ICC.

After considering this and other conversations with the North Vietnamese leaders, the Soviet embassy prepared its own evaluation of the situation in Indochina. In the document entitled "Some Issues of the Implementation of the Geneva Agreements on Indochina," the embassy at the outset stated its firm conclusion that there was some understanding among the United States, England, and France on securing the division of Vietnam into two parts. The embassy also noted the existence of contradictions among the Western powers as well as between the Western powers and India. While the United States was sending economic and military assistance to Indochina with the aim of building up a strategic base against China and India, France did not want to withdraw from the region completely and was trying to preserve its political and economic position. And the British were trying to assume in South Vietnam "the functions of mediators between Diem (i.e., the Americans) and the French, pretending to play a role of 'peacemakers' . . . in order to strengthen their influence in that region. In reality, the British are following the lead of the Americans."[42] The Soviet embassy suggested that the growth of U.S. influence in Indochina could be countered by strengthening the influence of the socialist camp and promoting peace in the region; the embassy did not suggest that Moscow's first priority should be the struggle for elections or the declaration that Diem's actions in the South were illegal and therefore null and void. The Vietnam question was being solved by a characteristic Cold War method: counter the strength of the enemy with our strength.

Later in the document, however, the Soviet diplomats in Hanoi did pay attention to the problem of elections. They noted their Vietnamese comrades' inclination to postpone elections as a "compromise solution of the question" in exchange for Diem's promise to participate in elections and pursue a foreign policy that excluded the interference of other powers in South Vietnam's domestic affairs (an obvious allusion to the United States). The embassy document also emphasized Diem's interest in the ICC. On the basis of these two observations, the embassy put forward its recommendations. It advised that Moscow use Diem's acceptance of the "articles of the Geneva Agreements profitable for him" as well as his interest in the ICC in order to "make him agree on political consultations with the DRV" and create a favorable situation for the ICC's activities in the South. In the embassy's view, it was also possible to agree with the British proposal about the postponement of the elections "since political consultations between North and South Vietnam have not begun as yet." The cochairs would have to envision the summoning of a new Geneva conference in case Diem rejected consultations with the DRV.[43]

Step by step, Moscow was reconciling itself to the eventuality that the most important political provision of the Geneva agreements about the 1956 elections would not be fulfilled. It was therefore important for the Soviets to keep in force other conditions of the agreements that preserved peace in the region, and during the London talks between Gromyko and Lord Reading, Moscow displayed its readiness for compromise as long as the foundations of the Indochina settlement were not undermined.

In general, almost all the countries involved in the situation in Indochina demonstrated their compliance with the latest regional developments. Apart from the United States and South Vietnam—whose hostility toward the Geneva agreements was well known—the British clung to the view that "since the Government in South Viet-Nam adhered unflinchingly to the position that it was not a party to the Geneva Agreement or Final Declaration and therefore under no obligation to discuss elections . . . there was nothing that could be done."[44] France had to bow to Diem's demands to withdraw militarily while it cherished hopes of retaining its presence in economic and cultural life of the region.[45] India also abstained from decisive actions. "In retrospect this seems a major concession on the part of Nehru, who should have insisted on a legal commitment by South Vietnam to elections at some date beyond mid-1956. If there was ever an opportunity to vehemently insist upon the implementation of the Geneva Agreements on Vietnam, it was at this time, before the deadline set in the agreements for elections and before the withdrawal of French troops from South Vietnam."[46] India possessed leverage on the elections issue—it could threaten its withdrawal from the ICC—but Nehru did not want to use it out fear of jeopardizing his own vision of peace on the Asian subcontinent.

The Communist powers—the Soviet Union, China, and Poland (as a member of the ICC)—eagerly complied with Hanoi's acceptance of postponed elections. In their recommendations before the Lord Reading–Gromyko talks in London and Khrushchev and Bulganin's April 1956 visit to Great Britain, the Chinese reiterated to Moscow their proposal for a new conference on Indochina and stated that "the Chinese government also shares the Vietnamese government's opinion that, in the case of necessity, it is possible to consider the question about the postponement of the general elections in Vietnam."[47]

The London talks reflected this general attitude. The two cochairs reached a tacit understanding that there was no point in holding a new conference and that reunification would have to be postponed indefinitely. They also absolved France of any further obligation with respect to the Geneva agreements. At the end of the talks, the cochairs issued letters addressed both to the DRV and the Republic of Vietnam (the official name of the Saigon government) as well as to France and the ICC.[48] The decisions contained in these letters "represented for the most part a patchwork, a vague reiteration of the provisions of the Geneva Agreements without specific deadlines or guarantees, hardly altering the situation in Vietnam, where a political impasse continued in more or less the same manner as before."[49] It did not help that at the same time the cochairs were negotiating prospects for peace in Indochina, two Soviet leaders—Khrushchev and Bulganin—came to London for the first high-level visit in the history of Soviet-British relations. The subject of Indochina did not occupy a prominent place during the London visit.[50]

Thus the Lord Reading–Gromyko talks sealed the fate of the Vietnam partition, which had come to resemble Germany and Korea. Such an outcome was of course most disappointing to Hanoi. It became clear that there would be no general election in July 1956 or in the near future. Furthermore, the Vietnamese Communists had to bow to the fact that no new conference would resolve the impasse in Indochina. Hanoi might very well have felt betrayed by its Communist allies on this issue. Even the Chinese, as soon as the London decisions were announced, dropped their demand for a conference.[51] Nevertheless, soon after the London talks, on May 11, Pham Van Dong addressed one more letter to Ngo Dinh Diem. "In a conciliatory tone as never thereafter,"[52] the North Vietnamese premier called for general elections, the result of which would be a coalition government. He suggested restoration and development of normal relations between the two zones as a preliminary step toward creating favorable conditions for elections. Diem rejected this approach as well.[53]

The Communist leaders in Hanoi found themselves in an uneasy situation. They had to explain to their people the latest developments on the question of the reunification of Vietnam. They had to justify their adherence to using peaceful means for achieving this goal even when it became clear that reunification was impossible given the intransigence of the Saigon regime. Leaders in the North had to resist their comrades' desire to resort to violence, especially after the South Vietnamese government repression of former Vietminh members and those suspected of supporting them. According to some estimates, twelve thousand were killed during 1955–1957 in South Vietnam.[54] A January 1956 presidential ordinance prohibited all political opposition. By the spring of that year, fifteen thousand to twenty thousand peasants labeled as Vietminh sympathizers had been detained in reeducation camps.[55] Newspapers were closed routinely. These actions as well as the general consolidation of the Saigon regime were made possible by U.S. support. In the first year after the Geneva conference, Diem received $322 million in aid from Washington.[56] This aid increased without interruption in the following years.

Because they encountered repression in the South when prospects of peaceful reunification were bleak, the Communist cadres remaining in the South after the Vietminh's withdrawal[57] questioned the North's policy and began to consider various military solutions to reunification. Sometime in March 1956, Le Duan, who headed the South Vietnamese Communists at the time, presented the 14-point plan of action that had been adopted by the Nam Bo regional committee. The plan recommended military action in combination with other activities in the South, the creation of support bases and more battalions, and the consolidation of the military organizations in districts (interzones) in South Vietnam. Hanoi turned down this plan as premature.[58] But the North Vietnamese leadership understood that it would not be able to contain these demands indefinitely. Ho Chi Minh implied this during his conversation with the Soviet ambassador. He confirmed that there were almost no prospects for political consultations with the South Vietnamese government or all-Vietnam elections, and, as a result, DRV cadres as well as ordinary people were now asking what should be done in order to achieve unification of the country. Especially concerned, in Ho's words, were the "many thousands of Vietnamese who had come from the South." They were asking when they would be able to return home, hence the basis for their discontent.[59]

Ho Chi Minh informed the Soviet ambassador that the Vietnamese Politburo had discussed the new situation in Vietnam, and Ho revealed what the Politburo believed were shortcomings of policy. The lack of foresight that "the French would kneel to the Americans so early" was mentioned as one shortcoming.[60] Ho also said that the Central Committee of the Lao Dong Party was preparing instructions about tasks and methods for the cadres working in the South. In conclusion, Ho Chi Minh repeated his assessment of the situation:

> The situation has become more complicated. The Workers' Party intends to concentrate its attention on the task of the strengthening of the DRV and the intensification of the struggle for the unification of the country. It is necessary to increase support of the democratic forces struggling in the South. The underground of the Workers' Party in the South had been preserved, in spite of fierce repression on the part of Diem, and the great losses that the party underground suffered, particularly in Interzone V. In the southern districts of the country the underground has been preserved better; there are clandestine armed forces [there].[61]

Moscow was not frightened by Ho Chi Minh's almost open admission of the possibility of armed struggle in the South. Soviet leaders were coming around to the view that as long as the status quo was preserved and developments in Indochina did not threaten to jeopardize international stability, there was nothing to worry about in South Vietnam. The Kremlin was even prepared to go so far as to agree on the formalization of the existence of two separate states in Vietnam, which was the implication of the discussion over the admission of South Vietnam to the United Nations.

On January 23, 1957, thirteen countries of the Western bloc introduced two draft resolutions in the special political committee of the UN General Assembly calling on the Security Council to consider the applications of South Korea and South Vietnam for membership in the United Nations. The next day the Soviet delegation objected to the resolution because it "suggested that South Korea and South Vietnam represented the whole of Korea and the whole of Viet Nam respectively." Moscow proposed instead that the Security Council consider simultaneous admission of the "Democratic Republic of Korea, South Korea, the Democratic Republic of Vietnam and South Vietnam."[62] The Soviet proposal mentioned "the states" of Vietnam, thus implying sovereign and independent status of the North and South.[63] Wang Bingnan, a Chinese diplomat, has written that Khrushchev had toyed with this idea since 1956 and it was well known in diplomatic circles in both the United States and China.[64]

The Soviet proposal apparently was made without prior consultations with the North Vietnamese. On January 25, 1957, DRV premier Pham Van Dong sent a protest to the Security Council and the General Assembly, drawing attention to the fact that the proposal by the thirteen countries was "at variance with the spirit of the Geneva Agreements of 1954"[65] and that an "attempt of the administration of South Vietnam—an administration that has only temporary power over the territory of one of the zones of Vietnam (according to article 14a of the Geneva Agreements on the cessation of hostilities in Vietnam)—to obtain South Vietnam's admission to the United Nations Organization represents an act aimed at the perpetuation of the division of Vietnam."[66] Pham Van Dong referred to the final communiqué of the conference of nonaligned nations at Bandung that stated that Vietnam could become a member of the UN only as an unified country. This communiqué, unlike the final declaration of the Geneva conference, had been approved by Saigon.

Did the Soviets not perceive the implication of their proposal to admit both zones of Vietnam as independent states? Their proposal revealed that they assumed there were no prospects for the unification of Vietnam in the nearest future. If not, why not therefore counter the Western resolution about the admission of South Vietnam with the more impartial suggestion to accept both parts of the country in the world body? But Moscow clearly failed to see the symbolism of this step as a de facto recognition of the Saigon regime.

During their meeting on January 30, 1957, Ho Chi Minh drew the Soviet ambassador's attention to the Soviets' symbolic act. He brought up Diem's declaration that the Soviet proposal for simultaneous admission to the UN of North and South Vietnam "means the recognition by the Soviet Union of the competence of the Diem government and, therefore, the liquidation of the Geneva agreements."[67] Thus, Ho implicitly accused Moscow of lining up with the

Saigon regime in undermining the Geneva agreements, the very agreements that the Soviets had helped to work out but to which they did not remain faithful. The Soviet ambassador made excuses for the actions of his superiors, reminded Ho that the Soviet Union was defending "vital interests" of the DRV, and tried to prove that the Soviet position in the United Nations did not "contradict the Geneva agreements and the struggle of the Vietnamese people for the peaceful unification of the country." If the Soviet Union vetoed the proposal about the admission of South Vietnam in the UN, he argued, the United States would do the same with respect to North Vietnam.[68]

Yet the Soviet excuses were weak and the Soviet foreign ministry admitted this internally. In a memorandum to Deputy Foreign Minister Nikolai Patolichev, head of the ministry's Southeast Asia Department, B. Volkov stated that the Soviet draft of the resolution at the UN did contradict "the well-grounded position of the Vietnamese friends." He expressed his concern that this proposal could "give cause for objectionable interpretations" of the Soviet position with regard to the Geneva agreements and suggested withdrawing this resolution while supporting Pham Van Dong's letter instead.[69] The Soviet delegation at the UN forestalled any new instructions, however, and even before new instructions came from Moscow, it declared that on the question of Vietnamese admission to the United Nations it would stand with the position of the DRV.[70] At the Security Council meeting on September 9, 1957, the Soviet representative vetoed the thirteen-power draft resolution and insisted that the question of admission be postponed until after the unification of Vietnam.[71]

Moscow, however, continued to base its policy on the recognition of the existence of two states on the territory of Vietnam. The Soviet ambassador in Hanoi, Mikhail Zimyanin, stated this plainly during a conversation with the Chinese chargé d'affaires, Li Zhimin, in the aftermath of the discussion at the UN. Although he denied that there were any disagreements between Moscow and Hanoi on the question of admission to the UN, Zimyanin spoke for the need to more closely coordinate the tactics of the struggle for the unification of Vietnam in the future. Zimyanin referred to the fact that Vietnam was divided into two states and this division would remain over a "more or less long period of time," but the Vietnamese Communists sometimes did not take this into account. As an example, the Soviet ambassador criticized "some Vietnamese comrades" who worked in South Vietnam and who proposed to organize armed uprisings against the Diem regime. Zimyanin called such an approach to the situation "oversimplified" and "non-Marxist" and justified Soviet policy as necessary in order to prevent South Vietnam from falling into the hands of the Americans.[72] It seems that Moscow was even prepared to grant recognition to the Diem regime if the North Vietnamese would not vehemently oppose the idea.

The Soviet leadership's Vietnam policy fell in line with the Kremlin's general policy in the Third World, inaugurated soon after Stalin's death and confirmed at the twentieth CPSU congress in February 1956. It looked back to "Lenin's vision of forging a united front between the nationalist aspirations of the developing world and the revolutionary, anti-Western objectives of the Soviet regime."[73] In part, it was a response to U.S. efforts to create an alliance system in Asia within the framework of the policy of containment. Moscow wanted to ensure the neutrality of as many countries as possible in the international struggle between capitalism and communism. Of course, the Soviet Union's principal targets were countries that professed a nonaligned approach to foreign policy, for example, Afghanistan, India, Indonesia, and Egypt;[74] but the Kremlin did not want to abandon hope that other countries, even such an anti-Communist countries such as South Vietnam, would leave the Western bloc and choose nonalignment.

The Soviet leaders already had in Cambodia a good example of a country in Indochina that, while remaining opposed to Communist ideology and developing relations with Washington, was not eager to align itself blindly with U.S. policy in the region. Although Laos still suffered from internal disorder and political instability, it was possible that it would follow Cambodia's policy as soon as it could establish a stable government. Why then did South Vietnam become an exception? Why, the Soviets wondered, should it refuse to enter a "peace zone" proclaimed by Khrushchev at the twentieth party congress, a "vast" zone that included "socialist as well as non-socialist peaceloving countries in Europe and Asia."[75] South Vietnam might be able to find its own place in it, the Soviets thought.

Such hopes with respect to South Vietnam might have existed in the minds of the Soviet leaders, considering their "great optimism concerning developments in the Third World" and "a lack of detailed information or ideological formulations concerning domestic developments in the Third World."[76] Such optimism was not totally baseless. The Soviet Union had never been a colonial country with overseas territories like Britain and France. Moreover, the USSR's "connections with colonialism" were much less visible than those of its rival, the United States.

> Moscow had one other advantage as well, which was that industrialization in the USSR had proceeded much more rapidly than in the capitalist west. For people suspicious of capitalism anyway because of its links to imperialism, this record of accelerated development— this lure of a short cut to economic prosperity and social justice— provided yet another incentive to look to Marxism-Leninism as a model.[77]

If the head of the South Vietnamese government had not been as staunch an anti-Communist and as fanatical a Catholic as Diem, who knows whether Soviet Third World policy would have succeeded in the South of Vietnam? But it is also necessary to remember that Soviet hands were tied by the regime in Hanoi, which followed closely Moscow's every step and vigorously protested every sign of rapprochement with the Saigon government, as the episode of admission to the UN had demonstrated. It was therefore hardly possible for Soviet leaders to realize a policy in the South of Vietnam similar to Soviet policies toward other Third World countries. It would have risked losing its friends in the North.

It became clear by 1957 that most of the countries involved in the 1954 Geneva conference had concluded that the division of Vietnam was, if not permanent, at least long lasting. China was no exception. Although the Chinese leaders formally assured Hanoi of their support for the policy of unification, they did nothing to translate such declarations into reality. For example, Beijing did not support the Soviet proposal to admit North and South Vietnam into the United Nations. But there were no reports of any Chinese protests on behalf of the North Vietnamese either.[78]

What did still remain of the Geneva agreements on Vietnam was the ICC, although its work by 1957 "was truncated, confined mainly to supervision of the cease-fire, checking the imports of war materials, and investigating complaints regarding violation of freedoms under articles 14(c) and (d)."[79] Nevertheless, the Communists were interested in the ICC's activities, however limited, for the commission represented the last obstacle before total disintegration of peace in Vietnam.

In the spring of 1957, however, the functioning of the ICC was further jeopardized. In its sixth interim report submitted in 1956, the commission drew attention to its inability to investigate complaints made by Hanoi about the Diem government's violation of article 14(c)—the requirement that both sides avoid repressions and discrimination against former Vietminh members or those who had cooperated with the Vietminh during the war against French. The commission put the blame on South Vietnam.[80]

On April 11, 1957, the commission sent the cochairs a letter that informed them of the decision of the South Vietnamese government not to respond to complaints about the violation of this article and not to allow ICC mobile teams to investigate such complaints. The commission asked the cochairs to consider this situation, which had led to the limitation of the ICC's functions in South Vietnam, and to instruct it as to further actions. The commission also stated that thereafter it could not undertake effective measures against violations of article 14(c) until the difficulties were removed. In addition to its letter to the cochairs, the commission adopted a decision not to pass on to the South Vietnamese government the complaints of the government of North Vietnam concerning the South's violations of article 14(c).[81] The Polish representative to the commission approved the letter to the cochairs and voted against the refusal to pass on the DRV's complaints to Saigon. He explained his actions to Soviet ambassador Zimyanin: "[H]aving agreed to sign the letter to the two chairmen, we took into account the situation of impotence in which the commission had found itself on the question about article 14(c), as well as a possibility of the alignment between the Indian and the Canadian [delegates] and the adoption of the decision by the majority."[82]

However, the Poles were not successful at excluding from the letter a reference to the ICC's inability to undertake effective measures against the violations of the article as long as the difficulties were not resolved. The North Vietnamese did not like this passage and at the last moment demanded that the letter not be signed. Pham Van Dong in a conversation with the Soviet ambassador presented Hanoi's interpretation of the Diem government's recent actions and the ICC's behavior. He accused the Indians of pursuing a policy that led to the "liquidation of the control over the fulfillment of article 14(c)." The North Vietnamese premier believed that the Indians and Canadians on the commission provided "great help to the American-Diemist clique," while the head of the Polish delegation did not understand this yet.[83] Concerned with the possible outcome of these developments, Hanoi appealed to Moscow to propose a meeting of the two cochairs to discuss the implementation of the Geneva agreements and the future activities of the ICC.[84]

Soviet foreign ministry officials seemed to share the concern of their Vietnamese friends, and they suggested that the USSR support the proposal for the meeting of the cochairs. They even tried to persuade the British to agree that the Soviet ambassador in Hanoi and the British ambassador in Saigon could play the roles of mediators in arranging consultations between the North and the South on the issue. The Soviets prepared a draft of instructions for cochair talks in London.[85] But, perhaps to their surprise, the Soviets discovered that the Chinese were not enthusiastic about this plan. The Soviet ambassador in Beijing reported to Moscow that "the Chinese friends believe that the conditions for the meeting of the two Chairmen have not ripened yet." Under these circumstances, the cochairs could only respond to the ICC letter with the demand to continue strict control over the Geneva agreements. The Chinese also proposed a letter from the cochairs to South Vietnam with the requirement that it continue its cooperation with the ICC and a letter from China and the Soviet Union to the Indian government with a request not to abandon its defense of the Geneva agreements.[86] The Soviet Foreign Ministry recommended that the Kremlin agree with the Chinese proposal. In accordance with this recommendation, Moscow suggested to the British that a joint message be sent to the South Vietnamese authorities and to the ICC with the request that the provisions of the Geneva agreements be observed. London, however, rejected the need for such a message and informed Moscow that it would do no more than acknowledge receipt of the commission's message.[87]

This whole episode demonstrated the Soviet anxiety about preserving at least the appearance that the Geneva agreements were functioning in Vietnam, even if they were reduced merely to the activities of the ICC. This guaranteed to the Soviets that the status quo in the region would not be changed. A memorandum prepared by the Foreign Ministry's Southeast Asia Department stated, "in spite of all attempts of the South Vietnamese authorities to deprive the Commission of the opportunity to carry out its activities efficiently, the very existence of the Commission in Vietnam is a paramount factor of maintaining peace between the two zones and a certain obstacle for the policy of violation of the Geneva Agreements pursued by the South Vietnamese regime."[88] The Soviet embassy in the DRV concurred with its superiors' opinion and recommended that the USSR support the commission's attempts to fulfill its functions "even in its present form" and declare all attempts to stop its activities "as a direct threat to the cause of peace in Southeast Asia."[89]

Also helping to preserve peace in Indochina was the development of good relations and the growth of Soviet influence in North Vietnam. On the basis of this influence, Moscow could keep the Vietnamese Communists from undermining the Geneva agreements and resorting to arms. Soviet influence was especially effective because Hanoi respected Soviet authority as the vanguard of the world communist movement and was interested in Soviet economic and military aid. Yet, initially, it was China that Moscow relied on in its policy toward Vietnam. At this time, there were no signs of disagreements and contradictions between the two Communist giants and the principle of sharing responsibilities was still on the agenda of the Soviet policymakers. The Kremlin did not refuse to develop relations with North Vietnam, but it was willing to share with Beijing the burden of aid to the DRV.

China was the greatest supplier of economic assistance to North Vietnam in the years after the Geneva conference. From 1955 to 1960, Chinese economic aid to the DRV amounted to twice as much as that from the Soviet Union (1,428 million *dong* from the PRC compared with 711.2 million *dong* from the USSR). More than 2,000 Chinese specialists worked in North Vietnam in 1956 compared with 658 Soviets.[90] Beijing's highest officials regularly visited the DRV; and Ho Chi Minh, Pham Van Dong, and other Vietnamese leaders sometimes visited Beijing several times a year. Their histories, cultures, and interests showed much in common. The leaders of the two countries shared many of the same views on domestic policies as well as on the international situation.

Notwithstanding its excellent relations with Beijing, Hanoi did not abandon its intent to develop close ties with the Soviet Union and counterbalance its alignment with China by cooperating with Moscow. The Soviet Union remained attractive in the eyes of the North Vietnamese leaders as it was a more powerful and developed country. In addition, traditional suspicion and even hatred toward the Chinese lingered among Vietnamese; sometimes these negative tendencies came out into the open. The Chinese ambassador to the DRV, Luo Guibo, complained to his Soviet counterpart that chauvinistic inclinations existed among the highest officials and even more often among the intelligentsia. In Vietnam, these chauvinistic inclinations were particularly strong against China. Luo Guibo was referring to local festivities dedicated to Vietnamese heroes who had fought against Chinese feudal lords and about the Vietnamese intent to prohibit theatrical plays written when Vietnam was a part of the Chinese empire.[91] When the Soviet ambassador touched on this subject with Ho Chi Minh, the Vietnamese leader agreed that there was a tradition of celebrating historical events related to the struggle against the Chinese. He also commented that chauvinistic propaganda could not be popular, however, among people who had witnessed the assistance that China had rendered to Vietnam.[92]

In this conversation with the Soviet ambassador, Ho Chi Minh admitted that there were anti-Soviet feelings in his country as well, but he did not explain why they existed. Because this conversation occurred in January 1957, it is possible that events of 1956 in the Soviet Union and other socialist countries had caused resentment in the DRV toward the Soviet Union.

The most important event of 1956 had been the twentieth congress of the Soviet Communist Party. The report delivered to the congress by Nikita Khrushchev and revelations made in his secret speech about Stalin's cult of personality seemed to shake the whole edifice of world communism.[93] For the Vietnamese Communists two things about Khrushchev's pronouncements might have been especially objectionable: the principle of peaceful coexistence and the repudiation of the inevitability of war between capitalism and communism,[94] and criticism of the cult of personality as incompatible with the party principle of the collective leadership. Peaceful coexistence meant that Moscow would avoid any risk of confrontation with the West and, consequently, would be overcautious with respect to Vietnam, trying to contain the militancy of the Communists in their struggle against the Diem regime. Eliminating the cult of personality did not please Ho Chi Minh personally because it threatened his position in the Vietnamese leadership.

The Kremlin understood that not all of its Communist allies would applaud the results of the CPSU congress. It decided, therefore, to send special envoys to the capitals of friendly regimes; these envoys would explain the congress's decisions and defend their correctness. Soviet Politburo member Anastas Mikoyan visited Hanoi in April 1956. Although documentary information about this visit is still not available, witnesses to his visit said that Mikoyan spoke in favor of building a strong and wealthy socialist state in the North, which would eventually be followed by the South. No joint communiqué followed the visit, which not only "suggests that the North Vietnamese and the Russians could not reach a unity of views"[95] but also indicates that no such communiqué had been planned by the Soviets and the Vietnamese owing to the working character of the visit.

Soon after Mikoyan's departure from Hanoi, the North Vietnamese leadership held the ninth plenary session of the Lao Dong Central Committee, which discussed the resolutions of the twentieth CPSU congress. The plenum's decisions were reported to the Soviet ambassador by Nguyen Duy Trinh, a member of the secretariat of the Lao Dong Party.

Trinh informed Ambassador Zimyanin that the Central Committee had decided to discuss the results of the CPSU congress without emphasizing the issue of the cult of personality. The first part of the plenum had been devoted to a discussion of the international situation in light of the decisions of the CPSU congress and related problems of foreign and domestic policies of the DRV. The second part focused on internal workings of the Lao Dong Party and the meaning of Khrushchev's report about the cult of personality.[96]

Zimyanin's memorandum of conversation about his talk with Trinh shows that Trinh's principal goal was to assure his Soviet comrades that there was no cult of personality in Vietnam. Trinh had assured Zimyanin that the principle of collective leadership dominated the activities of the Communists in the DRV. All important problems were discussed in the Lao Dong Politburo and plenary sessions. The question that stirred the most anxiety at the ninth plenum was whether the popularity of Ho Chi Minh should be interpreted as respect to the *Vozhd'* or as the cult of personality. The Vietnamese Communists finally concluded that there were "some elements" of a cult although these elements were not "of a systematic and serious character."[97]

The discussion among the Vietnamese Communists at the plenary session and their criticism of the cult of personality was apparently more a demonstration of loyalty to the Soviet ally than a sincere stance. Apart from their attitude to Stalin (whose sizable picture in Hanoi's International Bookshop remained in place until March 1962[98]), the DRV leaders had serious misgivings about the applicability to their country of Khrushchev's methods in the USSR. They feared that if they followed Khrushchev's direction it might jeopardize the leading role of the party in the struggle against Saigon and in the consolidation of the Communist regime in the North. In his conversation with the Soviet ambassador, Nguyen Duy Trinh admitted that there had been repressions during the agrarian reform against even the heads of local party organizations. There had also been ideological errors and abuses.[99] When the Vietnamese leaders decided to follow the Soviet example—and the Chinese example to some degree[100]—and admit their errors openly and liberalize ideological restrictions, they had encountered their most severe crisis since 1954.

For example, in November 1956, the North Vietnamese government had to quell an uprising in Nghe An province that had arisen as a result of repression against the peasantry during the agrarian reform in 1954–1955. The peasant unrest coincided with the intensification of dissent among intellectuals inspired by the decisions of the twentieth CPSU congress and the Chinese hundred-flowers policy. Peasants demanded not only material improvements but also freedom of expression. Bernard Fall wrote, "[n]one of the 'sacred cows' of the regime" escaped criticism of the Vietnamese intelligentsia: "The Viet-Nam People's Army was accused of being anti-intellectual; the Russian experts of being overbearing and of driving around in big cars; the Party of antagonizing the peasantry and allowing corruption to flourish among its members."[101] There appeared several publications that started to discuss themes of individual freedom and the pursuit of democracy.[102] Furthermore, the Communist leadership in the North faced pressure from comrades who felt it necessary to pay more attention to the struggle in the South. Le Duan, who was assigned by the Vietnamese Politburo to remain in South Vietnam, in August 1956 wrote his thesis, "The Path of the Revolution in the South of Our Country," in which he "clearly pointed out" that the path of the liberation of the South could only be a violent revolution.[103]

Vietnamese leaders had every reason to blame these difficulties on their Soviet and Chinese comrades. From this time on, perhaps, they chose not to follow the lead of their powerful allies in domestic policy, always referring instead to the specific situation of their country. It was, however, more difficult to differ from their allies in the sphere of foreign affairs. Hanoi clearly could not openly discount the principle of peaceful coexistence, but the North Vietnamese supported it only if it did not contradict their plans with respect to the South. They continued to regard South Vietnam not as an independent state recognized by foreign powers but only as the other part of one country, temporarily divided. In their view, then, the principle of peaceful coexistence did not apply.

The Vietnamese Communists also did not accept Khrushchev's declaration about how various countries could achieve socialism. While informing the Soviet ambassador about the ninth plenary session of the Lao Dong Party, Nguyen

Duy Trinh did not say a word about Ho Chi Minh's speech at the plenum. Trinh's silence about Ho's speech is understandable because Ho had not excluded the possibility of resorting to arms to achieve unity:

> Although it is possible that certain countries may achieve socialism by peaceful means, we must understand that in those countries where the administrative machinery, the military powers and the secret police of the bourgeois class are still powerful, the proletariat must prepare for an armed struggle. While noting the possibility of achieving the territorial unification of Vietnam through peaceful means, we must not forget [that] the American imperialists and their lackeys still occupy one-half of our national territory and are preparing for war. This is why, while holding high the flag of peace, we must be prudent and vigilant.[104]

But Ho's words did not in fact contradict Khrushchev's judgment of the ways to achieve socialism. First, the Soviet leader had noted that the Soviet Communists did not regard violence and civil war as the only way to overthrow capitalism, but he did not discard those tactics completely. Also, in his pronouncement he was mostly referring to developed capitalist countries, in which the working class had an "opportunity to inflict a defeat to the reactionary, anti-popular forces, to win over a solid majority in the parliament and to convert it from an organ of bourgeois democracy into a tool of really popular will."[105] Thus Khrushchev's thesis about peaceful achievement of socialism had nothing to do with Vietnam. Strictly speaking, the Vietnamese Communists, when admitting the possibility of armed struggle for unification, did not violate any of the guidelines proclaimed by Moscow; nevertheless they were eager to conceal their views because they could not but understand that such views ran counter to the interests of the Soviet leaders, who wanted to try rapprochement with the West, and counter to the similar trend in China, where Mao Zedong had stated in his speech at the eighth congress of the CCP in September 1956 that "the current international situation is turning better. We figured that war is unlikely to break out."[106] Because the trend among their allies did not seem to benefit them, the Vietnamese Communist leadership found it expedient to wait until the mood changed in the capitals of their allies; in the meantime, they concentrated on the development of cooperation with Moscow and Beijing in various spheres, including the military.

The North Vietnamese leaders' decision to bide their time complemented their strategy aimed at the development of the economy of the North and the buildup of socialism so as to make the North a base for the unification of the country.[107] In this, Hanoi could expect enthusiastic support of its Communist allies. While the West strove to make South Vietnam a "'showcase' that would outshine the North,"[108] the Soviets and Chinese were also eager to demonstrate the advantages of the system that was being created in the DRV with their help.

During Ho Chi Minh's visit to Moscow in the summer of 1955, the Soviet Union had promised to render the DRV assistance amounting to four hundred million rubles. In early 1956, a half year later, Pham Van Dong informed the Soviet ambassador that this sum had been depleted.[109] Moscow was helping with a number of projects to build up North Vietnam.[25] To create industrial sites, Moscow sent industrial equipment and assisted in drawing plans for economic development. Approximately 275 experts were sent to the DRV, including members of geological expeditions and medical units. The Soviets provided the North Vietnamese with various goods as well as food. A shortage of rice had occurred because Vietnam's rice-producing regions were located in the southern zone.[110] It became necessary to discuss prospects for further Soviet–North Vietnamese economic cooperation. This was one objective, among others, of Mikoyan's visit to Hanoi in April 1956.[111]

By mid-1957, the results of Soviet aid to North Vietnam had become noticeable. A memorandum prepared for Mikoyan sometime in the summer of 1957—two years after the first agreements for economic cooperation were signed between the two countries—stated that the Soviet specialists had "fully fulfilled" their obligations. They had put into operation five industrial enterprises, among them a tin mining and processing factory at Tinh Tuc that could produce 650 tons of tin yearly, a tea factory, a hydroelectric power station, and two lines of electricity transmission. The Soviets organized geological exploration for apatite, wolfram, zinc, lead, uranium, and other deposits. They modernized the port of Haiphong and helped organize production of cement and coal mining in Hon Gay. In addition, Moscow invited 249 Vietnamese specialists to the Soviet Union for further training.[112]

Economic aid was not the only area of Soviet–North Vietnamese cooperation. At its sixth plenum, the Lao Dong Central Committee had recognized the task of developing the army into a modern and regular one as a necessary condition of dealing effectively with the new revolutionary situation in the country. Hanoi therefore sought Soviet support in the military sphere as well. The issue of modernizing the army was again under consideration of the twelfth plenary session of the Lao Dong Central Committee in March 1957 when General Vo Nguyen Giap, the DRV minister of defense, again pointed out that the People's Army of Vietnam must be developed into a modern and regular army in order to be able to effectively carry out its mission of protecting the North and unifying the country.[113] This was also the main subject of Giap's conversation with Zimyanin on the eve of Ho Chi Minh's unofficial visit to Moscow in the summer of 1957. Giap discussed at great length the shortcomings of the North Vietnamese army. He complained that the army was not well adapted to the conditions of Vietnam, that the creation of new branches of the services occurred too slowly, and that many errors had been made during the introduction of conscription.

Giap then disclosed a part of the PAV general staff's report that was devoted to the assistance of fraternal countries, and he drew attention to the need for cooperation. The thrust of his conversation was that the present level and forms of assistance to the army were not enough. The Chinese, who had played the leading role in providing expertise and training for the Vietnamese, themselves admitted that the buildup of the modern army was a new problem for them. They did not possess the necessary knowledge and were not familiar with the new military equipment that was delivered from the Soviet Union. Therefore, Giap stated, it would be useful if Soviet experts were dispatched to North Vietnam "for a certain period of time."[114] The general also spoke about sending a PAV representative to Moscow to discuss plans for the modernization of the North Vietnamese army.

Ho Chi Minh apparently also touched on this issue during his unofficial visit to Moscow in July 1957.[115] Although details of his discussions in Moscow remain unknown, one result was a trip by Giap and a group from the Vietnamese military to Moscow in November of that year. Ambassador Zimyanin indicated to Foreign Minister Andrei Gromyko that the purpose of this secret military visit, which took place from November 14 to December 2, was "getting to know the life of the Soviet Union and the activities of the Soviet army."[116]

At about this time "a publicity blackout" on Giap's activities caused some Western observers (and, later, scholars) to suspect that there was some kind of struggle within the Vietnamese Politburo—either between the pro-Chinese faction and the pro-Soviet faction, to which Giap allegedly belonged; or between Giap and Le Duan, who had returned by that time to Hanoi from the South and who did not have good relations with the defense minister.[117] Instead, the silence about Giap could be explained by his trip first to China and, then, to the Soviet Union, during which he discussed issues of military cooperation with the North Vietnamese allies. If Giap's position in the North Vietnamese leadership was precarious, the Soviet ambassador knew nothing about it because, in that same letter to Gromyko, he referred to Giap as "one of the most promising political leaders in the DRV."[118]

Ho Chi Minh was also absent from the public arena at this time. During his July visit to Moscow he was invited to return in November on the occasion of the fortieth anniversary of the October Revolution.[119] But later he asked the Kremlin if it would be possible for him to come earlier, on October 19, so he could rest on the outskirts of Moscow before the festivities. The Soviet leadership had been informed about Ho's request by a letter prepared in the Foreign Ministry and in the international department of the CPSU Central Committee:

> Taking into account that the flight of Com. Ho Chi Minh after illness from Beijing to Moscow requires a special concern over his health, the embassy finds it expedient to send from Moscow to Beijing a doctor to accompany Com. Ho Chi Minh as well as to deliver for him in Beijing a set of warm clothes.[120]

Ho Chi Minh, who was in his late 60s, obviously wanted to be in good shape for participating not only in the October festivities but also in the meeting of representatives of Communist parties that was timed to coincide with the anniversary. Designed as a demonstration of the unity of the Communist movement after the twentieth congress of the Soviet Communist Party in February 1956 and the dissolution of the Cominform one month later, this meeting instead marked the beginning of a serious crisis in world communism that manifested itself in the growing rift between Moscow and Beijing. This rift had profound consequences for Vietnam.

6. If the Fractured Friendship Collapses

Si fractus illabatur orbis,
Impavidum ferient ruinae.

Horatius[1]

You never trust the Chinese! You only trust the Russians!
[To you] the Russians are the first-class [people]
whereas the Chinese are among the inferior
who are dumb and careless.

Excerpt from a conversation between Mao Zedong and
Yudin, Soviet ambassador to China

July 22, 1958[2]

Frictions in Soviet-Chinese relations existed well before the conflict between Moscow and Beijing became evident to Communist allies and, to a lesser extent, the West. The Chinese leaders had much to complain about concerning Soviet policy toward China, from the days of the Comintern to the very moment when the Chinese Communist Party dealt the final blow to the Guomindang and established a Communist regime in all of China except for Taiwan and a number of small offshore islands.[3] The Chinese Communists' coming to power only heightened their inferiority complex with respect to the Soviets, whom they suspected of chauvinism and of wanting to subdue their country. Although Moscow and Beijing signed the Treaty of Friendship, Alliance, and Mutual Assistance in 1950 and developed bilateral relations in many areas, the Chinese leaders remained suspicious about the Soviets' real objectives with respect to China. Mao Zedong, for example, could not forgive and forget Stalin's behavior during the Sino-Soviet negotiations in late 1949 and early 1950. The Soviet dictator treated "the revolutionary leader from the 'Central Kingdom,' as the inferior 'younger brother.'"[4] Mao's attempt to prove himself a theoretician by discussing with Stalin issues of communist theory encountered Stalin's contempt.

Yet Mao and his colleagues concealed their chagrin because Stalin—his arrogance and patronizing notwithstanding—remained for them Lenin's heir, a "powerful, though imperfect, incarnation of the revolutionary Gospel."[5] In addition to this reverence toward the Soviet dictator, the Chinese leaders understood that "acquiring Soviet aid was highly desirable, if not necessary, so as to resolve the nation's immediate economic problems."[6] Communist China also needed Moscow's support and encouragement in its situation of almost complete international isolation. At the same time Mao resented any notion that China ought to be a Soviet satellite. He wanted Moscow to treat his regime as an equal partner.

Mao's dream might have been realized after Stalin's death. The new Soviet leaders' visit to China in the fall of 1954 resulted in the elimination of the most irritating features of bilateral relations under Stalin. Nikita Khrushchev proposed abandoning the practice of joint Soviet-Chinese ventures, which he regarded as similar to those of the imperialist countries.[7] Khrushchev agreed to withdraw Soviet armed forces from their naval bases in Lushun. All in all, Khrushchev seemed to understand the Chinese feelings of inferiority and their desire for equality with their Soviet partners. For his part, Mao Zedong felt himself equal if not superior to the new Soviet leader owing to his longer experience at the top of the Communist Party hierarchy. But the great expectations of the Chinese leaders born during the first years after Stalin's death were not realized.

Khrushchev, while making concessions on some issues of Sino-Soviet cooperation, was not at all eager to compromise on the idea that the Soviet Union was "the vanguard of the world Communist movement" and "the first country of the victorious socialism" whose destiny was to serve an example for all other peoples who would follow the same path. Besides, the new Soviet leader was suspicious of Mao's aspirations and designs. He remembered Stalin's mocking remarks when he likened Mao Zedong to a radish—red from above but white inside.[8] It was therefore unthinkable for Khrushchev to accede to Mao's pretension of inheriting Stalin's role of theoretician and spiritual leader of the communists. As a result, after his first visit to China in 1954, Khrushchev firmly concluded that a conflict between Moscow and Beijing was unavoidable.[9]

But there was another reason why, even in the heyday of the Sino-Soviet alliance, distrust and bitter feelings continued to poison the atmosphere of bilateral relations. Although he had denounced Stalin's abuses of power and his cult of personality, Khrushchev could not overcome Stalin's old method of dealing with other Communist parties. Khrushchev, like Stalin, believed that whatever had been done in Moscow should serve as a directive for the whole communist movement. In other words, despite all the revelations about the exigencies of

Stalin regime, Moscow pretended to remain the ruling center for all communist allies. François Fejtö noted in his book on the Sino-Soviet conflict that there was a contradiction between the liberal and reformist contents of the decisions of the twentieth CPSU congress and the Stalinist methods of their implementation.[10] Considering the sensitivity of the Beijing leadership to China's independence and its desire to play a role in the socialist camp equal to the Soviet Union, this Soviet contradiction only added to Beijing's determination to revolt.

In addition, Mao disagreed with almost all of the principal ideas put forth at the congress of the CPSU. Mao distrusted the policy of peaceful coexistence and criticized the Soviet belief that the dictatorship of the proletariat could be established by peaceful means.[11] But Mao Zedong was most hostile toward the denunciation of Stalin. Although Mao criticized the Soviet dictator's mistakes, especially when they were committed with respect to China, Mao regarded him as a "great Marxist-Leninist revolutionary leader." He adopted a "seventy-thirty ratio" methodology, claiming that Stalin's achievements should account for 70 percent and his mistakes for 30 percent.[12]

In addition, Mao, who had endured Stalin's arrogance and maltreatment, defended the Soviet dictator and tried to emphasize his historical role because of his own desire to occupy Stalin's place in the world communist movement and his reluctance to dismantle his own cult of personality in China. In previous years Mao associated himself too closely with the Soviet dictator to be able to reject this relationship outright. Thus, for Mao, following Khrushchev's example and denouncing Stalin meant condemning himself and undermining the foundations of his authority in China. Mao insisted that Stalin's errors were secondary compared with his achievements[13] and, later, Mao distinguished between correct and incorrect personality cults.[14]

In general, the Chinese leader believed that Khrushchev's speech "made a mess"[15] and shattered Soviet positions among other Communist parties. This situation seemed to favor Mao and his aspirations for competing with Moscow for the leadership of the communist world; and the crises in Poland and Hungary during which the Chinese leader played an important role in containing Soviet intervention, in the first case, and blessing it, in the second, had consolidated Mao's positions.[16] "Although in public Mao continued to maintain that Moscow remained the center of the socialist camp, he really believed that it was he who was more qualified to dictate the principles underlying relations between and among socialist countries."[17] Mao's belief in his rightful position might have acquired new impetus as a result of the struggle within the Soviet leadership. The anti-party plot of 1957, although it consolidated Khrushchev's position in the country and in the party, seriously weakened his position in Chinese leaders' eyes.

Nevertheless, when the leaders of the Communist parties from many countries gathered in Moscow in November 1957, Mao displayed his loyalty toward Moscow. More than that, he called other Communist leaders to recognize the USSR's leadership role. Perhaps he was expressing his gratitude for the Soviet decision, made at the same time, to provide China a training model of an atomic bomb and related equipment.[18] If so, Mao did everything at the Communist parties meeting to discourage the Soviets from this step.

First of all, nobody in the Soviet leadership, including Khrushchev himself, believed in the sincerity of Mao's acknowledgement of the USSR's leading role. Khrushchev suspected a double game on the part of the Chinese. "If all other parties acknowledge the role of the leader as belonged to the one party," he wrote in his memoirs, "then the leader could be changed. Today [there is] one leader, tomorrow—another. We believed that the Chinese were preparing a basis for their future claims to such a role."[19]

Mao also literally shocked the Soviets by his pronouncements concerning war and revolution. He emphasized that "the Communists should not be frightened by the prospect of a nuclear war started by the imperialists but should realize that such a war, although carrying a high price, would bring the imperialist system to its final conclusion."[20] He repeated his famous slogans about the "east wind which is prevailing over the west wind" and imperialists as paper tigers.[21]

In the same vein, the Chinese protested against a peaceful transition to socialism. At the conference they disseminated a memorandum that both conceded that it was useful to include the passage about a peaceful socialist revolution in the text of the conference's documents and argued that the communists should not insist too much on peaceful revolution, for this could lead to weakened militancy on the part of the proletariat and to the confusion of the Communist parties with the socialists in the eyes of revolutionary masses.[22] Only after long debates were the Communist leaders able to compromise. Having obtained Chinese support for the policy of peaceful coexistence, the Soviets conceded on the issue of the transition to socialism and accepted that, under certain circumstances, there could be a nonpeaceful transition to socialism.

The November 1957 Moscow conference of the leaders of the Communist and Workers' Parties thus revealed several points of disagreement between the Soviets and the Chinese that were based on the rivalry between Moscow and Beijing over the leadership of the world communist movement. In 1957 a compromise between the CPSU and the Chinese Communist Party was still possible, but it was based on a weak foundation and quickly crumbled into acute conflict.

After the conference, Mao Zedong continued to assert his dominant role as the new Communist ideologue, at least, for Asian Communist parties. On December 7, 1957, he told the Czechoslovak military delegation that it was China's responsibility to develop a new theory and practice of communism in Asia.[23] Mao regarded any step by the Soviet Union to acquire geopolitical positions in Asia as an attempt to undermine China's role as a first-class power. When Moscow approached Beijing in 1958 with the suggestion that they jointly build a powerful long-wave radio station linking the Chinese navy with the Soviet navy in East Asia and establish a joint flotilla of nuclear-powered submarines for a common defense of the Far East, Mao not surprisingly was outraged. He summoned the Soviet ambassador, Pavel Yudin, and railed against the inferior treatment of his country by the Soviets. "You never trust the Chinese," Mao exclaimed. "You only trust the Russians! [To you] the Russians are the first-class [people] whereas the Chinese are among the inferior who are dumb and careless. . . . With a few atomic bombs, you think you are in a position to control us through asking the right of rent and lease."[24]

After making Khrushchev rush to Beijing and offer his apologies for the misunderstanding,[25] Mao asserted his independence of Moscow in the area of foreign policy and in August and September of 1958 ordered a large-scale shelling of a Guomindang-controlled island—Jinmen (Quemoy)—off the coast of Fujian province. He had not informed Moscow about the details of this operation or about its ultimate goal.[26] As a result, Moscow expressed support and solidarity with China while it could only guess what the Chinese were striving for by confronting the United States in a crisis that could lead to nuclear war. Only during Soviet foreign minister Andrei Gromyko's unscheduled visit to Beijing in September 1958 did Moscow learn that Mao did not plan to invade Taiwan or to involve China in a direct military confrontation with the United States. Although Mao had domestic as well as foreign policy reasons for the shelling, the Chinese leader clearly wanted to teach the Soviets that the era of Moscow's ability to dictate to China was over, and henceforth China did not intend to coordinate all its international actions with the Soviet Union.[27]

The events of the summer of 1958 were a turning point in the development of the Soviet-Chinese conflict. For the first time after his accession to power, Mao Zedong openly defied Soviet prestige and disregarded the interests of his powerful ally. Although on the surface relations between the two countries remained friendly and cooperation in various areas continued, undercurrents of disagreement, suspicion, and mistrust were destroying the foundation of the Sino-Soviet alliance.[28]

The two sides diverged on issues of foreign policy as well as on domestic reform. Beijing did not want to accept the Soviet concept of peaceful coexistence, which the Chinese leaders regarded as capitulation to the West. The Chinese believed that this Soviet policy stemmed from the Soviets' erroneous approach toward international relations in general. Zhou Enlai submitted his evaluation of Moscow's policy to Mao Zedong and the Chinese Communist Party leadership in early 1957 and wrote that the Soviet leaders:

> spend more time and effort on coping with specific and isolated events than on evaluating and anticipating situations thoroughly from different angles. They explicitly demonstrate weakness in considering and discussing strategic and long-term issues. As far as tactics are concerned, on the other hand, lacking clearly defined principles, they tend to be on such a loose ground in handling specific affairs that they will fail to reach satisfactorily the strategic goals through resolving each specific conflict.[29]

In return, Moscow disapproved of what it regarded as the PRC's adventurist international policy. The Soviets criticized Beijing for its lack of understanding of the new correlation of forces in the world and for its opposition to the idea of full and complete disarmament. They derided the Chinese idea of imperialists as paper tigers and of the possibility of nuclear war. This criticism was translated into practical steps by the Soviet leadership. While Khrushchev was ready to support China during the 1958 Taiwan Strait crisis, he strongly opposed the Chinese in their conflict with India in August 1959 although officially the Soviet government occupied a neutral position.[30] Moscow regarded China's initiation of the conflict with India on the eve of Khrushchev's visit to the United States as an attempt by the Chinese to frustrate an expected amelioration of U.S.-Soviet relations.[31]

But especially strong criticism was voiced by Moscow with respect to the domestic reforms begun in China after the eighth plenary session of the Chinese Communist Party in May 1958. Moscow regarded China's Great Leap Forward as a result of Chinese self-conceit and arrogance in their assessment of the success of their economic development in 1958.[32] The Soviet leaders also were not optimistic about people's communes. They assessed Mao's agrarian reform as an "attempt to jump over a large historic stage of socialist development, to declare Communism on the primitive basis in the backward Chinese village."[33] The Soviets tried to convey to Beijing their doubts about Chinese reforms in industry and agriculture but, as expected, these warnings only stimulated Chinese resentment. The Chinese ambassador to Moscow, Liu Xiao, reported to his superiors in October 1958 that the Soviet leaders "lacked a profound understanding of the application of our Party's strategy and tactics in [economic affairs] and the new thoughts and new practices that have emerged in our [economic] development." Such issues as people's communes and China's rapid transformation toward Communism were "incomprehensible" to them.[34] But what the

Soviet leaders especially worried about was that the Chinese example might be attractive to other countries and even to the people of the Soviet Union. In his memoirs Khrushchev wrote that some Soviet newspapers in the territories on the border with China raised the issue of the USSR copying the experience of the people's communes. "We should admit this frightened us," Khrushchev confided and told how the Bulgarian Communists followed the Chinese example until the Soviets taught them that this example could not be applied in the conditions of the European socialist countries.[35] The Chinese had begun to compete with their Soviet allies for ideological influence within the socialist camp. Soon this competition spread to the Third World.

By 1960 Moscow recognized the importance of strengthening its influence in developing countries of Asia, Africa, and Latin America. The principle of the division of responsibilities with Communist China adopted by Moscow in its foreign policy toward Third World in the mid-1950s proved to be obsolete now, even before disagreements between the two Communist giants led to conflict. Moscow realized it could not allow Chinese prestige to grow at the expense of Soviet influence in the newly independent countries as well as in the national liberation movements. If the Soviet Union and Communist China acted in unison toward the Third World initially, their differing views of their leaderships on the principal international issues gradually eroded their cooperation and pulled the two countries apart in their policies toward the Third World.

In 1958, the Soviet embassy in Beijing had already reported on the "tendency" of the Chinese friends "to solve the issues concerning Asia independently."[36] In 1959–1960, the embassy reported to Moscow about China's "tendency toward retreat from the internationalist policy, common to the whole socialist camp." More than that, according to the Soviet diplomats, Beijing had undertaken steps "that could inflict damage to the common cause of the working class." The Chinese leaders emphasized the special position of their country in the socialist camp, drawing attention to its closeness to the countries of Asia, Africa, and Latin America due to the specific historical experience. The Chinese belittled the support of other socialist countries, first of all, that of the Soviet Union, while they tried to present China as the only faithful ally of the people who were struggling for their independence and the country best able to promote national liberation movements. They popularized Mao Zedong's ideas about the predominant role of national liberation movements in the struggle against imperialism, neglected Soviet proposals in the UN on the complete abolition of colonialism, and spoke against Soviet proposals on disarmament. Furthermore, Beijing spared no effort to convince Third World leaders that only the Chinese Communist Party was a truly revolutionary party as opposed to the CPSU, which was "falling away from class positions."[37]

The "huge number" of various delegations from Asia, Africa, and Latin America that came to Beijing served to demonstrate Chinese activity in this area of foreign policy. For example, in 1960, more than 90 African delegations visited China, and all the Chinese leaders were involved in welcoming them. Mao Zedong received representatives from Africa, Asia, and Latin America 34 times, and Liu Shaoqi received delegations 37 times. But Zhou Enlai, with 111 such meetings, outdid both leaders. "At the same time," Soviet diplomats noted sourly, "the Chinese leaders extremely rarely met with representatives of the Soviet Union and other socialist countries."[38]

Thus, by 1960, Communist China, instead of being an ally, had become a rival to the Soviet Union. However, an open split had not yet occurred. Neither Moscow nor Beijing was prepared to completely abandon its policy of cooperation and expose contradictions to the outside world. The Soviets particularly demonstrated their eagerness to preserve the status quo in bilateral relations; and Khrushchev, who had just returned from an official visit to the United States on September 15–27, 1959, went to Beijing, allegedly to celebrate the PRC's tenth anniversary but, in reality, to discuss with his Chinese counterparts the pressing problems of bilateral relations and to try to bridge the widening gap between the two countries.

During his meeting with the Chinese leadership on October 2, Khrushchev spoke of the necessity for the socialist countries to "avoid everything that might be used by reactionaries in order to push the world into the 'Cold War' again." He criticized the Chinese actions against Taiwan and India and complained about an abnormal situation in which "we, the Chinese allies, do not know what the Chinese comrades will undertake tomorrow in the sphere of foreign policy." He accused the Chinese of not understanding the policy of peaceful coexistence and said that they complicated "the positions of the socialist camp by their incorrect actions."[39] The Chinese responded with their own accusations. They criticized Khrushchev for his denunciation of Stalin's cult of personality without prior consultation with Beijing and for seriously complicating the situation in the world Communist movement with the decisions of the twentieth CPSU congress. Through the Chinese foreign minister, Chen Yi, they criticized the Soviet position toward the Sino-Indian conflict, calling Moscow's policy "time-serving" as opposed to the consistent policy of China.[40] It turned out that, instead of leading to improved of relations between the two countries, the Soviet-Chinese negotiations led to even more serious discord, which was about to come to light.

In fact, fragmentary information about the disagreements between the Soviet Union and China had reached the West before the split in the Communist world became an established fact. Khrushchev himself, in spite of his position as an avowed defender of Chinese interests in his encounters with the West, had to admit in a conversation with Averell Harriman, the former ambassador to the Soviet Union, that differences existed in the views of the two countries on a number of issues.[41] However, since such revelations were accompanied by Soviet declarations in support of China, U.S. officials were circumspect in their evaluation of the scope of Sino-Soviet differences and warned against an overly optimistic approach. For example, in a memorandum prepared at the time of Khrushchev's September 1959 visit to the United States, the State Department's Bureau of Intelligence and Research reported to Secretary of State Christian Herter that: "While available evidence does suggest that the Sino-Soviet relationship at the present time may be subjected to unusual strains, it would be premature to conclude that the problems cannot be resolved at least to the extent of preventing a serious weakening of the alliance itself."[42] It took a full year before the director of the CIA, Allen Dulles, could provide the U.S. administration with more or less reliable information on the Sino-Soviet conflict. He reported at a meeting of the National Security Council on September 7, 1960, that "Communist China and the USSR have been quarreling for about two years," and he outlined five issues of disagreement between the two countries.[43] Thus, despite their public pronouncements about a consolidated international communism, U.S. officials were well aware of the lack of a communist monolith in the sense of a concentrated and optimized threat.[44]

By the time the news of Sino-Soviet discord reached Washington, the discord had long ceased to be a secret to the members of the socialist camp. Among the Communist leaders who followed most attentively the developments in Sino-Soviet relations were the North Vietnamese.

For North Vietnam, more than any other Communist country, the quarrel between the Russians and the Chinese posed great problems. The DRV could not openly align itself with Moscow, as most East European countries did, or with Beijing, as Albania did. The problem for North Vietnam was much more complicated than the geographic proximity of China because it involved many factors, such as historical background of the relationship between the two countries, the more recent experience of Vietnam's cooperation with both the Soviet Union and China, the division of Vietnam in two parts and the task of the unification of the country, and, of course, the ideological preferences of the Hanoi leadership.

The Vietnamese, at first glance, had much in common with the ideology of their Chinese neighbor. Ho Chi Minh, like Mao Zedong, had suffered greatly from Stalin's arrogance and distrust of the Asian communists. At the same time, Ho did not completely support Khrushchev's denunciation of Stalin and was inclined to agree with Mao's 70-30 ratio in his assessment of the Soviet dictator's achievements.[45] Like Mao, Ho's greatest concern was his special position on the question of the personality cult—the role of the leader who concentrates power in order to achieve the tasks of the regime. Ho believed that he, as the Vietnamese leader, must direct developments in his country until the goal of unification was achieved, much as Stalin had held all the strings of government during the war against Nazi Germany.

The same goal dictated the North Vietnamese attitude toward peaceful coexistence and the peaceful transition to socialism. Both of these Soviet concepts contradicted the plans for the South that Hanoi was working out after the 1954 Geneva conference on Indochina. Those plans never excluded the possibility of resorting to war if all other methods proved to be fruitless.[46] But everybody understood that a war in Vietnam would unavoidably be waged not only against the Saigon regime but also against its U.S. supporters because the United States would be involved in one form or another. Hence any revolution in the South would likely not be peaceful but would lead to a local war that could endanger the policy of peaceful coexistence pursued by the Soviet Union. Therefore, the Vietnamese might well have felt relief when, at the 1957 Moscow conference of the Communist parties, the Soviets had to concede under Chinese pressure that under certain circumstances there could be a nonpeaceful transition to socialism.[47]

This affinity of views did not presuppose unconditional support for Chinese policies on the part of Hanoi, however. Experience had taught the Vietnamese Communists to be careful in following the lead of Beijing. Examples of questionable Chinese policies include the disastrous agrarian reform in North Vietnam that had been advised and supervised by Chinese instructors and the liberalization of ideology and propaganda along the lines of Mao's hundred-flowers campaign.[48] The North Vietnamese leadership justified its decision to abandon the slavish imitation of China by referring to specific conditions that existed only in Vietnam.

Hanoi's attitude toward the Soviet Union was more utilitarian. No one would deny Hanoi's ideological closeness to Moscow, but ideology was by no means the only factor that pushed the North Vietnamese leaders to seek Soviet advice and support. The Soviet Union was a powerful industrial country that could assist Hanoi not only morally but also materially. China was not capable of competing with the advanced technology and skill that Moscow could provide to the DRV. Hanoi also regarded the Soviet Union as a counterbalance to Chinese influence and command. As a result, despite their disagreement with some aspects of Soviet foreign policy and theory, Ho Chi Minh and most of his subordinates never risked open dissent from Moscow's pronouncements.

Thus the DRV's situation was precarious. Dependent on Beijing as well as Moscow, the North Vietnamese had to pursue a middle course and avoid, for as long as possible, taking sides in their disputes. The result was a tactic "of responding to pressure from the Soviet Union and China by offering verbal support but taking no action."[49]

The growing Sino-Soviet estrangement threatened to jeopardize North Vietnam's ability to achieve a balance. The North Vietnamese leadership understood that in the case of an open rift both allies would demand a clear-cut alignment. Furthermore, Hanoi regarded any sharpening of contradictions within the Communist bloc as damaging the cause of the unification of Vietnam because Communists would be diverted from a unified front vis-à-vis the imperialist powers. It is therefore not surprising that the North Vietnamese were most unhappy about disputes between the Soviets and the Chinese and were most eager to mediate the disagreements.

The role of the Vietnamese Communists as mediators would reveal itself later, in 1960, when at a Moscow conference a last attempt was made to preserve the unity of the socialist camp. Meanwhile both allies developed their relations with the DRV, but China gained the lead. Sino-Vietnamese economic cooperation continued to broaden and intensify. On March 31, 1958, a new protocol on Chinese aid to the DRV and an agreement on assistance to North Vietnam for the construction of 18 industrial projects during 1958–1961 were signed by the two countries. These industrial projects were to be built with part of the 800 million *yuan* that the Chinese committed to the Vietnamese as a gift in 1955.[50] Issues of Sino-Vietnamese economic cooperation were actively discussed by Pham Van Dong during secret negotiations in Beijing in the fall of 1958, and in the first months of 1959 during an official visit to the Chinese capital of a DRV delegation headed by Le Thanh Nghi, minister of industry and director of the industrial section of the DRV's office of the premier. The Soviet embassy in Beijing reported that these negotiations resulted in a long-term credit of 300 million *yuan* at 1 percent interest for 10 years beginning in 1967.[51] The Chinese also gifted the North Vietnamese with another 100 million *yuan* to be used for economic development.[52] China was also North Vietnam's leading trading partner; 27.3 percent of the North Vietnamese trade was with the PRC.[53]

Sino-North Vietnamese military cooperation was well established. China assisted the People's Army of Vietnam in establishing antiaircraft, engineering, tank, and infantry units. The Chinese also supplied the PAV with assault guns; military vehicles; and engineering, communications, and reconnaissance equipment.[54]

The Soviet foreign ministry noted that in the realm of culture, China's influence in the DRV was growing. Hanoi and Beijing had signed an agreement that envisaged the development of cultural exchanges; however, the Soviet foreign ministry stated, "in practice cultural ties surpass the planned framework."[55]

The DRV imported a large number of Chinese books, many of which were translated into the Vietnamese. Between seventy and one hundred delegations from North Vietnam traveled to China every year, and China hosted the majority of the Vietnamese who were sent abroad for education (957 out of 1711 in 1959).[56]

Compared with China, the Soviet Union lagged far behind in its cooperation with the DRV. Although cooperation between the two countries developed in economic as well as in military and cultural matters, and Moscow provided ever-growing assistance to the DRV, the scope of this assistance could not compete with China's. This situation was the result of the Soviet policy of division of responsibility, initiated soon after the Geneva conference, and in 1957–1959 Moscow still saw no reason to modify it. In vain the Soviet diplomats in Hanoi appealed to their superiors, drawing their attention to the "growing role and importance of the Democratic Republic of Vietnam, which stands at the extremity of the socialist camp in Southeast Asia and becomes an immediate object of provocations on the part of American imperialists and their lackeys." They even emphasized the importance of the DRV for the policy of neutralization of other countries in Indochina and for "dragging them away from the sphere of the activity of the United States."[57] The Kremlin did not budge. Janos Radvanyi, a Hungarian diplomat who later defected to the West and who was a member of his country's delegation to North Vietnam in 1959, remembers his delegation's meeting with Khrushchev on its way back from Indochina. When Munnich, the Hungarian prime minister, "enthusiastically" tried to tell the Soviet leader "about some of the highlights of our Hanoi visit, Khrushchev all but yawned in his face." Instead, most of his talk was devoted to West Berlin and China.[58]

Evidently, Khrushchev did not yet see in Indochina a pressing issue that demanded his attention. The Soviets were convinced that "the Geneva agreements on Indochina keep their legal force and represent an important instrument of preserving peace in that region." Soviet diplomats supported this optimistic view by their analyses of the attitudes of the main participants in the 1954 Geneva conference. The two principal opponents of the Geneva agreements, the United States and South Vietnam, were avoiding a direct violation of the Geneva agreements and were cooperating with the ICC. France, although it continued to refuse to fulfill its obligations under the agreements, was concerned with the growing U.S. penetration into Indochina and wanted to counterbalance it by augmenting its own influence. The British, in spite of their opposition to all-Vietnamese elections and their tacit support of U.S. policy in Southeast Asia, had to take into account their interests in the region and their obligations as a cochair of the Geneva conference. These considerations served to "keep, in general, England in the framework of the struggle for the observance of the Geneva agreements." Even the Canadian position was not, in the Soviet view, wholly pro-American.[59]

This assessment of the developments in Indochina permitted Moscow to consider a step such as the establishment of direct relations with the Saigon regime. In its political report for 1958, the Soviet embassy in Hanoi recommended that Moscow "already at the present time . . . discuss measures aimed at the maintaining of economic and cultural relations between South Vietnam and the countries of the socialist camp (*apart from the DRV*)."[60] This proposal was justified by the need for the Soviets to have first-hand information about the situation in South Vietnam. At the same time the Soviets, acting through the ICC and the Polish representatives to it, pressed their North Vietnamese allies to continue attempts to establish direct communications with the regime in the South.

During 1958 plans were nurtured for a meeting of representatives of the two parts of Vietnam in the demilitarized zone. The South Vietnamese consented to such a meeting and the date of the meeting, January 12, 1959, was agreed to by both sides. Despite their agreement to avoid publicity, however, Hanoi broadcast the information on the forthcoming negotiations and asserted that Saigon had consented only under pressure of public opinion. Hanoi's revelation immediately incited a flow of protests from Saigon as well as from Washington and London. The Americans and the British demanded a postponement of the meeting, saying it was untimely.[61] As a result, this important event that might have led to the some sort of collaboration between the North and the South did not take place.

On the one hand, Hanoi had spoken in favor of the development of relations between the zones; and Pham Van Dong's letter of December 28, 1958, that spelled out a four-point program that could have become a basis for the normalization of relations with South Vietnam could be taken as proof of North Vietnam's intentions. On the other hand, the North Vietnamese had jeopardized the very step that could help to realize improved relations. In fact, by the end of 1958 Hanoi had decided to abandon its policy of reliance on only peaceful means in order to achieve the unification of the country, and it raised violence to a level equal with the political and the propaganda struggle.

In December 1958 and January 1959, the Central Committee of the Lao Dong Party held its fifteenth plenary session.[62] Unlike previous party sessions that had gathered in Hanoi after the 1954 Geneva conference and that had been devoted to the topic of peaceful unification, this plenary session came to the conclusion that "the main direction of the development of the revolution in South Vietnam is that of violence."[63] This meant a combination of the political struggle of the popular masses with an armed struggle aimed at "the overthrow of the power of imperialists and feudal lords and the establishment of the revolutionary power of the people."[64] In his closing address, Ho Chi Minh emphasized that the southern region of Vietnam was a part of "our country's revolution," while the revolution in Vietnam was a "part of the world's revolution." Ho declared that armed struggle was a supplement to political activity. "Peace does not mean that we do not prepare our military forces," Ho declared. "If we organize our political strength well, when the need comes to resort to arms, it will not be difficult."[65]

Thus, the decisions of the fifteenth plenum constituted a major departure from the prior policy of the Lao Dong Party toward the South. It is not surprising, therefore, that Hanoi did not announce its decisions until May 1959. But even when its decisions were made public, their wording was apparently so vague that the Soviet embassy did not at first recognize their impact on Soviet policy in the region. The embassy's annual report for 1959 simply noted that "for the first time in the postwar period a vitally important problem of the reunification of the country was considered in the whole and in some aspects. The plenum outlined revolutionary tasks for the whole country and as it is applied to North, as well as to South Vietnam."[66] Although the Chinese were well informed about North Vietnamese intentions to reconsider their strategy toward the South,[67] the Soviets remained ignorant. In conversations with Soviet officials, the Vietnamese "friends" deliberately misled Moscow, revealing only decisions of the fifteenth plenum that emphasized the importance of peaceful struggle. For example, one member of the Vietnamese Politburo, Pham Hung, told the Soviet ambassador in Hanoi, Leonid Sokolov, in June 1959 that the "plenum arrived at the unanimous opinion that it is necessary to unfold a political struggle aimed at the overthrowing of the Diem regime by peaceful means and, at the same time, to take into account a possibility, under certain internal and external conditions, of the fulfillment of this task by means of arms." He reiterated Hanoi's adherence to the Geneva agreements because they "represent an important basis for the unfolding of the revolutionary struggle in South Vietnam."[68] Thus Moscow heard from the Vietnamese what it wanted to hear and did not perceive the intensified struggle in the South as a threat to its Indochina policy.

This struggle was gaining momentum, however, and uprisings took place in various parts of South Vietnam. In the summer of 1959, sixteen thousand members of an ethnic minority in Tra Bong launched an uprising under the leadership of the district party committee and the provincial party committee. In January of 1960, forty-seven villages in Ben Tre province revolted simultaneously. Also beginning in 1960, concerted uprisings swept across the province of Nam Bo.[69] North Vietnam began training cadres to be sent to the South on an impressive scale.

In May 1959, the South Vietnamese government adopted Law 10/59, which intensified repression against communists and those who were suspected of supporting them; and in 1960 the South announced a doubling of the number of U.S. instructors in Vietnam serving in the U.S. military assistance advisory group (MAAG). These measures cemented Hanoi's determination to broaden the struggle against the Diem regime. Hanoi made special efforts to provide the South Vietnamese guerrillas with arms, ammunition, and other support for operations against the South Vietnamese armed forces. Hanoi decided to build a system of roads that could link the North Vietnamese with their southern comrades-in-arms. Starting in August 1959, the DRV sent to the Communist insurgents in the South ever-growing number of rifles, bayonets, explosives, and other matériel. In December 1959, the Lao Dong Central Committee approved for the first time the dispatch of a team of twenty-five regrouped southern cadres, who had been based in the North after the Geneva settlement, to cross back over the demilitarized zone to assist in the training of anti-Diem forces.[70] By this time, Hanoi had received China's blessing for its military plans in the South.[71]

These developments did not go unnoticed by Soviet leaders, who were aware that "the population of the South in the recent months began to pass from political and economic forms of the struggle to the armed struggle" and that "in a number of regions (especially in the extreme South) real fighting raged" between local guerrillas and South Vietnamese government troops. They also knew that there were "revolutionary bases" in South Vietnam, established after the Geneva conference.[72] But Moscow did not accurately perceive the extent of North Vietnamese involvement in these developments. Hanoi assured its Soviet allies that, in spite of the difficulties that the North Vietnamese experienced in keeping their comrades in the South from resorting to arms, "the general line of the [Lao Dong] Party in the South remains as before," that is, the preservation of peace "at any price."[73]

Moscow was therefore surprised when, during a May 1960 visit to the USSR, Vo Nguyen Giap, the DRV minister of defense who had been regarded as the most faithful Soviet ally in the North Vietnamese leadership, openly spoke to the Soviet deputy foreign minister, Georgii Pushkin, in favor of a revision of the Geneva agreements. Giap wanted to modify the part that concerned the ICC, which the Kremlin considered "an important factor of peace and further observance of the Geneva agreements in Vietnam, Laos, and Cambodia."[74] Hanoi, however, with its new outlook on violence, saw the ICC as an impediment to its plans for armed struggle in the South. Giap criticized the recent decisions of the ICC regarding Law 10/59 and the increase of the number of U.S. military advisers in Vietnam[75] and stated, on these grounds, that "the International Commission is becoming more and more a body supporting the interests of the South Vietnamese authorities. The activity of the International Commission, though it retains its significance for the cause of keeping peace in Indochina, practically starts to become, in some respects, disadvantageous to us." He added that the ICC's stationary groups "in reality are of no benefit: they are not capable of imposing any limits on South Vietnam and, at the same time, they lay restraint on the DRV."[76]

The full extent of Hanoi's departure from previous policy was revealed during the June 1960 visit to Moscow of Le Duan, who brought with him for the approval of the Soviet comrades abstracts of the Lao Dong Central Committee report to the forthcoming Vietnamese Communist Party congress. Although it was normal practice for Soviet allies to visit Moscow to receive the Kremlin's blessing before important events, Le Duan's trip to the Soviet capital was determined not so much by considerations of loyalty as by the North Vietnamese desire to secure Soviet economic support for building socialism in the DRV. During his conversation with the Soviet ambassador on May 17, Pham Van Dong openly linked the issue of aid with Le Duan's visit.[77] Le Duan, with the same goal, also stopped off in Beijing on his way to Moscow.

The Soviets supported the Vietnamese Communists in their plans for a socialist buildup in the North and readily agreed to sign an agreement with the DRV. The Soviet Union assumed obligations to assist the North Vietnamese in the production and processing of tropical crops, provide technical assistance in agriculture, and build a tea factory and enterprises for processing coffee and canning fruits. Moscow also provided a long-term loan of three hundred fifty million rubles to cover the supply of Soviet equipment, machines, and other material.[78]

Moscow had no objection to reported plans[79] of the Vietnamese Communists to outline at their upcoming congress the course of the socialist revolution in the North. What caused concern on the part of the Soviet leaders was the other part of the twofold task of the Workers' Party of Vietnam, that is, the people's democratic revolution in the South. Although Le Duan stressed that the Vietnamese strongly adhered to the course of peaceful unification of the country, "for it corresponds to the wishes of the people of our country," Hanoi warned that "if American imperialists and their underlings in the South, contrary to the wishes and desires of our people, as well as of the peoples all over the world, take a risk to unleash aggressive war, our people with sympathy and support of the peoples of the world, one and all, will rise to the struggle for their defeat and thus will realize the unification of the country."[80] The section of the abstracts of the Lao Dong Central Committee report entitled "The Struggle for the Realization of the Unification of the Motherland, for the Completion of the People's Democratic Revolution in the Whole Country" elaborated Hanoi's militancy. Analysts in the Soviet Foreign Ministry concluded that this section "represents essentially clear directions to unfold armed struggle in South Vietnam aimed at the overthrow-ing of the regime of Ngo Dinh Diem."[81]

This news was an unpleasant surprise for Moscow. The Hanoi leadership had concealed from the Soviet comrades its plans concerning the South. North Viet-namese leaders seemed to have decided to abandon their policy of support of the Geneva agreements and to do this openly. Moscow did not agree with Hanoi's rationale. The Soviets criticized the overly optimistic views of their friends in Hanoi on the situation in Indochina and doubted that "the United States and the bloc of SEATO nations could allow the unification of Vietnam on democratic foundations and thus agree to the loss to the socialist camp of such a first-class strategic position as South Vietnam."[82] The Soviet Union, as a great power, had to take into account geopolitical considerations, not only ideological preferences.

Moscow did not object to Vietnamese Communist intentions to initiate and support the armed struggle in the South. It became clear from Le Duan's report, however, that Hanoi was going to announce its intention from the podium of the congress. The Soviets predicted that this would mean a declaration of war to the Saigon regime and would be perceived as indirect aggression by the members of SEATO. Washington and Diem could then expedite the suppression of the liberation movement in the South. The Soviets believed that the more justifiable course was the one the North Vietnamese had followed theretofore—that the DRV had nothing to do with the armed struggle in South Vietnam and that the guerrilla war there was a result of the mass discontent of the South Vietnamese and their desire to replace the Diem regime with one that would guarantee in-dependence, democracy, and progress. Because of this ongoing policy, the So-viets claimed, "the DRV occupies now the advantageous position of the coun-try who legitimately renders moral support to the right of the population of South Vietnam to choose a democratic regime instead of the dictatorial govern-ment of Ngo Dinh Diem."[83] This traditional DRV policy was especially well-grounded in Soviet eyes because the North Vietnamese, as they had claimed be-fore, did not need to provide arms to the guerrillas in the South, where arms were plentiful.[84]

The highest Soviet officials argued for the continuation of this policy during their meetings with Le Duan in Moscow. But, unfortunately, they were not the only advisers to the North Vietnamese in policy toward the South. In mid-May, North Vietnamese and Chinese leaders had a number of discussions—first in Hanoi, then in Beijing—concerning the revolutionary struggle in South Viet-nam. Zhou Enlai told his Vietnamese counterparts that the South must be liber-ated. Although the Chinese believed there must be a combination of political and military struggle, Beijing firmly supported the Vietnamese position in favor of armed struggle in the South and pledged to assist Hanoi in it.[85]

In May Moscow was informed about Zhou Enlai's visit to the DRV. The Soviet leaders tried to find out through their ambassador in Hanoi what was discussed during the visit of the Chinese premier to the North Vietnamese capital. Ambassador Sokolov "carefully" raised this issue during his conversation with Pham Van Dong, and Dong "eagerly" informed his interlocutor that "we elucidated at great length the problems of socialist reforms in the North of Vietnam, our difficulties in economic development, as well as the issue of the development of the patriotic revolutionary movement in the South." Pham Van Dong had made it clear to Zhou Enlai that the DRV would need further Chinese aid for its economy, perhaps even on a larger scale. In his turn, Zhou Enlai let it be understood that "the Chinese government agrees in advance to render necessary assistance of sufficient proportions."[86] This news did not help alleviate Soviet concerns. It became obvious to the Kremlin that China had acquired a strong position in North Vietnam and was playing an increasingly important role in the life of the DRV. Now the Soviet leaders would have to pay increased attention to the reports of their diplomats in Hanoi about Chinese influence in North Vietnam.

The Soviet embassy informed Moscow that the Vietnamese and Chinese Communist parties were engaging in permanent contacts in the form of consultations and mutual supplies of information. "Preparing for the Third WPV Congress, the Vietnamese friends have consultations with the Chinese Communist Party CC . . . on all principal propositions" of the political report. In foreign policy, both countries "regularly exchange opinions on all main problems of the international situation and render active support to each other, particularly in their relations with the countries of Southeast Asia and Far East."[87]

Especially impressive was Sino–North Vietnamese economic cooperation. The Chinese provided 52.9 percent of socialist aid to the DRV,[88] and they were prepared to increase the volume of this aid, as Zhou Enlai's visit to Hanoi demonstrated. Moscow suspected that Beijing's eagerness to help North Vietnam was part of a larger strategy to tie North Vietnam, along with Communist Korea and Mongolia, to China.[89] The Soviet leaders viewed any demonstration of support for China in Vietnam with concern, especially when the Sino-Soviet conflict flared up again in the spring of 1960.

In April 1960, the Chinese Communist Party newspaper *Renminh Ribao* and the theoretical journal *Honqi* commemorated Lenin's ninetieth birthday by publishing articles by Chinese leaders who expounded on the principal problems of communism and the international situation. This Chinese propaganda criticized the Soviet thesis about war and peace as a vital problem of mankind, denied that it was possible to avert war, and justified the increase in international tensions as a favorable factor for the acceleration of the world revolutionary process. In response, the CPSU Central Committee circulated a memorandum among Communist and workers' parties in which the Soviets condemned these Chinese arguments. This did not deter the Chinese leaders from strongly criticizing the Soviet Union at a meeting in Beijing of the World Federation of Trade Unions.

Such outright defiance toward Soviet prestige only added fuel to the fire of conflict. Soviet leader Khrushchev seethed with indignation. He decided to use the participation of the Communist parties of other countries, including the Chinese party, in the third congress of the Romanian Communists in Bucharest in June 1960 for the clarification of the positions of the sides in the conflict. At the congress in Romania, Khrushchev accused the Chinese Communists of reneging on what had been agreed at the 1957 Moscow conference of the Communist parties and was able to rally most Communist leaders to the Soviet position. Khrushchev also had the opportunity to discuss the disagreements between Moscow and Beijing directly with the members of the Chinese delegation headed by Peng Zhen. These discussions took place in Moscow, where the Chinese delegation stopped on its way to Bucharest, as well as in the Romanian capital. Khrushchev's meetings with the Chinese made it clear that the conflict had gone too far to be easily overcome. The Soviet leaders concluded that their former allies "have chosen the road of the revision of the main principles of the [1957 Moscow] Declaration and the Manifesto of Peace."[90] Frol Kozlov, a member of the Soviet Communist Party Presidium, warned his colleagues at a CPSU plenum that the actions of the "Chinese comrades," if not rebuffed in a timely way, "could create serious difficulties for the implementation of the peace-loving course of the socialist camp and for the building of socialism in such a huge country like China."[91]

It is noteworthy that Kozlov spoke about the obstacles that could arise for Soviet policy in the international arena. Soviet leaders were well aware that Chinese "erroneous" views could exert an influence on foreign communists. It is impossible to say with certainty whether the Kremlin's fears were based on its recent negotiations with the North Vietnamese concerning the political report to their congress, but the Soviets could not help but suspect the Chinese hand in some of the Vietnamese arguments. Soviet officials, for example, noted the passage in Le Duan's abstracts of the political report that justified the intensification of the revolutionary struggle in South Vietnam: "[S]ince the socialist camp is stronger than the imperialist camp and is getting stronger each day" and "the forces of peace are prevailing over the forces of war," there existed "exceptionally favorable conditions for the struggle" in the South. In other words, Hanoi maintained that "the armed revolutionary movement in the South should not worry about the involvement of international imperialism, for the correlation of forces do not favor the latter."[92] With this radical view on the world situation, the North Vietnamese leaders were convinced that their "people would not understand an appeal for coexistence with this enemy."[93]

Vietnamese Communist leaders were also apprehensive about the aggravation of the crisis between Moscow and Beijing. Because the DRV needed support and assistance from both allies and taking sides in their dispute would unavoidably lead to the loss of support from one or the other, the only solution for the Vietnamese was to try to preserve close relations with the Soviets as well as the Chinese, without alienating either of them. This policy had its limits, however, because as the gap between the opponents widened and each pressured the DRV, it would become more and more difficult to occupy a neutral position. The North Vietnamese leadership began to undertake efforts to reconcile its allies.

Before the conference in Bucharest, Hanoi perhaps did not recognize the seriousness and the scale of the Sino-Soviet dispute. But Le Duan attended the third congress of the Communist Party of Romania, witnessed the heated exchanges between Khrushchev and Peng Zhen, and certainly informed his colleagues in the Lao Dong Party.[94] Soon after Le Duan's return from abroad, the DRV deputy foreign minister, Ung Van Khiem, who was also a member of the Lao Dong party Central Committee, met with the Soviet chargé d'affaires, N. I. Godunov. At their meeting, they touched upon the issue of the conflict between the Soviet Union and China, among other problems. Khiem offered that his colleagues were "concerned to some extent" over the differences of the viewpoints of the CPSU and the Chinese Communist Party "on cardinal questions of the present international relations." Khiem referred to the interest of the Vietnamese Communist cadres in this issue and remarked that the Vietnamese Central Committee had not yet made a final decision on it. Khiem then spoke at length about the importance his party attached to the question of unity in the communist movement: "Our Central Committee always adhered to the necessity for all Communist parties to have identical views on the main problems of the present, which is a solid guarantee against committing mistakes in practical activities and against the appearance of deviationist tendencies."[95] The Vietnamese deputy foreign minister asked the Soviet diplomat for any additional information on this problem. But a Soviet diplomat, despite his prominent position in the embassy hierarchy, could not enlighten his counterpart on as thorny a question as the Sino-Soviet quarrel. The only thing he dared to do was comment on the official communiqué of the Bucharest conference "along the lines of an editorial from *Pravda*."[96] It became clear to the Hanoi leadership that this issue needed to be discussed at a higher level. In August, Ho Chi Minh made a secret trip to Moscow.[97]

After visiting the Soviet capital, the Vietnamese leader went to Yalta, where he met with Khrushchev. He of course discussed with the Soviet leader the forthcoming congress of his party, but his main preoccupation no doubt was an attempt to reconcile the Soviets and the Chinese. His efforts led nowhere. Khrushchev constantly interrupted the soft-spoken Ho, and he did not budge from his anti-Chinese position.[98]

In the meantime, the Vietnamese Communists were preparing for the third congress of their party. In late July and early August of 1960, after being in session more than two months, the eighteenth plenum of the Lao Dong Party adjourned.[99] On August 14, a party conference was convened as a dress rehearsal for the forthcoming congress; the conference approved principal reports and resolutions of the congress and outlined the list of future leaders of the Workers' Party of Vietnam. On September 5, Ho Chi Minh opened the third congress of the Lao Dong Party and delivered an introductory speech.

The principal event of the congress was Le Duan's report. Le Duan, the number-two person in the Lao Dong Party, reviewed developments in Vietnam in the nine years that had passed since the previous party congress and outlined the tasks that the party should resolve in the forthcoming years. According to Le Duan, the Vietnamese Communists must "develop the cause of socialist buildup in the northern part of the country; strengthen North Vietnam, establishing it as a reliable stronghold of the struggle for the unification of the Motherland; . . . liberate South Vietnam from the severe yoke of the American imperialists and their lackeys; realize the unification of the country on the basis of independence and democracy; and establish a peace-loving, united, democratic, and flourishing Vietnam."[100] Thus from the outset Le Duan openly spoke about the liberation of the South, though without specifying means. Recurring throughout Le Duan's report was the hatred of the Vietnamese toward the Americans and Ngo Dinh Diem. Le Duan never missed an opportunity to emphasize the importance of the overthrow of the Saigon regime as a task equal to the socialist reconstruction in the North. In one place he even claimed that the successful development of North Vietnam depended on the elimination of the threat from the South.[101]

The North Vietnamese clearly had taken into account only part of the Soviet recommendations. Although they did not openly speak of Hanoi's support for the struggle in the South, all their pronouncements blessed the struggle. After Le Duan's speech no one doubted that the DRV stood behind the insurgents in the South. Moscow noted the fact that, while the North Vietnamese approved of the revolutionary struggle in South Vietnam, they were silent about the principles that had been put forward by the Soviet leaders at the most recent CPSU congresses and at the conference of the Communist parties in Bucharest. Soviet officials attributed this to Chinese influence on "some problems of the building of socialism in the DRV, as well as issues of the struggle for the unification of Vietnam."[102]

The North Vietnamese were careful not to demonstrate at the congress their preference toward either ally. Ho Chi Minh, Le Duan, and other Vietnamese leaders never mentioned China without mentioning the Soviet Union and vice versa. They congratulated the Soviets on their overfulfilment of the seven-year plan and emphasized the success of the Great Leap Forward in China. They thanked both countries for the help and support they had provided to the DRV, and they stressed the necessity of the "strengthening of solidarity, unity, fraternal mutual aid of the countries of the socialist camp" as the main condition of the successes of communism.[103] Sometimes, some observers noticed,[104] the North Vietnamese might even have been more enthusiastic about the Soviet Union, but this was perhaps overcompensation for their actual neglect of Soviet opinion on the struggle in the South. In any case, it was not great enough to alienate China.

Hanoi was concerned that the tensions between the Soviets and the Chinese would be repeated at the Lao Dong Party's congress. That possibility certainly existed. Delegations from both countries came to the DRV. The Chinese delegation was headed by Li Fuchun, Beijing's top economic official; and the Soviet delegation was headed by a full member of the CPSU Central Committee Presidium, Nuritdin Mukhitdinov. A member of the East German delegation to the congress, Willie Rumpf, confided to the counsellor at the Soviet embassy in the DRV that his delegation had learned about the Chinese intention to use the Vietnamese Communist forum for unleashing criticism of the Soviets. The East German delegation had even prepared a speech to rebuff any Chinese attacks. The Chinese, however, were restrained in their pronouncements at the congress. What were the reasons for Chinese restraint? The German delegate suggested that Beijing had decided to wait until the Moscow conference of the Communist parties that was scheduled for November 1960.[105] The Soviets likewise avoided open criticism of China. Perhaps it was a result of Ho Chi Minh's August meeting with Khrushchev in Yalta and their secret agreement: the Vietnamese leader, having failed to reconcile the two parties, obtained from Khrushchev, at least, a promise to restrain his representatives' emotions against the Chinese for the time being.[106] But it was obvious to everybody that, despite this temporary truce, a showdown between Moscow and Beijing was imminent.

After the Bucharest conference, tensions between the two countries continued to heighten. On July 16, 1960, the Soviet Union notified Beijing that all Soviet advisers and experts in China would soon be withdrawn. Khrushchev justified this decision by citing the poor treatment received by the Soviet citizens who worked in the PRC: they were not trusted and "literally scoffed." Khrushchev said that the Chinese "deliberately discredited our technical proposals, our machines, our equipment."[107] As a result, within one month, almost fourteen hundred Soviet advisers and experts left China. Moscow cancelled twelve agreements on economic and technological aid and abrogated more than two hundred projects for scientific and technological cooperation.[108] In July, Soviet authorities prohibited dissemination in the Soviet Union of the magazine *Friendship* published by Beijing and ceased publication of *The Soviet-Chinese Friendship* destined to be circulated in China by the USSR.[109]

Khrushchev concurrently suggested holding bilateral negotiations between the CPSU and the CCP in order to discuss controversial issues. In reply, Beijing sent Moscow a letter that was essentially a response to what the Soviets had circulated at the Bucharest conference. In their letter, the Chinese leaders, although changing the formulation of some of their views, continued to attack the Soviets and even accused them (and this especially aroused indignation in Moscow) of abandoning Marxism-Leninism and the 1957 Moscow declaration.[110]

The Sino-Soviet negotiations nevertheless took place on September 17–22. The Chinese delegation was headed by Deng Xiaoping. On the Soviet side, the delegation included CPSU Presidium members Mikhail Suslov, the leading Soviet ideologist; Frol Kozlov; Otto Kuusinen; Boris Ponomarev; and Yuri Andropov. The Soviet ambassador to the PRC, Stepan Chervonenko, was also present. But the five days of talks did not lead to reconciliation. In fact the Chinese tried to blame all the disagreements between the two countries on Khrushchev personally. The Soviet leaders assessed the negotiations as a "reconnaissance in force" on the part of the Chinese.[111]

Soon a commission that included both Soviet and Chinese representatives was assigned to work out drafts of final documents for the conference of Communist parties. The Chinese continued to expound their differing views at these sessions as well. They also demonstrated their unwillingness to come to agreement during direct talks—initiated by the Soviets and held on November 9—between Khrushchev and Liu Shaoqi, who headed the Chinese delegation at the conference.[112]

There was a real danger that the conference, instead of demonstrating the unity of the world communist movement and reconciling opposing views, might lead to an even deeper crisis. The Vietnamese felt this imminent failure most acutely. Ho Chi Minh continued to play the role of mediator. When the Chinese failed to subscribe to the final declaration, refused to recognize the importance of the twentieth CPSU congress, and disagreed with the condemnation of any actions that undermined communist unity (Khrushchev was adamant about the latter two propositions[113]), Ho visited Khrushchev and tried to persuade him to concede in order to avoid a split. The Soviet leader refused and instead proposed that Ho Chi Minh and other leaders who vacillated between Moscow and Beijing try to convince the Chinese of the correctness of the Soviet position. "And they went, and especially Ho Chi Minh insisted on this," reported Khrushchev at the CPSU plenum that discussed the results of the Moscow conference. "I was urging him: go, Comrade Ho Chi Minh, go. And this had an effect, finally the Chinese agreed on concessions."[114] Khrushchev all but admitted that Ho Chi Minh's efforts (though apparently not only Ho's) helped prevent a complete failure of the Moscow meeting and, consequently, an irreparable split in the world communist movement.

Schism was averted, and Hanoi preserved its freedom to pursue a middle course between the two parties without alienating either of them. The feeling of relief was reflected in the "almost hysterical reception of the news" in the North Vietnamese capital. From December 6 onward, Hanoi Radio broadcast the final documents of the Moscow conference in full and in part, day after day. Praises for the declaration continued interminably, and "no adjective was considered too extravagant by the broadcasters and journalists."[115] North Vietnamese leaders rightfully regarded the outcome of the conference as their victory, and they did not want to think about the shortcomings of the Moscow declaration that was a result of a compromise and, as Allen Dulles put it during a meeting of the National Security Council on December 8, 1960, could "be cited by both parties to substantiate the ideological views they had previously held."[116]

It is unlikely that Hanoi did not understand the weaknesses of the truce reached in Moscow. But North Vietnam got some breathing space and perhaps sincerely believed that the fragile peace between the leading Communist countries was, after all, better than a quarrel, especially as a crisis in Laos threatened to explode into a hot war.

7. Crisis in Laos

I have not the slightest interest in this
affair, because this affair itself is small,
but there is much noise around it.

Nikita S. Khrushchev to Mao Zedong
October 2, 1959[1]

Until the late 1950s, events in Vietnam overshadowed developments in Laos, a neighboring country also part of the Geneva agreements. Preoccupied with the issues of the Vietnamese elections and the strengthening of each half of Vietnam, the great powers did not pay much attention to that small and underpopulated land with few strategic advantages. True, the U.S. politicians were more attentive to Laos and probably more prescient than were their Soviet counterparts for they continued to supply aid to the royal Lao government (RLG) under the 1950 agreements and even established an aid mission, the United States operations mission (USOM), in January 1955. Moreover Washington included Laos in the list of the countries, along with South Vietnam and Cambodia, that were to be defended by SEATO in case of aggression by an outside power. The main concern of the U.S. government was, of course, the Laotian army, but the United States undertook efforts to strengthen the country's economy as well. As a result, Laos soon received more U.S. aid per capita than any other Southeast Asian country.[2] These measures should have guaranteed the country against a possible Communist takeover, especially since in Geneva the pro-Communist resistance movement known as the Pathet Lao had been granted control of two Laotian provinces, Sam Neua and Phong Saly, as regrouping areas.

Moscow, unlike Washington, did not provide any direct assistance to Laos mainly because the Soviet Union did not have diplomatic relations with the country. Even if it had, the pro-Western Laotian government under the premiership of Katay Dan Sasorith would not have encouraged cooperation between Moscow and Vientiane. The Pathet Lao received support from the Vietnamese Communists, who shared with their Laotian comrades what remained of Chinese and Soviet aid to the DRV. This practice had been established during the war with the French. Owing to North Vietnamese support, the Pathet Lao, which had had only three companies in January 1954,[3] was transformed into a strong political and military organization with an army, training centers, and provincial administration under its control, a control that was strengthened when the two provinces were conveyed to it.

Moscow's only interest in Laos was that it remain neutral and free of U.S. military bases, according to the provisions of the final declaration and the declaration of the Laotian government approved by the Geneva conference.[4] As long as these conditions remained in force, Moscow was prepared to reconcile itself to Vientiane's orientation toward the West. In their desire to enforce the Geneva agreements and to eliminate any pretext for U.S. involvement in Laos, the Soviet leaders were even ready to sacrifice the interests of their Laotian sympathizers. They constantly pressed the Pathet Lao and its Vietnamese allies to negotiate with the RLG in conformity with the solutions reached at Geneva. In its instructions for Ho Chi Minh's visit to Moscow in July 1955, the Soviet Foreign Ministry stated its intention to "emphasize that the most correct way of settlement in Laos is that of direct negotiations between the Royal government and the Pathet Lao and of mutual concessions."[5]

Soviet leaders enjoyed Chinese support for their approach to the Laotian problem. Beijing was more interested than Moscow in favorable developments in Laos, not least because China had a common border with Laos and any threat from Laos would be most immediate. During the Geneva conference, Zhou Enlai was anxious to secure on China's southern borders a buffer that consisted of independent and neutral states whose territories were free of any military installations. Zhou did not conceal this objective from his Western counterparts.[6] It is therefore not surprising that after Geneva Beijing tried to avoid any event that could provide justification for the United States to establish bases in countries bordering China. The Chinese, like the Russians, were not eager to sacrifice long-term security in favor of illusory prospects of a Communist Laos under the control of the Pathet Lao. China therefore supported negotiations between the Lao government and the Pathet Lao and the eventual reintegration of the two provinces under the Pathet Lao's control. Facing their allies' firm position on this principle, the Vietnamese had to comply even if they had reservations.

The process of reconciliation in Laos, however, was not as smooth and efficient as the Soviets and Chinese would have liked. Negotiations between the RLG and the Pathet Lao dragged on and failed to produce an agreement. As a result, a general election took place on December 25, 1955, without the Pathet Lao's participation. It is unclear whether Hanoi was behind such stubbornness on the part of the Pathet Lao, but on December 24 the North Vietnamese condemned the imminent elections as undemocratic and "entirely contrary to the letter and spirit of the Geneva agreements." At the same time they professed the desire to develop good neighborly relations with Laos.[7] In addition to the failure of the Pathet Lao to reach agreement with the RLG, the Soviets learned with uneasiness that the Pathet Lao was developing a guerrilla movement in Laos and had even scored successes. The North Vietnamese were displaying no concern over this course of events. While they did not exclude the possibility of agreement between the RLG and the Pathet Lao, they were not against the preservation of the status quo. The North Vietnamese were willing to allow some RLG representatives in the administration of the provinces of Phong Saly and Sam Neua, controlled by the Pathet Lao, but they would not allow their transfer to RLG authority.[8]

The situation changed for the better in March 1956 when Prince Souvanna Phouma became the new Laotian prime minister and declared his intention to bring about national reconciliation in accordance with the Geneva agreements. On August 1, talks between Souvanna Phouma and his half brother, the leader of the Pathet Lao, Prince Souphanouvong, took place in the Laotian capital of Vientiane and eventually led to agreement between the RLG and the Pathet Lao on almost all principal issues. The Pathet Lao agreed to the restoration of the power of Vientiane in the two provinces and the extension of RLG command over Pathet Lao fighting units. On December 28, the two princes agreed that in a future coalition government, which would be formed prior to supplementary elections, the Pathet Lao was to be given two portfolios.

Some observers suspected that the Pathet Lao's tractability during the negotiations in August–December 1956 was the result of pressure exerted on its leaders by the Soviets and the Chinese.[9] At least it corresponded with the line both Communist powers were following on the Laotian question. In fact, soon after concluding the negotiations with Souphanouvong, Souvanna Phouma went to China and the DRV for official visits. In China he spent a week and received from his hosts full approval for the agreements reached at the Vientiane talks. The Chinese stressed their desire to develop friendly cooperation with Laos on the basis of the five principles of peaceful coexistence but did not press for the immediate establishment of diplomatic relations between the two countries. The Vietnamese followed the Chinese example. They hailed the Sino-Laotian joint statement and also expressed their desire to base their relations with Laos on the five principles of peaceful coexistence.[10] The Soviet Union joined in the Communist countries' efforts toward rapprochement with Souvanna Phouma. As early as June 7, 1956, the Soviet ambassador to Thailand, I. N. Yakushin, met with his Laotian counterpart and discussed with him the prospects for the establishment of diplomatic relations between the two countries. Nothing resulted from these meetings, however, perhaps owing to Souvanna Phouma's fear of alienating the United States, on whose aid Laos relied heavily.

Despite the promising developments in Laos in the second half of 1956, the situation changed for the worse in early 1957. Souphanouvong did not return to the Laotian capital until February 4. In the meantime the RLG, under the influence of former premier Katay Sasorith who had visited the United States, demanded additional guarantees from the Pathet Lao as proof of good faith. Vientiane also demanded that the integration of the Pathet Lao forces should precede rather than follow the formation of the coalition government.[11] In response, the leader of the Pathet Lao demanded that the RLG accept Chinese aid, which was virtually a condition of the Pathet Lao's further cooperation with Vientiane. Both sides refused to compromise.

It has been unclear to observers and scholars why Souphanouvong abandoned the tactics of compromise and who, if anyone, was behind his demand. Beijing did not pressure Souvanna Phouma to accept Chinese aid. Was North Vietnam behind Souphanouvong's demand?[12] Although the picture of what happened in January and February of 1957 remains incomplete, we now know that the Red Prince—as Souphanouvong was called because of his sympathy for Communism—did travel in January to Hanoi where he and his comrades had discussions with the North Vietnamese leaders about further tactics in negotiating with the RLG. Soviet ambassador Mikhail Zimyanin was informed of Souphanouvong's visit by Pham Van Dong.[13] Several days after his conversation with Dong, Zimyanin met with the Chinese ambassador in the DRV, Luo Guibo, and confided his concern over the Vietnamese attitude toward the Laotian issue. According to the Soviet ambassador, "the Vietnamese comrades are not in a hurry" in their dealings with Souphanouvong and for him to put into practice the agreements with the RLG, particularly about the coalition government. But Zimyanin pointed out that "the delay in the resolution of this question could be dangerous for the Pathet Lao forces, for it creates conditions for the direct involvement in the situation in Laos of the U.S.A."[14] Zimyanin could have been implying that the main reason for Souphanouvong's tactic of delay was the North Vietnamese opinion that representatives of the Pathet Lao were not promised important portfolios in the future government. Although the Soviet ambassador did not deny the necessity of striving for important government positions, he believed that it would be better to do this in Vientiane; hence the suggestion that Souphanouvong return to Laos quickly.[15] Luo Guibo agreed with Zimyanin.

Apparently Hanoi turned a deaf ear to the views of its allies, and Souphanouvong waited until February 4 to return to Laos and put forward new demands that stalled the process of reconciliation. It also seemed that Souphanouvong's demands were not fully coordinated with Beijing by the North Vietnamese and their Laotian friends. Although during Souvanna Phouma's visit to China in August 1956 Zhou Enlai had announced the PRC's readiness to provide aid to Laos, the Chinese ambassador told Zimyanin that he reminded the North Vietnamese and Laotians that Zhou "never told them that China will render economic assistance to Laos before the formation of the coalition government." Moreover, the Chinese ambassador had queried Beijing, and Beijing had replied that it would be difficult for China to replace the U.S. economic assistance to Laos.[16] Both ambassadors agreed on the necessity of settlement in Laos and the formation of a coalition government.

Nevertheless, the Pathet Lao and its Vietnamese supporters continued to drag out negotiations with Vientiane on the coalition government, using as a pretext Souvanna Phouma's refusal to accept Chinese aid. The Chinese ambassador in Hanoi believed that the Pathet Lao and the North Vietnamese used this delay for the reorganization of their forces and the strengthening of their positions in the two Laotian provinces under contention. The Chinese ambassador rejected the accusation that Souvanna Phouma was tilting toward the United States and expressed his opinion that "Phouma is the best premier for the negotiations and it is necessary to avoid creating difficulties for him."[17] To bolster Chinese support of the negotiated settlement in Laos, Zhou Enlai on May 13 told the DRV ambassador to China, Nguyen Khang, that "Laos must be neutral and there should not be a revolution in Laos at this point in time."[18] Perhaps this declaration, wrapped in revolutionary language, impressed Hanoi; but soon after, the government of Souvanna Phouma was toppled and a political crisis took place in Laos that lasted from May 31 until August 9, 1957.

The Chinese, who were concerned with the course of events in Laos and feared that it would lead to U.S. interference, blamed the "erroneous tactics of the Vietnamese and Laotians comrades."[19] They continued to press for the formation of a coalition government, which they regarded as a guarantee of Laotian neutrality. The Soviets supported Beijing in its efforts to prevent the disruption of the negotiating process and tried to persuade the Pathet Lao that it was possible to continue negotiations even with a pro-Western leader such as Katay.[20] Fortunately for the Soviets and the Chinese, on August 9 the national assembly approved a government headed once again by Souvanna Phouma.

The situation in the summer of 1957 clearly demonstrated to Moscow and Beijing how precarious the balance of forces in Laos was and how dangerous any delay in the formation of the coalition government could be. But if the great Communist powers regarded Laos only from the perspective of the preservation of regional equilibrium in Indochina, the North Vietnamese had other considerations. The DRV kept in mind its interests in South Vietnam and approached the situation in Laos from that point of view. Consequently, the DRV continued to hinder negotiations between Souvanna Phouma and the Pathet Lao while it tried to improve the Pathet Lao's position in the country. When, in early September 1957, Souphanouvong again visited Hanoi to discuss his tactics in the negotiations on the coalition government, the Vietnamese were still of the opinion that the Pathet Lao was too weak to influence the process of the formation of the government. Thanh Son, head of the committee on Laos and Cambodia of the Lao Dong Central Committee, discussed with the Soviet and Chinese ambassadors the weakness of the Pathet Lao and stressed that the struggle in Laos was expected to be long and complicated.[21]

It became obvious that greater pressure was needed to persuade the North Vietnamese comrades to change their stalling tactics. Therefore, in September 1957 Zhou Enlai met with Ho Chi Minh, who was returning home via Beijing after his trip to socialist countries, and expounded on the Chinese position on Laos. Zhou stated in plain words that the Laotian problem should be approached as a general task of the strengthening of peace in Asia, not as the problem of two provinces in Laos; and Zhou said that it was impossible to eliminate the Americans from Laos with the help of only the Pathet Lao. The Chinese premier again pointed out that not a socialist revolution—not even a bourgeois revolution—was possible in Laos, where one could talk only about a feudal-nationalist revolution. Zhou Enlai warned Ho against a military solution to the Laotian problem because this could lead to U.S. involvement and, as a result, to the consolidation of U.S. positions and the establishment in Laos of U.S. bases. He also confided that, in case Washington interfered, socialist countries would not be able to render military support to the Pathet Lao as they had in Korea. Therefore, any delay of the settlement in Laos would be "fraught with dangerous consequences." Zhou Enlai stressed that it was necessary to use Souvanna Phouma's premiership and "apply all efforts for reaching agreement with him, while making maximal concessions." The Chinese premier reiterated his government's objective to have a neutral or even "semineutral" Laos that would be free of military bases on its territory.[22] It is possible that a conversation with Ho Chi Minh along similar lines took place in Moscow as well.

Pressure by the DRV's Communist allies bore fruit. Negotiations between the RLG and the Pathet Lao resumed on September 16 and quickly led to an understanding on the formation of the coalition government. This understanding was formulated as a joint communiqué signed by Souvanna Phouma and Souphanouvong on November 1, 1957. The communiqué was supplemented by military agreements completed the next day. The sides agreed that, on the day of the formation of the new government, the Pathet Lao would return the two northern provinces under the RLG's control; the Pathet Lao fighting units would be integrated into the Royal Laotian Army; units in excess of fifteen hundred men to be integrated would be disbanded; the Pathet Lao would surrender all weapons in their possession; and the Pathet Lao's political organization, the Neo Lao Hak Xat (NLHX), would operate as a legal political party in Vientiane. Finally, both sides reaffirmed that Laos would adhere to a policy of neutrality.[23] On November 19, 1957, the national assembly of Laos gave its unanimous approval to the new government, which included two Pathet Lao members.

The legalization of the NLHX and its transformation into a governmental party gave rise to new problems that confronted the Pathet Lao and its allies. Not abandoning their revolutionary goals, Pathet Lao members tried to combine legality with underground methods to further the revolutionary goals. They decided to demobilize a number of military cadres from eight-thousand-member fighting units and send them to various provinces where they would work as civilians.[24] This gave the Communists an opportunity to recruit new followers in those provinces that had been immune to their propaganda and, at the same time, reliable and battle-hardened cadres were at hand in case of need.

The Pathet Lao soon learned that it is one thing to be in opposition to the legal government and criticize the current situation in the country while putting forward attractive slogans; but it is another thing to implement those slogans as members of the government. Soon after the formation of the Souvanna Phouma–Souphanouvong coalition, the Vietnamese detected a decrease in the popularity of the NLHX. Ho Chi Minh openly talked about this during a January 1958 meeting with the Soviet chargé d'affaires. He said, "Before the signing of the agreements with the royal side, Pathet Lao forces had enjoyed strong sympathy among broad popular masses, who expected certain improvements in their life. However, their expectations have not been realized, and their sympathy toward the Pathet Lao began to cool down gradually. The situation is still good so far, but it can change to the worse for the Pathet Lao by the election scheduled for May 1958."[25] The Vietnamese leader also was concerned over disagreements within the Pathet Lao leadership and its lack of unity.

The Soviets and Chinese preferred a strong Pathet Lao to influence Souvanna Phouma, prevent him from leaning too much on U.S. support, and compel him to pursue a policy of neutrality. In his conversation with the new Chinese ambassador to the DRV, He Wei, the Soviet chargé d'affaires A. M. Popov, warned about the complicated situation in Laos that could "be fraught with a serious danger" and pointed out that, in connection with this, the Laotian "comrades now need our help, and it is necessary to be in a hurry with it."[26]

Whether owing to the efforts of the Pathet Lao allies or the fact that disappointment with the NLHX was not as widespread as feared, in the supplementary elections to the national assembly in May 1958 the NLHX gained a convincing victory. It won nine seats out of twenty-one that were contested. Another four seats were won by the neutralist party, Santiphab (Peace), led by Souvanna Phouma's protégé, Quinim Pholsena. Some observers were convinced that "the Pathet Lao was about as surprised by its strong showing as the Western candidates themselves were."[27]

The NLHX victory notwithstanding, the election unleashed events that practically undermined all Communist plans with regard to Laos. As early as March 20, 1958, Souvanna Phouma addressed the ICC established in Laos in conformity with the Geneva agreements; he stated that the Geneva agreements had now been fully implemented and asked for the termination of the commission's activities after the May election, which he considered as the last act in the application of the agreements. On May 15, Souvanna Phouma informed the ICC that the election had been held successfully and therefore there was no reason for continuing ICC activities.[28]

Souvanna's eagerness to get rid of the ICC is explained, on one hand, by his disillusionment with the commission's policy in Laos and, on the other, by his desire to eliminate all non-Laotian influences in the country.[29] The Canadian delegation in the ICC supported Souvanna on this issue. However, the Indian and Polish delegations objected. The Poles in their objections followed other socialist countries that had perceived the commission as an obstacle to unfavorable developments in Laos and a guarantor of the Pathet Lao's positions. Therefore the Polish delegate tried to prove that besides the task of national reconciliation the ICC in Laos had other obligations such as the supervision of the import of arms, munitions, and military equipment. The Polish delegate also required prior consultation with the ICCs in the other two countries as well as a consideration of the situation in Cambodia and Vietnam before deciding to reduce the ICC's activities. The Indian delegation hesitated because the Geneva agreements had made no provision for dissolving any of the three commissions.[30] After much debate and considering India's ambiguous attitude,[31] on July 19 the commission decided to adjourn sine die. The Polish member dissented.

The ICC's decision dealt a severe blow to Soviet plans with respect to Laos. Moscow regarded the international commissions as an important part of the Geneva agreements that represented a sort of guarantee of their implementation. The Chinese and the Vietnamese generally shared this view. It is therefore not surprising that the Communist countries resisted the commission adjournment. They strongly criticized the Polish members who, according to the new Soviet ambassador in the DRV, Leonid I. Sokolov, "occupied only a defensive position in the question of struggle for the preservation of the commission in Laos."[32] Then Moscow attempted a diplomatic maneuver during the negotiations in London on August 26, but the British, with the support of the United States and France, rejected Soviet references to SEATO aggression,[33] and the matter was left in suspension for the time being. In November the Soviets had to inform Hanoi that "it appears inexpedient to raise at the London negotiations . . . the proposal that the two cochairmen recommend the preservation in Vientiane of a reduced secretariat of the commission or of its part." Moscow decided to leave this issue at the discretion of the ICC itself.[34]

What worsened the situation in Laos was Souvanna Phouma's failure to form a new government after the May elections. The government was formed on August 15, by Phoui Sananikone, a staunch anti-Communist who soon abandoned the neutral policy of his predecessor. He established closer relations with the regimes of South Vietnam and Thailand and allowed the installation of a Taiwanese consulate general in Vientiane, thus reversing the country's earlier stand of noncommitment on the China issue.

These foreign policy steps were matched in domestic affairs. Phoui gave four posts in his government to members of the pro-Western Committee for the Defense of National Interests (CDNI). Souvanna Phouma himself was eased out and went overseas as Laotian ambassador to France. Phoui did not conceal that he was eager to fight the danger of communism in Laos. He openly warned that "we must guard against the most threatening danger which will undermine our independence and unification. This danger is Communism."[35] Accordingly, the North Vietnamese expected political repressions against the NLHX and the Pathet Lao to begin very soon. One DRV Foreign Ministry official, in a conversation with the Soviet chargé d'affaires, A. M. Popov, drew attention to the reactionary character of the new Laotian government and spoke about the possibility of a resumption of Lao government attacks against "progressive forces."[36]

The North Vietnamese were worried about the ability of their Laotian comrades to adjust their tactics to the new situation. DRV deputy foreign minister Ung Van Khiem felt that although the friends in Laos had much experience in the struggle among the population, they needed help and advice with respect to issues of policy. Communication with the Pathet Lao after the ICC's adjournment was complicated because the Polish delegation in the ICC apparently served as an important channel between Hanoi and Vientiane.[37] The North Vietnamese had to be cautious about maintaining contacts with members of the NLHX in order to avoid accusations that both the NLHX and the Pathet Lao were but puppets in Hanoi's hands.[38]

Neither the Pathet Lao nor its Communist allies were prepared for events as they developed in Laos after the national assembly elections in May 1958, and it took some time for them to work out strategy that corresponded to the new conditions. Those conditions were becoming more and more difficult for the Pa-

thet Lao. In a letter sent to Hanoi from Laos in late October 1958, Laotian revolutionary leaders complained about mounting repressions against them and
murders and arrests of NLHX members in various provinces of Laos. They drew
attention to the growing U.S. involvement in Laotian internal affairs. In particular, they referred to the import from the United States of more than sixty tons
of armaments that included the newest antiaircraft weapons. These facts, wrote
the Laotian friends, demonstrated the U.S. intention to transform Laos into its
military base. The reference to bases was obviously aimed at the Chinese, for
whom U.S. bases on their borders caused alarm. In closing, the letter supplied
information about a meeting of the Central Committee of the People's Party of
Laos, the clandestine Marxist organization behind the NLHX and headed by
Souphanouvong's long-time associate, Kayson Phomvihan. The party had decided to organize armed struggle as it maintained, at the same time, formal cooperation with Phoui's government. The Laotian Communists also wrote of
plans to gather the party's members and sympathizers in the mountains on the
border with the DRV and establish a revolutionary base there.[39] A Chinese
diplomat who provided this information to his Soviet colleague said that the
Vietnamese rejected these plans of their Laotian friends. It was only a question
of time, however, before Hanoi's growing militancy would cause the Lao Dong
Party to reverse its decision.

Chinese officials in the DRV also disagreed with the Pathet Lao's opinion that
all possibilities for legal activities had been exhausted. The Chinese continued
to hope for the resumption of the ICC as a deterrent to Western designs.[40] The
RLG–Pathet Lao negotiations of 1957 made it seem unlikely, however, that Beijing could prevent Hanoi from adopting a militant stand with regard to Laos.
The subsequent diplomatic row between Laos and North Vietnam—Hanoi accused Vientiane of violating the DRV border—only confirmed this view.

The diplomatic dustup began on December 28, 1958, with Pham Van Dong's
protest to Phoui Sananikone regarding alleged Laotian violations of Vietnamese
territory and air space since October 13. This message was followed by a flow
of accusations and counteraccusations concerning intrusions upon each other's
territory. It is now known that Hanoi's diplomatic ruckus was aimed at con-
cealing secret movements of North Vietnamese troops in Laos. Western intelligence sources were learning that armed units from North Vietnam had started
moving into the Tchepone area of Laos on about December 20, 1958.[41] Members of these units dug entrenchments and took positions in the highly sensitive
area just west of the demarcation line between North and South Vietnam.[42]
These actions, combined with the meetings of the fifteenth plenum of the WPV
Central Committee in Hanoi that adopted the decision to begin an armed struggle in South Vietnam, clarify that Laos would unavoidably occupy a prominent

place in the strategic plans of the Lao Dong leadership in the South. The resumption of armed struggle in Laos was regarded positively in the DRV capital because it cloaked Hanoi's preparations for war against Saigon. It is quite probable also that the diplomatic war initiated by the DRV against Laos in early 1959 aimed at pushing the RLG to resort to a tougher policy inside the country to justify this struggle.

The North Vietnamese succeeded in their designs. On January 14, 1959, the national assembly of Laos voted to give Phoui's government special powers for one year. Ten days later, Phoui formed a new cabinet that did not have any NLHX representatives in it. On February 11, 1959, Phoui Sananikone added fuel to the fire when he declared that he considered "the application of the Geneva agreements as fully accomplished and that, therefore, Laos was no longer bound by its provisions."[43] Although six days later the Laotian government issued a new communiqué that essentially negated everything that had been said in the February 11 statement, Hanoi must have felt satisfied. The armed struggle in Laos and North Vietnam's support of that struggle were now fully justified in the eyes of the Chinese and Soviet allies.

Beijing was the first to change its policy toward Laos. In February 1959, the Chinese wrote to the Lao Dong Party explaining their views on the Laotian situation. They said, under the circumstances "when the reactionary forces are trying to begin a broad offensive against progressive forces of the country, further concessions on the part of the Neo Lao Hak Xat can only inflict damage to the developing patriotic movement." The Chinese Communist Party Central Committee also drew attention to the necessity of preparing the Laotian comrades for armed struggle. The Chinese took the view that "one should not fear armed struggle, for in the present conditions it will be of defensive character."[44] Although in the letter the Chinese subordinated armed struggle to other forms of activity, it obviously was just a temporary reservation.

Having obtained Beijing's blessing, the North Vietnamese quickly adopted a decision along similar lines. It was conveyed to the Soviet ambassador on March 9.[45] Although Deputy Foreign Minister Ung Van Khiem referred numerous times to legal forms of the struggle that, in his words, were still valid and he even tried to create the impression that Hanoi was more cautious than its Chinese friends in its approach to armed struggle, his interpretation was mainly a tribute to the well-known Soviet reluctance to approve any drastic actions that could destroy a fragile equilibrium in Indochina.

Moscow nevertheless had to bow before the logic of events in Laos. It became increasingly clear to Soviet decision makers that the Laotian government headed by Phoui Sananikone and under the strong influence of the pro-U.S. CDNI would hardly continue to adhere to the course of neutrality and independence prescribed for Laos by the Geneva agreements. What most alarmed the Soviets was the growing U.S. involvement in the situation, which the Soviets could regard only as another attempt by Washington to undermine the 1954 settlement and its resulting regional balance and to establish "aggressive" U.S. plans for this region. The Soviet embassy reported from the DRV that "American imperialists and their protégés in Laos are successful, to an extent, in the realization of their plans of liquidation of democratic achievements of the Laotians after many years of the national liberation struggle, in the creation of obstacles to the development of Laos along the road of peace and neutrality." The Soviet embassy believed that the principal objective of the U.S. efforts was to use Laos "as an important strategic springboard for staging armed provocations against the PRC and the DRV, exerting pressure on neutral Cambodia, suppressing the national liberation movement in Laos itself, as well as in the whole region of Southeast Asia."[46] In other words, in Moscow's eyes, the United States could subvert peace in Indochina in a roundabout way through Laos.

Yet Moscow was still reluctant to approve the resumption of armed struggle in the country and attempted to restore the status quo through the ICC. The Soviet government sent two notes to the British cochairs, on February 26 and March 21, 1959, suggesting that the cochairs request the ICC in Laos to resume its activities as soon as possible. The British response to the Soviet appeal was expectedly negative.[47]

In the meantime the situation in Laos developed according to the worst scenario. An attempt by Phoui's government in mid-May to integrate fifteen hundred Pathet Lao soldiers, forming two battalions, in the national army was only partly successful. Although the First Battalion that was settled south of Luang Prabang agreed to integration, the Second Battalion deserted on May 19 to the jungles, taking with them their families and belongings.[48] They then moved to the Lao–North Vietnamese border and, as Pham Van Dong "smilingly" informed the Soviet ambassador, all its soldiers reached the DRV safe and sound. Hanoi had alerted its border guards about such a possibility.[49] In fact, on June 12 the Soviets learned that the Second Battalion had crossed the border and settled on North Vietnamese territory.[50] It was suspected that the whole operation with the Pathet Lao battalion had been authorized by Hanoi, and Souphanouvong had been bypassed entirely in the operation.[51] Although in Soviet reports there was no direct evidence of North Vietnamese involvement, the very fact that the DRV leadership possessed complete information of what was transpiring in Laos could be regarded as evidence that Hanoi had been involved. These events were used by Vientiane for new repressions against NLHX and the Pathet Lao leaders. In an interview on May 21, the Laotian foreign minister, Khamphan Panya, declared the RLG's intention to outlaw the NLHX.[52]

Souphanouvong and other NLHX members were first placed under house arrest and later, in July, were arrested and moved to a police camp on the northern outskirts of Vientiane.

Developments in Laos in May–July of 1959 put an end to the relative peace in the country. They also strengthened the determination of Hanoi and Beijing to render support to the armed struggle of the Pathet Lao in order to withstand what they considered U.S. machinations. As early as May 25, the Chinese deputy foreign minister, Zhang Wentien, apprised the Soviet ambassador in China, Pavel Yudin, that at that moment fighting units of the Pathet Lao were waging defensive guerrilla war since "civil war was initiated by the royal government of Laos itself." The Chinese diplomat declared that his leaders considered these defensive actions on the part of the Pathet Lao as necessary and approved of them.[53] By late July the Chinese had assessed that the armed struggle was playing a leading role in the events in Laos, and Hanoi and Beijing were preparing to render necessary assistance to the Pathet Lao.[54] Ung Van Khiem informed the Soviet chargé d'affaires that the primary tasks were the strengthening and broadening of revolutionary bases in various parts of the country and the formation of three to five new Pathet Lao battalions. "It is necessary," stated Ung Van Khiem, "to complete the work of arming the Pathet Lao forces as soon as possible, before the beginning of the rainy season."[55]

Fighting between the government troops and the Pathet Lao was already under way in July in the provinces of Xieng Khouang and Sam Neua, where the Pathet Lao were traditionally strong. Then, after a brief lull, military activities resumed toward the end of August in widely scattered areas of the country adjoining the Vietnam border. On August 26, 1959, the U.S. government decided that it would provide Vientiane with "emergency aid" in the form of weapons and money.[56] In this situation the Soviet Union had no choice other than to follow the lead of its Chinese and North Vietnamese allies in support of the armed struggle of the Pathet Lao. Nevertheless Moscow made it clear to Beijing and Hanoi that this struggle should be aimed at the "strict implementation of the Geneva and Vientiane agreements," not at the overthrow of the existing government. In addition, the action must be limited to guerrilla fighting combined with political activities among the population. In the Soviet view, the broadening of military action would bring no good,[57] and Khrushchev strongly emphasized this at the end of an uneasy conversation with Mao Zedong on October 2. If warfare were to intensify, the Soviets anticipated possible U.S. interference. The Soviet leader argued that the Americans could appear on the borders of North Vietnam and easily "crash" the DRV border, while the Soviets would have no time to undertake retaliatory measures. Khrushchev appealed to Mao to join him in persuading the North Vietnamese to act with restraint.[58]

The Soviets were also concerned lest the support provided to the Pathet Lao by China and North Vietnam become known to the West, especially in view of the RLG's September 4 request to the United Nations to send an emergency force to Laos to halt aggression by the DRV. On September 5 the DRV deputy foreign minister, Ung Van Khiem, met with Soviet chargé d'affaires Popov and Chinese ambassador He Wei and begged for support. "First of all, we hope," stated Khiem, "that the Soviet government gives instructions to its representative in the Security Council to expose the lie with respect to the DRV and to impose a veto during the vote on this issue, following the experience of discussions of the Korean question."[59] Moscow also should try to dissuade the British from supporting the RLG's request.

In spite of Soviet opposition, the Security Council met on September 7, discussed Phoui's charges against North Vietnam, and decided that a subcommittee composed of Argentina, Italy, Japan, and Tunisia be sent to Laos to investigate Vientiane's claims of foreign aggression. The subcommittee's appointment was considered a procedural issue so as to avoid a Soviet veto. The majority on the Security Council favored the Western position, and the Soviet representative had to satisfy himself with formal protests against such a decision.[60]

Having failed to prevent UN involvement in the Laotian conflict, Moscow wanted to make certain that the Security Council mission would not find any evidence of the DRV's participation in military operations in Laos. Soviet diplomats in Hanoi and Beijing therefore inquired among their Vietnamese colleagues whether Vientiane's accusations had any substance. The Vietnamese assured the Soviets that PAV troops did not participate in armed struggle in Laos and that this struggle was waged only by the Laotian comrades. True, the DRV helped the Pathet Lao by sending food and weapons, but not manpower. Even the arms that Hanoi provided for Laotian guerrillas were of American and French origin captured by the Vietminh during the first Indochina war. Those North Vietnamese who had been dispatched earlier to Laos with training missions were withdrawn from the country, and after that Pathet Lao cadres had to go to the DRV themselves to get support and advice.[61] The only evidence that could be used against the DRV were weapons captured from PAV deserters who fled to Laos as well as any cartridge cases and uniforms made in North Vietnam.[62]

The UN mission was not able to find firm evidence in support of the Phoui government's allegations against North Vietnam. It could conclude only that certain operations against the RLG "must have had centralized coordination." Bernard Fall, who was in Laos at that time as a correspondent for several U.S. and French newspapers, wrote: "It is . . . noteworthy that the UN report does not make any mention of the possibility that such 'centralized coordination' might have come from non-Laotian elements outside the Pathet Lao,"[63] even though the mission was of a "solidly pro-American character." In other words, Fall noted, "if there were any evidence that a Communist invasion had taken place, that mission would certainly not have been loath to report on it at great length."[64]

While the U.N. fact-finding mission failed to register any proof of Communist powers' involvement in Laos, there was ample evidence of U.S. penetration in that country, which had only increased with the resumption of hostilities. On July 23, in response to the request from Phoui's government, the United States announced that it was dispatching additional technicians to conduct an emergency training program aimed at expanding the Royal Lao Army from 25,000 to 29,000 men.[65] Washington poured into Laos an ever-growing amount of money and aid, predominantly military aid. As a result of this aid, the per capita cost to the United States of a Laotian soldier was more than $1,000 per year as against a worldwide average of $848, annual costs in Pakistan of $485, and in Greece of $424.[66]

U.S. activity in Laos could not remain a secret from Moscow. The Soviet embassy in Hanoi reported that U.S. military advisers "worked out plans of 'mopping-up operations,' took part in the formation of new units of the royal Army, pursued on-site inspections, etc." The U.S. military ousted the French from training the Laotian army, and the army was almost completely transferred into the hands of U.S. instructors.[67] The result was the consolidation of U.S. influence in Laos and an incipient coalition composed of South Vietnam, Thailand, Laos, South Korea, and Taiwan. In other words, Moscow regarded U.S. efforts as aimed at building up a belt of pro-U.S. regimes on the southern borders of China and near the DRV that would greatly impair the existing balance and pose a direct danger for the Soviet Asian allies.

Despite this concern, Moscow's attitude toward developments in Laos was not totally devoid of optimism. Throughout the summer of 1959, according to British sources, the Soviet position was that the Russians would like to see the Laotian situation stabilized.[68] For the Kremlin, Laos apparently did not have any value beyond the framework of the Geneva agreements and was only one of the factors important for maintaining peace in Indochina. Soviet leaders did not lose hope of convincing Washington that the best possible solution for every country involved in those agreements was to keep Laos neutral, independent, and free from the military presence of an outside power. The Soviets were even prepared to see Laotian neutrality weighted toward the West, like Austria, rather than have a conflict that could destroy the whole Geneva edifice. This position corresponded fully with Khrushchev's policy of peaceful coexistence, which he advocated during his visit to the United States in September 1959.

Khrushchev's U.S. visit had had a generally favorable effect on the international situation and was regarded by Moscow as a sort of guarantee against unexpected developments in Laos. At least the Soviet embassy in Hanoi was eager to interpret it as such in its annual report for 1959:

[T]he thaw in international relations started after Com. Khrushchev's trip to the USA has wielded and will continue to wield substantial and direct influence on the further events in Laos. In fact, the U.S. governing circles do not already dare to act openly, they are hiding behind the UN cover, are searching for new, more flexible ways for the implementation of their plans in Laos.[69]

In some respects, this assessment was not totally unjustified. For example, on December 25 the Laotian army under the command of a CDNI member, General Phoumi Nosavan, a U.S.-backed strongman in Laos, tried to stage a coup d'état against the Sananikone government. The U.S. ambassador in Laos, accompanied by the ambassadors from Great Britain, France, and Australia, called on the Laotian king and made it clear that this far exceeded Western plans in Laos and the premiership of Phoumi Nosavan, who was closely associated with a "hard" policy, was not acceptable.[70] As a result, the premiership was entrusted to Khou Abhay, a sixty-seven-year-old court official of moderate views.[71]

This was but only a brief interlude in the growing crisis in Laos. Abhay headed a care-taker government for the period before the new nationwide legislative elections, and these elections, which finally took place on April 24, 1960, were notorious for violations and manipulations. By changing eligibility requirements and gerrymandering electoral districts, the RLG excluded most of the NLHX candidates. The leadership of the Pathet Lao was still in jail awaiting trial and could therefore not take part in the electoral campaign. Repression against NLHX members and the suppression of their propaganda only added to the overall atmosphere of political oppression.[72] As a result, the candidates from the CDNI won the majority of seats in the national assembly, with the remainder going to candidates who were close to the CDNI. The neutralists and the NLHX won no seats and were defeated even in such strongholds of the Pathet Lao as the provinces of Sam Neua and Phong Saly. This outcome was also in many cases due to large-scale fraud and election rigging that reached such proportions that in one district the government candidate got two thousand more votes than there were registered voters.[73]

The election victory of the anticommunist candidates alarmed the Pathet Lao leaders and their allies in Hanoi and Beijing. Prince Souphanouvong and his NLHX colleagues who were detained in the Phone Kheng police camp had every reason to expect repressions from the new government and began to prepare for their escape. The North Vietnamese prepared to cooperate. For months Souphanouvong and his associates, while tending their little garden and doing physical exercises in the police camp, discussed politics with their guards. As a result, on May 23, 1960, when they decided to break out of prison, not only did they not meet any resistance, but the majority of their guards followed them right out of town and into the jungle hideouts.[74] Even Hanoi could not hope for an outcome better than this operation.[75]

After he escaped from the camp, Souphanouvong traveled three hundred miles on foot, visiting Pathet Lao bases in each province,[76] and he was eagerly awaited in Hanoi where the North Vietnamese wanted to adjust their plans for Laos according to the new situation and coordinate them with the Pathet Lao leaders.[77] But the Red Prince had not reached Hanoi by August 9, when they heard about the coup in Vientiane carried out by Kong Le, commander of the Second Paratroop Battalion, who was "sick and tired of it all"—the graft and corruption, the fratricidal war, the loss of Laotian values, and foreign control of Laotian affairs.[78] The coup was almost bloodless and afterwards Kong Le formed a provisional executive committee that included, among others, Souvanna Phouma, who was to govern the country until a new government could be assigned.

No one had anticipated this turn of events. Nevertheless, both Hanoi and Beijing were quick to greet the coup and state that the policy of peace and neutrality were compatible with Laotian aspirations. The Chinese also hailed the coup as a blow to U.S. imperialism.[79] When, on August 15, it was announced that the former government was voted out by the national assembly and the king had appointed Souvanna Phouma to form a new government, the Communist powers were more than pleased. They expected that Souvanna Phouma would continue on the course of peace and neutrality that he had followed before. More than that, Moscow hoped that he had become wiser and more tractable in his attitude toward Communist countries. Instructions were even sent to the Soviet ambassador in Cambodia, Aleksandr Abramov, in August to probe the issue of the establishment of diplomatic relations with Laos. The Soviet feelers were successful, and in September Souvanna Phouma addressed, through Abramov, his government's proposal to the Soviet Union to continue negotiations on the question of diplomatic relations that had begun as early as 1956. On October 7, 1960, Moscow and Vientiane published communiqués on the establishment of diplomatic relations between the two countries.[80]

Souvanna Phouma's negotiations with his political rivals inside Laos were not so fruitful. General Phoumi Nosavan, the leader of the CDNI who initially had agreed to enter Souvanna's government as deputy prime minister and interior minister but then reversed his decision, flew back to his stronghold in Savannakhet, in the south of the country, and announced the formation of a revolutionary committee headed by Prince Boun Oum. He embarked on military plans to retake Vientiane by force, but his first offensive failed and his troops were forced by Kong Le's paratroopers to retreat down the Mekong Valley to the south bank of Ca Dinh river.[81]

The external situation was also complicated for Souvanna Phouma. Although it first recognized his government, the United States soon shifted the bulk of its aid to Phoumi Nosavan because Washington regarded the new government in Vientiane as heavily dependent on the Pathet Lao and the North Vietnamese. After mid-September, an increased number of flights by Air America—a Central Intelligence Agency front—manned by U.S. crews brought military supplies to Savannakhet. At the same time, Thailand imposed an unofficial blockade on Vientiane. This soon had a drastic effect on the capital's economy. Vientiane was running out food, fuel, and other necessary supplies.[82]

This situation was in many respects a result of the policy of polarization pursued by the United States in Laos. This policy reflected the Pentagon's and the CIA's inclination to support Phoumi Nosavan out of the conviction that "the entire American defense posture in Southeast Asia, and more particularly in South Vietnam and Thailand, depended on unconditional support to anti-Communists in Laos."[83] Souvanna Phouma's maneuvers after his accession to power—his negotiations with the Pathet Lao and the establishment of diplomatic relations with the Soviet Union—convinced policymakers in Washington that it was necessary to counterbalance them with measures that would undermine the position of the new government and would eventually lead to its downfall. It was therefore not surprising that the day after the announcement of the establishment of Soviet-Lao relations, the United States withheld its cash grant to the government in Vientiane. Washington sent to Laos the assistant secretary of state who was responsible for Far Eastern affairs, J. Graham Parsons, to inform Souvanna Phouma that to retain U.S. aid he should suspend negotiations with the NLHX, reconcile with the Phoumi Nosavan faction, and transfer the Laotian capital to Luang Prabang.[84] Neither the conditions nor the messenger, who had been "the most ardent and vocal advocate of the 'hard line' on Laos,"[85] was met favorably by Souvanna Phouma. Therefore, instead of bowing to U.S. demands, the Laotian premier turned for support to the Soviet Union and other Communist countries. U.S. efforts in Laos had been excessive.

Unlike the U.S. government, the Soviet Union acted subtly and carefully toward Laos. Instructions given to Aleksandr Abramov, the first Soviet ambassador to Laos, who was also ambassador to Cambodia, for his first visit to Vientiane reflect this. Abramov was instructed to emphasize during his meeting with Souvanna Phouma that Moscow fully supported the new government's program that proclaimed a policy of neutrality, observance of the Geneva agreements, development of relations "with all states without any differentiation," as well as national reconciliation and unity of Laos by means of negotiations. Moscow also instructed its ambassador to offer Soviet economic aid to Laos if Laos requested it officially. Aid to Laos would not differ from assistance rendered to other underdeveloped countries: credits and loans on favorable terms, construction of industrial and cultural objects, and supplies of food and goods.

The Soviet leaders handled with care the issues of the 1954 Geneva agreements. The ambassador was instructed not to raise questions on the implementation of these agreements in Laos at his own initiative, but he was to hint, in case such questions were touched upon by the Laotians themselves, that it would be in the interest of Souvanna Phouma to declare Laos's adherence to the Geneva agreements. The ambassador could also imply that the resumption of activities by the ICC would favorably influence political settlement in the country and guarantee a policy of neutrality.[86]

Soviet flexibility and U.S. rigidity bore their respective fruits. Confronted with Washington's unacceptable demands, the military danger from Phoumi Nosavan's faction, and the growing shortage of economic resources in Vientiane, Souvanna Phouma announced at a press conference on October 27 that he had in principle accepted Soviet aid.[87] Abramov, who had a long talk with Souvanna upon his arrival in the Laotian capital and who emerged from it smiling, had every reason to state: "Had the Americans been our best friends, they could not have acted otherwise."[88]

In the meantime, various Laotian factions continued fighting with each other. On November 10, the forces of Phoumi Nosavan gained control over Luang Prabang and captured the Laotian king. Viktor Likhachev, head of Soviet Foreign Ministry's Southeast Asia Department, had to inform the Soviet deputy foreign minister, Georgii Pushkin, that only two provinces out of twelve were under control of the Vientiane government. Likhachev considered the situation in the country "critical."[89] The Soviet official saw in the Pathet Lao's intransigence during the negotiations on the formation of the coalition government one of the important reasons for the growing isolation of Souvanna Phouma. Likhachev wrote with concern that the month that had passed since the start of the negotiations had not brought substantial progress. Souphanouvong and Kayson Phomvihan did not want to limit themselves to the understanding reached earlier and wanted more. Accordingly, they were prepared to have long talks. "It is noteworthy," Likhachev pointed out, "that the leaders of the Pathet Lao regard as the principal objective of their delegation not to reach an agreement, but to 'push to the left' the Souvanna Phouma government."[90] The Pathet Lao also refused to transfer to the government's control the province of Sam Neua and other regions occupied by fighting units of the Pathet Lao. As a result, the prestige of Souvanna Phouma was being undermined.

Likhachev in his memo predicted the worst prognosis for events in Laos, from the Soviet viewpoint. Likhachev believed that without Souvanna Phouma a new government would be too leftist to get the king's approval and could rely only on the Kong Le and the Pathet Lao forces:

> The result would be the official formation in Savannakhet of a reactionary countergovernment, approved by the king, which would command almost all Laotian army and would have recognition and broad material support from the United States and SEATO. In essence, the situation would go back to the status when, on one hand, there were Pathet Lao fighting units composed of five battalions and, on the other, a twenty-five-thousand-strong Laotian army, acting on the order of the lawful, that is, approved by the king, Laotian reactionary government . . . . The result of such a development would be a civil war in Laos under unfavorable conditions for the Pathet Lao and the transformation of Laos into a factor that would undoubtedly be used by the imperialist circles of the United States to the detriment of our struggle for the relaxation of international tension, disarmament, etc.[91]

Moscow wanted to keep the Pathet Lao as a strong political force in a government headed by a neutralist politician such as Souvanna Phouma who had been chosen in order to avoid the transformation of Laos into a factor for instability in Indochina. The Soviet solution was concessions on the part of the Pathet Lao and completion of the negotiations "on the basis of the restoration, to the full extent, of principles and provisions of the Geneva and Vientiane agreements."[92] Finally, Likhachev recommended the use of Chinese and Vietnamese friends, who were in Moscow participating in a conference of Communist and workers' parties, to arrange consultations on these issues.

It is not known whether such consultations really took place, but Likhachev's recommendation came a little late. On November 16, it was announced that the NLHX and Souvanna Phouma had reached an agreement on the basis of the 1957 accords. Final details of this agreement were settled at a personal meeting of Souvanna Phouma with Souphanouvong.

But a coalition government without the participation of the Nosavan faction could not prevent the deterioration of events in Laos resulting in military conflict. The country was divided into two camps, each enjoying support and encouragement from opposing Cold War blocs. If one accepts the definition of an international crisis as "a sequence of interactions between the governments of two or more sovereign states in severe conflict, short of actual war, but involving the perception of a dangerously high probability of war,"[93] it is obvious that by the end of November 1960 the situation in Laos had acquired all the characteristics of an international crisis.

In early December, the Communist powers started delivering aid to Souvanna Phouma in response to his request for supplies of petroleum and oil that had been conveyed to Moscow sometime during the last ten days of November.[94] The request had stipulated that the aid should be sent via Hanoi, and on November 23, 1960, Likhachev met with the North Vietnamese ambassador to Moscow, Nguyen Van Kinh, to discuss this issue.[95] On December 3, a Soviet test flight staffed by a Russian crew landed in Vientiane for the first time. No cargo was on board, but the flight attracted many curiosity seekers, journalists, and diplomats. After it was decided that there would be two flights a day and other problems were settled,[96] regular flights delivering fuel from Hanoi to Vientiane began on December 4.

The North Vietnamese, who were concerned with developments in Laos, were of the opinion that economic aid was not enough. On December 4, Pham Van Dong stated to the counsellor of the Soviet embassy that it was the DRV that was primarily interested in providing assistance to Laos and that this assistance must be immediately forthcoming for Laos was changing so rapidly that "a situation might arise when nobody is to be helped."[97] The DRV premier seemed to be implying that it was necessary to deliver weaponry and munitions to Kong Le's units and the Pathet Lao. Hanoi was alarmed by news of a coup d'état being prepared in Vientiane amid the offensive against the Laotian capital organized by the troops loyal to the Savannakhet group.

In a few days North Vietnamese fears were justified. On December 8, the commander of the Vientiane military region, Colonel Kouprasith Abhay, seized control of the capital and forced Kong Le and his men to withdraw westward. Kong Le's forces were able to regain their positions, however, and reoccupied Vietniane. Now the Chinese were alarmed and pushed the Soviets into action. The same day that the news about the coup apparently reached Beijing, Chinese foreign minister Chen Yi met with Soviet chargé d'affaires Nikolai Sudarikov and raised the issue of sending arms to the government of Souvanna Phouma. Chen pointed out that it was best to deliver weaponry to Vientiane by air, and he informed the Soviet diplomat that Beijing was ready to provide the airport in Nanning for Soviet transports. However, since the situation in Vientiane was very unstable and Kong Le might not be able to control the Laotian capital, the best plan, according to the Chinese foreign minister, would be to deliver arms to Hanoi and wait until the situation was clarified.[98]

The following day Sudarikov participated in a reception at the airport for the Chinese delegation returning from the Moscow Communist parties conference. In the midst of the formalities, he was invited to talk to Zhou Enlai, who assured the Soviet diplomat that the Chinese would do their best in facilitating the transport of Soviet aid through the territory of Communist China. He underlined the need to accelerate deliveries of arms, ammunition, and fuel to the government of Souvanna Phouma in Vientiane. The crisis in Laos apparently caused the Chinese to forget their disagreements with Moscow. Sudarikov noted that all members of the Chinese Communist Party Politburo who greeted him were in good spirits and expressed satisfaction with the outcome of the Moscow conference.[99]

The Soviets did not need urging to provide military assistance to Laos. Sudarikov's remarks during his conversations with the Chinese officials show that Moscow had already undertaken measures to satisfy the needs of their Laotian friends. By December 10, eleven railway cars of weapons and thirty-five of oil and gasoline had been moved to the Soviet-Chinese border, ready for delivery to Laos.[100] Because it was necessary to deliver this aid to Laos in the shortest possible time, it was transported by railway through Chinese territory to Nanning and then airlifted to Hanoi and Vientiane.

All these efforts notwithstanding, the situation in Laos continued to deteriorate for Souvanna Phouma who, having failed to reach an agreement between the warring factions, departed Vientiane for Phnom Penh, the capital of Cambodia. British officials in Vientiane believed that one reason he had fled was his disagreement with the leftists in his government on the necessity of asking the Soviets for arms.[101] There were some grounds for this assertion since Quinim Pholsena, who remained the senior cabinet member in Vientiane, flew to Hanoi the next day aboard a Soviet transport and requested that the North Vietnamese send his government arms and ammunition; in his words, "Souvanna Phouma did not believe in the strength of the people." Pholsena declared that he and his associates believed in the strength of the people and their victory. Pholsena returned to Vientiane that same day, bringing with him nine tons of arms.[102]

But this infusion of military aid did not stop the course of events unfavorable for the neutralists and the Pathet Lao. On December 12, the national assembly withdrew its support for the Souvanna Phouma government and set up a new regime under General Phoumi Nosavan and Prince Boun Oum, which was immediately recognized by the United States and Thailand while the Soviet Union sent a note to the United States protesting its intervention in the internal affairs of Laos. At the same time, severe fighting took place in Vientiane between rightist and neutralist forces, resulting in the defeat of those supporting neutrality. Kong Le had to retreat northward. But the battle for Vientiane, as this episode was called, did not significantly improve the military situation in favor of the Nosavan–Boun Oum government. Although they were now outside of Vientiane, Kong Le's paratroops kept their weapons and discipline, and the Pathet Lao forces had not participated in the fighting for Vientiane at all. The combination of Kong Le's paratroops and guerrilla units of the Pathet Lao only increased their maneuverability and gave them command over the countryside. Soon they captured such strategically important areas as Xieng Khouang and the Plain of Jars.

Both the Chinese and the Vietnamese constantly prevailed upon the Soviets for fresh supplies of weapons and ammunition for Kong Le and the Pathet Lao. The Chinese deputy foreign minister, Jien Yunqiuan, said, "Now any delay with assistance can lead to a great detriment for the patriotic forces of Laos."[103] The Soviet Union was not deaf to these pleas and increased its deliveries to Laos. According to the U.S. State Department, during the battle for Vientiane, Soviet IL-14 aircraft flew in howitzers, ammunition, gasoline, combat rations, and other war matériel. Soviet heavy transport aircraft were passing over China to Hanoi and Haiphong, maintaining the airlift into Laos.[104] In his retreat Kong Le was supported by a constant stream of Soviet supply drops.[105]

It was becoming clear that Laos was plunging into a civil war with international repercussions. Chen Yi predicted in his conversation with the Soviet chargé d'affaires that, "the struggle of the patriotic progressive forces against reactionary pro-American forces in Laos apparently would lead to the diarchy in the country and to its split in two parts—northern and southern." Chen said that this struggle would be prolonged and it was therefore necessary to render assistance to those who supported Souvanna Phouma and Kong Le.[106] By that time the Soviet leaders might have recognized that the continuation of armed struggle in Laos would result in a conflict that unavoidably involved the United States and the Soviet Union and that buried all existing hopes for stabilization in Indochina. Thus, the Kremlin believed that a diplomatic settlement of the Laotian problem, probably at a conference with the participation of all interested states, seemed to be the only solution. Khrushchev first mentioned this in September 1960; the Cambodian leader, Prince Norodom Sihanouk, revived the idea in his speech in Beijing on December 19.[107]

The problem of an international conference was closely linked with the ICC in Laos, which had adjourned sine die in the summer of 1958. Since then, Moscow had continued to insist on the resumption of its activities. On December 15, 1960, Indian prime minister Jawaharlal Nehru, in a note to the Geneva cochairs, proposed that the ICC for Laos be reconvened. The British supported this proposal and addressed it to the Soviet government. In response, on December 22, the Soviet Union delivered a note to the British government proposing the convocation of a conference of the interested powers and the resumption of the ICC's activities in Laos.[108]

The Soviets expected a favorable reception by both allies and rivals for the idea of the conference and the resumption of the ICC's activities. As recently as November 1960 in a conversation in Moscow between Le Duan and Mikhail Suslov, a member of the CPSU Presidium and chief ideologist of the Soviet Communists, Le Duan insisted on the expediency of contacting India on the question of resuming the ICC in Laos.[109] He was joined on December 16 by Pham Van Dong, who addressed a telegram to Khrushchev in which he spoke of the dangerous developments in Laos and called for "positive and effective actions" that would lead to the "saving of the present situation in Laos, the guaranteeing of the policy of peace and neutrality of the royal government of Laos."[110] Hanoi was not opposed to Sihanouk's idea of the neutralization of Laos and Cambodia. Pham Van Dong noted both the positive and negative sides of Sihanouk's proposal and stressed that the DRV was ready to support all that was positive in Sihanouk's program.[111] Beijing likewise supported the idea of a neutrality zone in Indochina, which Sihanouk had put forward during his December 14–26 visit to the PRC. Always preoccupied with the danger of U.S. bases on their southern borders, the Chinese could not but see in the neutrality-zone idea a guarantee against a threat from this direction. Chen Yi confirmed this in his conversation with the Soviet chargé d'affaires.[112] As a result, North Vietnam and China assented when, on January 1, 1961, Sihanouk wrote to the two cochairs and other heads of states appealing for a new enlarged conference on Laos.

Having obtained the consent of its allies, Moscow was hopeful that the United States would not oppose the idea of the conference. The basis for such a hope was grounded in the victory of John F. Kennedy, the Democratic Party candidate in the 1960 U.S. presidential election. Soviet leaders expected that the new U.S. administration would reverse the policy of its Republican Party predecessors on a number of issues, including Laos. The Soviet ambassador in Washington, Mikhail Menshikov, confided to a close associate of Kennedy that, "[h]is principals—especially Khrushchev—believed the coming into power of a new American administration presented an opportunity to resolve existing and dangerous differences between our countries. The atmosphere had changed. Psychologically, it would be easier for the U.S.S.R. to deal with the new Administration than with the old one."[113]

While the Kennedy administration was working out its own position on Laos, nuances appeared in the approach of various countries toward the issue of the conference. Although Great Britain and India stressed that the immediate objective should be the cessation of hostilities and the reconvening of the ICC, the

Soviet Union, China, and North Vietnam insisted that a conference should precede all these steps.[114] Although Khrushchev declared in his January 20, 1961, letter to the British prime minister that his government was ready to undertake steps needed to convene a conference and to reactivate the commission,[115] he drew London's attention to the fact that the existing situation in Laos differed from conditions in 1954 and that it was the conference that should be the priority for the cochairs if they wanted to settle the conflict in Laos. This argument was repeated in Moscow by the Soviet deputy foreign minister, Vasilii Kuznetzov, in his conversation with the British ambassador, Frank Roberts, the next day. In response to Roberts's reasons why having the ICC in Laos was enough, Kuznetzov stated that a conference was necessary for not only the two cochairs and members of the ICC but also all interested countries to discuss the existing situation in Laos. At such a representative conference it would also be possible to discuss objectives and tasks of the commission as well as ways and opportunities for achieving them.[116] Kuznetzov also expressed Moscow's conviction that the only legitimate government in Laos was that of Souvanna Phouma, and he rejected any attempt at compromise with the Laotian king on the grounds that the king was a captive of the rebels.

While Kuznetzov, a high-ranking Soviet diplomat, expounded on these views to the British ambassador, there was actually no unity among the Communist powers themselves on the issue of the ICC in Laos. The Chinese opposed reconvening the ICC before the conference because, as Zhou Enlai explained to the Soviet chargé d'affaires, the commission would unavoidably have to deal with the rebel clique of Phoumi–Boun Oum, which was unacceptable.[117] Beijing was also concerned about the ambivalent position of India, lest the ICC become a tool of the West. On these grounds the Chinese did not fully concur with the Soviet proposal to reconvene the ICC outside Laos—for example, in New Delhi—in order to facilitate preparations for the conference. They also insisted that the ICC's sole obligation would be "to discuss the question of the resumption of its activities" and that this provision be included in the ICC document. In an oral message spelled out by Deputy Foreign Minister Zhang Hanfu during his meeting with Sudarikov, Beijing drew the Soviet leaders' attention to the possibility that, after having obtained access to Laos, the ICC could demand a ceasefire if the "rebellious clique of Phoumi–Boun Oum" prevailed over the "patriotic forces." "This would not favor the development of the patriotic forces of Laos and the strengthening of Phouma's government," the Chinese concluded.[118]

Unlike the Chinese, it seemed that Hanoi did not fear a resumption of ICC activities in Laos. Vo Nguyen Giap informed the Soviet ambassador, Leonid Sokolov, that the Lao Dong Party's Politburo did not oppose the resumption of the ICC's activities or its dealing with the Souvanna Phouma government, the Pathet Lao, and the government of Boun Oum all at the same time. The North Vietnamese believed the commission should stay in a neutral zone where neither the Pathet Lao forces nor Phoumi Nosavan's units were located. Giap did not even object to the possibility that the ICC could impose the cease-fire although he admitted that it was not to the Pathet Lao's advantage.[119]

North Vietnam's friends coordinated their positions with Hanoi's intention to use the opportunity to prolong the fighting in Laos. Vo Nguyen Giap declared during the same conversation with Sokolov that "the best way to prepare the conference [on Laos] would be offensive and the capture of Luang Prabang."[120] Since the Pathet Lao did not possess enough resources for such an offensive, the North Vietnamese regarded the reconvening of the ICC as a way to win time in the still unstable situation in the country. A few days later, Pham Van Dong was even more outspoken. He stated to the Soviet ambassador that "the convening of the conference would depend, to a great extent, on the military situation in Laos, that is, the new successes achieved by the Kong Le and Pathet Lao forces could accelerate [the opening of] this conference."[121] In the view of the DRV premier, it was necessary to take into account the fact that the conference would not be convened soon. In the meantime, "the patriotic forces" would proceed to strengthen their positions. Pham Van Dong repeated this several times during the conversation, while he also spoke of the need to prevent the spread of the Laotian conflict to other territories and of the preservation of peace in Southeast Asia.

The North Vietnamese did not conceal that they were sending their cadres to Laos. A total of 12,000 North Vietnamese troops were in Laos, serving as military advisers, political commissars, and instructors. Hanoi increasingly regarded developments in Laos and Vietnam as a united struggle against the common enemy,[122] a fact that could hardly please the Soviet comrades who were trying to find a solution to the Laotian problem in order to exclude Laos as a factor in the Vietnam problem.

Because their allies' views on reconvening the ICC differed but were not resolutely negative, the Soviets proposed an interim solution on February 18: that the Commission meet immediately in New Delhi—not in Laos—and that it should work out instructions that would then be issued by the cochairs.[123] It was clear to the Western countries that such a solution would only delay achieving a cease-fire in Laos. The British again insisted that an armistice ought to precede a conference, and it seemed that discussions on this question—almost a chicken-and-egg situation—had reached a deadlock.

The new U.S. administration could have played a decisive role, but the legacy of the Republicans complicated Kennedy's approach to the problem of Laos.

While Eisenhower regarded U.S. intervention as preferable to any other solution,[124] the new president considered Laos "not a land 'worthy of engaging the attention of great powers,' that the effort to transform it into a pro-Western redoubt had been ridiculous and that neutralization was the correct policy."[125] Accordingly, the new administration was negative about its predecessors' actions in Laos in 1960, blaming them for giving the Soviet Union an excuse to intervene in Southeast Asia and for letting North Vietnam make "major gains" there.[126] In sum, the State Department concluded in its memorandum on Laos that the Kennedy administration "inherited a thoroughly confused and almost insoluble Laos problem, albeit explosive. Whatever the last administration hesitated to do as a 'last act' with respect to Laos was equally difficult for the new administration to take as first act."[127]

In addition, Washington had to take into account the views of its European allies. The British as well as the French were critical of U.S. policy toward Laos under the Eisenhower administration and, especially, the unconditional adherence of the United States to Phoumi Nosavan and his faction. Both London and Paris were apprehensive about a military conflict over Laos and made it clear to Washington that as SEATO members they would not be prepared to get involved in this conflict.[128] In addition, the British and French were more flexible than Washington in their interpretation of the concept of neutrality. Winthrop Brown, the U.S. ambassador to Laos, explained to the new president that Britain and France "were prepared to go much farther with a neutral Laos accepting aid from the Soviets and having Pathet Lao in the government and not taking an anti-communist posture than we would. They felt that the only hope of uniting the country was to support Souvanna Phouma, and the British at least were willing to accept Pathet Lao in the government."[129] The latter two conditions had almost been anathema in Washington.

Thus the Kennedy administration faced a dilemma: either continue the pro-Phoumi Nosavan policy in Laos and prepare for an eventual clash with the Communist powers over a country outside immediate U.S. geopolitical interests or agree on a Laotian government headed by Souvanna Phouma that would pursue a policy of neutrality not fully compatible with Western interests in Southeast Asia. Characteristically, Kennedy chose a middle course while he attempted to find a solution more acceptable to the United States. In other words, Washington did not stop considering military contingency plans relating to Laos but, at the same time, it put forward several diplomatic proposals.

Its first proposal was to establish a commission composed of neutral nations with the aim of investigating the situation in Laos; this would replace the reconvening of the ICC. Washington suggested including Cambodia and Burma as well as maintaining "suitable flexibility for additions."[130] It was clear that, by proposing such a commission, the United States took into account its Laotian allies' vow "never" to accept again the return of the ICC to Laos.[131] In addition, as the State Department explained in its cable, "while neutral and sometimes troublesome, Cambodia and Burma are anti-Communist domestically, are alive to Communist threat, desire a non-Communist Laos in their own self-interest and have themselves taken initiatives consistent with approach we have in mind. Moreover, Soviet Bloc actively wooing them and would find it difficult completely rebuff their efforts on behalf of peace."[132]

The U.S. administration broached this proposal with the Soviets, whose reaction was crucial to U.S. plans in Laos. On February 20, 1961, Dean Rusk, the new U.S. secretary of state, met with Soviet ambassador Mikhail Menshikov and informed him about the neutral-nations-commission proposal. Menshikov's immediate reaction was cool, to say the least. He interpreted this proposal as one-sided and insisted on the expediency of an international conference.[133] A week later, the Soviet ambassador delivered his government's response to the U.S. proposal: Moscow considered it an abandonment of the Geneva agreements and maintained that there was no legal ground for such a step. The Soviets suspected that one of Washington's aims was to eliminate "socialist Poland" from the commission and declared that the "cooperation of all countries is required and not the imposition of another group."[134] Nikita Khrushchev reiterated this view in his conversation with Llewellyn Thompson, U.S. ambassador to Moscow. Khrushchev described the U.S. proposal as unrealistic, expressed his support for Sihanouk's call for a fourteen-nation conference, and insisted on a mechanism "devised along lines of 'Polish-Canadian-Indian Commission.'"[135]

During the Khrushchev-Thompson conversation, Khrushchev expounded Soviet views about the settlement of the Laos crisis. "We welcome, [Khrushchev] said, a Laos that pursues neutral policy on model of Austria." The Soviet leader tried to persuade Washington of the acceptability of the choice of Souvanna Phouma as head of the Laotian government, saying Souvanna was "not Communist, nor candidate of Communists but rather man like Sihanouk or Nehru and would not, in Khrushchev's opinion, follow pro-Soviet policy."[136]

Khrushchev's assertion probably helped the United States eventually modify its position on Laos. With the rejection of the proposal for a neutral-nations commission by the very countries—Cambodia and Burma—that were expected to form its core and the absence of an impressive military success for the Phoumi forces in Laos, President Kennedy went before television cameras on March 23 and read a statement on Laos at the beginning of a news conference. Kennedy stated that the United States "strongly and unreservedly" supported "the goal of a neutral and independent Laos, tied to no outside power or group of powers, threatening no one, and free from any domination." He warned, however, that his country and its SEATO allies would not remain indifferent if "armed attacks by externally supported Communists" did not cease. He spoke in favor of the "constructive negotiation" and supported the British call for a cease-fire and convocation of an international conference on Laos.[137] Behind Kennedy were maps illustrating the extent of Pathet Lao domination at various stages of the conflict. The third map demonstrated the situation as of March 1961: a red area on it showed the territory controlled by the Pathet Lao covering the entire region in and around the Plain of Jars. Although inaccurate,[138] this map sought to justify the administration's decisions relating to Laos, decisions that had been taken at a White House meeting two days earlier. Decision makers had created a two-track strategy, that is, they envisaged the preparation for military actions along with the pursuit of negotiations.[139]

The Soviets nevertheless expressed their satisfaction that the United States had changed its position on the settlement of the crisis in Laos. During his meeting with Kennedy in late March, Foreign Minister Andrei Gromyko of the Soviet Union assured the U.S. president that Moscow would exercise restraint in its actions in Laos "in order to avoid exacerbation of situation with consequent danger of spreading of conflict" and expected such a restraint from the U.S. side. Kennedy noted that "Gromyko's presentation was a serious one and devoid of the deliberate evasion."[140]

Yet Moscow's subsequent steps dispelled whatever optimism the West nourished with regard to the Soviet attitude. On April 1, in response to the British aide-mémoire of March 23, 1961, Moscow suggested that Great Britain and the Soviet Union issue an appeal for a cease-fire simultaneously with the commencement of the international conference. The Soviets obviously still held to the views expressed in their note of February 18.[141] Furthermore, the Kremlin delayed its response to the drafts presented by Ambassador Roberts of Great Britain, which contained an appeal for a cease-fire in Laos, a report to Nehru concerning the ICC, and an announcement of the conference. Only on April 16 did Gromyko reciprocate with the Soviet drafts,[142] and his response apparently was precipitated by the U.S. demonstration of its determination to intervene on a greater scale in Laos. Confronted with North Vietnamese support for the expansion of the Pathet Lao military campaign into the region of route no. 9 and southern Laos,[143] Washington issued an order to U.S. personnel in Laos lifting all restrictions on their participation in combat operations and permitting them to wear uniforms.[144] On April 19 the United States transformed its military advisory personnel in Laos from a civilian programs evaluation office (PEO) to a military assistance advisory group (MAAG).[145]

The Kennedy administration interpreted the Soviet stalling tactics as aimed at avoiding a "major overt move until it is too late" for the United States "to move in," as well as a "collapse of the morale of the FAL [Forces Armées de Laos] forces and of the present government."[146] Moscow's policy had to take into account the opinions of its North Vietnamese and Chinese allies. Both Hanoi and Beijing held to the view that the military situation favored the Pathet Lao and, accordingly, were reluctant to accede to moves that could frustrate the mounting Communist offensive. North Vietnamese Politburo member Nguyen Chi Thanh informed Soviet ambassador Sokolov on March 25 that his colleagues in the Lao Dong Party believed that the Pathet Lao offensive was developing satisfactorily and that the fighting spirit of the Communist troops was at a high level. Therefore, Thanh stated, "the WPV CC Politburo adopted a decision to continue military actions."[147]

The Chinese expressed almost identical views in a telegram to Moscow on March 31, 1961. They accused the United States of insidious plans regarding Laos, aimed at strengthening Nosavan's "rebels," splitting the "patriots," and striking a blow to "progressive Laotian forces." The Chinese believed that the West wanted to tie up progressive Lao forces by means of the ICC. At the same time, the Chinese claimed that the West was not interested in the conference itself and would be satisfied if such a conference were not held at all. Under such circumstances, Beijing said, it was armed struggle that played the most important role. Although the Chinese did not exclude that under certain conditions it was possible to consider political methods of struggle, "the highest principle for us should be the further growth of strength of the Laotian people." "In the present situation," the telegram continues, "when patriotic progressive forces of Laos gained a significant momentum, it would be advantageous for them to stop the war under the condition that this would not limit them in the development of their strength."[148] In other words, the Chinese were against any action that would jeopardize the success achieved by the Pathet Lao forces.

To understand the Soviet attitude toward Laos, a summary of Moscow's views as they had developed by April 1961 might be useful. Laos was not a major priority in Soviet foreign policy plans. Khrushchev himself made this clear in his letter congratulating Kennedy on his victory in the 1960 presidential election. The Soviet leader did not even mention Laos by name but, instead, wrote of the necessity "to continue efforts to solve such a pressing problem as disarmament, to settle the German issue through the earliest conclusion of peace treaty and to reach agreement on other questions, the solution of which could bring about an easing and improvement of the entire international situation."[149] Later, Soviet officials more than once assured the Americans of their desire to eliminate the Laotian problem as an obstacle on the way to agreement with the United States on more important international issues. Such statements reflected a real Soviet interest, as the Soviet Foreign Ministry's internal documents clearly demonstrate. A March 14, 1961, memorandum entitled "On Laos" states: "The principal task with respect to Laos is the struggle for the liquidation of a hotbed of international tension in that region and neutralization of that country." And further: "The policy of peace, neutrality and national reconciliation [in Laos] objectively serves the interests of our camp."[150]

Yet Moscow, like Washington, implemented its Laos policy as a two-track policy. On one hand, the Soviets were prepared to search for a peaceful settlement to the Laotian crisis while, on the other hand, they were ready to render all possible assistance to the "patriotic forces of Laos."

On the diplomatic front, the Soviet Union was preoccupied principally with organizing an international conference, either with the participation of only those countries that had taken part in the previous Geneva conference or with the inclusion of additional states proposed by Prince Sihanouk. On tactical grounds, Moscow also regarded as necessary the reactivation of the ICC in Laos. Pursuing these goals, the Soviets were concerned lest their Asian friends would not ruin Soviet plans aimed at the settlement of the Laotian crisis. That is why they insisted on flexibility on the part of the Pathet Lao, including the Pathet Lao's policy toward Souvanna Phouma, whom they regarded as the most acceptable politician in Laos at that time. Moscow rejected the leftist slogans of the Laotian Communists as well as their excessive demands, which the Soviets believed would "not only weaken the united broad front of struggle against the rebels, but also complicate our struggle for the neutralization of Laos."[151]

At the same time, the Soviet Union continued to provide military and economic aid to the pro-Communist forces in Laos. Military aid, according to the Soviet Foreign Ministry's Southeast Asia Department, was "one of the decisive factors of success of the national-patriotic forces of Laos in their struggle against the rebels." Aid included cannons, mortars, recoilless guns, various types of machine guns, small arms, tanks, armored troop carriers, artillery workshops, ammunition, and medical supplies.[152] The Soviets were evidently interested in the consolidation of the Pathet Lao's positions and wanted to avoid any deterioration in favor of Nosavan's group, and this was regarded as an important prerequisite of the future negotiations. The Soviet ambassador in the DRV intentionally stated to Ho Chi Minh that a "military success will help us at the fourteen-power conference, as, in the past, the victory of the Vietnamese people at Dienbienphu had helped in the conclusion of the Geneva agreements."[153] As a consequence, the Soviets did not want the ICC to impede the consolidation of the Pathet Lao positions, and they insisted that ICC members gather outside Laos. Furthermore, the Soviets wanted to limit the ICC's activities as well, especially initially.

Thus the Soviet leaders had much in common with the Chinese and the North Vietnamese in their approach to the crisis in Laos. They all apparently shared the concern that the cease-fire and resumption of the ICC's activities would reverse the Laotian situation in favor of the anti-Communist forces without settling the conflict itself. But Moscow was less preoccupied with the question of keeping the Pathet Lao's gains intact, regarding those gains mainly as future diplomatic bargaining chips useful as concessions. The Chinese and, especially, the North Vietnamese differed from this Soviet point of view. During his April 1961 visit to Moscow, the DRV deputy prime minister and member of the Lao Dong Politburo, Nguyen Duy Trinh, underlined in his conversation with the Soviet deputy foreign minister, Georgii Pushkin, that it was necessary to do one's best so that "the Pathet Lao has an opportunity for strengthening its positions in the future and, in addition, the administration in the regions now under control of the Pathet Lao remains in their hands."[154] A similar view was formulated in a telegram from Beijing on April 12 in which the Chinese leaders drew attention to the necessity for the Souvanna Phouma government and the Pathet Lao fighting units to "strengthen their positions . . . and to achieve the unification into one coherent area of all those places that are now under their control."[155]

The substance of the differences among the Communist powers was in the Soviet opposition to a general tendency on the part of the USSR's Asian allies to downplay the importance of the earliest settlement of the Laotian crisis as well as the allies' related desire to postpone the conference and put forward new demands to the West. The Chinese and the North Vietnamese were not as concerned as the Soviet Union about the danger of broadening the conflict. For China, this corresponded with Mao's recent approach toward foreign policy issues that favored the growth of confrontation with the West and even possible nuclear showdown. The U.S. fiasco at the Bay of Pigs in Cuba in April 1961 only strengthened Mao. Laos became, in the eyes of the Chinese, a trump card in the struggle against the United States. On April 19, Zhou Enlai in a conversation with the Soviet chargé d'affaires, Nikolai Sudarikov, touched upon the situation in Laos in connection with Cuba. Zhou said that "it would not be bad if it becomes a little more strenuous." In other words, Laos could be a response to recent U.S. actions in the Western hemisphere. Zhou insisted that the Soviets be firm in their positions on the international conference and agreed on concessions to the British only if all Soviet proposals were accepted. Otherwise it would be better to stall.[156] Such views were met with full understanding in Hanoi.

China and the DRV were in agreement about conditions for a cease-fire in Laos. They both thought that the cease-fire should be negotiated by the warring Laotian parties. Neither the two cochairs nor the ICC could order or impose a cease-fire; the cochairs could only appeal to the Laotians to cease hostilities.[157] Furthermore, Beijing and Hanoi insisted that the ICC be permitted in Laos only after imposition of the cease fire,[158] for they both feared that, once in Laos, the ICC could check on the implementation of the cease-fire and prevent the Pathet Lao from violating it with impunity.[159] These demands were antithetical to the Western requirements that the cease-fire should be imposed before the conference and should be verified by the ICC.

Moscow's attempts to find a compromise to these and related issues evidently delayed the Soviet response to the British proposals in April. The Soviets might also have been waiting for a firsthand account to be received during the visit to the USSR of Souvanna Phouma and Souphanouvong, who were there on April 16–21.[160] In this light, the assertion of Marek Thee, a member of the Polish delegation to the ICC, that the Soviet government did not possess a correct understanding of Laotian realities and had not consulted with the Chinese and North Vietnamese on the ICC's tasks cannot be accepted as completely reliable.[161] Consultations among the Soviet Union, China, and North Vietnam, with the involvement of the Laotians, took place throughout April and covered the range of issues concerning settlement in Laos; and the Kremlin had sufficient information about the opinions of its Asian allies. It is also unlikely that the Soviets were deluded about developments in Southeast Asia. It is therefore unclear why Deputy Foreign Minister Pushkin was so optimistic in his conversation with the Polish ICC delegation that arrived in Moscow for prior consultations with Soviet comrades. Marek Thee reported that Pushkin offered "a rather simplistic formula for the initial tasks of the Commission" and suggested that the conference on Laos "would last no longer than six weeks."[162] It is possible that Pushkin was expressing Soviet wishful thinking and the desire to settle the conflict in Laos as soon as possible.

In any case, on April 24, the Soviet Union joined Great Britain in issuing the cochairs' messages that appealed to the three parties in Laos to cease hostilities, invited the ICC to reassemble, and proposed that the interested parties gather at a conference.[163] This opened the final stage of preparation for the fourteen-power conference on Laos.

The primary objective for the Soviet leaders in late April was to confirm that the hostilities in Laos would be over by the time the ICC delegation arrived there. The dates proposed by Pham Van Dong, May 5–6,[164] did not satisfy the Soviets, especially in light of the two British warnings that any further military moves by the Pathet Lao would endanger the chances of the conference and that the cease-fire should become effective at once.[165] Moscow pressed Hanoi for an earlier deadline, not later than May 3–4.[166] The North Vietnamese conceded, and the military operation they had begun together with the Pathet Lao on April 11 was successfully completed by 8:00 a.m. on May 3, 1961. Pathet Lao forces supported by the North Vietnamese by that time controlled the provinces of Sam

Neua, Phong Saly, Xieng Khuang, a large part of Luang Prabang, the Plain of Jars, and highways 7, 8, 9, and 12.[167]

Finally on May 11 the three delegations representing the warring Laotian groups convened in the schoolhouse at the village of Ban Namone for their first meeting.[168] This meeting, although it was marked more by its cordial atmosphere than by any formal agreement, justified the ICC report to the cochairs that a general de facto cease-fire existed.[169] The ICC report eliminated a significant obstacle to the opening of the conference in Geneva.

In the meantime, the Soviets held last-minute preparatory talks with their allies in order to work out a coordinated Communist position at the conference. At the talks scheduled for May 9, because Moscow wanted to make sure that the principal points of the Soviet position coincided with those of the Chinese and North Vietnamese, the Soviet Foreign Ministry planned to query its allies: What do the Asian Communist delegations regard as the principal task of the international conference on Laos? Do they agree with the objectives formulated by the Soviets, for example, the restoration of peace in Laos, the independence and neutrality of Laos with full guarantees for the interests of the Pathet Lao? What issues should be discussed by the conference and what must be left to the Laotians? In their preparatory talks, the Communist delegations were also to discuss certain provisions of the declaration on the neutrality of Laos, which the Soviet Union was going to present in Geneva.[170] Although the records of these preparatory talks have not been made available to the author, the Chinese views on the eve of the Geneva conference on Laos, which were generally shared—except for some nuances—by the North Vietnamese, are in an aide-mémoire delivered to the Far East Department of the Soviet Foreign Ministry by the PRC embassy in Moscow. In it, the Chinese government expressed its general agreement with the Soviet opinion that it was necessary to use "to the end" the favorable conditions that existed at that time for guaranteeing the independence and neutrality of Laos and, simultaneously, to do their best in defending the interests of the "national patriotic and popular democratic forces in Laos." The Chinese believed that sufficient conditions existed for the successful implementation of this task: the United States had suffered its third defeat in the East (Korea and the Geneva conference on Indochina were the first two); the progressive forces in Laos had achieved impressive victory; and the socialist camp together with national democratic movements in Asia, Africa, and Latin America enjoyed superiority over the imperialists. The Chinese felt that these favorable conditions should be used for a "gradual revolutionizing of this region." But because the victory of the progressive forces in Laos had not yet been consolidated, the Chinese conceded that, "it was necessary, basing on tactical considerations, to strive for a peaceful situation in Laos, even a temporary one."[171]

Thus the Chinese repeated their previous arguments concerning settlement in Laos. They continued to regard the Geneva conference on Laos only as an instrument to strengthen the NLHX positions and to guarantee its future domination of Laotian politics. Hence Beijing's primary objective at the conference would be the establishment of the neutrality and independence of Laos "with the purpose of helping the progressive forces of Laos to develop further with the reliance on their own resources." The Chinese advised their Communist allies to pay the most attention to the guarantees of noninterference in the internal affairs of Laos because it was such interference on the part of the United States that after 1954 became the principal method of undermining the Geneva agreements.[172] Accordingly, Beijing—unlike Moscow—rejected Austrian neutrality as a model for Laos on the grounds that such neutrality "could hamper the development of revolutionary forces" in Laos.[173]

Because the consolidation of the Pathet Lao's positions was uppermost in the minds of the Chinese (and North Vietnamese) at the conference, they were not in a hurry, as were the Soviets, to reach an agreement on Laos within six weeks. Moreover, they were prepared to halt negotiations and return to armed struggle whenever the situation in Geneva or in Laos appeared propitious. The Chinese deputy premier and foreign minister, Chen Yi, who headed the PRC delegation at the conference, reaffirmed these views during his stopover in Moscow on the way to Geneva.[174]

The Soviets could not agree with some of the positions of Beijing and Hanoi. The Soviets were concerned over approaching Southeast Asia as a weak link in the capitalist chain that should be revolutionized. The Soviets were critical of the Chinese admission that armed struggle could possibly be resumed in Laos.[175] The Kremlin, however, concluded that the differences in the views on Laos of the Communist powers were not about principle, and some of them could be reconciled with the Soviet position. On other issues the Soviet delegation would remain aloof, neither supporting nor rejecting them.[176] Moscow hoped that in the course of the negotiations the Soviet delegates would prevail over their Chinese and North Vietnamese allies and advance Soviet ideas about the settlement. Directives to the Soviet delegation therefore advised paying "special attention to the maintenance of permanent contacts and consultations with the delegations of the PRC, the DRV, and the PPR [Polish People's Republic]."[177]

Adhering to these directives proved to be a difficult task, one that fell upon the shoulders of Deputy Foreign Minister Georgii Pushkin, who had to wage a two-front struggle throughout the conference—trying to win over the rivals as well as the allies. One might wonder which front was the more exhausting.

8. Back to Geneva

Strange sight this Congress! destined to unite
All that's incongruous, all that's opposite.

George Byron
The Age of Bronze, XVI, 1, 2

The Soviet delegation went to Geneva with firm instructions to use "to the end" favorable conditions to settle the Laotian crisis on the basis of "mutually acceptable decisions" that would facilitate the "restoration of peace and calm in Laos" and guarantee the "real independence and neutrality of that country." The delegation was also told to "do its best so as to guarantee the interests of the national patriotic and national democratic forces of Laos."[1] Conditions seemed to be favorable indeed, the Soviet diplomats soon confirmed. Moscow was well aware that there was no unity of views among the United States, Great Britain, and France on the methods of settlement.[2] The Soviets learned that Paris and London were apprehensive of Washington's plans to use armed force in Laos and were more inclined to find a peaceful means to resolve the Laotian crisis. The U.S. position had likewise undergone significant change in the months preceding the conference, and Kennedy's determination to send U.S. troops to Southeast Asia was not as firm as Eisenhower's. Moscow received signals that Washington regarded Laos as a "lost position" and was not opposed to neutralization of Laos, or even its partition.[3]

In fact, the Kennedy administration did not exclude the division of Laos as a compromise solution during the course of negotiations, and the U.S. delegation at Geneva was so instructed.[4] Secretary of State Dean Rusk regarded such a solution "a better outcome than unity under leadership responsive to the Communists."[5] To the Soviets, who had already tested this in Berlin, Korea, and Vietnam, partition would also not be an unacceptable outcome of the Geneva conference. On the eve of his summit with President Kennedy in Vienna, Khrushchev confided to his Czechoslovak friends that a partitioned Laos could be advantageous to the socialist camp and to the Laotian revolutionary forces; in his words, such a solution was profitable in the long run. "On the one hand," the Soviet leader reasoned, "the Americans will once again unmask themselves before the whole world as an international gendarme. And, secondly, the revolutionary forces will consolidate and strengthen their position inside the country. Then we will see what happens later."[6]

Although at first all the conference's major participants shared their desire to settle the crisis in Laos as soon as possible, several issues prevented them from gathering at the Palais des Nations in Geneva on May 12, 1961, as scheduled. First was a controversy over representation at the conference. The Soviets and their allies insisted that all three contending forces in Laos, including the Pathet Lao, be equally represented in Geneva. The Western delegations objected to the Pathet Lao's admission to the conference because participation would imply its de facto recognition. They suggested instead an empty seat for Laos, with the Lao groups coming to it when called upon to speak.[7] This proposal was absolutely unacceptable to the Communist powers, which had to defend the interests of their Laotian allies. Foreign Minister Andrei Gromyko pointed out to Secretary of State Rusk that the "Pathet Lao after all were real Lao forces" and called his counterpart to look at the map of Laos to convince himself.[8] Rusk conceded only that the delegates from the Laotian factions were representatives from (not of) Laos, but since Washington did not want to appear to be the force that would wreck the conference before it even started, the U.S. delegation had to give in.

Although it seemed now that all obstacles to the conference had been removed, the Soviets unexpectedly encountered problems inside their own camp. The Chinese firmly opposed assigning to India the task of proposing that the USSR and Great Britain act as chairs of the conference. At the meeting of the four Communist delegations on May 15, the head of the Chinese delegation, Foreign Minister Chen Yi, expressed his dissatisfaction that Gromyko had agreed with Lord Home, his British counterpart, on this issue and demanded that this task be carried out by a representative of another country, not by V. K. Krishna Menon, the Indian delegate.[9]

Although unexpected, this Chinese démarche was not a complete surprise and reflected the fact that during the preceding two years relations between the two countries had worsened and would soon lead to an armed conflict. However, the Chinese defended themselves by asserting that the Geneva conference on Laos was merely a continuation of the previous conference of 1954 and hence there was no need for a new proposal about cochairs, which must remain the same. Counterarguments by other delegations seemed only to annoy Chen Yi, who was known for his hot temper.[10] He was especially upset by Polish foreign minister Adam Rapacki's remark that the Chinese were overly preoccupied with formal, rather than political, considerations. Chen Yi accused the Poles of excessive criticism of China's position during preliminary negotiations in Moscow and declared that China did not recognize Poland's right to assess Beijing's actions.[11]

The fire in the Chinese attack against the Poles was probably aimed primarily at Moscow, perhaps as a warning that the Chinese were not going to be the complacent allies the Russians would like them to be. One day before, in a conversation with Gromyko, Chen Yi had spoken of the importance of unity between the Soviet Union and China and suggested holding bilateral Soviet-Chinese consultations separately from similar meetings of all the Communist delegations because, he said, "it is sometimes easier for the representatives of the PRC and the USSR to come to agreement separately, rather than in the presence of representatives of other socialist countries."[12] Chen Yi's outburst the next day may have demonstrated that he believed this was really the case. Gromyko was obviously stunned by the wrangle between the allies but, nevertheless, remained adamant in his position concerning India, and Chen Yi had to yield.[13]

The discussion at the consultative meeting of the Communist delegations had demonstrated that China was determined to play one of the leading roles at the Geneva conference and was not prepared to yield easily to Soviet pressure. Everything including the size and composition of the Chinese delegation—numbering some fifty men and women who occupied more seats in the spacious council chamber of the Palais des Nations than any other delegation[14]—was to prove the seriousness of Beijing's intentions. Accordingly the Chinese wanted to have a voice in major decisions made by the Soviet Union on behalf of other Communist delegations. For example, in his conversation with Gromyko, Chen Yi expressed China's desire to be acquainted with the draft of the declaration on the neutrality of Laos, which the Soviet delegation was planning to present at one of the first sessions of the conference in order to have an opportunity to make a necessary revisions in this and other documents.[15] The Soviet foreign minister had to agree, although reluctantly, while he referred to the lack of time remaining before the opening of the conference.

Two days later the Chinese delegation presented its proposals concerning the Soviet drafts. In addition to Chinese suggestions about international control over the introduction of arms and military equipment into Laos and over future general elections, the Chinese insisted on the inclusion of the requirement that all Guomindang troops be withdrawn from the territory of Laos. Remnants of Chiang Kaishek's units had operated in the Laos-Burma border area ever since they were driven out of Yunnan by the Communist forces in 1949. They were primarily engaged in farming and opium smuggling, but occasionally these troops conducted operations against China in collaboration with Taiwanese and U.S. intelligence agencies.[16] Communist China was of course concerned by the presence of enemy forces in the close vicinity of its borders and was determined to eliminate them by means of international agreements.

The Soviet point of view, which was expounded to the Chinese deputy foreign minister, Zhang Hanfu, by the deputy head of the Soviet delegation, Georgii Pushkin, held that the inclusion of such a provision in the text of the Geneva agreements proposed by the Communist delegations "could only complicate the reaching of the agreement." Pushkin said the West could use it as a pretext to refuse to settle the Laotian question.[17] For the Soviets, the issue of Guomindang troops represented an unnecessary irritation to the United States and could be omitted; but Pushkin encountered strong resistance from the Chinese, who decided to teach Pushkin and, by implication, Moscow, a lesson in revolutionary vigilance. "I would like to say," Zhang Hanfu stated, "that in our opinion in the course of the preparation of the draft of the agreement it is not expedient to guess whether it is acceptable to the United States and other Western countries or not. In any event, the Chinese delegation is guided not by these considerations, but by its desire to guarantee peace in Southeast Asia."[18] If the United States wanted to wreck the conference, Zhang Hanfu continued, they could find many pretexts, not necessarily the Guomindang bands. Another member of the Chinese delegation, Qiao Guanhua, even presented the elimination of Chiang Kaishek's units in Laos as a part of the struggle against imperialism.

Pushkin was evidently taken aback by the intransigence of the Chinese. He retorted that the Soviet people need not be persuaded about the necessity of struggle against imperialism. "To make the Western countries to agree on the agreement advantageous to the socialist countries, to the democratic forces of Laos," the Soviet diplomat argued, "is not only struggle, but also victory. The question is how to wage this struggle, which tactical line to follow." From this perspective, the issue of Guomindang troops was counterproductive because the situation might arise that all other provisions of the agreements would be acceptable to the West except for this particular issue. In that case, the Communist delegations would have to abandon it, which would prove to be politically disadvantageous.[19] The Soviets felt that because one of the articles of their draft required the withdrawal of all foreign military personnel from Laos, the question of Chiang Kaishek's units was covered.

This debate again demonstrated how different were the approaches to the Laotian problem in Moscow and in Beijing. While the Soviets did not consider Laos a vital issue to their foreign policy and were prepared to be satisfied with an Austria-like neutral Laos or even with a divided country in order to eliminate the danger of a global conflict involving the Soviet Union and the United States, the Chinese wanted a friendly country on their borders and guarantees that it would not be again transformed into a future springboard for U.S. aggression against the People's Republic. The Chinese did not regard neutralization as a permanent solution to the Laotian problem and instead hoped for the augmentation of their influence in Laos.[20]

These considerations lay behind China's refusal to accept partition as a possible solution to the Laotian question. In an aide-mémoire sent to Moscow on May 10, the Chinese leaders argued against both the complete integration of the provinces under the Pathet Lao's control and the division of Laos. The Chinese considered integration under Pathet Lao control not to the advantage of the Pathet Lao; but division, the Chinese thought, would "tie our hands."[21] Beijing would not want even a part of Laos to fall under the control of the Boun Oum–Phoumi Nosavan government because of the U.S. presence there. That portion of Laos, along with South Vietnam and Thailand, would create a coalition of enemy regimes with unpredictable consequences on the southern Chinese borders. By contrast, a neutral Laos under the government of Souvanna Phouma, even with the participation of the Savannakhet group, would be more favorable for China.

The discordance of Soviet and Chinese views on the settlement of the conflict in Laos was influenced by the growing estrangement between the two countries, which broke into an open rift after the twenty-second CPSU congress in October 1961, while the Geneva conference was under way. But despite heated discussions between the Soviets and the Chinese on the eve of the Geneva conference and sometimes during its course, never did the conflict of the Communist parties prevent the cooperation of the two delegations in Geneva, at least to the extent visible to other participants. For example, Arthur Lall, a member of the Indian delegation, wrote in his book on the 1961 Geneva conference: "While later revelations showed that already the ideological and other differences between the Chinese and the Soviets were great, neither the Chinese nor the Soviets, by their words or actions, gave the slightest indication of any divergence of views in regard to the problems before the conference. If the Chinese took, in general, a more forthright and extreme position than the Soviets, the latter backed them up, or at any rate never uttered a word in opposition to the Peking government."[22]

Such harmony stemmed mainly from the fact that both Moscow and Beijing wanted to see the Laotian conflict settled, notwithstanding their differences on the ways and methods of the settlement. To achieve their overall goal, they closely coordinated their steps at the conference and discussed various actions during bilateral negotiations as well as at periodic meetings of all the Communist delegations. In fact, the clash of views that occurred at the first such meetings was not at all characteristic of the gatherings of Communist diplomats. Usually the Soviets and the Chinese peacefully found common ground in their approach to the current conference issues. Thus the deadlock that arose in mid-May was broken; and on May 16 Prince Sihanouk of Cambodia, at whose initiative fourteen governments gathered in Geneva to discuss the question of Laos, opened the conference at 5:00 p.m.

Yet it was obvious from the beginning that the going would not be easy. At the opening session, contrary to the agreed schedule, Chen Yi made a speech in which he identified the United States as the main culprit in the crisis in Laos. Chen's speech contained eighteen direct references to the United States and most of them were highly critical.[23] Everyone at the Palais des Nations understood that this attack could not go unanswered by Dean Rusk, and the next morning the U.S. secretary of state, in a more subtle speech, condemned China as the main threat to peace in Southeast Asia.[24] Thus, a confrontation between the United States and the PRC was emerging at the conference; it would not improve the prospects for a settlement of the crisis.

In addition, Washington was not satisfied with the situation on the battlefield in Laos. Although the ICC had reported before the conference that an effective cease-fire had been established between the warring parties and negotiations at Ban Namone had taken place, sporadic fighting continued. The Pathet Lao and neutralist forces concentrated their efforts on the elimination of pro-Nosavan strongholds at their rear. Toward the end of May, U.S. intelligence reported heavy Pathet Lao attacks in the area of Ban Padong, which was held by Meo tribes loyal to the Boun Oum government.[25] As a result, the U.S. delegation insisted on discussing the conditions of the cease-fire in Laos and the control over it. The Communist delegations, on the other hand, wanted to initiate discussion of general issues of Laotian neutrality and its guarantees. The tone was set by Gromyko's speech on the same day as Rusk's reply to Chen. The Soviet foreign minister presented to the conference the Soviet drafts of a declaration on the neutrality of Laos and of an agreement on the withdrawal of foreign troops and military personnel from the territory of Laos and the mandate of the ICC.[26] Reflecting the Soviet desire to move the conference from a propaganda exercise to a discussion of questions of substance, Gromyko's proposals encountered resistance from Western delegations that suspected Moscow and its Asian allies of supporting the Pathet Lao's offensive.

However, the Soviets too were concerned with the skirmishes on the battlefield and with their effect on the negotiations. And the Chinese generally shared this concern. At the meeting of the Communist delegations on May 23, Gromyko insisted on not giving the Westerners a pretext to accuse them of a lack of desire to observe the cease-fire.[27] Chen Yi agreed with his Soviet colleague and recommended advising the Laotian "friends" not to undertake new military operations. "We could cause accusations," Chen asserted, "that here, in Geneva, we are demanding meetings and a discussion of the question of peaceful settlement in Laos, while in Laos itself, our friends initiate military actions. Of course, when rebels attack . . . it is necessary to repulse them. Yet, at one's own initiative, one should not create military conflicts." The Chinese minister also called for flexible tactics.[28]

Soviet diplomats in Southeast Asia followed the recommendations of their Communist colleagues in Geneva and tried to warn their clients in the region against drastic actions on the battlefield while the negotiations were under way. They addressed their requests to the North Vietnamese, who were really responsible for planning and conducting operations in Laos, including the operation at Ban Padong. An official of the Soviet embassy in Laos, A. A. Skoryukov, met on June 4 with the DRV chief military adviser in Laos, General Thau Tian, and pointed to the necessity for prudence in conducting operations against pro-Nosavan troops "so as to avoid giving an opportunity to the United States to use them with the purpose of wrecking the Geneva conference."[29] In addition to concern over the prospects of the Geneva conference, Moscow evidently kept in mind the adverse effect that such violations could have on the meeting between Khrushchev and Kennedy that occurred at that time in Vienna.

Laos was not the only subject on the agenda of the Vienna summit although the West hoped that the meeting of the Soviet and U.S. leaders would help facilitate the negotiations in Geneva. The possibility of such a meeting had been raised in the first communications between Moscow and Washington soon after Kennedy's election as U.S. president. In his letter to Khrushchev of February 22, 1961, the new president expressed his desire to meet with the Soviet leader "for an informal exchange of views" on basic problems that existed between the two countries, as well as on issues of the international situation.[30] Khrushchev accepted this proposal in his letter of May 16 and suggested Vienna as a possible venue for the summit and June 3–4 as the dates.[31] In the same letter Khrushchev named the situation in Laos as one of the subjects for the leaders' negotiations, placing it ahead of the problems of disarmament and Germany. And, as Pushkin did during negotiations with the Polish representatives to the ICC, Khrushchev expressed his desire to see the Laotian problem resolved, as soon as possible, so that "from the moment of our meeting with you we could with pleasure state that the settlement of the problem of Laos had become a fact."[32]

Khrushchev's statement in his letter to Kennedy was however in striking contrast with Khrushchev's later intimation to the Czechoslovak leaders with whom he met near Bratislava on his way to the Austrian capital. Speaking on the question of Laos, the Soviet leader stated that "we will hardly come to agreement on this question. . . . We could not agree on their demands." He claimed: "This would mean the negation of successes achieved by the revolutionary forces. Neutral states, such as India, Cambodia, and others, are afraid of the quick advancement of the revolutionary forces and have made up their mind virtually against us."[33] Such a change of mood evidently reflected Khrushchev's disappointment with the lack of success at Geneva and Western demands for imposing strict control over the cease-fire in Laos. Compared with the optimistic and militant predictions about Germany that he confided to the Czechs at the same meeting, Khrushchev's assessment of the prospects of the Laotian discussion looked defeatist, especially considering his readiness to accept the partition of Laos. But this defeatism could only be explained by the fact that the Soviet leader was more interested in a favorable solution to the German question, which he considered of primary importance, and was prepared to accept—however grudgingly—any kind of palliative for the problem of Laos. The long sessions he devoted to the discussion of various actions by the Soviet Union in Germany and the rather scarce synopsis of choices on the Laotian problem only emphasized Khrushchev's "imbalance of interests."

While the Soviet leader was skeptical about prospects for agreement with the U.S. president, Kennedy cherished a hope that the summit with Khrushchev would help create a framework for Soviet-U.S. relations in the future. This hope was based on his overall approach to international politics. According to Arthur Schlesinger Jr., the U.S. president:

> saw the world as in a state of uncontrollable change, rushing in directions no one could foresee. The equilibrium of force, he believed, was now roughly in balance between the United States and the Soviet Union . . .; and the overriding need, he felt, was to prevent direct confrontations between Russian and American power in the chaotic time ahead. He intended to propose, in effect, a standstill in the cold war so that neither great nuclear state, in the inevitable competition around the planet, would find itself committed to actions which would risk its essential security, threaten the existing balance of force or endanger world peace.[34]

In his desire to discuss with Khrushchev international problems purely on the grounds of geopolitics, Kennedy overlooked the ideological component of the Soviet leader's thinking, which remained strong regardless of his pragmatic inclinations. Kennedy neglected the substantial analyses of the Kremlin's views made by U.S. ambassador to Moscow, Llewellyn Thompson, a "pragmatic idealist" who developed intimate relations with Soviet officials.[35] Thompson wrote in one of his dispatches designed to educate the new U.S. administration about the Soviet Union and its leaders:

> Khrushchev probably most pragmatic and least dogmatic of all, but he basically as devout believer as any. He is reported once to have said something to the effect that if Communism did not demonstrate its superiority and prevail throughout world, his life would have lost its meaning. . . . As they [the Soviet leaders] look around world they can find plenty of evidence which they can use to justify to themselves their belief in class struggle. They pose everything in these terms and do not accept that our support of rightist or reactionary governments motivated by our fear [of] their attempt [to] obtain world domination for power reasons, and instead see it in terms of exploiters banding together to maintain exploited in subservience.[36]

The discussions between Kennedy and Khrushchev in Vienna justified Thompson's opinion. Whenever the U.S. president raised the subject of the balance of forces in the world and the necessity for both countries to avoid upsetting it, the Soviet leader referred to the facts that proved, in his view, that it was the United States that tended to disrupt the world order to prevent the spreading of Communist ideas around the world. Khrushchev even lectured his U.S. counterpart on the futility of any efforts to build a dam on the way of ideas. He accused Washington of supporting "rotten and anti-popular" regimes in Asia and Latin America,[37] criticized U.S. actions against Cuba and China,[38] and justified liberation wars as "sacred wars" supported by the Soviet Union.[39] Discussions on Berlin and disarmament were likewise unproductive.[40]

The U.S. president left the Austrian capital "tense and tired,"[41] disappointed with the results of his meetings with Khrushchev. The only outcome that might have alleviated Kennedy's frustration was an agreement on Laos. It turned out that neither the United States nor the Soviet Union wanted to be involved in the situation in that country. Khrushchev bluntly told his U.S. counterpart that the "Soviet Union has no vested interest in Laos, either political or economic, or of any other nature. That country is far from Soviet borders." Khrushchev subscribed to Kennedy's statement that the "United States wishes a government in Laos which would not be involved either with the United States or with the USSR, but would rather be genuinely neutral" and spoke in favor of finding a solution.[42] However, he brushed aside U.S. complaints about violations of the cease-fire and insisted that other questions should not be delayed because of this. He also rejected the idea of the ICC becoming "a kind of supergovernment administering the country" but assured Kennedy that the "USSR will exert efforts to solve the Laotian question."[43] Both leaders agreed that their countries "should use their influence so as to bring about an agreement among the forces participating in the Laotian struggle."[44]

Yet reaching that agreement proved difficult to accomplish because the forces involved in the Laotian crisis were beyond the direct command of the leaders of the two great powers. Fighting in the area of Ban Padong went unimpeded, all admonitions of Soviet diplomats notwithstanding. The Left continued their attacks and occupied the stronghold on June 6. This was a major setback for the government forces, and the fall of Ban Padong led to a crisis at the Geneva conference. Western delegations regarded the event as a flagrant violation of the cease-fire, and they interrupted negotiations. The conference was suspended for several days. The U.S. representatives held Moscow responsible "because of its role in supplying PL [the Pathet Lao] by air with military supplies and equipment."[45] By suspending the negotiations they wanted to impress on the Soviet government that pressure on its allies was necessary in order to stop the fighting and continue the talks.

But Moscow did not possess enough leverage to dictate its will in Laos. Marek Thee, a Polish member of the ICC in Laos who was a witness to what was happening in 1961–1962 in that country, asserted that "the Indochinese were masters of their own strategy."[46] Most decisions and plans for Laos were worked out in Hanoi. Not only were the North Vietnamese responsible for military actions in Laos, they were also directly involved in combat operations against Phoumi Nosavan and his troops. By mid-summer 1961, there were about eight thousand North Vietnamese troops grouped into thirteen infantry battalions and one artillery unit in Laos.[47] These units of the PAV were the vanguard of the Pathet Lao army that comprised a force of fifteen thousand armed with Soviet and Chinese weapons.[48] Hanoi did not conceal from Moscow its role and contribution of troops to the fighting in Laos. The DRV chief military adviser in Laos, General Man, revealed to a Soviet diplomat that "all the victories over the Boun Oum armies have been achieved by us. The royal troops [under the command of the Souvanna Phouma government] and the Pathet Lao armies have served us but a cover, that is, a mask."[49]

The North Vietnamese did not think highly of the fighting abilities of their Laotian comrades-in-arms, whom they characterized as afraid of artillery fire and hand-to-hand combat, slow in rushing to the attack, and fast to retreat. There were even accidents when the Pathet Lao soldiers who remained behind the advancing PAV units shot at their backs.[50]

Because they were carrying the main burden of the combat operations in Laos, the North Vietnamese had the upper hand in determining strategy with respect to the Laotian crisis. They were in charge of all military, political, and economic questions. Hanoi had its people in not only the Laotian army but also in administrative organs of the provinces controlled by the Pathet Lao. Pathet Lao leaders undertook no action without first consulting their North Vietnamese mentors.[51] And the advice from the DRV was often at variance with what was conceived in Moscow.

According to the Polish representatives to the ICC in Laos, Hanoi tended to regard the Laotian crisis in isolation from general developments in the world and from the process of Soviet détente with the West. On the other hand, the North Vietnamese closely linked developments in Laos to what was happening in South Vietnam. One of the highest DRV officials openly drew the attention of Marek Thee to this relationship, claiming that events in Laos "influence favorably the rise of revolutionary movement in South Vietnam and *will help the earliest unification of Vietnam.*" The North Vietnamese emphasized that "we must by all means help Laos and, first of all, patriotic forces of Laos as the major driving force of these events."[52]

Moscow could not but be concerned about such an approach by the Vietnamese friends. Whereas Moscow regarded the settlement in Laos as a necessary precondition for the stabilization of the situation in Indochina, Hanoi wanted to use the Laotian crisis to instigate precisely the processes the Soviets wanted to prevent. The North Vietnamese were not completely opposed to the solution of the problem of Laos, but they supported only a solution that allowed them to continue their activities in South Vietnam.

Consequently, Hanoi was skeptical about what success at the Geneva conference meant and favored delays in the diplomatic negotiations, which they believed would help consolidate the NLHX position in the country. DRV leaders insisted on the retention by the Pathet Lao of the territories under its control and upheld demands that key positions in a future coalition government go to its representatives. They denied the possibility of a durable reconciliation between the warring parties in Laos and admitted only the prospect of a temporary armistice.[53] The North Vietnamese therefore did not display much enthusiasm about the outcome of the Vienna summit between the Soviet and U.S. leaders. They claimed that the Khrushchev-Kennedy agreement "did not change actual priorities or the long-range appraisal of events."[54] As a result, the news about the understanding reached in Vienna did not deter the Pathet Lao and their North Vietnamese allies from the capture of Ban Padong, which caused such damage at the Geneva talks.

The situation was even more complicated for Moscow because the Chinese shared most of Hanoi's views on the Laotian settlement. Like Hanoi, Beijing was suspicious about Moscow's inclination to compromise with Washington. Even before the Geneva conference, Chen Yi warned that China should be on the alert against the Soviet tendency for such a compromise.[55] It is therefore not surprising that Chinese reaction to the Vienna summit was rather restrained. Beijing did not speak directly in support of the Soviet Union and, instead, tried to convey an impression that nothing useful resulted from the Khrushchev-Kennedy talks.[56] The Soviet embassy in the PRC attributed this attitude to Beijing's conviction that one should not negotiate with U.S. imperialism and to Beijing's desire to present itself as the most devoted revolutionary leader actively engaged in the class struggle. At the same time, the Soviet embassy admitted that the Chinese might have been chagrined because they learned about the U.S.-Soviet summit from newspapers and were not informed of it by Soviet leaders well in advance.[57] This fact could not have helped good relations between the two Communist powers.

The Chinese supported Hanoi's view on the expediency of dragging out the negotiations in Geneva. Chen Yi raised this during his conversations with the Soviet leaders during a stopover in Moscow on his way back from Switzerland in early July.[58] Chen said that the delay in the negotiations was advantageous to the Communist powers because it provided an opportunity for strengthening the patriotic forces in Laos. He revealed Chinese plans to train the Pathet Lao troops in the meantime and concluded that even the resumption of hostilities in Laos was also to the advantage of the Communist powers because "it would give us an opportunity to drive out aggressors and rebels from the territory of the country."[59]

Although Chen Yi claimed that Khrushchev and Gromyko approved of this approach, it is quite unlikely that they remained complacent about the militant positions of their Asian allies. To the Soviets, the only justification for a delay of the settlement in Laos was the Chinese foreign minister's reference to the need for time to consolidate the alliance between the Pathet Lao and Souvanna Phouma[60] and to form a coalition government. And early July seemed unpromising for achieving these ambitions.

On June 22, 1961, the leaders of the three factions in Laos—Souvanna Phouma, Boun Oum, and Souphanouvong—met in Zurich and reached an agreement on the basic principles of the future external and internal policy of Laos as well as procedures for the formation of a government of national union. Participants in the Geneva conference regarded the Zurich meeting as an important step forward on the way to national reconciliation in Laos and the settlement of the crisis. The Zurich agreement did not lead to positive results, however. Instead, on the first of July, the leader of the rightist forces, Phoumi Nosavan, declared in Bangkok that he doubted the success of the negotiations between the warring parties, and he provided information about the military preparations of his government in case the talks failed and no solutions were reached.[61] Nosavan's statement had its effect on the Pathet Lao. Souphanou-vong, who had never been enthusiastic about a coalition with the rightist forces,[62] only hardened his suspicion of an agreement of the opposing forces in Laos. While in Moscow, where he went after Zurich, Souphanouvong remained unmoved by Khrushchev's attempts to convince him of the need for a peaceful solution to the Laotian problem and, instead, he seemed to follow a hard line with the Soviet leader.[63] During his visit to Beijing, Souphanouvong openly favored more radical methods, declaring at a reception given by Zhou Enlai, "We are proponents of the faster realization of progressive actions; to use the Chinese expression, we are for 'great leaps forward'."[64]

Declarations like Souphanouvong's, made by the Pathet Lao leaders with the support of their Chinese and North Vietnamese allies, not only dimmed prospects for the formation of a coalition government in Laos but also jeopardized the existing cooperation between the NLHX and Souvanna Phouma's faction. Hanoi's distribution in Laos of aid provided by the Communist countries, primarily the Soviet Union, also jeopardized cooperation. Starting in the spring of 1961, Moscow received a constant flow of complaints from the Souvanna Phouma government about North Vietnamese handling of Soviet aid and its uneven distribution among the government troops and the Pathet Lao. The neutralists suspected that Hanoi sent the bulk of arms and materials to the pro-Communist forces, while the remainder—not always as good—went to them. Souvanna Phouma himself raised this in his May 10 conversation with the Soviet chargé d'affaires in Laos, Vasilii Chivilyov, when he claimed that his troops received little or nothing of the Soviet shipments to Laos. "We have understood from the conversation," Chivilyov reported to Moscow, "that it was the Vietnamese who distribute aid and the bulk of it is passed to the Pathet Lao."[65] When confronted, DRV officials referred to the difficulties with transportation, the lack of sufficient means of delivering aid, and the fact that the Pathet Lao took a more active part in combat operations in Laos and accordingly needed more arms and ammunition. Souphanouvong supported the North Vietnamese logic: "There is nothing surprising," reasoned the Red Prince, "that the governmental forces have received less, since they are located predominantly in the rear area and are not engaged in military actions. Besides, their number is less than the Pathet Lao troops."[66]

Nevertheless, complaints continued and Soviet diplomats soon discovered that Hanoi had duped not only the neutralists but the Pathet Lao as well. Information provided to Chivilyov by leading members of the Souvanna Phouma government, Khamsouk Keola and Sisoumang, showed that the Vietnamese kept much of the Soviet aid for themselves while they sent to Laos outdated arms and ammunition that belonged to the PAV. For example, the Kong Le troops received arms that were used by the Vietminh at the time of Dienbien-phu.[67] Chivilyov's information was confirmed by other sources. The Czech am-bassador to the DRV confided to his Soviet counterpart that "the Vietnamese friends" retained the weapons delivered by Czechoslovakia specifically for Sou-vanna Phouma and sent to Laos old foreign arms. "The Vietnamese do the same with other equipment," confided the ambassador, including items from the So-viet Union.[68]

Moscow stepped in to prevent the Souvanna Phouma–Pathet Lao alliance from falling apart because of the problem of aid. Khrushchev himself touched upon this issue during his negotiations with Ho Chi Minh in August 1961 in Pitzunda, near Sochi. He strongly criticized the North Vietnamese approach and warned the DRV leader about the consequences of alienating Souvanna Phouma. He bluntly said to Ho: "Depriving Souvanna Phouma of weapons, you are playing into American hands." Khrushchev brushed aside Ho Chi Minh's excuses that the number of the Pathet Lao troops exceeded those of the govern-ment forces. "That is an arithmetical approach to the matter," Khrushchev re-torted, "and it is absolutely inapplicable when politics is the question. In poli-tics, it is necessary to consider phenomena not from an arithmetical, but from a political, point of view. What the Vietnamese comrades are doing now frightens Souvanna Phouma. As a result of such a policy, we have almost lost him."[69] The Soviet leader's argument was further strengthened by a detailed August 31, 1961, memorandum to the Chinese and Vietnamese friends on the problem of Laos, which called the attention of the Soviet allies to political errors commit-ted in the cooperation between the NLHX and the neutralists.[70] The memo charged that Souvanna Phouma had received inadequate support, and it de-manded a reversal of this treatment. Moscow again expressed its dissatisfaction with Hanoi's handling of Soviet aid to Laos and cited examples of its misman-agement.[71]

Following the Soviet memorandum, a consultative conference was held in Hanoi from September 22 to 25 that addressed the issues of the alliance between the neutralists and the Pathet Lao as well as problems of Soviet aid to Laos. At the conference, the North Vietnamese and the representatives of the NLHX con-tinued expressing their radical views on the coalition government, which they tended to regard as necessary only for a temporary stabilization in the country; they continued to emphasize the development of guerrilla struggle. Neverthe-less, estimated the Soviet diplomats who attended, the discussions in Hanoi helped the Laotian friends determine "their attitude toward Souvanna Phouma, Kong Le, [and] the formation of coalition government which had not been con-sistent and clear before."[72] The Soviet embassy reported to Moscow that, as a result of the conference, the participants agreed with the Soviet views on the questions under the discussion and occupied "generally correct positions." The Soviet ambassador in the DRV, Suren Tovmasyan, stressed the need to follow the agreed policy in Laos, which was aimed at the unity of the NLHX and the neutralists. "It was this agreed line," reminded Tovmasyan, "together with rendering effective economic and military aid to Laos from our countries, as well as supporting Prince Souvanna Phouma as the central figure capable of rallying patriotic forces, that helped the patriotic forces achieve positive results at the first stage of the struggle."[73] The Soviet ambassador once again called for the formation of a coalition government at the earliest possible time; this reflected the preoccupation of the Soviet leaders who believed the absence of such a government was the main stumbling block to the success of the negotiations at Geneva.

The Geneva conference by this time had long exceeded the duration of six weeks that had been anticipated by Moscow. For a prolonged period, participants in Geneva were unable to find solutions on procedural issues, that is, What should be negotiated first? The neutrality of Laos or conditions of cease-fire and control? The Soviet Union and other Communist delegations insisted on discussing Laotian neutrality, especially because the Soviet draft of the declaration on neutrality had been tabled during the first days of the conference. The United States, in turn, was concerned with numerous violations of the cease-fire in Laos and demanded that the conference's primary aim should be strengthening peace in Laos and clarifying the role of the ICC. Although in the meantime the participants did discuss Soviet proposals on neutrality, on the withdrawal of foreign troops from Laos, and on the functions of the ICC as well as proposals by France and India on the same issues, the deadlock remained unbroken.

The Soviets suspected that U.S. intransigence on the question of the priority of the issues grew out of Washington's desire to use the conference as an exposé of the Communist countries' lack of cooperation on the settlement of the Laos conflict. Georgii Pushkin, who headed the Soviet delegation in the absence of Foreign Minister Gromyko, confided to Zhang Hanfu, who replaced Chen Yi at Geneva, that the Americans in the course of discussions on the issues of control were going to "pick us to pieces on the questions of the cease-fire, the withdrawal of foreign troops, etc."[74] He believed that the Communist delegations should not budge from their position even though the negotiations might be transformed as a result, "into a conversation between deaf mutes."[75] At the same time, Pushkin spoke of the need to prepare for the second phase of the conference; thus he did not exclude some eventual compromise.

Pushkin himself provided the basis for this compromise. In a July 12 conversation with his U.S. counterpart, W. Averell Harriman, who headed the U.S. delegation, Pushkin suggested discussing proposals on neutrality and control as a "single entity" in the order in which they appeared in the tabled drafts, with the provisions on which the delegates disagreed being put aside for further consideration.[76] Thus by moving from one provision of each document to another and setting all disagreements "in one basket" for later bargaining the conference had a chance of entering a "serious phase of horse trading and compromise."[77]

After discussing this proposal at formal meetings of the major delegations, the two cochairs of the conference prepared "Proposals of the Co-Chairmen on the Procedure for Further Work of the Conference," that was read at the July 19 session. In addition to the announcement of the completion of the general discussion and the beginning of a detailed consideration of the draft proposals presented as a basis of a settlement of the Laotian crisis, the "Proposals" suggested holding "restricted meetings" attended by only the heads of delegations and their advisers and experts. Other points of the document conformed with Pushkin's proposal to Harriman.[78]

Thus, thanks to the Soviet efforts, the conference participants finally moved to a discussion of questions of substance, which took place throughout the fall of 1961 at plenary and restricted sessions as well as during private meetings of the six delegations (British, Soviet, U.S., Chinese, French, and Indian) and confidential conversations between the heads of delegations. Pushkin and Harriman were especially active in engaging in informal discussions of controversial issues during the second phase of the Geneva conference. Pushkin reported to the collegium of the Soviet Foreign Ministry that it was during these conversations between the Soviet and U.S. representatives that agreements on most problems were reached; they were then confirmed at the meetings of other delegations.[79]

Both the Americans and the Soviets demonstrated a keen interest in how to guarantee the neutrality of Laos. During a meeting with Pushkin on September 12, Harriman found out that—the preferences of its Asian allies notwithstanding—Moscow did not object to the Western kind of neutrality based on the example of Finland.[80] Having conceded on this question, however, the Soviets continued to oppose the protection of Laos by SEATO, which they regarded as an aggressive alliance. Pushkin paid no heed to Harriman's explanations that an agreement of the parliaments of the member states of the bloc was required to discontinue this protection. Pushkin also rejected a compromise, suggested by Harriman, that would permit the Laotian government to declare its rejection of SEATO protection; SEATO members would then take the declaration into account and promise their noninterference in internal affairs of Laos. Pushkin felt that such a compromise was not enough, and he stated that "if the United States really wants an agreement on the Laotian question, it should revise its position" on SEATO.[81]

Harriman expressed U.S. concern over the North Vietnamese use of Laotian territory for penetration into South Vietnam; this concern only increased at the end of the rainy season in Southeast Asia when Washington expected an increase in Hanoi's activities in the area.[82] In addition, the Americans were aware of the presence of North Vietnamese troops in Laos and insisted on their withdrawal. Pushkin assured his U.S. counterpart that "North Viet-Nam ready to live up to agreement" on Laos, and the Soviet Union was prepared to guarantee it. He even proposed a sort of a quid pro quo to the United States. In a conversation with Harriman on October 25, the Soviet diplomat suggested that "if the Western countries give us a satisfactory formula on the issue of defense of Laos on the part of SEATO, we are ready to agree to the inclusion in the declaration of the thirteen powers participating in the conference, at the appropriate place, the following provision on the nonuse of the territory of Laos: 'They (the thirteen states participating in the 1961 Geneva conference) assume the obligation not to use the territory of Laos with the purpose of interference in internal affairs of other countries'."[83] Harriman admitted that this formula was acceptable.

This and other suggestions Pushkin made during his conversations with Harriman were undoubtedly approved by his superiors in Moscow. Pushkin read a letter to Harriman on October 10 in which Khrushchev himself expressed his satisfaction with the course of discussions. The Soviet leader professed his adherence to a "fully sovereign and neutral Laos" and emphasized the importance of U.S.-Soviet efforts to this end. "If US and USSR act jointly on Laos question," the letter read, "this will have decisive influence on getting agreement. It will have favorable influence not only in reducing tension in Laos and in SE [Southeast] Asia, but, to certain degree, throughout world."[84] This particular passage demonstrated how eager Moscow was, after the confrontation over Berlin that had led to the division of the city by the construction of a wall, to eliminate the hostile atmosphere through settlement of the Laos issue, even at the price of the interests of its Chinese and Vietnamese allies.[85]

The North Vietnamese and the Chinese suspected that the Soviets were liable to collude with the United States behind their backs. In his internal report on the Geneva conference, Zhang Yan, a senior associate of Chen Yi, stated that the Soviet Union wanted to reach a compromise with Washington in order to demonstrate the success of its policy of peaceful coexistence. Zhang reported that during the conference the Soviet delegation was in a hurry to conclude an agreement without making sure that the Pathet Lao was in a strong military position at the negotiation table. The Chinese explained the Soviet behavior by citing the Soviet desire to limit China's intervention in Laos and thereby limit China's influence.[86] This was possibly true, especially in light of the growing estrangement between Moscow and Beijing that led to Zhou Enlai's walkout from the twenty-second CPSU congress in October 1961, which demonstrated the rift between the two parties. However, concern about the preservation of peace in Indochina on the basis of the 1954 Geneva agreements was equally prevalent in the Kremlin's thinking.[87] And Moscow, using its diplomatic prowess and exerting pressure on its militant friends, maneuvered among its allies in order to achieve this goal.

While Pushkin was demanding greater concessions from the West, in his private conversations with his colleagues from China and Vietnam as well as during the meetings of all Communist delegations at the conference, he tried to convince them that Western concessions were acceptable or at least were worth taking into account. For example, the Soviet representative had told Harriman that a unilateral declaration by the Laotian government about its rejection of SEATO protection combined with a declaration of noninterference by the members of SEATO was not enough to solve this problem. At a meeting of Communist delegations on October 13, however, he insisted that such a proposal was quite satisfactory, for "this concession on the part of Western countries means our considerable victory and a blow to SEATO.[88]

Pushkin also remained vigilant lest unilateral actions of the Soviet allies did not undermine agreements already reached by the conference. When the North Vietnamese representative, Nguyen Co Thach, told Pushkin of a Chinese recommendation to keep some DRV troops in Laos after the settlement, Pushkin reacted negatively. "The idea of keeping DRV troops in Laos after the conclusion of the agreement at Geneva is a very questionable thing," he stated to his counterpart. "We have to count on political work in Laos, on internal democratic reforms in that country, not on a military solution of this problem. If we sign an agreement at Geneva, we should unconditionally observe the neutrality of Laos. Therefore, there must be no DRV troops in Laos."[89]

While pressuring its allies to reach an agreement on Laos that would be acceptable to the USSR, Moscow also used the reward of Soviet aid to assure compliance. Notwithstanding the protestations of Soviet diplomats in Geneva, the USSR did not cease its military shipments to Laos. Soviet weapons and ammunition continued to arrive in the DRV, and the North Vietnamese then transported them to Laotian territory. In November 1961 alone, the Laotians received 38 Soviet tanks,[90] most of which were apparently delivered to the Pathet Lao. Not long before, the Pathet Lao delegation to the CPSU congress in Moscow had received assurances from Soviet leaders that the Soviet Union would continue to provide open, as well as secret, assistance to the "patriotic forces" in Laos,[91] assistance that, at Laotian request, included mortars, guns, firearms, ammunition, and transport.[92]

In addition to encountering resistance from its Communist allies in its efforts to reach agreement on Laos, the Soviet Union also enjoyed their cooperation. Despite differing approaches to many issues concerning Laotian settlement, China and North Vietnam shared with Moscow a common concern over the danger of war in Indochina. Beijing was especially anxious to see the conflict on its southern borders resolved because that would eliminate a pretext for the U.S. presence in the close vicinity of China. It was also important for the Chinese leaders to demonstrate their willingness to cooperate with the international community on the pressing issues of war and peace in order to increase China's prestige in the world and reassert its traditional influence in Southeast Asia.[93]

Soviet efforts finally bore fruit and, by the end of November, participants at the conference reached an agreement on almost all aspects of the Laotian problem. At the meeting of the Communist delegations on November 29, Pushkin announced that "practically, the conference has already completed its work and what remains can be resolved in one day."[94] At the forty-third restricted session, on December 18, 1961, the cochairs presented to the conference the tentative texts of the declaration on the neutrality of Laos and of the accompanying protocol on the functions of the ICC.[95] But for these conference documents to be enforced, it was necessary that the coalition government of Laos make its own declaration on neutrality and confirm its desire to cooperate with the ICC.[96] There was still no coalition government in Laos, however. All negotiations among the rival Laotian factions in Zurich, then at Ban Hin Heup in Laos, and later in Geneva in January 1962 came to nothing because of the intransigence of the Boun Oum–Nosavan faction.

Both the Soviets and the Chinese displayed their concern about the lack of success in forming a coalition government. In his report in Moscow in late December 1961, Pushkin emphasized that for the completion of the settlement of the Laotian question "it is necessary to undertake all measures in helping the Laotian friends to form, as soon as possible and under acceptable conditions, the government of national union, to work out the declaration on the neutrality of the country and to send to Geneva a unified Laotian delegation for the signing of the adopted decisions."[97] Beijing concurred with the Soviet determination to finish with the Laotian crisis. Chinese deputy foreign minister Jie Penfei assured a Soviet diplomat that China's "unfailing course" was the achievement of an agreement in Geneva and the formation of a coalition government headed by Souvanna Phouma.[98] The Communist allies were determined to exert pressure on the United States to this end. In a conversation with William Sullivan, aide to the head of the U.S. delegation, Averell Harriman, Pushkin did not conceal that the Soviets believed the only reason why the Laotian crisis was not yet settled was the "'Nosavan clique' and its supporters, among which he listed US military advisers, who were counseling stubborn resistance rather than cooperation. . . . He [Pushkin] advised pressure be brought on Phoumi by curtailment US financial assistance."[99]

Washington no less than Moscow was interested in the settlement of the Laos crisis. However, as the Soviets had problems with the intransigence of their Asian allies, the Americans had similar problems of their own. Phoumi Nosavan consistently refused to comply with Washington's demands to come to agreement with Souvanna Phouma, and Nosavan accused the Kennedy administration of betrayal.[100] To bring its client into line, Washington had to authorize its ambassador to Laos, Winthrop Brown, to exert pressure on Nosavan to make him more amenable to cooperation. Brown reported to his superiors: "1) I have no pressures left to use on Phoumi and Boun Oum. 2) I have made all the threats that words alone can convey. Though my words have been general, they have been interpreted as saying aid would be cut off."[101] The ambassador recommended imposing military sanctions on Nosavan; however, it was difficult for the Kennedy administration to follow his advice because it was receiving at the same time information on the Pathet Lao's preparations for a military offensive. In fact, toward the end of January 1962, fighting broke out around the village of Nam Tha in northwest Laos, not far from the Laos-China border. Contrary to the advice of his U.S. backers, Nosavan had built up a large concentration of troops there, and in the last week of January 1962, his fighters carried out small-scale offensive operations in the area in an effort to cut the Pathet Lao supply lines between northern and southern Laos.

Communist forces had to respond; they had to counter Nosavan's military operations in the rear of the Pathet Lao. In addition, Nosavan's small offensive provided the Pathet Lao and its North Vietnamese supporters an opportunity to influence militarily the course of negotiations on the coalition government, for they believed that success in the armed struggle against the Boun Oum–Nosavan faction would encourage Nosavan to negotiate. The Chinese agreed. They also believed that a military advance was a precondition for a political solution and that military and political instruments should be used simultaneously. In a January 28, 1962, conversation with Souphanouvong in Beijing, Zhou Enlai stated: "It will be fine if a coalition government can be organized. . . . You must be prepared to carry out struggle within the coalition government. In any case, to increase your own strength is the most important matter. The final settlement will be decided by force."[102]

Soon after that, Hanoi began preparations for the military campaign. Seven battalions and a number of other units from the North Vietnamese 316th, 335th, and 330th brigades crossed into Laos to fight alongside the Pathet Lao–neutralist Souvanna Phouma government forces at Nam Tha.[103] Pathet Lao leaders asked for assistance from China as well. Beijing immediately directed its Kunming Military Region to implement an aid program, and the military region assigned 2,149 soldiers, 1,772 civilian workers, 203 trucks, and 639 horses and mules to collect and transport military supplies to the Pathet Lao.[104]

Moscow was aware of the planning for Nam Tha and apparently agreed that a military blow might push Nosavan to the negotiating table. Early in March, the Soviet ambassador in the DRV, Suren Tovmasyan, participated in a conference in Hanoi that decided the situation in Laos was not yet ripe for the formation of a coalition government, efforts must be made to overcome the difficulties, and the most important tasks for the NLHX were to strengthen the alliance with Souvanna Phouma's neutralists and expand its military and political forces.[105] The Communist Party of the Soviet Union reached similar conclusions to the Laotian problem and sent letters stating this to the parties of China, North Vietnam, and Laos, which the Soviet ambassador to Laos, Aleksandr Abramov, carried from Moscow. The letter to Hanoi, which Abramov showed to Marek Thee, cited the Vietnamese comrades' belief in the necessity for undertaking military actions in defense of the liberated areas of Laos and forcing the adversary into negotiations aimed at the establishment of a coalition government favorable to the national-patriotic forces. The letter stated that the Soviets accepted this conclusion, shared by the Chinese and Laotian comrades, and treated it with due understanding, for they were nearer Laos and knew local conditions better.[106]

Marek Thee regarded this as "a clear statement of disengagement as far as internal Laotian developments were concerned,"[107] and he believed the Soviet leaders had been disengaging since the autumn of 1961. Although the USSR's gradual disengagement was undoubtedly a result of Moscow's assessment of the overall situation in Indochina and was based on the Kremlin's foreign policy priorities and the situation in Sino-Soviet relations, the Soviet leaders could have genuinely believed that military success for the Communist forces would facilitate diplomatic negotiations.[108]

If so, they were correct. On May 6, 1962, the Pathet Lao–North Vietnamese forces captured Nam Tha. Despite Washington's announcement on May 11 about dispatching troops to Thailand and sending elements of the U.S. Seventh Fleet to the Gulf of Siam, Washington had been made to understand that the longer the negotiations over a coalition government continued, the greater the likelihood of more incidents like Nam Tha. The U.S. administration confronted Nosavan with this and pressed him for concessions.[109] At the same time, the Kennedy administration received firm assurances from Moscow that Khrushchev continued to adhere to the concept of a settlement in Laos and had "not changed his policy of achieving an independent and neutral Laos."[110] As a result, negotiations between the three factions resumed in Laos, and the three Laotian princes finally reached agreement on a coalition government at a meeting at the Plain of Jars on June 12. On June 23, the date of its formation, the new Government of National Union issued a statement of neutrality, announcing that Laos would not "recognize the protection of any alliance or military coalition, including SEATO."[111] The fourteen participants in the Geneva conference signed the Declaration on Neutrality of Laos and adopted a protocol containing provisions about the role of the cochairs and the ICC. The Geneva conference on Laos thus completed its work.

During the final days of the conference, however, one important meeting took place between the head of the U.S. delegation, Averell Harriman, and Ung Van Khiem, the foreign minister of the Democratic Republic of Vietnam. At the start of the conversation Harriman brought up the agreements on Laos and affirmed his country's determination to carry them out "in the letter and in the spirit." After this statement, he asked whether the North Vietnamese were going to do the same thing. Ung Van Khiem informed his counterpart that the DRV government had assured Souvanna Phouma "that they would abide carefully by the terms of the Laos agreements. They would do nothing which was contrary to the provisions of those agreements."[112] Yet he warned that if the United States did not refrain from attempts to "instigate anti-communist forces in Laos," it would discover "that the NLHX was a very strong organization which could defend the interests of the Lao people."[113]

At the initiative of the North Vietnamese foreign minister, the conversation then turned to Vietnam. He accused the United States of intervening in South Vietnam, an intervention that had prevented the reunification of the country in 1956. "US intervention had in recent years grown worse until it was now a fact that American forces were mercilessly killing Vietnamese citizens."[114] Brushing aside Harriman's counterarguments that the United States had increased its military presence in the South only because of the increased guerrilla activity directed from the North, Ung Van Khiem insisted that there was a popular revolt against the regime in South Vietnam and there were "no North Vietnamese airplanes, ships or motor vehicles which can bring guerrilla forces or weapons into Vietnam."[115]

The conversation concluded with an obvious warning to the U.S. government. Responding to Harriman's reminder that "clear undertakings on the part of the US Government and on the part of the North Vietnamese to carry out scrupulously all the provisions of the Geneva Agreements on Laos would result in peace in Laos," Ung Van Khiem expressed his hope that "Governor Harriman would not forget the second part of the conversation, and particularly what the Foreign Minister had had to say about American military intervention in Vietnam."[116]

For the North Vietnamese, the agreements on Laos had settled nothing. Hanoi was of course interested in the resolution of the Laotian crisis; ongoing chaos could result in open Western military involvement in the form of SEATO's full support for Nosavan and a war with unpredictable consequences for the Pathet Lao. On the other hand, continued instability in Laos was not disadvantageous to the DRV because under cover of internal struggle in Laos the North Vietnamese could maintain permanent contacts with their comrades in South Vietnam and provide them the resources necessary for guerrilla war against the Saigon regime and its U.S. supporters. Settlement could limit Hanoi's freedom of action for it implied certain obligations and international control.

A situation of neither war nor peace was therefore most preferred in the eyes of the North Vietnamese leadership as long as the Vietnamese problem remained unresolved. Hanoi's preference for a fluctuating situation likely caused disillusionment in Moscow over the future of the Laos agreements. In the spring of 1962, Asian experts in the Soviet Foreign Ministry prepared a report that described the role of Laos in the North Vietnamese strategy toward South Vietnam. The ministry report noted that the Vietnamese friends' orientation toward armed struggle in the South was influenced by the "favorable situation," which included "the maintenance of an open way from the DRV to South Vietnam through some southern provinces of Laos that are under control of Pathet Lao forces." The Vietnamese friends in this way dispatched troops, arms, and ammunition. They even used the Soviet planes engaged in the airlift to Laos. "During the summer of 1961," the report said, "the friends have transferred to the South three fully equipped infantry battalions and a significant number of officers for twenty battalions. . . ."[117]

Knowing of Hanoi's activities in Laos and its position toward the settlement there, the Soviet leaders could hardly have had illusions about the effectiveness of the agreements reached at Geneva. Nevertheless, they displayed their satisfaction with the agreements[118] and were determined to observe them strictly, perhaps with the lurking hope that their allies would follow their lead.[119] As soon as the Geneva conference on Laos ended, the Soviet Union cancelled its deliveries of supplies to Laos and dismantled the airlift. In reply to the Chinese, who urged the USSR to continue its assistance to the pro-Communist forces in Laos, Deputy Foreign Minister Vasilii Kuznetzov on September 3, 1962, handed a note to the Chinese embassy elaborating on the Soviet position. The note insisted on the need to concentrate on a political struggle in Laos and denounce U.S. actions there. It praised the Geneva agreement and emphasized the importance of observing it. The note therefore rejected requests for Soviet military aid to the NLHX and asserted that "any of our steps which might violate the Geneva agreement would create difficulties for the socialist countries in other international problems, too. We would put in the hands of our enemies a great political trump, enabling them to say in their propaganda that socialist countries do not meet their obligations." How would Soviet initiatives on Berlin look, asked the note, if Moscow began to violate the recently signed Geneva agreement?[120]

If the conference on Laos had been immediately followed by negotiations on the settlement of the Vietnam problem, an exit from this situation could have been found. Both Hanoi and Beijing supported Vietnam negotiations. As early as May 1961, on the eve of the conference on Laos, Chinese foreign minister Chen Yi raised the question of Vietnam during a meeting of the heads of Communist delegations. "To us, the posing of the question of South Vietnam," Chen stated in response to Polish foreign minister Rapacki, "is quite understandable. It is explained by the situation which exists in Vietnam. We find it necessary . . . to raise questions of South Vietnam and Taiwan after the resolution of the question of Laos."[121] Thus, for the Chinese, the issue of Vietnam was but a part of a wider problem of divided countries.

The North Vietnamese also nourished hopes that a favorable resolution of the conflict in Vietnam would come on the heels of the conference on Laos. Ung Van Khiem tried to discuss this issue during his conversation in Geneva with Harriman. Pham Van Dong broached the subject of a neutral zone in Indochina, including South Vietnam, during his meeting with Souvanna Phouma, and he confirmed the North Vietnamese interest in a conference that would ratify this idea.[122]

Although plans for some sort of a conference on Vietnam were discussed in the Kennedy administration at this time,[123] Washington was too afraid to lose South Vietnam to Communists to agree on its neutralization. Instead, the U.S. government considered military schemes aimed at the strengthening of the Saigon regime. As a result, time passed and the situation in Indochina remained explosive. The settlement of the Laotian crisis, though it cleared the air somewhat, did not have a positive influence on processes in the region. Quite to the contrary: the deepening of the crisis in Vietnam undermined the Geneva agreements on Laos. Neither Hanoi nor Washington abandoned its plans to use Laotian territory for armed confrontation in South Vietnam. While the North Vietnamese continued to maintain their routes through Laos for pouring arms, ammunition, and troops into the South, the United States supported its clandestine forces in Laos under Operation Momentum initiated in early 1961.[124]

Thus Moscow's hopes to consolidate prospects for peace in Indochina by means of the settlement in Laos proved to be futile. In the early 1960s, armed struggle in South Vietnam became the focal point of the developing situation in Indochina.

9. A Disposition to War

For War, consisteth not in Battle only,
or the act of fighting; but in a tract of time,
wherein the Will to content by Battle is
sufficiently known. . . . So the nature of War,
consisteth not in actual fighting, but
in the known disposition thereto, during all
the time there is no assurance to the contrary.

Thomas Hobbes, *Leviathan*, chap. 13

Debates over John F. Kennedy's policy toward Vietnam continue today. One group of scholars has attempted to prove that Kennedy, who avoided sending combat troops to South Vietnam and resisted pressure from the U.S. military for such a step, would ultimately have disengaged from Southeast Asia had he survived the gunshots in Dallas and been reelected in 1964.[1] These assertions are rejected by those who emphasize the consistency of the Vietnam policy during the Kennedy administration and the president's full knowledge and approval, which led to greater U.S. involvement in the Indochina conflict.[2] However useful these debates are for our knowledge of the past, they remain hypothetical because Kennedy after all did not survive his trip to Dallas in November 1963, and it was the new U.S. president, Lyndon B. Johnson, who made a series of fateful decisions concerning U.S. participation in the Vietnamese conflict.

Nevertheless, for a better understanding of Soviet policy toward the Vietnam conflict as it developed in the early 1960s, it is necessary to reconstruct briefly the sequence of decisions and actions by the U.S. government and then analyze their impact on decision making in Moscow.

Commitment, credibility, consequences, and counterinsurgency—these were the watchwords of the Kennedy administration Vietnam policy, which was based on the conclusion that South Vietnam's survival was vital for U.S. national security.[3] The Eisenhower administration—predecessor of the Kennedy administration—left Kennedy a legacy that regarded Indochina in terms of the domino theory: the fall of any one country to Communists would inevitably lead to the collapse of a whole region and to the U.S. loss of influence. Kennedy and his associates could put forward no other theory in place of the primitive domino comparison (involving chess or even poker) primarily because, as Robert S. McNamara, Kennedy's secretary of defense, stressed several times in his memoir, the new administration had "sparse knowledge, scant experience, and simplistic assumptions" about the crisis in Southeast Asia.[4]

President Kennedy regarded the situation in Vietnam through the prism of the balance of power that existed in the world by the time of his election to the U.S. presidency. At the same time Kennedy was convinced of the advantage that Western values had over Communism. This conviction was shared by other members of his administration. Considering the existing equilibrium between the Western and the Communist camps fragile, the Kennedy administration was determined to prevent any change in favor of the rivals. Any distinction between key regions and peripheral areas did not matter very much.[5] The zero-sum ratio was uppermost in the Cold War competition.

It is not surprising, therefore, that Kennedy could not allow the loss of South Vietnam to the Communists, especially after he had suffered humiliation as a result of the Cuban invasion fiasco and agreed to the neutralization of Laos, which was already regarded by U.S. conservatives as an unjustified concession to Communism.[6] The further strengthening of relations between the Soviet Union and Cuba, as well as "a new wave of Soviet provocations in Berlin" added to Washington policymakers' conviction that, in McNamara's words, it was "reasonable to consider expanding the U.S. effort in Vietnam."[7]

The U.S. president was nevertheless ambivalent as to which course of action should be adopted toward South Vietnam. This ambivalence was very much influenced by the lack of unity within the Kennedy administration itself. One group of advisers, whose mouthpiece in the early days of the new administration was Col. Edward Lansdale—Graham Greene's "ugly American," with his long history of experience in covert operations in Asia—pressed for unqualified support for Ngo Dinh Diem as well as the dispatch of U.S. combat troops to South Vietnam. This group had the strong and growing backing of the U.S. military establishment and tacit support from Secretary of Defense McNamara and Secretary of State Rusk. This group developed a so-called conspiracy complex stemming from an aversion to any changes that, in their eyes, resulted from the "mysterious influence or control of internal and external 'enemy' agents." Paul Blackstock, author of a book on subversion and its forms, wrote that "these changes had created an explosive undercurrent of frustration in conservative circles, especially among military leaders who fought a losing battle against native nationalist movements in Southeast Asia and Algeria. In such circumstances, nothing could be more plausible than to ascribe failure exclusively to 'the Communist Conspiracy.'"[8]

Another group of Kennedy advisers, represented initially by the U.S. ambassador in Saigon, Elbridge Durbrow, did not oppose Diem but insisted that U.S. military aid to South Vietnam be tied to reforms there. Some in Washington favored a coup d'état against Diem. The person who first advocated a coup was the director of the State Department's Bureau of Intelligence and Research, Roger Hilsman. Later he was joined by such influential figures as W. Averell Harriman and the new U.S. ambassador to South Vietnam, Henry Cabot Lodge Jr., among others.[9]

The U.S. establishment also included a few people who questioned the rationale for U.S. policy in Indochina. They refused to see South Vietnam as a country important for U.S. national interests and rejected as simplistic the view that Ho Chi Minh and his regime were puppets of Moscow and Beijing; they argued instead that it was nationalism that was prevailing in the minds of Asian leaders, not communism. An eminent economist, teacher and author who was serving as U.S. ambassador in New Delhi, John Kenneth Galbraith, was among this group. He worried over growing U.S. military commitment in Vietnam and, in a letter to the president, asked: "Incidentally, who is the man in your administration who decides what countries are strategic? I would like to have his name and address and ask him what is so important about this real estate in the space age."[10]

With such a divergence of opinions among his closest advisers, Kennedy—instead of making clear-cut decisions—chose to improvise, temporize, split the difference. His administration "took the minimum steps judged necessary to stabilize the situation, leaving its resolution to the longer future, while always conscious that harder decisions lay ahead."[11] Robert Kennedy, who occupied the post of attorney general in his brother's administration and was close to many foreign policy decisions, described his elder brother's policy as "We'd cross that bridge when we came to it,"[12] implying that Washington postponed crucial decisions on Vietnam until the situation became intolerable from the U.S. strategic point of view.

Yet even those decisions that Kennedy did adopt played a fateful role in the later U.S. policy toward Vietnam. Although withstanding military pressure in favor of sending combat troops to South Vietnam, he significantly increased U.S. presence and influence in that country. In November 1961, the U.S. president agreed to a greater role for U.S. advisers in the South Vietnamese struggle against Communist guerrillas on their territory. Kennedy substantially strengthened the advisory role of the U.S. Air Force in Vietnam and authorized the course that resulted in dispatching nearly sixteen thousand U.S. military personnel to Vietnam within the next two years.[13] In addition to sending military personnel, Washington decided to render military assistance to the South Vietnamese armed forces. Saigon was receiving U.S. aircraft, armored personnel carriers, and other equipment, and the United States provided South Vietnam with financial support for increasing its army to two hundred thousand. Americans were also closely involved in activities of the Diem regime such as the strategic hamlet program, initiated by Diem in the spring of 1962, which resulted in the forced resettlement of thousands of peasants in something resembling concentration camps. The strategic hamlet program led to increased estrangement of the rural population and its support of the Communist guerrillas.[14] An indication of the increased U.S. role in South Vietnam was the transformation on February 8, 1962, of the U.S. military assistance advisory group (MAAG) into the U.S. military assistance command in Vietnam (MACV) under General Paul D. Harkins.

These Kennedy administration actions added up to a clear violation of the 1954 Geneva agreements. The United States had abandoned its former course of compliance with the Geneva Accords and ignored its obligation to "refrain from the threat or the use of force to disturb them."[15] As early as the end of 1961, the strength of the MAAG in South Vietnam was three times the number allowed in the Geneva agreements.[16] The development of Vietnam policy in the Kennedy administration makes futile any discussion of whether Kennedy "would have pulled us out of Vietnam," as McNamara, one of the architects of the U.S. Vietnam policy, argued in his memoir.[17] Whatever Kennedy's intentions, he had set up a policy that would be difficult to discard later. The difficulty was exacerbated by the fact that Washington's actions triggered changes in the policies of other countries that had played an important role in the Vietnam affair and that now had to reconsider their approach toward the Vietnam conflict in response to the U.S. actions. One of the most prominent of those countries was the Soviet Union.

Moscow was concerned with the prospect of deterioration in the situation in Indochina. Hanoi's militant pronouncements made Moscow apprehensive, and Soviet leaders tried to restrain their North Vietnamese allies from taking what Moscow regarded as premature action aimed at the instigation and support of armed struggle in the southern half of Vietnam. Soviet leaders were successful in discouraging the DRV leaders from openly endorsing this struggle at the third congress of the Workers' Party of Vietnam in September 1960, when the Chinese sharply criticized the Soviet "appeasement" policy toward the West. Moscow made a concession to Beijing in approving only the struggle of indigenous movements in the Third World, which the Communists called national liberation movements because they fought for the liberation, sovereignty, and independence of their countries from foreign dominance. On January 6, 1961, however, when Khrushchev spoke at a meeting of the party organizations of the Higher Party School, the Academy of Social Sciences, and the Institute of Marxism-Leninism of the CPSU Central Committee, he subordinated the struggle of indigenous movements to the general problem of war and peace. The Soviet leader warned about the danger of the local wars that could grow into a world conflict and stressed that it was necessary to fight against world wars and against local wars.[18]

In its efforts aimed at the settlement of the Laotian conflict, Moscow likewise tried to prevent the disruption of peace in Indochina as well as demonstrate that the Vietnam problem could be resolved along lines similar to the settlement in Laos, that is, by neutralization. At the 1961–1962 Geneva conference, the Soviets not only contained the revolutionary zeal of the Chinese and North Vietnamese to fight imperialism; they also tried to convey explicitly to the West— for example, during Khrushchev's meeting with Kennedy in Vienna—as well as implicitly that Moscow did not regard Indochina itself as an area of strategic importance and, accordingly, it was prepared to search for an arrangement that would satisfy both opposing camps.

News from Washington about U.S. military plans for South Vietnam therefore could not be received in the Kremlin without disappointment and disdain. It must have been discouraging for Moscow to discover that all its efforts aimed at the preservation of peace in Indochina had borne no results. Moreover the Soviets now felt compelled to engage on two fronts, in the West and in the East— in the East trying to discourage North Vietnam from war. In early October 1961, the Soviet embassy in the DRV informed Moscow that the Kennedy administration continued "to follow the former political course [in Vietnam]: to prevent peaceful unification of the country, to put brakes on the development of the patriotic movement in the South, and to tie South Vietnam to itself even more strongly." The embassy explained the increase in U.S. aid to South Vietnam by citing the U.S. government's concern about losing "this strategically important region as a result of the growth of the patriotic movement in the country."[19]

Soviet diplomats in Hanoi pointed to recent U.S. steps in South Vietnam—for example, Vice President Johnson's visit to Saigon; and the establishment of a special committee to cooperate with the Pentagon and General Lansdale, which was to be headed by Sterling Cottrell,[20] who the Soviet diplomats described as "a well known expert on the struggle against guerrillas"—as evidence of Washington's support for Diem's regime. They drew the attention of their superiors to the increase in casualties among the guerrillas as a result of Saigon's punitive expeditions arranged with the "active support of the Americans." They reported that Diem, in addition to his military measures against guerrillas, intensified political struggle against the Communists and the patriotic movement "on the advice of the Americans."[21] The embassy's report referred to all these facts in order to support the conclusion that it was the punitive measures of the Saigon regime that had provoked the intensification of the armed struggle in South Vietnam.

Hanoi, the embassy reported, on the contrary occupied a rather reasonable position: North Vietnamese leaders believed the ouster of the Americans from Vietnam and the overthrow of Diem should be undertaken by the South Vietnamese themselves, without "direct military interference on the part of the DRV." A new South Vietnamese government adhering to the principle of neutrality would initiate negotiations with Hanoi on the ways to realize peaceful unification of the country.[22] The embassy did admit that the North Vietnamese undertook measures to strengthen guerrilla bases to the south of the seventeenth parallel, formed "large military units" such as battalions and regiments and supplied them with arms and equipment, and used Laotian territory to help carry out some of these activities. Soviet diplomats in the DRV justified these actions by citing the increasing U.S. and South Vietnamese suppression of the patriotic movement in the South.[23]

The Soviet embassy in Hanoi had obviously taken at face value the declarations of the North Vietnamese leadership about its desire, following the example of Laos, to settle the Vietnam conflict by peaceful means. The diplomats did not see a contradiction between such declarations and the intensification of guerrilla operations in South Vietnam authorized and supported by the North. Therefore, the embassy's recommendation, made in its October 1961 political letter signed by Ambassador Suren Tovmasyan, corresponded with its overall context:

> Not excluding the possibility of the Vietnamese friends' appeal to us for help to the patriotic forces in the South, the Embassy finds it possible to consider preliminarily a question of what kind of arms, ammunition, and other equipment of American manufacture the Soviet Union could provide to the South Vietnamese patriots through the DRV.[24]

The embassy's interpretation of the developments in Vietnam did not fully coincide with Moscow's assessment of the situation. The Soviet Foreign Ministry, undoubtedly basing its views on information received from other sources, including intelligence, did not fail to draw Tovmasyan's attention to this discrepancy. The ministry criticized its embassy in the DRV for the "tacit acceptance of the logic of the North Vietnamese actions in the South," for relying too heavily on North Vietnamese propaganda that emphasized only one aspect of the problem—the intensification of U.S. involvement in Vietnam—while it underestimated facts that led to the conclusion that the Vietnamese friends were "choosing the way of transition toward active armed struggle in the South, trying to realize the policy of unification of Vietnam by military means."[25] At the same time, the ministry in Moscow believed that the Soviet diplomats in the DRV underestimated U.S. determination to suppress the liberation movement in South Vietnam as well as U.S. assistance to the regime of Ngo Dinh Diem. Moscow asked "whether the transition toward an open armed struggle against the Ngo Dinh Diem regime would not put the revolutionary forces of South Vietnam under threat and, on the other hand, whether this would not lead to an even deeper U.S. intervention in South Vietnam that is fraught with the complication of the political situation in that region and could lead to the transformation of South Vietnam into a sharp ganglion of international tension."[26] The Soviet Foreign Ministry doubted the expediency of even a preliminary consideration of military aid to the South Vietnamese guerrillas.

Soviet reaction to Vietnam developments clearly reveals Moscow's apprehension about the Vietnam situation. Nikita Khrushchev expressed Moscow's concern in a November 10, 1961, letter to President Kennedy in which the Soviet leader criticized U.S. support of Ngo Dinh Diem and U.S. economic and military assistance. Khrushchev referred to reports of "some news agencies" about Washington's intention to send U.S. troops to South Vietnam, and he stressed that this action would not improve the situation in Indochina. Khrushchev warned Kennedy: "Sending troops to suppress national-liberation movements in other countries is by no means a way that corresponds to the interests of peace and, besides, what are the guarantees that the American troops would not get tied up in South Vietnam. I think that such a perspective is most real." According to Khrushchev, this type of involvement would only add to the difficulties both countries had to deal with in the international arena.[27]

The Soviet leader's prophesy must have struck a sour note for Kennedy because it came at a time when the U.S. administration was considering a recommendation from General Maxwell Taylor, the president's military representative who had just returned from his mission to Saigon, to introduce U.S. combat forces in the South to prevent the fall of South Vietnam to Communism.[28] The initial number of U.S. troops necessary to fulfill this task was estimated at eight thousand to ten thousand.[29] Although one cannot say for sure, it is quite probable that Khrushchev's letter influenced Kennedy's decision to not send U.S. troops to South Vietnam.

Moscow's appeal to the common sense of U.S. policymakers did not have much effect, however. Washington's November 1961 decisions, though short of committing combat troops, became "a vitally important step toward 'Americanization' of the conflict."[30] One month later the Soviet Foreign Ministry noted that the United States was continuing its military preparations. A memorandum prepared by the ministry's Southeast Asia Department on the basis of information from military intelligence and the Soviet civilian intelligence service (KGB) reported how the United States kept on alert in the area of the Philippines one aircraft carrier with thirty-nine low-flying attack aircraft that could carry nuclear weapons, twenty-eight jet fighters, and other planes. The United States also had in the Philippines one cruiser, four destroyers, one frigate with antiaircraft guided missiles, one helicopter carrier, and several ships of the Seventh Fleet that carried up to fifteen hundred paratroopers and twenty helicopters. Under such conditions, the memorandum concluded, the continuing efforts of North Vietnam to intensify armed struggle in the South "without corresponding political education of the masses in the situation when the United States undertakes active measures for military support of Ngo Dinh Diem could have negative consequences, internal as well as international." This policy could lead to the suppression of the national liberation movement in South Vietnam, on the one hand, and the development of the war in the South into an international conflict, on the other.[31] Thus, in addition to its efforts aimed at persuading the U.S. administration to stop its interference in Vietnam, Moscow obviously had to apply even more pressure to its Vietnamese friends to convince them to take a less militant line in their policy toward South Vietnam. Yet prospects for Soviet success in pressuring the North were diminishing.

Soviet-Vietnamese cooperation in various spheres appeared to continue unabated after the 1960 Moscow conference of Communist parties. In 1961, as before, the Soviet Union retained its strong position among socialist countries for economic assistance provided to the DRV.[32] The number of delegations traveling back and forth between the two countries increased, according to the Soviet embassy in the DRV, and they included industrial, youth, and military delegations.[33] In June, a Soviet military delegation visited Hanoi to study how to strengthen the DRV military potential.[34] Also in June, soon after the Vienna meeting between Khrushchev and Kennedy, North Vietnamese premier Pham Van Dong visited Moscow to discuss questions of Soviet-DRV cooperation and the international situation. The Soviet leader gave a breakfast in the Kremlin in honor of the DRV delegation, at which he declared that North Vietnam had in the Soviet Union a "trustworthy and staunch friend in the struggle for the buildup of socialism and for peaceful unification of the country."[35] The DRV premier was followed by Ho Chi Minh who, as usual, visited the Soviet Union in August to have a vacation in Crimea where he met Khrushchev for a lengthy discussion on the international situation and problems of the world communist movement.[36] As was tradition at these meetings, both leaders assured each other of their mutual respect and amity.

These leaders' declarations, however, concealed their growing estrangement, a process under way since Hanoi's reorientation toward a military solution to the Vietnam problem evident as early as the 1960 Moscow Communist parties conference, when the North Vietnamese supported many Chinese declarations that contradicted the principles of Khrushchev's internal and external policies. After the conference, the North Vietnamese leaders kept silent about decisions that had stressed the role of the Soviet Communist Party as the vanguard of world communism. Instead, they began to call the CPSU "the center of the international communist movement, and the USSR the center of the socialist camp." The Soviets immediately perceived this modification as a "demonstration of insincerity" on the part of the Vietnamese friends.[37]

North Vietnam's insincerity was especially evident in Hanoi's policy toward South Vietnam. Aware of the Soviet negative attitude toward intensification of armed struggle there, the North Vietnamese tried to avoid discussing this subject during their contacts with Moscow and accordingly refused to elaborate on their plans in the South. They apparently did not inform their Soviet friends in advance about the December 20, 1960, formation of the National Liberation Front of South Vietnam (NLFSV) for no report from the Soviet embassy in Hanoi mentioned this event until after it had taken place. In 1961, the Soviet diplomats in the DRV began complaining that they had "limited opportunities for receiving complete and timely information on the situation in the South." They asked Moscow to send them necessary materials that could be used in their conversations with North Vietnamese officials.[38] By failing to provide the Soviets with information on developments in South Vietnam, Hanoi was in fact refusing to get preliminary approval for its actions from Moscow.[39]

Moscow suspected that behind the deterioration of the Soviet position in the region lay the concurrent growth of Chinese influence on the policy of the North Vietnamese leadership. The widening gap between how Moscow and Beijing approached international relations was detrimental to the Soviet role in the Indochinese conflict. As predicted by U.S. analysts in their reports on Sino-Soviet relations, the 1960 Moscow conference "did not produce a complete agreement, or one which is likely to be lasting. The estrangement seems likely to continue."[40] Although the 1960 conference did temporarily stop the public recriminations between the two parties, it did not reconcile their divergent objectives. The Soviet embassy in China reported that after the conference the Chinese position did not undergo serious modification. Beijing refused to criticize itself for erroneous views. Mao's cult of personality remained strong. In the middle of

1961, the embassy registered indications of China's abandonment of its course toward reconciliation with the Soviet Union. Chinese leaders ceased to emphasize the importance of the unity of the Communist movement, kept silent about the draft of the new CPSU program that was to be adopted at the forthcoming congress of Soviet Communists, and started to talk again about Chinese Marxism.[41] The period after the 1960 Moscow conference until fall 1961 was clearly a lull before a storm.

The storm raged at the twenty-second congress of the Soviet Communist Party, which took place from October 17 to October 31, 1961. At the congress, Khrushchev vigorously denounced Albania for its adherence to Stalinism and for opposing the Soviet policy of de-Stalinization. Zhou Enlai rose in defense of the Albanian comrades; he delivered a speech on October 20 in which he criticized Khrushchev for his public denunciation of the Albanians and pointed out that such public criticism did not help the unity of the Communist movement, disagreements should be aired privately, and errors should be rectified during negotiations between respective parties. The Chinese leader also spelled out his party's disagreement with the program proposed to the congress that contradicted many provisions of the 1957 declaration and the 1960 statement. He left the podium without shaking hands with Khrushchev. The next day Zhou Enlai laid two wreaths at the mausoleum on Red Square that still had the names of Lenin and Stalin on its façade. One of the wreaths bore the inscription: "To Iossif Vissarionovich Stalin, the Great Marxist-Leninist."[43] Failing to resolve differences with the Soviet leaders, Zhou Enlai left Moscow on October 23, before the congress closed.

After this open breach between the leadership, Sino-Soviet relations continued to deteriorate rapidly despite reconciliation efforts from both sides from time to time. One consequence of the rift was the transformation of China from an ally to a rival of the Soviet Union in Indochina. Even before the conflict, Chinese influence in the DRV was relatively strong. Within the North Vietnamese leadership, Beijing had an influential pro-Chinese lobby that was eager to follow the Chinese example in many instances. Hanoi shared with Beijing its dislike of Soviet criticism of Stalin's cult of personality, Moscow's policy of rapprochement with the West, and Moscow's denunciation of the Albanian Communists.[43] The developing conflict between China and the Soviet Union only strengthened the Chinese leaders' desire to consolidate their position in neighboring North Vietnam.

Building upon the ideological affinity of the Chinese and North Vietnamese, Beijing tried to guarantee its influence in the DRV by binding North Vietnam to China economically. Communist China had always played an important role in assisting "democratic Vietnam," and by 1962 it led all other countries in economic cooperation with the DRV, leaving the Soviet Union behind in some areas. For example, in trade, aid, credits, and technical assistance to North Vietnam, China was out in front of other socialist countries. Furthermore, Chinese credits and economic and technical assistance were concentrated in the key sectors of the North Vietnamese economy. Beijing helped the DRV in the largest construction projects and in light industries, in the creation of a network of railway lines, and in irrigation. The Chinese usually equipped the factories and enterprises they built in Vietnam with their own machines and tools, which guaranteed continuing North Vietnamese dependence on advice and support from China. In 1962 the Soviet embassy in the DRV pointed out in its review of Sino-Vietnamese relations that "[e]conomic relations with the PRC which play such an important role in the development of the DRV people's economy are one of those levers by means of which China is able to influence, to some degree, foreign and domestic policy of [North] Vietnam."[44]

Beijing's expansion in its neighboring country in the early 1960s also came in the form of visits of various delegations from China to the DRV. The number of delegations grew rapidly, prompting the Soviet embassy to express concern over the intensification of China–North Vietnam contacts. The embassy reported to Moscow that the Chinese delegations were "very representative." In the period from October 1961 to March 1962 alone, Hanoi hosted Chinese military and trade delegations, trade union representatives, railway specialists, artists, and athletes.[45] Moscow must have been most concerned about the development of military contacts between Hanoi and Beijing. A Chinese military delegation led by Marshal Ye Jianying, which visited the DRV in December 1961, was the highest-powered military delegation to North Vietnam to date. It included a PRC air force commander, representatives of the general staff of the People's Liberation Army (PLA) and the PLA's political department, and a number of senior officers.[46] Various sources reported that the delegation came to North Vietnam not solely for the celebration of the seventeenth anniversary of the PAV but also for discussions on the prospects of armed struggle in the South.[47] Soviet diplomats regarded the visit of the Chinese military delegation as a manifestation of the "aspiration of the Chinese comrades to somehow demonstrate to the leaders and the people of the DRV the PRC's readiness to lend them all-out support in case of a possible armed conflict over South Vietnam."[48]

North Vietnamese leaders eagerly reciprocated the Chinese visits. Perhaps most irritating to Moscow was that visits of the Vietnamese comrades to China took place before or after their trips to the Soviet Union and East European countries. The Kremlin suspected that the Vietnamese not only asked for advice of the Chinese leaders but also informed them of what was transpiring during negotiations with the Soviets and their European allies. Therefore, it does not seem strange that Khrushchev warned Ho Chi Minh, whom he met in Sochi in August 1961, that the Vietnamese leader "should not pass over to the Chinese comrades what was told to him in confidence, for this would lead to the deepening of the present discord, not the rapprochement between the CCP and CPSU."[49]

Soviet observers reached the conclusion that relations between China and North Vietnam were strengthening and China's importance was gradually growing.[50] But Moscow definitely retained some leverage in the DRV, and Chinese influence in Vietnam had certain limits. For example, Hanoi was not fully satisfied with Chinese economic aid because the factories built with Chinese help and the equipment provided by China were mostly obsolete or at least could not compete with the more modern machines and tools sent by the Soviet Union and East European countries.[51] As a result, Hanoi sought a continuation of economic cooperation with Moscow and always emphasized how important Soviet aid was to the DRV.

China and North Vietnam also had differing approaches toward the development of the North Vietnamese economy. Because of the failure of Hanoi's program of agrarian reform—which had adhered to Chinese principles—Hanoi was cautious in following other examples of its northern neighbor. Attempts by some provincial leaders to establish people's communes in the DRV were not approved by the Central Committee of the Workers' Party of Vietnam. And North Vietnamese enthusiasm about great leaps forward was shattered as China entered a sharp downturn in its economy in the early 1960s.[52]

Even in ideology, where the correspondence between Hanoi and Beijing was most apparent, the Chinese did not enjoy unquestioned authority. Although one group in the DRV leadership was striving for a closer rapprochement with China—the Soviet embassy included Vietnamese Politburo members Truong Chinh, Hoang Van Hoan, and Nguyen Chi Thanh in this faction—the Soviet embassy emphasized that the "pro-Chinese feelings" of these leaders did not prevent them from supporting the development of Soviet–North Vietnamese friendship and did not cause the Vietnamese to play off one country against the other.[53] Furthermore, influential North Vietnamese leaders—Ho Chi Minh, Pham Van Dong, and Vo Nguyen Giap—remained firm defenders of relations with the Soviet Union. Giap did not even shy away from expressing pro-Soviet sentiments before the highest-level visiting Chinese military delegation. One observer remembered that Giap "barely remained within the bounds of politeness" while delivering his speech at a banquet for the visitors. Giap counterbalanced all flattering references to the Chinese PLA with still more flattering references to the Soviet army and praised Soviet "advanced military science."[54]

Other North Vietnamese leaders followed Giap's example in their encounters with Chinese visitors.[55]

Hanoi therefore still tried to maintain its policy of balancing between the powerful allies and did not want to antagonize either of them, leading officials from the Soviet Foreign Ministry's Southeast Asia Department to be optimistic about the further development of Soviet–North Vietnamese relations. In their view, Moscow only needed to take the "proper initiative" to broaden multiple contacts with the DRV, which "could have in the present conditions an important positive significance."[56] Increased contacts and influence would be useful not only for bilateral relations but ultimately for peace in Indochina, which the Soviets were eager to preserve.

Soviet leaders, however, were not prepared to follow the proposals of the officials of the ministry's Southeast Asia Department. Preoccupied with other pressing problems, primarily their relations with the West as well as their quarrel with China, the Soviets were reluctant to be proactive with respect to Vietnam. Khrushchev could not even find time to visit the DRV although his visit would certainly have had a positive effect on bilateral relations. In 1961, in response to Ho Chi Minh's invitation to him to come to North Vietnam, Khrushchev said, "We are busy now with the preparation of the [party] congress and the solution of the German problem. When we resolve it, we will have more time and it will be possible to consider [sic] the issue of the trip to Vietnam."[57]

Thus, at a time when both the United States and the DRV were intensifying activities leading to the undermining of peace in Indochina, Moscow pursued an increasingly passive policy in the region. Soviet leaders seem to have resigned themselves to the consequences of their North Vietnamese and Chinese allies' policies. What were the reasons for the Soviets' apparent passivity? The Soviet position undoubtedly was influenced by the Sino-Soviet rift and its impact on Soviet-Vietnamese relations. Another reason was Moscow's lack of interest in that region and Moscow's belief that it was devoid of strategic importance for the Soviet Union.

Moscow's policy was also affected by the Soviet failure to garner the support of other countries responsible for the situation in Southeast Asia for Soviet efforts to counter recent belligerent tendencies in the region. Great Britain, a cochair of the 1954 Geneva conference, was unwilling to challenge the United States over Vietnam. F. A. Warner, head of the Southeast Asia Department at the British Foreign Office, summarized his government's attitude: "The policy which we have agreed with the Americans is to avoid international discussion on Vietnam until the military situation has been restored."[58] The result was that although London continuously questioned the rationale for U.S. moves in

Southeast Asia, it never confronted its powerful ally with its clear-cut opposition to U.S. policy and did not want to put forward any alternative.

Soviet leaders were also skeptical about the position of France. Georgii Pushkin, who headed the Soviet delegation at the Geneva conference on Laos, referred to the role of the French delegation at the conference when he confided to the Chinese deputy foreign minister, Zhang Hanfu, that "The French display a striking conservatism on all issues. Apparently, they are overburdened with defeat in [their] colonies, in particular, the Algerian problem which tied them hand and foot."[59] In addition, Moscow was receiving indications of Paris's negative assessment of the effectiveness of the Geneva settlement. Louis Dauge, the French representative to the United Nations, commented that the Geneva Accords did not "stir up in France fond memories" and it was hardly possible "to start up this rusty mechanism."[60]

Soviet decision makers therefore were not surprised when their initiative on the neutralization of Vietnam met with failure. The evolution of the Soviet neutralization initiative illustrates the USSR's growing passivity toward Indochina.

The idea of a neutral South Vietnam had emerged some time before the Geneva conference on Laos and was discussed among various countries including China and the DRV as part of a more general proposal for a peaceful settlement of the Vietnam conflict and of the establishment of a neutrality zone in Indochina comprising Laos, Cambodia, and South Vietnam. As the negotiations on Laos neared an end, both Western and Communist diplomats raised the subject of neutralization during private conversations and in public pronouncements. For example, in April 1962, a senior North Vietnamese official suggested publicly that the "Laotian model" could be considered as a possible solution of the Vietnamese problem at a new Geneva conference on Vietnam.[61] Expectations were very high among many delegates at Geneva that such a conference would immediately follow the successful conclusion of the Laos conference.[62]

Moscow generally favored the ideas of a new conference and the neutralization of South Vietnam. The Southeast Asia Department of the Soviet Foreign Ministry included in its plan for 1962 the following point:

> In the nearest future it would be expedient to put forward a thesis on a possible convocation of an International Conference on South Vietnam and then, after consultations with the Chinese and Vietnamese friends, to unleash a campaign in support of this proposal. The objective of such a conference would be to work out concrete measures on the suppression of U.S. interference in the internal situation in South Vietnam and to guarantee the implementation of the

1954 Geneva agreements. At the conference it would also be possible, with the concurrence of the Vietnamese friends, to raise the issue of a possible neutralization of South Vietnam with corresponding guarantees.[63]

Almost simultaneously with the 1962 plan, the Foreign Ministry issued directives to the Soviet ambassador to the DRV to look into North Vietnamese attitude toward the issue:

> [O]n the one hand, the Vietnamese friends, in the framework of the National Liberation Front of South Vietnam, officially speak in favor of a peaceful unification of Vietnam and admitted the neutralization of South Vietnam as the first step. . . . On the other hand, using the situation that has arisen in spring and summer 1961 in connection with the developments in Laos, the Vietnamese friends in practice have undertaken measures aimed at the intensification of armed struggle against the Diem regime, while not taking into account direct military support to Ngo Dinh Diem on the part of the United States.[64]

Similar instructions had apparently been given to Moscow's ambassadors in Washington, Beijing, and other capitals.[65]

By August 1962, shortly after the Geneva settlement on Laos, Moscow had acquired enough information on the issue for Anatolii Chistyakov, the head of the Southeast Asia Department at the Soviet Foreign Ministry, and Ambassador Suren Tovmasyan to submit a memorandum to Deputy Foreign Minister Georgii Pushkin. In their memo they admitted that, in general, there were "some objective conditions" for a peaceful settlement of the Vietnam problem: the U.S. agreement on the negotiated solution of the crisis in Laos, the ambivalent positions of the principal U.S. allies Great Britain and France, and the recognition by the Vietnamese friends that it was possible to bargain with imperialists. Their memorandum also revealed Moscow's vision of Indochina after the Geneva conference on Laos:

> A peaceful solution of the South Vietnamese question at the present time is acquiring a particular urgency because the observance of the Geneva agreements on Laos by South Vietnam, Thailand, *as well as by the DRV,* will be dependent, to a considerable degree, on the situation in South Vietnam, and it goes without saying that this would be the consolidation of the achieved successes in the matter of the preservation of peace in Southeast Asia.[66]

The authors then contradicted their promising remarks by referring to information received from Soviet embassies in countries involved in the situation in Indochina. Chistyakov and Tovmasyan wrote that those countries were not prepared to agree on a negotiated settlement of the Vietnam problem. Washington did not want the neutralization of South Vietnam, according to the Soviet embassy in the United States, out of fear that the idea would be supported by a number of Asian countries. London would not venture to quarrel with the United States on this issue. The French would follow suit. Even India would not definitely support neutralization. The Soviet's Communist allies' position was no more encouraging. Hanoi, though not opposing the idea of a conference on Vietnam, believed that conditions for it were not yet ripe and was planning to use this issue mostly as a propaganda tool. The Chinese also paid only lip service to Prince Sihanouk's initiatives on the settlement of the conflict in Vietnam. Therefore the conclusion reached by Chistyakov and Tovmasyan was logical: "The socialist countries should work out a single program of settlement of the South Vietnamese problem in advance. *However, an initiative in raising this issue as well as the issue of the convening of an international conference on South Vietnam should be relegated to the DRV.*"[67]

Their conclusion fully reflected the Soviet tendency toward disengagement evident in its Indochina policy from mid-1961 onward, a tendency based on a pragmatic evaluation of the situation in and around the region. When the principal participants in the conflict opposed negotiations and other countries involved avoided taking firm positions, Moscow also chose to be an onlooker and avoided putting forward initiatives concerning negotiations so as not to quarrel with the Vietnamese or provoke further accusations on the part of the Chinese—apparently important considerations for the Soviets.

Moscow was well informed about the DRV's attitude toward negotiations. Unlike Western observers who had taken at face value both Hanoi's public pronouncements and the secret revelations made by unidentified North Vietnamese diplomats about their country's desire to find a peaceful settlement of the Vietnam problem,[68] the Soviet leaders possessed first-hand information that they received from the highest levels of the DRV leadership. Examples of such information included a letter Ho Chi Minh sent to Moscow on behalf of the Central Committee of the Workers' Party of Vietnam on May 25, 1962, that contained an exposure of North Vietnamese policy toward South Vietnam. Ho wrote that Hanoi followed a two-pronged course, simultaneously intensifying both the political and military struggles with a single purpose: "to force the enemy back, step by step, and to achieve partial successes, to wear out and to eliminate most of the enemy's manpower."[69] Diplomacy was only a part of this strategy, and the military component was predominant: Although the DRV regularly called for negotiations in 1961–1963, Hanoi at the same time sent to the South more than 40,000 people and thousands of tons of ammunition and equipment including 165,000 guns, and it mobilized during that period 73,000 people for the revolutionary armed forces that by 1964 totaled 150,000.[70]

While it was undertaking efforts to intensify the struggle in South Vietnam, Hanoi wanted to avoid U.S. intervention in the conflict and the spread of the war in the region. It was with this concern in mind that the North Vietnamese contemplated diplomatic initiatives such as an international conference on Vietnam, an idea Hanoi raised from time to time to demonstrate to the world that it was not opposed to a negotiated settlement. But diplomacy was subordinated to the war against the Saigon regime. "The friends believe," the Southeast Asia Department of the Soviet Foreign Ministry stated in its memorandum of December 25, 1962, "that the more the war is dragged out, the more the enemy would suffer a defeat and he would be persuaded of the impossibility to win over the patriotic forces. In that case he would agree on a peaceful settlement."[71] Thus, negotiations were to be an outcome of the armed struggle in the South; during the struggle they were purely a tool of propaganda designed to prevent U.S. involvement in Vietnam.

Moscow surmised correctly that this strategy for the South had been worked out by Hanoi under the strong influence of the Chinese allies. In fact, while warning the North Vietnamese leaders against large-scale military operations in South Vietnam, Beijing insisted on protracted guerrilla warfare and promised its support in arms and equipment. For example, in the summer of 1962, China agreed to give the DRV, free of charge, ninety thousand rifles and guns that could equip two hundred thirty infantry battalions. These weapons were to be shipped through the DRV to the guerrillas in the South.[72]

At the same time, the Kremlin with its pessimistic attitude toward developments in Indochina and its decision to give up attempts to influence those developments, expressed hopes that the war in the region could still be averted with the help of the machinery established by the 1954 Geneva conference, which neither of the rivals had ventured to renounce completely. The ICC was at the center of that machinery. Moscow's directives to the Soviet ambassador in the DRV in early 1962 pointed out that the ICC had not yet exhausted its potential and its activities "meet the interests of the preservation and consolidation of peace on the Indochinese peninsula" and could be used to the advantage of the DRV.[73]

The obvious purpose of these Soviet assertions was to conceal Moscow's passivity, indecisiveness, and vacillations about events in Indochina and cover Moscow's retreat in a situation when none of the direct participants in the conflict regarded the Geneva agreements as an obstacle to their plans in Vietnam. The

Soviets were even ready to close their eyes to the fact that the ICC had ceased favor the DRV as a result of India's changing attitude toward Hanoi's policy in South Vietnam in 1962 and its growing suspicion about North Vietnam's support for subversive activities in the South. The Indian delegation more and more often aligned itself with the Canadians, thus leaving the Polish representatives in the minority.

A diplomatic bombshell exploded on June 2, 1962, when the ICC sent the cochairs a special report signed by India and Canada with a dissenting statement by the Polish commissioner. The report accused both the DRV and South Vietnam of violations of "fundamental provisions of the Geneva agreements . . . resulting in ever increasing tension and threat of open hostilities."[74] These violations took the form of the virtual military alliance between the United States and the Saigon regime on the one hand, and Hanoi's increasing support for the struggle against the South Vietnamese government, on the other.

Although the ICC's special report condemned both sides, the reaction of the North Vietnamese authorities was especially negative. They issued denunciations and denials and attacked the ICC report and the commission itself. The brunt of the attack was directed against the Indian chairman of the ICC, G. Parthasarathi.[75] Hanoi's denunciations of the ICC concerned the Soviet leaders, who worried with the Poles that the North Vietnamese wanted to cut off the commission's activities in Vietnam. Moscow also disapproved of Hanoi's accusations against India on the grounds that they would lead to Delhi's further alienation and its closer alignment with the West. Soviet diplomats, together with their Polish colleagues, tried to persuade the North Vietnamese of the advantages of the continuation of the ICC's activity in Vietnam. A report of the USSR embassy in Hanoi shows that the Soviets reiterated to DRV officials the need to maintain cooperation with the ICC, improve relations with the Indian delegation, and smooth over several problems in Hanoi's relations with the commission. Moscow still regarded the ICC as "a containing factor which helps the preservation of peace in Vietnam."[76]

As Moscow tried to convince the North Vietnamese of the advantages of cooperation with the ICC, the Soviet Foreign Ministry was working out plans to provide support to the National Liberation Front of South Vietnam, an organization established by Hanoi to facilitate its activity in the South. The Soviets were evidently attracted by the relative moderation of the NLFSV, which envisioned an independent and neutral South Vietnam governed by a coalition government. The Soviets were also sympathetic to the front's objective of rallying the support of various South Vietnamese social strata and political organizations—implying a political rather than a military struggle—to form an effective opposition to the Diem regime.[77] Moscow was not concerned, however, by the fact that the establishment of the NLFSV did not prevent the development of armed struggle. The front in fact soon became a useful cover for Hanoi's military plans in the South.

Soviet support to the NLFSV was limited mostly to diplomacy. Moscow planned to facilitate the NLFSV's entry into the international arena and its recognition as a representative of the South Vietnamese people.[78] Soviet influence brought the front invitations to take part in various congresses and conferences organized by Soviet-controlled associations and organizations such as the seventh congress of the International Union of Students in Leningrad, the sixth assembly of the World Democratic Youth Federation in Warsaw, and the fifth congress of the International Association of Journalists in Budapest. Some East European countries began to consider permitting NLFSV permanent missions in their capitals.[79]

The Soviet Union also was on the itineraries of NLFSV delegations. On July 5, 1962, a front delegation arrived in the Soviet Union to participate in the World Congress for General Disarmament and Peace. It was received at the Soviet Afro-Asian Solidarity Committee, evidently to find out the NLFSV's positions on controversial issues of war and peace. What the Soviets heard could not have pleased them more; they reported that "the NLFSV delegation occupies the position of complete and unreserved support" of the policy of the Soviet Communist Party and the USSR government on all issues touched on during the conversations. Front representatives reportedly shared Soviet views on complete disarmament, the struggle for peace, and the strength of imperialism; and they fully approved Soviet policy toward South Vietnam.[80] The Soviets detected not the slightest desire on the part of the delegates to express views that differed from Moscow's interpretation of Soviet-Chinese relations, the cult of personality, and other controversial issues. In all their public presentations and private conversations, the NLFSV delegation emphasized the vanguard role of the Soviet Union in the socialist camp and expressed its appreciation for the support of the Soviet people and their government.[81]

When the NLFSV delegation visited Hanoi and Beijing later that year, however, the South Vietnamese Communists hardly mentioned the Soviet struggle for peace.[82] It became clear that the NLFSV visitors to the Soviet Union, under Hanoi's instructions, had deliberately made pronouncements that would please the Kremlin in order to obtain additional support—not only diplomatic support—from Moscow.

North Vietnamese hopes for Soviet support of their struggle in South Vietnam were not realized, at least in the coming year. Events surrounding the Cuban missile crisis in October 1962 discouraged Moscow from any risky moves in the area of foreign policy. The Cuban crisis demonstrated to Soviet leadership how dangerous a conflict between the superpowers armed with nuclear weapons could be. Soviet leaders, who had to rely on questionable allies, decided to avoid their country's involvement in situations in remote areas of the globe in which U.S. national interests, real or imaginary, were at stake.[83]

The Cuban missile crisis had a great impact on the Soviet attitude toward the conflict in Indochina. It accelerated the process, already under way, of the Kremlin's abandonment of an active policy in the region. If Moscow had earlier tried somehow to influence the situation with reminders about the Geneva Accords and the possibility of peaceful negotiations in the form of an international conference, during the period after October 1962 the Soviet Union remained mostly a bystander to the dangerous developments in Vietnam.

Khrushchev, who had been advocating the policy of disengagement from Vietnam, was more than ever prepared to sacrifice the illusory prospects of a Communist victory in Southeast Asia in favor of détente with the West. He did not want to risk another showdown with the United States after the failure of his Cuban adventure. In addition, his political standing within the Soviet leadership was now diminished. Because of the growing dissatisfaction among the Soviet Communist Party's bureaucrats over his domestic policy, any and new ill-considered steps in the international arena could cost Khrushchev dearly.[84] He also suspected the North Vietnamese leaders of duplicity because they refused to take sides in the Sino-Soviet dispute and align themselves with Moscow. All these factors probably contributed to the Soviet unwillingness to meddle in the conflict in Vietnam.

Khrushchev therefore turned a deaf ear to warnings of his Asian experts about the possible negative consequences of Soviet restraint during the Vietnam conflict. For example, the Foreign Ministry's Southeast Asia Department drew the attention of its superiors to the fact that Soviet restraint was "interpreted in the United States as the unwillingness to get embroiled" in the conflict. Such an assessment could give birth to "dangerous illusions on the part of the American military clique whose high level representatives declare boastfully that within a brief period of time they will achieve a complete 'pacification' of South Vietnam and liquidate the guerrilla movement in that country."[85]

Another consequence of Soviet disengagement was Hanoi's accelerated drift toward China and the further erosion of the Soviet position in the DRV. By 1963 China was prepared to make a major commitment to North Vietnam. During a May visit to the DRV, one of the PRC's leaders, Liu Shaoqi, assured Ho Chi Minh, "We are standing by your side, and if war breaks out, you can regard China as your rear."[86] This assertion was coupled by new promises of assistance to the "heroic struggle" of the Vietnamese Communists against the Diem regime.

Encountering Moscow's lack of desire to support its policy toward South Vietnam, Hanoi had to abandon its previous policy of balancing between the two Communist allies. It threw itself into the arms of China. Le Duan, in a speech at the Nguyen Ai Quoc party school in March 1963, commemorating the eightieth anniversary of Karl Marx's death, openly defied fundamental tenets of the Soviet theory of communism and revolutionary struggle. He argued that "the proletariat has no alternative but to use violence to demolish the bourgeois state apparatus and to establish one of its own." Le Duan also questioned the concept of peaceful evolution toward socialism and pointed out that "the working class and Marxist-Leninist parties, while seeking to make revolution by peaceful means, must make active preparations for the seizure of power by violence." He criticized aid supplied by the Soviet Union to bourgeois nationalist regimes like India and Egypt, and he called for the exposure of the Yugoslav revisionists as a requirement "essential to the smooth progress of the people's revolutionary cause in nationalist countries."[87] Le Duan's speech was so much to the liking of Beijing that it was printed in full by the *People's Daily* and broadcast by the New China News Agency.[88]

Later Hanoi joined China in its criticism of the Limited Test Ban Treaty signed by the Soviet Union, the United States, and Great Britain in July 1963. On August 6 and 9, *Nhan Dan,* the WPV newspaper, published editorials in which it supported China's opposition to the treaty and demanded complete and total nuclear disarmament. In September, the Vietnamese Communist theoretical journal *Hoc Tap* denounced the treaty as "the result of a deal struck by the leaders of nuclear power" and said it contradicted "the peace-loving peoples of the world."[89]

Despite Hanoi's apparent adherence to Chinese policies, North Vietnamese leaders had not completely abandoned their hopes for cooperation with the Soviet Union and for obtaining Moscow's support in their struggle for the unification of Vietnam. Perhaps this was one of the reasons why Hanoi, after firmly deciding in favor of armed struggle in the South, did not cease its efforts in searching for a peaceful settlement of the conflict.

Beginning in August 1963, the West began receiving indications about the possibility of some kind of diplomatic accommodation between Hanoi and Saigon. On August 10, Ngo Dinh Nhu, South Vietnamese president Diem's influential brother, confided to two British diplomats, Lord Selkirk and Donald Murray, that he had had regular meetings with representatives from North Vietnam. He described a group of patriotic individuals in Hanoi who were more nationalist than communist and who sought a solution to the problem of Vietnam. Nhu claimed that some from this group had visited him.[90] Soon the news about the Diem government's contacts reached Washington, and William Colby of the CIA detailed them during a discussion that took place at the State Department with the participation of highest officials of the Kennedy administration. Colby said that, in Nhu's contacts with the North, Nhu was acting through French representatives in Saigon.[91]

In fact, the French ambassador to Saigon, Roger Lalouette, was among those who believed that neutralization was the best solution for South Vietnam and that this could be negotiated with the NLFSV and perhaps Hanoi.[92] Another person who shared these views was Mieczyslaw Maneli, the Polish delegate to the ICC in Vietnam. Maneli also encouraged Diem's brother to seek contacts with the North Vietnamese. In early September talks with Nhu, Maneli pretended to be authorized by Pham Van Dong to act as intermediary.[93] Maneli reported his activities to his superiors in Warsaw as well as to the Soviet embassy in Hanoi.[94]

Washington believed that rumors about a possible deal between Hanoi and Saigon were credible and that the Diem government was seriously interested in some form of rapprochement with the North. Of course, unification was not considered an immediate goal of the negotiations; hopes centered on some kind of cease-fire or neutralization.[95] U.S. officials also suspected that Nhu, perhaps with the tacit approval of Diem himself, wanted to acquire room to maneuver vis-à-vis the United States and increase the South's leverage to resist U.S. pressure for political reforms in South Vietnam.[96]

Why was the North Vietnamese leadership interested in exploring prospects of negotiations? Although the idea of negotiations served mainly as a propaganda tool for Hanoi, the Vietnamese Communist leaders had never discarded the possibility that negotiations with Saigon could lead to some kind of accommodation with the southern regime, the eventual establishment of a coalition government in South Vietnam, and U.S. withdrawal from Indochina. North Vietnamese leaders believed that such an opportunity would arise only in a situation of sharp contradictions and clashes between the United States and the Diem regime as well as within the Diem government itself.[97] Because contradictions between Washington and Saigon reached a high point in August and September 1963, and some officials in the Kennedy administration seriously considered the ouster of Diem and his family from power,[98] Hanoi believed that the situation could not have been more propitious for initiating contacts with the Diem regime.

The Soviet attitude toward the North-South exchanges in 1963 is not clear, mainly because of the lack of declassified documentary sources in the Russian archives. But it is not difficult to infer, given Moscow's general disposition toward negotiated settlement and its previous efforts to stimulate North Vietnamese contacts with the Diem regime. The Kremlin had long advocated negotiations between the North and the South that could lead to some kind of under-standing, particularly if this would result in U.S. withdrawal from the region. How feasible was such an outcome in Moscow's eyes? Moscow had been in-formed about the contacts between the North Vietnamese and Ngo Dinh Nhu[99] and might have tacitly approved the Polish diplomat's mediation to facilitate them.[100] In this, the Kremlin followed a pattern that would become its modus operandi after the United States began its direct military involvement in the war in Vietnam: the Soviets acted through their East European allies when they found it inexpedient to intervene openly.

Would the Soviets have played more active role later if initial negotiations be-tween Hanoi and Saigon had encouraged real prospects of peaceful settlement? This is an open question because these prospects never became a reality. Alarmed by the possibility of a Diem-Ho deal and the eventual withdrawal of the United States from South Vietnam as well as dissatisfied with the Saigon regime's intransigence and its growing anti-Americanism, Washington favored a coup d'état against Diem in order to bring to power in South Vietnam more tractable rulers.[101] The coup took place on November 1, 1963. Diem and Nhu were arrested and soon shot; Nhu was knifed several times as well.[102]

The overthrow of Diem had important consequences for the Vietnam situa-tion. Most immediate was that the North Vietnamese leaders opted once and for all for a military solution to the conflict. In December 1963 the ninth plenum of the WPV Central Committee took place in Hanoi, and it placed armed struggle above all other forms of Communist activities in South Vietnam and called for the creation of powerful military units there.[103] At the same forum, the North Vietnamese Communists completed their party's separation from the Kremlin's international line. In his speech at the plenum, Le Duan dismissed the Soviet strategy for the socialist camp as defensive and instead praised Mao Zedong's theory of revolutionary war.[104] Hanoi's switchover to China led to some changes in North Vietnamese leadership. The plenum dismissed from important posts a number of party officials who were known for their pro-Soviet and anti-Chinese sentiments; some were transferred to economic bodies of the govern-ment, others were dismissed on grounds of poor health.[105] Soviet influence in Vietnam fell to its post-1954 nadir.

Soviet diplomats fought on the front lines of Hanoi's change in attitude. Mieczyslaw Maneli observed during two official receptions in Hanoi in those years how Pham Van Dong deliberately ignored the Soviet ambassador, Suren Tovmasyan. Maneli described Tovmasyan as "a caged tiger. He was helpless because he could not 'teach' these goddamned Vietnamese the way his col-leagues in the 1940s and 1950s did in Warsaw, Prague, Budapest, and Sofia. He lost his 'freedom' and 'dignity,' because in Hanoi he was a 'paper tiger.'"[106]

Yet even then the North Vietnamese leaders were not prepared to break with their Soviet ally completely. They still nourished hopes for obtaining support from the USSR, the most powerful of the Communist countries. They also understood the importance of unity in the Communist camp for the success of their struggle for the reunification of Vietnam. Therefore Ho Chi Minh continued to urge a Sino-Soviet dialogue and to send letters to both rivals. His efforts proved futile, however. Mao's reply on December 27, 1963, to Ho's several letters was not encouraging. Although not rejecting outright negotiations with the Soviets, the Chinese leader expressed pessimism that reconciliation would soon be achieved and claimed that it would take more than ten years to achieve an outcome that was "favorable to revolution and to a true solidarity."[107]

Moscow was no more responsive to Hanoi's overtures; in addition, Khrushchev was evidently irritated by the decisions of the ninth plenum of the Workers' Party of Vietnam. He openly warned the North Vietnamese leaders who visited Moscow in January 1964 about the consequences of WPV adherence to Chinese precepts that did not "meet the interests of the unity and cohesion between the WPV and the CPSU, the interests of the socialist camp and the world communist movement as a whole."[108] Thus Soviet-Vietnamese relations remained frozen. Only after the commencement of the hot war in Vietnam's Tonkin Gulf six months later did the North Vietnamese–Soviet ice begin to melt in the name of proletarian solidarity.

Conclusion

It is easier to make war than to make peace.

Georges Clemenceau
July 20, 1919

The two deaths in November 1963 had a significant impact on the development of the conflict in Vietnam. The overthrow of Ngo Dinh Diem on November 1, 1963, contrary to expectations of U.S. policymakers, did not lead to greater stability in South Vietnam. Quite the opposite occurred, for the coup d'état in Saigon was soon followed by another, without improvement in the prospects for prevailing over the internal insurgency. As a result, a few months later, Secretary of Defense Robert McNamara had to report to President Johnson that "conditions in South Vietnam had unquestionably worsened since the coup" against Diem. The South Vietnamese regime remained unable to win political backing or legitimacy; furthermore, it could not even rely on its own army.[1]

The desperate situation in South Vietnam alarmed Vice President Lyndon B. Johnson, who became president after John F. Kennedy's assassination in Dallas on November 22, 1963. Johnson, who had from the outset voiced strong doubts about the necessity of overthrowing the Diem regime, was determined to prevent the fall of South Vietnam to Communists. He pursued the policy of his predecessor in Vietnam but with more vigor and insistence.[2] Soon after he became president, he said in strongly personal terms: "I am not going to lose Vietnam. I am not going to be the President who saw Southeast Asia go the way China went."[3] These words foretold increased U.S. involvement in the Vietnam conflict.

Already U.S. involvement was not limited to South Vietnam and the support and encouragement of the Saigon regime. The U.S. administration carried out various operations against the DRV in order to convince the Communist leadership of the futility of its efforts to conquer the South and to retaliate for the

North's support of the Vietcong. Covert U.S. operations within the so-called OPLAN 34A included the insertion of airborne commandos into the North, sabotage, diversionary operations, and the collection of intelligence.[4] Land operations were supplemented with patrols along the coast of Vietnam, under the code name DeSoto, conducted to gather information on North Vietnamese coastal defenses.

During 1964, however, it became apparent to Washington that covert operations against North Vietnam would not bring the desired results. McNamara, who returned from a trip to South Vietnam in March of that year, described OPLAN 34A as "a program so limited that it is unlikely to have any significant effect." Other members of the U.S. administration held similar views.[5] Policymakers in Washington began to consider planning major military actions against the DRV, which included the bombing of North Vietnamese territory. Referring to his March 1964 visit to Saigon, McNamara admitted, "While I did not recommend increased American military involvement, I did agree to begin planning for U.S. air attacks in the North." He sent such options to President Johnson.[6]

In early 1964, the situation in Indochina had reached a danger point and was on the verge of breaking out into open hostilities between the opposing parties. The determination of the North Vietnamese leadership to pursue unification of Vietnam by any means, including the overthrow of the Saigon regime—expressed in the decisions of the ninth plenum of the Workers' Party of Vietnam in December 1963—made the commencement of war a question of months, if not days. The incidents in the Gulf of Tonkin during the first days of August 1964 that caused retaliatory U.S. strikes against North Vietnam were a prologue to open U.S. intervention in the conflict.[7] A resolution adopted by the U.S. Congress on August 7, which granted Johnson broad powers to conduct combat operations in the region, removed the last obstacles on the way to war. In February 1965, Johnson gave the order to begin the bombing campaign against the DRV, and in March the first U.S. military contingents landed in South Vietnam. The Vietnam War had begun.

The Soviet Union remained for the most part a passive observer. Even the Tonkin Gulf incident stirred only a weak reaction from the Soviet leaders, who confined themselves to press comments about U.S. "aggressive actions." Nikita Khrushchev sent President Johnson a formal letter with warnings about the danger of war in Indochina.[8] It appears that Moscow had decided that whatever was happening in Vietnam was beyond its influence, a position that reflected the Soviet leadership's deep disillusionment with its policy toward the conflict in Indochina.

This disillusionment went back to the 1954 Geneva agreement, which the Soviets regarded as a guarantee against war in Southeast Asia for a more or less prolonged period of time. While recognizing the weaknesses of these agreements, Soviet leaders believed that adhering to them could help transform the agreements into an important component of regional peace. For example, prospects for peace would be enhanced if the United States complied with the decisions of the Geneva conference and refrained from violating them, if the French maintained a presence in the region, and if Vietnam were divided into two parts because the Soviets believed that had been a proved solution to disputes between the two opposing camps during the Cold War.

Soviet efforts to bring peace to Southeast Asia were dictated not so much by a peaceful disposition on the part of the Soviet leaders but by their desire to eliminate this thorny issue from Moscow's relations with the West. Although not averse to a Communist victory in the region, the Kremlin ascribed to Indochina no geostrategic importance and did not want the crisis there to be an impediment to the process of détente with the United States and its allies. This lack of interest in Indochina also explains why, after the Geneva conference, Soviet leaders were eager to delegate the primary responsibility for the fledgling Communist state in North Vietnam to their Chinese allies, thus making the Chinese their agents in Asia.

However, the edifice created with Soviet help in Geneva began crumbling almost from the outset. The United States did in fact avoid open violation of the Geneva Accords, at least during the Eisenhower administration, but it supported and encouraged actions of the Ngo Dinh Diem regime in South Vietnam that were aimed at disrupting the implementation of the accords. Claiming that his government did not sign the Geneva agreements, Ngo Dinh Diem refused to hold consultations with Hanoi on an all-Vietnamese election and proclaimed an independent state in the South of the country with himself as its president. Although these events were not of great concern to Soviet policymakers, who seemed to be more preoccupied with strengthening the DRV as a sovereign and independent state than with preparing conditions for reunification, the consequences of Diem's violations of the Geneva Accords and the tacit approval of the United States were important.

Unlike their Soviet comrades, Hanoi's leaders were determined to achieve the unification of Vietnam according to the provisions of the agreements reached in Geneva. Although they had yielded to the pressure of their powerful allies in Moscow and Beijing in favor of the division of the country, the North Vietnamese Communists never ceased to regard this division as temporary and never abandoned their plans to unify the country under their authority. After the Geneva conference they tried to achieve this objective by peaceful means, through negotiations with Saigon and general elections. As it became more and more obvious to them that Ngo Dinh Diem with the support of his U.S. advisers was not inclined to come to terms with Hanoi on the issue of reunification, the DRV leaders became increasingly militant and began to regard the support of the insurgency in the South by human and material means as the only way to overthrow the Saigon regime and attain a unified Vietnam.

In its quest for peace, Moscow could not limit its efforts to discouraging the North Vietnamese from their military plans in the South; Soviet leaders also had to appeal to the other countries involved in the Geneva settlement in order to prevent conflict in Southeast Asia. Yet, at the end of the 1950s, it seemed that no other Geneva participant was prepared to undertake measures aimed at reviving the 1954 accords on Indochina. The U.S. objective of transforming South Vietnam into a bastion of anticommunism in the region had led to greater political and, later, military involvement of Washington on the side of Saigon. Even a neutral South Vietnam was anathema to U.S. policymakers who regarded neutrality as only a prelude to the inevitable eventual submission of the country to the Communists.

Great Britain, as a cochair of the Geneva conference along with the Soviet Union, did not want to quarrel with its U.S. ally over an issue of minor importance compared with Western solidarity and cooperation. Whenever the issue of Vietnam arose during the course of international negotiations, London aligned itself with the United States, accusing the Communists of being the principal violators of the settlement or resorting to purely formal declarations in support of the Geneva agreements. France was paralyzed by its defeat in the first Indochina war and its eventual loss of its influence in the region. No one had expected French power to disintegrate so rapidly in its former Indochinese colonies, particularly Vietnam. Ngo Dinh Diem openly aligned his regime with the Americans who had replaced the French as the principal advisers in all spheres of life in the South. As a result, France's voice was hardly audible in Vietnamese politics, at least until the early 1960s when France's president, Charles deGaulle, put forward his initiatives on the neutralization of Indochina.

But the most severe blow to Soviet policy in Indochina was struck by Moscow's Chinese allies. The Sino-Soviet dispute over the tenets of Marxism-Leninism and the place of the two countries in the world communist movement had seriously affected the Kremlin's actions in the conflict in Vietnam. By the early 1960s, Soviet leaders had to take into account the fact that they now faced in Asia not an ally to whom it was possible to delegate responsibility for local affairs but a rival that was waiting for any blunder by Moscow that it might exploit to reap a profit for itself. Moreover, this rival, thanks to the Soviets' own strategy of the division of responsibility, enjoyed great influence over decision making in Hanoi and used it contrary to the direction advocated by Moscow.

Confronted with so many adverse factors in the early 1960s, Moscow evidently decided in favor of disengagement from Indochina, an inclination already apparent during the Geneva conference on Laos in 1961–1962 that was one of the USSR's last active attempts to avert war in the region. Soviet detachment contributed to the subsequent failure of the agreements on Laos and, ultimately, to the outbreak of war in Vietnam. Had Moscow in fact used all measures at its disposal to help prevent a regional conflict from growing into a serious international crisis? If not, what prevented the Soviets from doing so?

It seems incontestable now, at the beginning of the twenty-first century, that Moscow was not interested in the war in Indochina, and throughout the period after the 1954 Geneva conference it demonstrated its desire to find a solution of the Vietnamese conflict. However, the very factor that made this conflict unattractive in the eyes of the Soviet leaders—the position of Indochina outside of the Kremlin's geostrategic interests—preordained the failure of Soviet policy aimed at settlement of the conflict. Indochina and Vietnam were on the periphery of the decision-making process in Moscow. The Soviet leadership never paid much attention to this issue, placing ahead of it problems relating to European affairs and détente with the United States. Never during the 1950s and early 1960s—that is, before the Vietnam War—in their negotiations with Western leaders had the highest officials of the Soviet Union discussed the issue of Vietnam with a sufficient degree of substance, as they did later during, for example, the Kosygin-Wilson talks in February 1967 and the Kosygin-Johnson talks at Glassboro in June of that same year. In the course of his visit to the United States in September–October 1959, Nikita Khrushchev did not mention the conflict in Vietnam at all although he paid much attention to such problems as Berlin, U.S. policy toward China, disarmament, and the maintenance of various kinds of cooperation with the United States. This negligence indicates that the Soviet leaders did not want to sacrifice their immediate concerns and preoccupations for possible advantages in a remote part of the globe. As a result, Moscow never seriously tried to influence the opinion of U.S. and other Western leaders on Vietnam through high-level diplomacy.

That some form of understanding with the United States on this issue could have been reached during the course of diplomatic talks by the leaders of the two countries was demonstrated during the Vienna summit between Kennedy and Khrushchev. In the Austrian capital both the Soviet premier and the U.S. president displayed determination to settle the conflict in Laos and felt an urgency to reach agreements to put an end to the Laotian civil war and guarantee Laos's neutrality and sovereignty. The decisions made in Vienna stimulated the negotiation in Geneva and the search for a solution to the Laotian question. The powers unfortunately did not follow the Laotian example in the case of Vietnam, and that deficiency became much of the reason for the failure of the Laotian settlement. Laos could not be solved without a corresponding solution of the Vietnam problem.

Undoubtedly, the personality of the Soviet leader, Nikita S. Khrushchev, had an impact on Moscow's policy toward the conflict in Vietnam. Flamboyant and impulsive, he lacked a consistent approach toward the outside world and often could not reconcile his contradictory attitudes about the processes in Indochina. Although he criticized Stalin for his arrogant attitude toward the Vietnamese Communists and their leader, Ho Chi Minh, Khrushchev essentially continued his predecessor's policy. He had never attached due importance to the conflict in Indochina, and he relegated the development of Soviet–North Vietnamese relations to a low place on his foreign policy agenda. During his eleven-year tenure as the first secretary of the CPSU Central Committee and his slightly shorter tenure as Soviet prime minister, he never found time to visit the DRV for a first-hand impression of the country and its leadership.

As the Sino-Soviet dispute sharpened, Khrushchev increasingly viewed the outside world through the lens of his quarrel with Mao Zedong. A follower of the traditions of the Bolsheviks, he categorized other Communist leaders according to their readiness to align with either Moscow or Beijing, and the ambiguous and ambivalent position of the North Vietnamese Communists in the Sino-Soviet dispute accordingly led to Khrushchev's growing suspicion about their real intentions. He regarded with disdain Ho Chi Minh's efforts to find a compromise and openly derided them. Khrushchev had a "litmus test of loyalty" for North Vietnam as well as for other countries: "If the DRV could not be counted as an ally against China, then the relationship should be downgraded."[9]

Khrushchev's disappointment with the North Vietnamese failure to comply with the Geneva agreements on Laos, which Moscow was obliged to guarantee, and Hanoi's continuing support of the insurgency in the South contributed to his unwillingness to become enmeshed in Indochina. In addition, the Cuban missile crisis had cooled his enthusiasm for testing the United States in remote areas of the world. Like an ostrich, he might have decided to eliminate the Vietnamese question from the Soviet list of priorities simply by ignoring it. The result was that, with the beginning of the U.S. bombing of the DRV and the introduction of U.S. troops in the South, the Vietnam problem that confronted Khrushchev's successors was already not a local conflict; it was an international crisis and war.

The new Soviet leadership that came to power after the October 1964 party coup d'état against Khrushchev had to revise its policy toward the conflict in Indochina because the situation there was rapidly moving toward armed conflict. Two objectives stood before Moscow: improve relations with the North Vietnamese, thus increasing Soviet credibility and influence in that country; and resume a dialogue with Washington and other Western capitals, thus facilitating a solution of the Vietnam problem. Soviet premier Alexei Kosygin worked on this twofold task and went to Hanoi in February 1965. But it was too late. While Kosygin was in the DRV, President Johnson gave orders to retaliate for the Vietcong assault against the U.S. base at Pleiku and start bombing the territory of the DRV. Years later Kosygin regretted that Washington had not consulted Moscow before this fateful decision.[10]

In spite of the shift in Moscow's attitude toward Vietnam after October 1964, its basic tenet remained as it had been under Khrushchev: eliminate the Vietnam problem from the Soviet foreign policy agenda so it is not an impediment to the solution of other issues of primary importance to the Kremlin—Soviet-U.S. relations and détente with the West.[11] It is in this light that one should regard all Soviet efforts with respect to the Vietnam War, which were the subject of the author's first book on the Soviet Union and the conflict in Indochina.

Bibliography

Primary Sources

Manuscript Collections

Great Britain
General Records of the Foreign Office. General Correspondence.
Public Record Office. Kew, England.

Russia
Arkhiv vneshnei politiki Rossiiskoi Federatsii (Archive of Foreign Pol-
icy of the Russian Federation). Moscow, Russia.
Fond 06, Secretariat of Vyacheslav M. Molotov.
Fond 022, Secretariat of Andrei A. Gromyko.
Fond 026, Secretariat of Vasilii V. Kuznetsov.
Fond 079, *Referentura* on Vietnam.
Fond 0100, *Referentura* on China.
Fond 0445, Geneva Conference of the Ministers of Foreign Affairs of
the USSR, PRC, USA, Great Britain, and France on Korea and In-
dochina.
Fond 0570, *Referentura* on Laos.
Rossiiskii Gosudarstvennyi Arkhiv Noveishei Istorii (Russian State
Archive of Contemporary History). Moscow, Russia.
Fond 5, Central Committee of the Communist Party of the Soviet
Union.
Rossiiskii Gosudarstvennyi Arkhiv Sotsial'no-Politicheskoi Istorii
(Russian State Archive of Social Political History). Moscow,
Russia.
Fond 45, Archive of Iossif Stalin.

United States

    Library of Congress, Manuscript Division. Washington, D.C.

       Papers of W. Averell Harriman.

       Papers of Souvanna Phouma.

    Lyndon B. Johnson Library. Austin, Texas.

       Papers of Lyndon B. Johnson, President, 1963–1969. Vice Presidential Security File.

       Papers of William P. Bundy.

    National Archives and Records Administration. Washington, D.C.

       Record Group 59.

Published Collections of Documents

France

L'Année politique. 1954. Revue chronologique des principaux faits politiques, diplomatiques, économiques et sociaux de la France et de l'Union française du 1er Janvier 1954 au 1er Janvier 1955. Paris: Presses universitaires de France, 1955.

Great Britain

Documents relating to British Involvement in the Indo-China Conflict, 1945–1965. Cmnd 2834. London: Her Majesty's Stationery Office, 1965.

Vietnam and the Geneva Agreements. Documents concerning the Discussions between Representatives of Her Majesty's Government and the Government of the Union of Soviet Socialist Republics Held in London in April and May 1956. Cmnd 9763. London: Her Majesty's Stationery Office, 1956.

Russia

Federal'naia Arkhivnaia Sluzhba Rossii. *Soveshchaniia Kominforma, 1947, 1948, 1949: Dokumenty i materialy* (Federal Archival Service of Russia. The conferences of the Cominform, 1947, 1948, 1949: Documents and materials). Moscow: ROSSPEN, 1998.

Ministerstvo inostrannykh del SSSR. *Sovetskii Soyuz–V'etnam: 30 let otnoshenii, 1950–1980. Dokumenty i materialy* (USSR Ministry of Foreign Affairs. The Soviet Union–Vietnam: Thirty years of relations, 1950–1980. Documents and materials). Moscow: Politizdat, 1982.

Partiia trudiashchikhsia V'etnama. *III syezd* (Workers' Party of Vietnam. The third congress). Moscow: Gospolitizdat, 1961.

Sovietskii Soyuz i vengerskii krisis 1956 goda: Dokumenty (The Soviet Union and the Hungarian 1956 crisis: Documents). Moscow: ROSSPEN, 1998.

United States

U.S. Department of State. *Foreign Relations of the United States, 1952–1954: Indochina.* Vol. 13. Washington, D.C.: U.S. Government Printing Office, 1982.

———. *Foreign Relations of the United States, 1952–1954: The Geneva Conference.* Vol. 16. Washington, D.C.: U.S. Government Printing Office, 1981.

———. *Foreign Relations of the United States, 1958–1960: Eastern Europe Region; Soviet Union; Cyprus.* Vol. 10. Washington, D.C.: U.S. Government Printing Office, 1993.

———. *Foreign Relations of the United States, 1958–1960: China.* Vol. 19. Washington, D.C.: U.S. Government Printing Office, 1996.

———. *Foreign Relations of the United States, 1961–1963: Vietnam, 1961.* Vol. 1. Washington, D.C.: U.S. Government Printing Office, 1988.

———. *Foreign Relations of the United States, 1961–1963: Vietnam, August-December 1963.* Vol. 4. Washington, D.C.: U.S. Government Printing Office, 1991.

———. *Foreign Relations of the United States, 1961–1963: Soviet Union.* Vol. 5. Washington, D.C.: U.S. Government Printing Office, 1998.

———. *Foreign Relations of the United States, 1961–1963: Kennedy-Khrushchev Exchanges.* Vol. 6. Washington, D.C.: U.S. Government Printing Office, 1996.

———. *Foreign Relations of the United States, 1961–1963: Laos Crisis.* Vol. 24. Washington, D.C.: U.S. Government Printing Office, 1994.

Secondary Sources and Published Memoirs

Anderson, David L. *Trapped by Success: The Eisenhower Administration and Vietnam, 1953–1961.* New York: Columbia University Press, 1991.

———, ed. *Shadow on the White House: Presidents and the Vietnam War, 1945–1975.* Lawrence: University Press of Kansas, 1993.

Ang, Cheng Guan. *Vietnamese Communists' Relations with China and the Second Indochina Conflict, 1956–1962.* Jefferson, N.C.: McFarland, 1997.

Arnold, James R. *The First Domino: Eisenhower, the Military, and America's Intervention in Vietnam.* New York: Morrow, 1991.

Bator, Victor. *Vietnam: A Diplomatic Tragedy: The Origins of the United States Involvement.* Dobbs Ferry, N.Y.: Oceana Publications, 1965.

Blackstock, Paul W. *The Strategy of Subversion: Manipulating the Politics of Other Nations.* Chicago: Quadrangle Books, 1964.

Boyevoi avangard v'etnamskogo naroda. Istoriia Kommunisticheskoi partii V'etnama (Militant vanguard of the Vietnamese people: History of the Communist Party of Vietnam). Translated from the Vietnamese. Moscow: Politizdat, 1981.

Brandt, Conrad. *Stalin's Failure in China, 1924–1927.* Cambridge: Harvard University Press, 1958.

Cable, James. *The Geneva Conference of 1954 on Indochina.* London: Macmillan, 1986.

Chen Jian. "China and the Vietnam Wars." In *The Vietnam War,* edited by Peter Lowe. London: Macmillan, 1998.

——— and Yang Kuisong. "Chinese Politics and the Collapse of the Sino-Soviet Alliance." In *Brothers in Arms: The Rise and Fall of the Sino-Soviet Alliance, 1945–1963,* edited by Odd Arne Westad, 246–294. Stanford: Stanford University Press, 1998.

Combs, Arthur. "The Path Not Taken: The British Alternative to U.S. Policy in Vietnam, 1954–1956." *Diplomatic History* 1 (Winter 1995): 33–57.

Conboy, Kenneth, and Dale Andradé. *Spies and Commandos: How America Lost the Secret War in North Vietnam.* Lawrence: University Press of Kansas, 2000.

Copper, John F., and Daniel S. Papp, eds. *Communist Nations' Military Assistance.* Boulder, Colo.: Westview, 1983.

Devillers, Philippe, and Jean Lacouture. *End of a War: Indochina, 1954.* Translated by Alexander Lieven and Adam Roberts. New York: Praeger, 1969.

Divil'kovskii, S., and I. Ognetov. *Put' k pobede: Ocherk bor'by za natsional'nuiu nezavisimost', edinstvo, mir i sotsializm vo V'etname (1945–1976)* (The path to victory: An essay on the struggle for national independence, unity, peace, and socialism in Vietnam [1945–1976]). Moscow: Politizdat, 1978.

Dobrynin, Anatoly F. *In Confidence: Moscow's Ambassador to America's Six Cold War Presidents, 1962–1986.* New York: Times Books, 1995.

Dommen, Arthur J. *Conflict in Laos: The Politics of Neutralization.* New York: Praeger, 1965.

Eden, Anthony. *Full Circle: The Memoirs of Anthony Eden.* Boston: Houghton Mifflin, 1960.

Fall, Bernard B. *Viet-Nam Witness, 1953–66.* New York: Praeger, 1966.

———. *The Two Viet-Nams: A Political and Military Analysis.* 2d rev. ed. New York: Praeger, 1967.

———. *Anatomy of a Crisis: The Laotian Crisis of 1960–1961.* Garden City, N.Y.: Doubleday, 1969.

Fejtö, François. *Chine-URSS-La fin d'une hégémonie: Les Origines du grand schisme communiste, 1950–1957.* Paris: Plon, 1964.

Fursenko, Aleksandr, and Timothy Naftali. *One Hell of a Gamble: Khrushchev, Castro, and Kennedy, 1958–1964.* New York: Norton, 1997.

Gaddis, John Lewis. *We Now Know. Rethinking Cold War History.* Oxford: Clarendon Press, 1997.

Gardner, Lloyd C. *Approaching Vietnam: From World War II through Dienbienphu, 1941–1954.* New York: Norton, 1988.

———. *Pay Any Price: Lyndon Johnson and the Wars for Vietnam.* Chicago: Ivan Dee, 1995.

Ghosh, Partha S. *Sino-Soviet Relations: U.S. Perceptions and Policy Responses, 1949–1959.* New Delhi: Uppal Publishing House, 1981.

He Di. "The Most Respected Enemy: Mao Zedong's Perception of the United States." In *Toward a History of Chinese Communist Foreign Relations, 1920s–1960s: Personalities and Interpretive Approaches,* edited by Michael H. Hunt and Niu Jun, 27–65. Washington, D.C.: Woodrow Wilson International Center for Scholars Asia Program, 1995.

Herring, George. *America's Longest War: The United States and Vietnam, 1950–1975.* 3rd ed. New York: McGraw-Hill, 1996.

Hess, Gary R. "Commitment in the Age of Counterinsurgency: Kennedy's Vietnam Options and Decisions, 1961–1963." In *Shadow on the White House: Presidents and the Vietnam War, 1945–1975,* edited by David L Anderson, 63–86. Lawrence: University Press of Kansas, 1993.

Honey, P. J. *Communism in North Vietnam: Its Role in the Sino-Soviet Conflict.* Westport, Conn.: Greenwood Press, 1973.

"'Ia veriu v velichie starshego brata.' Besedy N. S. Khrushcheva s Kho Shi Minom" ("'I believe in the greatness of the elder brother.' Conversations of N. S. Khrushchev with Ho Chi Minh"). *Istochnik* 2 (1998): 76–91.

Isayev, M. P., and A. S. Chernyshev. *Istoriia sovietsko-v'etnamskikh ot-noshenii, 1917–1985* (The history of Soviet-Vietnamese relations). Moscow: Mezhdunarodnye otnosheniia, 1986.

Joyaux, François. *La Chine et le règlement du premier conflit d'Indochine (Genève 1954)*. Paris: Publications de la Sorbonne, 1979.

Kanet, Roger, ed. *The Soviet Union and the Developing Nations*. Baltimore: Johns Hopkins University Press, 1974.

Kapitsa, M. S. *Na raznykh parallelyakh. Zapiski diplomata* (On various parallels: The memoirs of a diplomat). Moscow: Kniga i bizness, 1996.

Khrushchev, Nikita S. *Otchetnyi doklad Tsentral'nogo Komiteta Kommunis-ticheskoi Partii Sovetskogo Soyuza XX syezdu KPSS* (Report of the Central Committee of the Communist Party of the Soviet Union to the twentieth congress of the CPSU). Moscow: Gospolitizdat, 1956.

———. *Vremia. Liudi. Vlast'. Vospominaniia v 4-kh knigakh* (Time. People. Power. Memoirs in four books). Moscow: Moscow News, 1999.

Kolko, Gabriel. *Anatomy of a War: Vietnam, the United States, and the Modern Historical Experience*. New York: Pantheon Books, 1985.

Lachs, Manfred. *Zhenevskiie soglasheniia 1954 g. ob Indokitaie* (The Geneva agreements of 1954 on Indochina). Moscow: Inostrannaia literatura, 1956.

Lacouture, Jean. *Pierre Mendes France*. Paris: Seuil, 1981.

Lall, Arthur. *How Communist China Negotiates*. New York: Columbia University Press, 1968.

Ledovskii, A. M. *SSSR i Stalin v sud'bakh Kitaia: Dokumenty i svidetel'stva uchastnika sobytii, 1937–1952* (The USSR and Stalin in the fortunes of China: Documents and evidence of a participant of events, 1937–1952). Moscow: Pamiatniki istoricheskoi mysli, 1999.

Li Xiaobing, Chen Jian, and David L. Wilson. "Mao Zedong's Handling of the Taiwan Straits Crisis of 1958: Chinese Recollections and Documents." *Cold War International History Project Bulletin* 6–7 (Winter 1995/1996): 208–227.

Logevall, Fredrik. *Choosing War: The Lost Chance for Peace and the Escalation of War in Vietnam*. Berkeley: University of California Press, 1999.

Maneli, Mieczyslaw. *War of the Vanquished*. New York: Harper and Row, 1971.

Mayers, David. *The Ambassadors and America's Soviet Policy*. New York: Oxford University Press, 1995.

McLane, Charles B. *Soviet Strategies in Southeast Asia: An Exploration of*

Eastern Policy under Lenin and Stalin. Princeton: Princeton University Press, 1966.

McNamara, Robert S. *In Retrospect: The Tragedy and Lessons of Vietnam.* Written with Brian VanDeMark. New York: Times Books, 1995.

Menon, K. P. S. *The Flying Troika: Extracts from a Diary by K. P. S. Menon, India's Ambassador to Russia, 1952–61.* London: Oxford University Press, 1963.

Mkhitarian, S. A., and T. T. Mkhitarian. *V'etnamskaiia revolutsiia: voprosy teorii i praktiki* (The Vietnamese revolution: Questions of theory and practice). Moscow: Nauka, 1986.

Moïse, Edwin E. *Tonkin Gulf and the Escalation of the Vietnam War.* Chapel Hill: University of North Carolina Press, 1996.

Neese, Harvey, and John O'Donnell. *Prelude to Tragedy: Vietnam, 1960–1965.* Annapolis, Md.: Naval Institute Press, 2001.

Newman, John. *JFK and Vietnam: Deception, Intrigue, and the Struggle for Power.* New York: Warner Books, 1992.

Niu Jun. "The Origins of the Sino-Soviet Alliance." In *Brothers in Arms: The Rise and Fall of the Sino-Soviet Alliance, 1945–1963,* edited by Odd Arne Westad, 47–89. Stanford: Stanford University Press, 1998.

"Peregovory N. S. Khrushcheva c Mao Tsedunom, 31 iulia–3 avgusta 1958 g. i 2 oktiabria 1959 g." ("Negotiations of N. S. Khrushchev with Mao Zedong, 31 July–3 August, 1958, and 2 October 1959"). *Novaiia i noveishaia istoriia* 1 (2001): 100–128; 2 (2001): 94–106.

Pike, Douglas. *Vietnam and the Soviet Union: Anatomy of an Alliance.* Boulder, Colo.: Westview, 1987.

Porter, Bruce D. *The USSR in Third World Conflicts: Soviet Arms and Diplomacy in Local Wars, 1945–1980.* Cambridge: Cambridge University Press, 1984.

Radvanyi, Janos. *Delusion and Reality: Gambits, Hoaxes, and Diplomatic One-Upmanship in Vietnam.* South Bend, Ind.: Gateway Editions, 1978.

Randle, Robert F. *Geneva 1954: The Settlement of the Indochinese War.* Princeton: Princeton University Press, 1969.

Rust, William J. *Kennedy in Vietnam.* New York: Scribner's, 1985.

SarDesai, D. R. *Indian Foreign Policy in Cambodia, Laos and Vietnam, 1947–1964.* Berkeley: University of California Press, 1968.

Schlesinger, Arthur M., Jr. *A Thousand Days: John F. Kennedy in the White House.* Boston: Houghton Mifflin, 1965.

Smith, R. B. *An International History of the Vietnam War.* Vol. 1, *Revolution versus Containment, 1955–1961.* New York: St. Martin's Press, 1983.

Snyder, Glenn H., and Paul Diesing. *Conflict among Nations: Bargaining,*

Decision Making, and System Structure in International Crises. Princeton: Princeton University Press, 1977.

Thee, Marek. *Notes of a Witness: Laos and the Second Indochinese War.* New York: Vintage Books, 1973.

Toynbee, Arnold. *Experiences.* New York: Oxford University Press, 1969.

Tréglodé, Benoît de. "Premiers contacts entre le Viet Nam et L'Union Sovietiqie (1947–1948): Nouveaux documents des archives russes." *Approches Asie* 16 (1999): 125–135.

———. "Les relations entre le Viet-Minh, Moscou et Pékin à travers les documents (1950–1954)." *Revue historique des armées* 4 (2000): 55–62.

Troyanovsky, Oleg A. *Cherez gody i rasstoianiia: Istoriia odnoi semyi* (Across years and distances: The history of one family). Moscow: Vagrius, 1997.

Truong Nhu Thang. *A Vietcong Memoir.* Written with David Chanoff and Doan Van Toai. New York: Vintage Books, 1985.

VanDeMark, Brian. "A Way of Thinking. The Kennedy Administration's Initial Assumptions about Vietnam and Their Consequences." In *Vietnam: The Early Decisions,* edited by Lloyd C. Gardner and Ted Gittinger, 24–36. Austin: University of Texas Press, 1997.

Warner, Roger. *Shooting at the Moon: The Story of America's Clandestine War in Laos.* South Royalton, Vt.: Steerforth Press, 1996.

Zhai Qiang. *China and the Vietnam Wars, 1950–1975.* Chapel Hill: University of North Carolina Press, 2000.

Zhang Shuguang. "Sino-Soviet Economic Cooperation." In *Brothers in Arms: The Rise and Fall of the Sino-Soviet Alliance, 1945–1963,* edited by Odd Arne Westad, 189–225. Stanford: Stanford University Press, 1998.

——— and Chen Jian. "The Emerging Disputes between Beijing and Moscow: Ten Newly Available Chinese Documents, 1956–1958." *Cold War International History Project Bulletin* 6–7 (Winter 1995/1996): 148–163.

——— and Chen Jian, eds. *Chinese Communist Foreign Policy and the Cold War in Asia: New Documentary Evidence, 1944–1950.* Chicago: Imprint Publications, 1996.

Zhang Xiaoming. "Communist Powers Divided. China, the Soviet Union, and the Vietnam War." In *International Perspectives on Vietnam,* edited by Lloyd C. Gardner and Ted Gittinger, 77–97. College Station: Texas A&M University Press, 2000.

Zhukov, Yu., I. Plyshevskii, and G. Rassadin. *Tri mesyatsa v Zheneve* (Three months in Geneva). Moscow: Pravda, 1954.

Notes

Preface

1. Arnold Toynbee, *Experiences* (New York: Oxford University Press, 1969), 89.

2. Ilya V. Gaiduk, *The Soviet Union and the Vietnam War* (Chicago: Ivan R. Dee, 1996).

3. Some reviewers went as far as discrediting the author's conception, pointing to the fact that most of documents the author used for this book were reclassified and therefore impossible to verify. They accused the author of "repetition of past Soviet interpretations of the conflict" and even blamed him for a wide use of documents from U.S. archives. Instead they themselves put forward the outdated conception of the Soviet Union as the principal villain in international relations, responsible for all crises and conflicts. See Richard C. Thornton's review in *American Historical Review* (October 1997): 1194–1195.

4. R. B. Smith, *An International History of the Vietnam War,* 3 vols. (New York: St. Martin's Press, 1983–1991).

5. Peter Lowe, ed., *The Vietnam War* (London: Macmillan, 1998).

6. Lloyd C. Gardner and Ted Gittinger, eds., *International Perspectives on Vietnam* (College Station: Texas A&M University Press, 2000).

7. Zhai Qiang, *China and the Vietnam Wars, 1950–1975* (Chapel Hill: University of North Carolina Press, 2000).

8. Among other works I would like to mention a very substantial contribution to the study of the Vietnam War made by Fredrik Logevall. His book *Choosing War: the Lost Chance for Peace and the Escalation of War in Vietnam* (Berkeley: University of California Press, 1999) presents the best example of an approach toward the conflict in Indochina as an international crisis.

9. See, among others, Anatoly Dobrynin, *In Confidence: Moscow's Ambassador to America's Six Cold War Presidents (1962–1986)* (New York: Times Books, 1995); Mikhail S. Kapitsa, *Na raznykh parallelyakh: Zapiski diplomata* (On various parallels: The memoirs of a diplomat) (Moscow: Kniga i Biznes, 1996); Andrei M. Ledovskii, *SSSR i Stalin v sud'bakh Kitaia: Dokumenty i svidetelstva uchastnika sobytii, 1937–1952* (The USSR and Stalin in the fortunes of China: Documents and evidence by a participant of events) (Moscow: Pamiatniki istoricheskoi mysli, 1999); Oleg A. Troyanovsky, *Cherez gody i rasstoianiya: Istoriia odnoi sem'i* (Across years and distances: The history of a family) (Moscow: Vagrius, 1997). See also the complete edition of Nikita Khrushchev's memoirs: Nikita S. Khrushchev, *Vremia, Liudi, Vlast'. (Vospominaniia v*

4-kh knigakh) (Time. People. Power. Memoirs in four volumes) (Moscow: Moscow News, 1999).

10. For example, R. B. Smith in his *An International History of the Vietnam War;* see also William Duiker, *U.S. Containment Policy and the Conflict in Indochina* (Stanford: Stanford University Press, 1994); George Herring, *America's Longest War: The United States and Vietnam, 1950–1975,* 3rd ed. (New York: McGraw-Hill, 1996), among others.

11. Douglas Pike, *Vietnam and the Soviet Union: Anatomy of an Alliance* (Boulder, Colo.: Westview Press, 1987).

12. Mari Olsen, *Solidarity and National Revolution: The Soviet Union and the Vietnamese Communists, 1954–1960* (Oslo: IFS, 1997).

13. Ang Cheng Guan, *Vietnamese Communists' Relations with China and the Second Indochina Conflict, 1956–1962* (Jefferson, N.C.: McFarland, 1997).

14. P. J. Honey, *Communism in North Vietnam: Its Role in the Sino-Soviet Dispute* (Westport, Conn.: Greenwood Press, 1973).

Notes to Chapter 1

1. See, for example, Sergei N. Goncharov, John W. Lewis, and Xue Litai, *Uncertain Partners: Stalin, Mao and the Korean War* (Stanford: Stanford University Press, 1993); Odd Arne Westad, ed., *Brothers in Arms: The Rise and Fall of the Sino-Soviet Alliance, 1945–1963* (Washington, D.C.: Woodrow Wilson Center Press, 1998).

2. Philippov (Stalin) to Ho Chi Minh, ciphered telegram to Soviet chargé d'affaires in Beijing Shibaev signed by Andrei Vyshinskii, February 1, 1950, Rossiiskii Gosudarstvennyi Arkhiv Sotsial'no-Politicheskoi Istorii, formerly RTsKhIDNI (hereafter cited as RGASPI) (Russian State Archive of Social-Political History), fond 45, opis' 1, delo 295, list 1.

3. Chen Jian, "China and the Vietnam Wars," in *The Vietnam War,* ed. Peter Lowe (London: Macmillan, 1998), 153.

4. S. Divil'kovskii and I. Ognetov, *Put' k pobede. Ocherk bor'by za natsional'nuyu nezavisimost', edinstvo, mir i sotsialism vo V'etname (1945–1976 gg.)* (The path to victory. An essay on the struggle for national independence, unity, peace, and socialism in Vietnam) (Moscow: Politizdat, 1978), 31.

5. Ibid., 35.

6. Charles McLane, *Soviet Strategies in Southeast Asia: An Exploration of Eastern Policy under Lenin and Stalin* (Princeton: Princeton University Press, 1966), 46.

7. *Istoriia Kitaia* (History of China) (Moscow: Moscow State University Press, 1998), 472–485.

8. McLane, *Soviet Strategies in Southeast Asia,* 266, 274.

9. Bernard B. Fall, *The Two Viet-Nams: A Political and Military Analysis,* 2nd ed. (New York: Praeger, 1967), 196. Emphasis in original.

10. Janos Radvanyi, *Delusion and Reality: Gambits, Hoaxes, & Diplomatic One-Upmanship in Vietnam* (South Bend, Ind.: Gateway Editions, 1978), 4.

11. Nguyen Vu Tung, "Coping with the United States: Hanoi's Search for an Effective Strategy," in *The Vietnam War,* ed. Peter Lowe, 31, 32.

12. See: *Soveshchaniia Kominforma, 1947, 1948, 1949: Dokumenty i materialy* (The

conferences of the Cominform, 1947, 1948, 1949: Documents and materials) (Moscow: ROSSPEN, 1998), 154, 157.

13. See Benoît de Tréglodé, "Premiers contacts entre le Viet Nam et l'Union Sovietique (1947–1948): Nouveaux documents des archives russes." *Approches Asie* 16 (1999): 125–135.

14. McLane, *Soviet Strategies in Southeast Asia,* 367.

15. See Conrad Brandt, *Stalin's Failure in China, 1924–1927* (Harvard: Harvard University Press, 1958).

16. Niu Jun, "The Origins of the Sino-Soviet Alliance," in *Brothers in Arms,* ed. Westad, 49.

17. Nikita S. Khrushchev, *Vremia. Liudi. Vlast'. Vospominaniia v 4-kh knigakh* (Time. People. Power. Memoirs in four books), vol. 3 (Moscow: Moscow News, 1999), 23.

18. Niu Jun, "Origins of the Sino-Soviet Alliance," 70.

19. According to Benoît de Tréglodé, Liu Shaoqi informed the Soviet chargé d'affaires in Beijing about the Chinese intention to recognize the DRV on December 25, 1949; see: Benoît de Tréglodé, "Les relations entre le Viet-Minh, Moscou et Pékin a travers les documents (1950–1954)," *Revue historique des armées* 4 (2000), 57. Nevertheless, Chinese documents indicate that Mao Zedong telegraphed his decision to China on this issue on January 17, 1950, and instructed his subordinates there to broadcast it on the next day; see Shuguang Zhang and Chen Jian, eds., *Chinese Communist Foreign Policy and the Cold War in Asia: New Documentary Evidence, 1944–1950* (Chicago: Imprint Publications, 1996), 138.

20. *Pravda,* January 31, 1950.

21. Philippov (Stalin) to Din (Ho Chi Minh), telegram, February 1, 1950, RGASPI, f. 45, op. 1, d. 295, l. 1.

22. Din (Ho Chi Minh) to Philippov (Stalin), ciphered telegram, February 7, 1950, Ibid., l. 2.

23. The exchange of telegrams between Philippov (Stalin) and Din (Ho Chi Minh), testifies that the Vietnamese leader came to Moscow in February 1950. However, B. de Tréglodé in his article, "Les relations entre le Viet-Minh, Moscou et Pékin," page 58, pointed to other dates of visits by the Vietnamese Communist leader. Tréglodé reports that Ho went to Moscow together with a Chinese delegation headed by Zhou Enlai and met Stalin for the first time on January 20, 1950. The possibility of the Russian documents relating to Ho's visit bearing falsified dates is highly unlikely, especially because they are confirmed by documents from Chinese archives, as well as the chronology of events based on them; see Chen, "China and the Vietnam Wars," 154). This confusion over Ho Chi Minh's visit to Moscow can also be seen in books published in the Soviet Union and Russia, where the dates of the visit are moved to an even earlier period—December 1949. Perhaps the Soviet and Russian authors confused the visits of the Chinese and the Vietnamese leaders, which in fact were very closely related. See, for example, M. P. Isaev and A. S. Chernyshev, *Istoriia sovetsko-v'etnamskikh otnoshenii, 1917–1985* (The history of Soviet-Vietnamese relations) (Moscow: Mezhdunarodnye otnosheniia, 1986), 61–62; and M. S. Kapitsa, *Na raznykh parallellyakh. Zapiski diplomata* (On various parallels. The memoirs of a diplomat) (Moscow: Kniga i biznes, 1996), 260. The truth awaits the declassification of the whole complex of materials—in Russian, as well as in Chinese and Vietnamese archives—relating to the Vietnamese leader's visit to Moscow.

24. Chen, "China and the Vietnam Wars," 154.

25. de Tréglodé, "Les relations entre le Viet-Minh, Moscou et Pékin," 58–59.

26. Khrushchev, *Vremia, Liudi, Vlast'*, 114.

27. McLane, *Soviet Strategies in Southeast Asia,* 436.

28. Chen, "China and the Vietnam Wars," 155.

29. Niu Jun, "Origins of the Sino-Soviet Alliance," 78n.

30. Ibid.

31. Din (Ho Chi Minh) to Philippov (Stalin), letter, October 14, 1950, RGASPI, f. 45, op. 1, d. 295, l. 4.

32. Ibid., l. 5.

33. Ibid.

34. Ibid., l. 4. Emphasis added.

35. Ibid., l. 5.

36. "Soviet Capabilities and Intentions," National Intelligence Estimate, November 11, 1950, National Security Archive, Washington, D.C.

37. Stalin to Liu Shaoqi, letter, February 2, 1951, RGASPI, f. 45, op. 1, d. 313, ll. 60–61. Soviet contacts with the Indonesian communists were maintained through the Chinese who hosted members of the so-called Provisional Central Committee (CC) of the Communist Party of Indonesia.

38. Ibid., ll. 58–59.

39. Ibid., l. 59.

40. McLane, *Soviet Strategies in Southeast Asia,* 465.

41. John Lewis Gaddis, *We Now Know: Rethinking Cold War History* (Oxford: Clarendon Press, 1997), 84.

42. Chen, "China and the Vietnam Wars," 156.

43. Din (Ho Chi Minh) to Philippov (Stalin), ciphered telegram, September 30, 1952, RGASPI, f. 45, op. 1, d. 295, l. 10.

44. Ibid., l. 11.

45. Philippov (Stalin) to Din (Ho Chi Minh), Ibid., l. 12.

46. Ho Chi Minh wrote to Stalin: "Dear and Beloved Comrade. I am awaiting your order so as to come, to kiss you, and to present a report on the question of Vietnam. In the expectation of the response, permit me to put forward one suggestion. While I will be making the report, it would be desirable that Com. Liu Shaoqi be present at the conversation." See V. Grigorian (head of the CPSU CC foreign policy commission) to A. N. Poskryobyshev (Stalin's aide), October 17, 1952, with Ho Chi Minh's letter to Stalin attached, RGASPI, f. 45, op. 1, d. 295, l. 14.

47. Ibid., l. 16.

48. Ibid., l. 18.

49. McLane, *Soviet Strategies in Southeast Asia,* 479.

Notes to Chapter 2

1. John Tahourdin (head of the Southeast Asia Department, Foreign Office), memorandum, March 19, 1954, Public Record Office (PRO), FO 371 112048.

2. Kapitsa, *Na raznykh parallellyakh,* 267.

3. *Pravda,* September 30, 1953.

4. François Joyaux, *La Chine et le règlement du premier conflit d'Indochine (Genève 1954)* (Paris: Publications de la Sorbonne, 1979), 90.

5. Isaev and Chernyshov, *Istoriia sovetsko-v'etnamskikh otnoshenii,* 61–63.

6. *Pravda,* August 9, 1953.

7. *Pravda,* September 30, 1953.

8. Robert F. Randle, *Geneva 1954: The Settlement of the Indochinese War* (Princeton: Princeton University Press, 1969), 4–5. Citation is on page 5.

9. Laniel cited the list of such presentations in his declaration at the French National Assembly on March 5, 1954; see: *L'Année politique. 1954. Revue chronologique des principaux faits politiques, diplomatiques, économiques et sociaux de la France et de l'Union française du 1er Janvier 1954 au 1er Janvier 1955* (Paris: Presses universitaires de France, 1955), 565.

10. The literature about the French war in Indochina is impressive and would require many pages. I therefore refer to only a few books published in the West: Peter M. Dunn, *The First Vietnam War* (New York: St. Martin's Press, 1985); Bernard B. Fall, *Hell in a Very Small Place: The Siege of Dien Bien Phu* (Philadelphia: Lippincott, 1966); Melvin Gurtov, *The First Vietnam Crisis* (New York: Columbia University Press, 1967); George C. Herring, *America's Longest War: The United States and Vietnam, 1950–1975,* 2nd ed. (New York: Knopf, 1985); Stanley Karnow, *Vietnam: A History* (New York: Viking Press, 1983); Alan J. Levine, *The United States and the Struggle for Southeast Asia, 1945–1975* (Westport: Praeger, 1995).

11. *L'Année politique,* 299.

12. James Cable, *The Geneva Conference of 1954 on Indochina* (London: Macmillan, 1986), 35.

13. John Foster Dulles to President Eisenhower, telegram, January 27, 1954, Dwight D. Eisenhower Library, Abilene, Kansas, Ann Whitman file, Dulles-Herter series, box 2.

14. Vyacheslav Molotov-Georges Bidault, memorandum of conversation, February 11, 1954, Arkhiv vneshnei politiki Rossiiskoi Federatzii (AVP RF), Moscow, fond 06, opis' 13a, papka 25, delo 7, list 25.

15. Vyacheslav Molotov-John Foster Dulles, memorandum of conversation, February 13, 1954, Ibid., l. 32.

16. See "Communiqué Issued at the Conclusion of the Quadripartite Meeting of the Four Foreign Ministers at Berlin," February 18, 1954, U. S. Department of State, *Foreign Relations of the United States (FRUS), 1952–1954: Indochina,* vol. 13 (Washington, D.C.: U.S. Government Printing Office, 1982), part 1, 1057.

17. Philippe Devillers and Jean Lacouture, *End of a War: Indochina, 1954,* trans. Alexander Lieven and Adam Roberts (New York: Praeger, 1969), 58.

18. V. M. Molotov, verbatim record of report on results of the Berlin conference of ministers of foreign affairs of the four powers at the plenum of the CPSU CC, March 2, 1954, Rossiiskii Gosudarstvennyi Arkhiv Noveishei Istorii (RGANI) (Russian State Archive of Contemporary History), fond 2, opis' 1, delo 77, list 75. Emphasis added.

19. Pavel Yudin-Zhou Enlai, memorandum of conversation, February 16, 1954, AVP RF, f. 0100, op. 47, 379, d. 7, l. 22.

20. Ibid.

21. Joyaux, *La Chine,* 105.

22. Vyacheslav Molotov-Zhang Wentien, conversation at reception, March 6, 1954, AVP RF, f. 06, op. 13a, p. 25, d. 7, l. 41–66

23. 186th meeting of the U.S. National Security Council, memorandum of discussion, Friday, February 26, 1954, *FRUS, 1952–1954,* vol. 13, pt. 1, 1080.

24. Ibid., 1080–1081.

25. *L'Année politique,* 340.

26. Kirill Novikov-Nguyen Long Bang, memorandum of conversation, February 26, 1954, AVP RF, f. 079, op. 9, p. 6, d. 5, l. 26.

27. Ibid., l. 35.

28. Ibid., f. 06, op. 13a, p. 25, d. 7, l. 45.

29. *FRUS, 1952–1954,* vol. 13, pt. 1, 1009n.

30. Tahourdin, memorandum, March 19, 1954, PRO, FO 371 112048.

31. H. A. F. Hohler, memorandum, Ibid.

32. Vyacheslav Molotov-Zhang Wentien, conversation, March 6, 1954.

33. Pavel Yudin-Hoang Van Hoan, memorandum of conversation, March 5, 1954, AVP RF, f. 0100, op. 47, p. 379, d. 7, l. 63.

34. The Vietnamese envoy's arguments, however, resembled those of the French prime minister in his speech before the National Assembly made on the same day of the conversation between the Soviet and Vietnamese ambassadors. But Joseph Laniel, unlike his adversaries, found it possible to resolve the Indochina problem on the basis of the existing situation, without dividing Vietnam. He suggested evacuating Vietminh troops from the Tonkin delta and creating around its periphery a sort of no-man's-land. He suggested that in central Vietnam, People's Army units should be concentrated in the established zones and, in the south of Vietnam where the Vietminh forces were much less numerous, they should be either disarmed or evacuated. See Joseph Laniel's declaration on Indochina before the National Assembly of France, March 5, 1954, *L'Année politique,* 567.

35. Tahourdin, memorandum, March 19, 1954, PRO, FO 371 112048.

36. The British ambassador in Saigon, Hubert Graves, reported to the Foreign Office on March 23, 1954: ". . . I believe French politicians are moving uneasily but perceptibly towards partition theory. . . . Partition would not be provoked by the French but it might be accepted." PRO, FO 371 112048.

37. Lloyd C. Gardner, *Approaching Vietnam: From World War II through Dienbienphu, 1941–1954* (New York: Norton, 1988), 176.

38. There exists an abundant literature on the siege of Dienbienphu and discussions within the U.S. government about intervening in the battle, including the use of atomic weapons (Operation Vulture). The classic work on the subject is Bernard B. Fall's *Hell In a Very Small Place* (1966). For more recent publications see John R. Nordell Jr., *The Undetected Enemy: French and American Miscalculations at Dien Bien Phu* (College Station: Texas A&M University Press, 1995), and John Prados, *The Sky Would Fall: Operation Vulture: the U.S. Mission in Indochina, 1954* (New York: Dial Press, 1983).

39. 192nd Meeting of the U.S. National Security Council, memorandum of discussion, April 6, 1954, *FRUS, 1952–1954,* vol. 13, pt. 1, 1260.

40. Ibid., 1182.

41. Gardner, *Approaching Vietnam,* 175.

42. Vasilii Kuznetzov-Charles Bohlen, memorandum of conversation, March 17, 1954, AVP RF, f. 026, op. 2, p. 4, d. 2, l. 42. See also Bohlen's report on this conversation in U.S. Department of State, *FRUS, 1952–1954: The Geneva Conference,* vol. 16 (Washington: U.S. Government Printing Office, 1981), 467–468.

43. AVP RF, Ibid. Bohlen recommended to the U.S. government that "in replying to

this aide-mémoire the point that the Chinese Communists were consulted by its own desire and not by any right should be reemphasized." *FRUS,* Ibid.

44. "Geneva Conference: Indo-China" W. D. Allen, memorandum, March 20, 1954, PRO, FO 371 112049.

45. These plans envisaged the writing of directives for the Soviet delegation, collecting documents of an analytical character, and preparing memoranda and reports on various aspects of the situation in Southeast Asia. An integral part of all these plans was collecting materials on U.S. involvement in the war in Indochina. Various preparatory materials are located in the fond 022 (Gromyko's Secretariat) in the AVP RF.

46. "Questions in Connection with the Forthcoming Geneva Conference," memorandum, top secret, March 15, 1954, AVP RF, f. 022, op. 7b, p. 106, d. 7, ll. 16–19.

47. Vyacheslav Molotov-Zhang Wentien, conversation, March 6, 1954.

48. Ibid. The North Korean foreign minister, Nam Il, also arrived in the Soviet capital for negotiations on the Korean phase of the conference.

49. "Plan of Talks [for Molotov] with Zhou Enlai and Ho Chi Minh," memorandum, top secret, April 4, 1954, AVP RF, f. 022, op. 7b, p. 106, d. 7, l. 23.

50. Ibid.

51. Ibid., l. 25.

52. Kapitsa, *Na raznykh parallellyakh,* 261–262.

53. Joyaux, in *La Chine,* page 91, argued:

> The eventual opening of the negotiations on Indochina . . . fully corresponded to the national interests of China: it would promote the relaxation of tensions in the Far East which was necessary for China's economic development, eliminate, in the case of success of the conference, the danger of a massive U.S. intervention in the conflict, give the Chinese government a possibility to put an end to ostracism whose victim it was in the United Nations Organization, illustrate the great-power status of the People's Republic on the international arena and, last, provide opportunity for trade negotiation with the West.

In this situation China's stakes obviously were too impressive to compromise in favor of the Vietminh.

54. "Draft of the Directives on the Issue of Restoration of Peace in Indo-China," memorandum, top secret, undated, AVP RF, f. 0100, op. 47, p. 389, d. 107, l. 5.

55. Ibid., l. 6–7.

56. "On Positions of the Western Powers. Conditions of the Cessation of Hostilities in Indochina," memorandum, top secret, undated, AVP RF, f. 022, op. 7b, p. 106, d. 7, ll. 27–31.

57. Randle, *Geneva 1954,* 125.

58. Anthony Eden, *Full Circle: The Memoirs of Anthony Eden* (Boston: Houghton Mifflin, 1960), 97.

59. John Tahourdin to Hubert Graves, diplomatic communication, March 10, 1954, PRO, FO 371 112048.

60. Southeast Asia Department, Foreign Office, "Policy Towards Indo-China," April 1954, Ibid., FO 371 112049. This paper received Eden's approval.

61. Cable, *The Geneva Conference,* 54.

62. For Eisenhower's and Dulles's slips of the tongue on this subject, see Gardner, *Approaching Vietnam,* 252–256. Gardner draws attention to the reasons why Dulles found

it possible to agree on partition. On the basis of documents from British archives, Gardner concludes on page 256 that "the Americans had something else in their mind when they talked about partition: a base for military operations to recapture the whole of Indochina."

63. "List of Counselors, Experts, and Members of the USSR Delegation," April 12, 1954, AVP RF, f. 0445, op. 2, p. 1, d. 1.

64. Devillers and Lacouture, *End of a War,* 124.

65. "List of Counselors," AVP RF, f. 0445, op. 2, p. 1, d. 1.

66. Vasilii Kuznetzov-A. Ledovskii-Wan Binnanh, memorandum of conversation, April 17, 1954, AVP RF, f. 0445, op. 2, p. 1, d. 1, l. 76.

67. Before arriving in Moscow, the Vietminh delegation stayed in Beijing where it received advice from the Chinese allies. In a conversation with Kirill Novikov on March 26, Vietnamese ambassador Nguyen Long Bang informed his Soviet counterpart that the DRV delegation had already come to Beijing where "together with the Chinese comrades it will be occupied with the preparation for the Geneva conference." See Kirill Novikov-Nguyen Long Bang, memorandum of conversation, March 26, 1954, AVP RF, f. 079, op. 9, p. 6, d. 5, l. 35.

68. Kirill Novikov-Alexander Lavrishchev-Pham Van Dong, memorandum of conversation, April 10, 1954, Ibid., l. 37–40.

69. Kirill Novikov-Alexander Lavrishchev-Pham Van Dong, memorandum of conversation, April 21, 1954, Ibid.

Notes to Chapter 3

1. Arnold J. Toynbee, *Experiences* (New York: Oxford University Press, 1969), 57.

2. Devillers and Lacouture, *End of a War,* 122.

3. Yu. Zhukov, I. Plyshevskli, and G. Rassadin, *Tri mesyatza v Zheneve* (Three months in Geneva) (Moscow: Pravda, 1954), 3. This book is based on news reports from Geneva by three *Pravda* correspondents.

4. For a very lively description of Zhou Enlai's arrival in Geneva, see Devillers and Lacouture, *End of a War,* 122.

5. *Pravda,* April 25, 1954.

6. Vyacheslav Molotov-Anthony Eden, memorandum of conversation, July 21, 1954, AVP RF, f. 06, op. 13a, p. 25, d. 8, l. 120.

7. Vyacheslav Molotov-Georges Bidault, memorandum of conversation, April 27, 1954, Ibid., l. 20.

8. Ibid., l. 21.

9. Eden to Foreign Office, diplomatic cable, April 27, 1954, PRO, FO 371 112057.

10. Ibid.

11. Vyacheslav Molotov-Georges Bidault, memorandum of conversation, April 28, 1954, AVP RF, f. 06, op. 13a, p. 25, d. 8, l. 19.

12. Dulles, like Eden, sent his superiors a detailed report about the first conversation between Molotov and Bidault. See *FRUS, 1952–1954,* vol. 16, 591–592.

13. John Foster Dulles-Vyacheslav Molotov, meeting, April 27, 1954, *FRUS, 1952–1954,* vol. 16, 579–580.

14. Ibid., 580.

15. Ibid.

16. Ibid., 613.

17. John Foster Dulles-Nguyen Quoc Dinh, meeting, May 2, 1954, Ibid., 666–667.

18. Jean Chauvel-Georges Bidault-John Foster Dulles, memorandum of conversation, May 2, 1954, Ibid., 668.

19. Georges Bidault-John Foster Dulles-Anthony Eden, memorandum of conversation, May 1, 1954, Ibid., 643.

20. W. Bedell Smith to Department of State, diplomatic cable, May 5, 1954, Ibid., 700.

21. Anthony Eden to Foreign Office, diplomatic communication, May 6, 1954, PRO, FO 371 112060. Emphasis added.

22. See, for example, one interpretation of what Molotov said to Eden after the Berlin conference: "the Westerners should be happy that they did not have to take into consideration Mao Zedong 'who is very tough, very tough.'" Joyaux, *La Chine,* 106.

23. John Foster Dulles to Department of State, diplomatic cable, May 1, 1954, *FRUS, 1952–1954,* vol. 16, 648.

24. Cable, *The Geneva Conference,* 85.

25. Gardner, *Approaching Vietnam,* 259.

26. *L'Année politique,* 200–201.

27. Khrushchev, *Vremia,* vol. 3, 115.

28. At a meeting of the U.S. National Security Council on April 6, President Eisenhower said that "even if Dien Bien Phu were lost to the French, it could hardly be described as a military defeat, since the French would have inflicted such great losses on the enemy." See *FRUS, 1952–1954,* vol. 13, part 1, 1253. Dulles confirmed this in late April in his letter to Bidault in which he stated, "[T]here is no reason why the fall of Dien Bien Phu, should it fall, should be regarded as materially and vitally altering the military position in Indochina." See John Foster Dulles to Department of State, diplomatic communication, April 24, 1954, Ibid., 1308.

29. See Khrushchev, *Vremia,* vol. 3, 115.

30. Record of the meeting of military advisers and experts of the delegations of the PRC, the DRV, and the USSR at the Geneva conference, May 19, 1954, AVP RF, f. 0445, op. 1, p. 1, d. 1, ll. 3–4.

31. During a conversation between John Tahourdin, of the British Foreign Office, and I. Borisov, a member of the Soviet delegation and member of the KGB, Borisov confirmed that "partition appeared to be the only possible solution to the problem." He repeated this twice. Eden wrote on the margins of this record, "I regard this as encouraging, for it is better than amalgamation which I feared that they would want." The foreign secretary was apparently afraid that the Soviets would demand a coalition government with the Vietminh's participation. PRO, FO 371 112060.

32. "2. In case the Western powers have agreed to our proposal about the participation of the Democratic Republic of Vietnam at the Geneva conference, the Soviet delegation should let the Vietnamese and Chinese delegations take the initiative in putting forward proposals about conditions of the armistice or the restoration of peace in Indochina." See "Plan of the Directives on the Issue of the Restoration of Peace in Indochina," top secret, undated, AVP RF, f. 0100, op. 47, p. 389, d. 107, l. 5.

33. Vyacheslav Molotov, "On the Restoration of Peace in Indochina," speech, fourth plenary session, Geneva, May 14, 1954, AVP RF, f. 0445, op. 1, p. 11, d. 46, ll. 28–50. The address was also published in *Pravda,* May 15, 1954.

34. AVP RF, f. 0445, op. 1, p. 1, d. 1.

35. Zhukov et al., *Tri mesyatza v Zheneve,* 122.

36. W. Bedell Smith-Vyacheslav Molotov, meeting, May 22, 1954, *FRUS, 1952–1954,* vol. 16, 899.

37. Randle, *Geneva, 1954,* 268.

38. AVP RF, f. 0445, op. 1, p. 10, d. 44, l. 56.

39. For details, see Randle, *Geneva, 1954,* chapter 13.

40. Vyacheslav Molotov-Georges Bidault, meeting, June 7, 1954, AVP RF, f. 06, op. 13a, p. 25, d. 8, l. 27.

41. Vyacheslav Molotov-W. Bedell Smith, memorandum of conversation, June 7, 1954, *FRUS, 1952–1954,* vol. 16, 1059.

42. Ibid., 1060.

43. Devillers and Lacouture, *End of a War,* 233.

44. Ibid., 234.

45. Randle, *Geneva, 1954,* 232.

46. Record of the meeting of military advisers and experts of the delegations of the PRC, DRV, and USSR at the Geneva conference, May 19, 1954, AVP RF, f. 0445, op. 2, p. 1, d. 1, ll. 2–5.

47. Record of the meeting of military advisers and experts, May 27, 1954, Ibid., ll. 7–9.

48. Record of the meeting of the military advisers and experts, May 28, 1954, Ibid., l. 11.

49. Record of the meeting of military advisers and experts, June 10, 1954, 10 p.m. to midnight, Ibid., l. 33.

50. Devillers and Lacouture, *End of a War,* 232.

51. Cable, *The Geneva Conference,* 93–94. During the meeting with W. Bedell Smith, Eden was clearly depressed. He pointed to the three points on which the Communists showed no intention of compromising (separate treatment of Laos and Cambodia, status and powers of the ICC, and the composition of the commission) and said, "we can get no further on these issues and should break within next few days." W. Bedell Smith-Anthony Eden, meeting, June 9, 1954, *FRUS, 1952–1954,* vol. 16, 1083.

52. Devillers and Lacouture, *End of a War,* 234–235; Randle, *Geneva, 1954,* 275–276.

53. Reinhardt (special adviser to the U.S. delegation) to Johnson (coordinator of the delegation), memorandum, June 10, 1954, *FRUS, 1952–1954,* vol. 16, 1110.

54. Ibid., 1126.

55. Randle, *Geneva, 1954,* 280.

56. Eden to Foreign Office, diplomatic communication, June 15, 1954, PRO, FO 371 112073.

57. Eden to Foreign Office, diplomatic communication, June 16, 1954, Ibid., FO 371 112073.

58. Randle, *Geneva, 1954,* 281–282.

59. Ibid., 281.

60. Vyacheslav Molotov-Georges Bidault, meeting, June 17, 1954, AVP RF, f. 06, op. 13a, p. 25, d. 8, ll. 29–33.

61. W. Bedell Smith-Vyacheslav Molotov, meeting, June 18, 1954, *FRUS, 1952–1954,* vol. 16, 1189.

62. Vyacheslav Molotov-Anthony Eden, memorandum of conversation, June 19, 1954, AVP RF, f. 06, op. 13a, p. 25, d. 8, ll. 37–38.

63. W. Bedell Smith-Vyacheslav Molotov, meeting, June 18, 1954, *FRUS, 1952–1954,* vol. 16, 1192.

64. Vyacheslav Molotov-Anthony Eden, memorandum of conversation, June 19, 1954, AVP RF, f. 06, op. 13a, p. 25, d. 8, 1.40.

65. John Foster Dulles to U.S. delegation, May 12, 1954, *FRUS, 1952–1954,* vol. 16, 778.

66. For details, see Gardner, *Approaching Vietnam,* chaps. 5–8.

67. John Foster Dulles to embassy in France, June 28, 1954, *FRUS, 1952–1954,* vol. 13, part 2, 1757. Emphasis added.

68. John Foster Dulles to President Eisenhower, draft memorandum, undated. *FRUS, 1952–1954,* vol. 13, part 2, 1774–1776.

69. Vyacheslav Molotov, "On the Results of the Geneva conference," draft report, June 24, 1954, RGANI, f. 2, op. 1, d. 94, 1. 8.

70. Ibid., 1. 22.

71. Vyacheslav Molotov-Anthony Eden, memorandum of conversation, June 19, 1954, AVP RF, f. 06, op. 13a, p. 25, d. 8, ll. 40, 43.

72. RGANI, f. 2, op. 1, d. 94, 1. 24.

73. *L'Année politique,* 390–391.

74. Zhukov et al., *Tri mesyatza v Zheneve,* 169, 172.

75. Ngo Dinh Diem, recently appointed prime minister by Bao Dai, believed this. See Douglas Dillon, U.S. ambassador in France, to the Department of State, diplomatic cable, June 21, 1954, *FRUS, 1952–1954,* vol. 13, part 2, 1727.

76. Devillers and Lacouture, *End of a War,* 247.

77. Joyaux, *La Chine,* 235–236.

78. Gladwyn Jebb, British ambassador in France, "Account of the French Note," undated, PRO, FO 371 112074, DF 1071/765G.

79. Ibid.

80. Devillers and Lacouture, *End of a War,* 260.

81. Vyacheslav Molotov-W. Hayter, meeting, July 4, 1954, AVP RF, f. 06, op. 13 a, p. 25, d. 8, 1. 59.

82. V. V. Vas'kov-Mao Zedong, memorandum of conversation, July 5, 1954, Ibid., f. 0100, op. 47, p. 379, d. 7, ll. 69–70.

83. Vyacheslav Molotov-Jean Chauvel, meeting, July 9, 1954, Ibid., f. 06, op. 13a, p. 25, d. 8, 1. 75.

84. Ibid., 1. 78.

85. Record of the meeting of the military advisers of the USSR delegation with the military expert of the French delegation, July 10, 1954, AVP RF, f. 0445, op. 1, p. 1, d. 1, 1. 79.

86. Ibid.

87. Vyacheslav Molotov-Pierre Mendès France, memorandum of conversation, July 10, 1954, AVP RF, f. 06, op. 13a, p. 26, d. 8, ll. 80–87.

88. Ibid., 1. 85.

89. Ibid., ll. 80–81.

90. Cable, *The Geneva Conference,* 116.

91. For details of negotiations among Mendès France, Anthony Eden, and John Foster Dulles concerning W. Bedell Smith's participation in the conference, see: *FRUS, 1952–1954,* vol. 13, part 2, 1800–1834. Dulles mentioned that one of the reasons for his re-

luctance to send Smith to Geneva was the possibility "that high-level U.S. representation at Geneva might so stiffen the French as to preclude their accepting any settlement offered by the Communists." In that case, in Dulles' words, the French "might then turn to us and ask us to participate unilaterally with them in continuing the war." 206th meeting of the U.S. National Security Council, memorandum of discussion, July 15, 1954, Ibid., 1836.

92. Randle, *Geneva, 1954,* 317–318.

93. Vyacheslav Molotov-Pierre Mendès France, memorandum of conversation, July 15, 1954, AVP RF, f. 06, op. 13a, p. 25, d. 8, ll. 96–97.

94. Ibid., l. 89.

95. Ibid., l. 90.

96. Anthony Eden to Foreign Office, diplomatic communication, July 17, 1954, PRO, FO 371 112079.

97. W. Bedell Smith to Secretary of State, diplomatic cable, July 18, 1954, *FRUS, 1952–1954,* vol. 16, 1429.

98. Vyacheslav Molotov-Zhou Enlai-Pham Van Dong, memorandum of conversation, July 16, 1954, AVP RF, f. 06, op. 13a, p. 25, d. 8, l. 102.

99. Ibid., l. 103.

100. Vyacheslav Molotov-Zhou Enlai-Pham Van Dong, memorandum of conversation, July 17, 1954, Ibid., l. 107.

101. Molotov had already proposed a commission composed of the three countries as well as the possibility of a five-member commission. As possible candidates for the tripartite commission, India, Poland, and Indonesia were mentioned. While putting forward this proposal, Molotov obviously took into account a conversation between his deputy, Andrei Gromyko, and Indian diplomat V. K. Krishna Menon, who was sent to Geneva by Nehru. Krishna Menon hinted that India would not agree to become a member of a commission together with Pakistan, whose membership was suggested by Molotov in his proposal of a commission composed of five countries. See Andrei Gromyko-V. K. Krishna Menon, memorandum of conversation, June 10, 1954, AVP RF, f. 022, op. 7v, p. 114, d. 2, ll. 40–42.

102. Vyacheslav Molotov-Zhou Enlai-Pham Van Dong, memorandum of conversation, July 17, 1954, Ibid.

103. W. Bedell Smith to Department of State, diplomatic cable, July 18, 1954, *FRUS, 1952–1954,* vol. 16, 1432.

104. Ibid., 1434.

105. Anthony Eden to Prime Minister Winston Churchill, diplomatic communication, July 18, 1954, PRO, FO 371 112079.

106. Joyaux, *La Chine,* 281.

107. W. Bedell Smith to Department of State, diplomatic cable, July 19, 1954, *FRUS, 1952–1954,* vol. 16, 1455–1456.

108. Joyaux, *La Chine,* 282.

109. Ibid., 284.

110. Randle, *Geneva, 1954,* 240.

111. Anthony Eden to Foreign Office, July 17, 1954, PRO, FO 371 112079.

112. Vyacheslav Molotov-Zhou Enlai-Pham Van Dong, memorandum of conversation, July 16, 1954, AVP RF, f. 06, op. 13a, p. 25, d. 8, l. 103.

113. John Foster Dulles to U.S. delegation, June 23, 1954, *FRUS, 1952–1954,* vol. 16, 1226.

114. Jean Lacouture, *Pierre Mendès France* (Paris: Seuil, 1981), 257.

115. Ibid., 258.

116. Cable, *The Geneva Conference,* 123.

117. Minutes of the final plenary session, July 21, 1954, AVP RF, f. 0445, op. 1, p. 6, d. 27, ll. 107–109.

118. See, for example, Randle, *Geneva, 1954,* chaps. 21–22; Manfred Lachs, *Zhenevskiie soglasheniia 1954 g. ob Indokitae* (The 1954 Geneva agreements on Indochina) (Moscow: Inostrannaia literatura, 1965).

119. See the arguments put forward by Randle, *Geneva, 1954,* 373–385; and Cable, *The Geneva Conference,* 129–132.

120. Vyacheslav Molotov-Pierre Mendès France, memorandum of conversation, July 10, 1954, AVP RF, f. 06, op. 13a, p. 26, d. 8, l. 86. Emphasis added.

121. Vyacheslav Molotov-Pierre Mendès France, meeting, July 21, 1954, AVP RF, f. 06, op. 13a, p. 25, d. 8, l. 123. For a French account of the conversation, see *Documents diplomatiques français. 1954. Annexes (21 juillet-31 décembre)* (Paris: Imprimerie nationale, 1987).

122. Vyacheslav Molotov-Pierre Mendès France, meeting, July 21, 1954, AVP RF, f. 06, op. 13a, p. 25, d. 8.

123. Cable, *The Geneva Conference,* 3.

124. W. Bedell Smith-Vyacheslav Molotov, meeting, May 22, 1954, *FRUS, 1952–1954,* vol. 16, 899.

125. Anthony Eden-Vyacheslav Molotov, record of conversation, May 5, 1954, PRO, FO 371 112060.

126. Ibid., FO 371 112077.

127. Khrushchev, *Vremia,* vol. 2, 247.

128. Oleg A. Troyanovsky, *Cherez gody i rasstoianiia. Istoriia odnoi sem'yi* (Across years and distances: The history of one family) (Moscow: Vagrius, 1997), 138.

Notes to Chapter 4

1. Ministerstvo inostrannykh del SSSR, *Sovetskii Soyuz-V'etnam: 30 let otnoshenii, 1950–1980. Dokumenty i materialy* (The Soviet Union-Vietnam: Thirty years of relations, 1950–1980. Documents and materials) (Moscow: Politizdat, 1982), 15.

2. Ibid., 12.

3. Ibid., 13.

4. Ibid.

5. Ibid.

6. Ibid., 9–11.

7. Ibid., 14.

8. Kirill Novikov-Pham Van Dong, memorandum of conversation, July 27, 1954, AVP RF, f. 079, op. 9, p. 6, d. 5, p. 60.

9. I. F. Kurdiukov (deputy head of the Department on Far Eastern Affairs)-Ma Le (aide to Zhou Enlai), telephone conversation, July 28, 1954, AVP RF, f. 0100, op. 47, p. 379, d. 6, l. 175. This conversation was devoted to arranging the visit of the two Asian lead-

ers with Molotov. Zhou Enlai's aide also raised issue of Zhou meeting with Georgii Malenkov "and someone else from the Soviet leadership." Pham Van Dong would have been invited to such a meeting as well.

10. Kapitsa, *Na raznykh parallelyakh,* 269.

11. Valerian Zorin-Nguyen Long Bang, meeting, August 4, 1954, AVP RF, f. 079, op. 9, p. 6, d. 4, l. 1.

12. Ibid.

13. Kirill Novikov-Nguyen Long Bang, memorandum of conversation, August 9, 1954, AVP RF, f. 06, op. 13a, p. 35, d. 158, l. 49.

14. For biographical information on A. A. Lavrishchev, see AVP RF, f. 079, op. 9, p. 6, d. 4, l. 2.

15. List of advisers, experts, and staff of the USSR delegation. AVP RF, f. 0445, op. 2, p. 1, d. 1, l. 89.

16. Alexander Lavrishchev-Nguyen Long Bang, memorandum of conversation, August 10, 1954, AVP RF, f. 079, op. 9, p. 6, d. 5, l. 64.

17. Nguyen Long Bang-Kirill Novikov-Alexander Lavrishchev, memoranda of conversation, August 9–10, 1954, AVP RF, f. 06, op. 13a, p. 35 d. 158, l. 49; and f. 079, op. 9, p. 6, d. 5, l. 65.

18. Kirill Novikov-Tueng (DRV charge d'affaires), memorandum of conversation, October 14, 1954, AVP RF, f. 079, op. 9, p. 6, d. 5, l. 68.

19. Kirill Novikov-Pham Van Dong, memorandum of conversation, July 27, 1954, AVP RF, f. 06, op. 13a, p. 35, d. 158, l. 45.

20. Kirill Novikov to Vyacheslav Molotov, memorandum, July 29, 1954, AVP RF, f. 06, op. 13a, p. 15, d. 156, ll. 1–2.

21. These Soviet ships are referred to in the Soviet Foreign Ministry's "The Democratic Republic of Vietnam. (Political situation)," June 29, 1954. This publication provided information about the transportation of Vietnamese Catholics from North Vietnam to the South. See AVP RF, f. 022, op. 8, p. 117, d. 30, l. 58.

22. Fall, *The Two Viet-Nams,* 173–174.

23. Ibid., 139, 152.

24. Kirill Novikov-Nguyen Long Bang, memorandum of conversation, October 28, 1954, AVP RF, f. 06, op. 13a, p. 35, d. 158, l. 54.

25. Vladimir Kuznetzov (Southeast Asia Department) to Vyacheslav Molotov, memorandum, January 11, 1955, AVP RF, f. 079, op. 10, p. 10, d. 15, l. 1.

26. Ibid., l. 2.

27. "Directives to the group of Soviet specialists sent on an official trip to the DRV in connection with the Decree of the Council of Ministers of the USSR dated January 19, 1955, on the rendering of help to the DRV in restoration of its economy," draft, January 27, 1955, RGANI, f. 5, op. 30, d. 120, l. 48.

28. Ibid.

29. AVP RF, f. 022, op. 8, p. 117, d. 30, ll. 27–28.

30. Vyacheslav Molotov to the CPSU CC, May 26, 1955, AVP RF, f. 06, op. 14, p. 12, d. 170, l. 8.

31. CPSU CC to the WPV CC, telegram (copy), May 28, 1955, Ibid., l. 11.

32. David L. Anderson, *Trapped by Success: The Eisenhower Administration and Vietnam, 1953–1961* (New York: Columbia University Press, 1991), 65.

33. Ibid., 68.

34. James R. Arnold, *The First Domino: Eisenhower, the Military, and America's Intervention in Vietnam* (New York: Morrow, 1991), 236.

35. Ibid., 242.

36. R. B. Smith, *An International History of the Vietnam War,* vol. 1, *Revolution versus Containment, 1955–1961* (New York: St. Martin's Press, 1983), 36.

37. Nikolai Bulganin-Kumar Menon, conversation, April 8, 1955, RGANI, f. 5, op. 30, d. 116, ll. 42–43. Emphasis added.

38. Nikolai Bulganin-Jawaharlal Nehru, meeting, June 8, 1955. Ibid., ll. 75–76. See also Indian ambassador K. P. S. Menon's account of this conversation in his memoir, *The Flying Troika: Extracts from a Diary by K. P. S. Menon, India's Ambassador to Russia, 1952–1961* (London: Oxford University Press, 1963), 116.

39. Vyacheslav Molotov to CPSU CC, memorandum, May 19, 1955, AVP RF, f. 06, op. 14, p. 12, d. 176, l. 1.

40. Andrei Gromyko (deputy foreign minister) to CPSU Central Committee, memorandum, June 15, 1955, AVP RF, f. 06, op.14, p. 12, d. 172, l. 4.

41. General Antonov to Valerian Zorin (deputy foreign minister), letter, June 10, 1955, AVP RF, f. 079, op. 10, p. 9, d. 8, l. 32.

42. Foreign Ministry to Alexander Lavrishchev (Soviet ambassador in Hanoi), diplomatic communication, June 14, 1955, AVP RF, f. 06, op. 14, p. 12, d. 172, l. 6.

43. "Directives for the Negotiations with the Governmental Delegation of the Democratic Republic of Vietnam," addendum to a draft of the CPSU CC resolution, undated, Ibid., l. 15.

44. Ibid., l. 17.

45. Hanoi was fully aware of the importance the Soviets attached to the development of the DRV's relations with France. Thomas Corcoran, U.S. consul in Hanoi, cabled the State Department describing the November 1954 reception celebrating the anniversary of the October revolution: at the reception Pham Van Dong expressed his country's "willingness settle economic and cultural relations with France on the basis of equality and satisfaction of interests for both sides." See Hanoi to Secretary of State, diplomatic cable, November 8, 1954, National Archives, record group 59, 651G.00/11-854, no. 372.

46. "Directives for the Negotiations," AVP RF, f. 06, op. 14, p. 12, d. 172, l. 19.

47. Ibid.

48. Ministerstvo inostrannykh del SSSR, *Sovetskii Soyuz–V'etnam,* 17.

49. "Plan of the Protocol Arrangements in Connection with the Arrival in the USSR of the DRV President, Com. Ho Chi Minh," Ibid., ll. 25–27.

50. "A Preliminary Program of Ho Chi Minh's Stay in the USSR," Ibid., ll. 28–29.

51. Vyacheslav Molotov to CPSU CC, May 19, 1955, AVP RF, f. 06, op. 14, p. 12, d. 176, l. 2.

52. AVP RF, f. 079, op. 10, p. 9, d. 8, l. 12.

53. Ho Chi Minh to Alexander Lavrishchev, "Questions To Be Discussed with the CPSU Central Committee," July 13, 1955, AVP RF, f. 06, op. 14, p. 12, d. 172, l. 58.

54. Vladimir Kuznetsov to Mikhail Suslov, July 13, 1955, RGANI, f. 5, op. 30, d. 120, l. 66.

55. See, for example, Paul W. Blackstock's *The Strategy of Subversion: Manipulating the Politics of Other Nations* (Chicago: Quadrangle Books, 1964) 52, for a discussion of "the deliberately planned manipulation of psychological and sociological factors by one

state intervening in the affairs of another" as an integral part of the policy aimed at undermining a rival regime.

56. Kirill Novikov to Vyacheslav Molotov, memorandum, December 29, 1954, AVP RF, f. 079, op. 9, p. 6, d. 8, l. 51.

57. Ministerstvo inostrannykh del SSSR, *Sovetskii Soyuz–V'etnam,* 15.

58. Ibid.

59. "Directives for the Negotiations," AVP RF, f. 06, op. 14, p. 12, d. 172, l. 16.

Notes to Chapter 5

1. *Documents relating to British Involvement in the Indo-China Conflict, 1945–1965* Cmnd. 2834 (London: Her Majesty's Stationery Office, 1965), 23.

2. Ibid., 107.

3. Ibid., 84–85.

4. Victor Bator, *Vietnam: A Diplomatic Tragedy: The Origins of the United States Involvement* (Dobbs Ferry, N.Y.: Oceana Publications, 1965), 137. Emphasis in original.

5. Smith, *An International History,* 29.

6. "The Agreement on the Cessation of Hostilities in Vietnam," July 20, 1954, AVP RF, f. 0445, op. 1, p. 11, d. 48, ll. 61–62.

7. *Documents relating to British Involvement,* 85.

8. Ibid., 17.

9. Ibid., 20.

10. Gardner, *Approaching Vietnam,* 282.

11. Arnold, *The First Domino,* 285.

12. Arthur Combs, "The Path Not Taken: The British Alternative to U.S. Policy in Vietnam, 1954–1956," *Diplomatic History* 1 (Winter 1995): 46.

13. Anderson, *Trapped by Success,* 125.

14. D. R. SarDesai, *Indian Foreign Policy in Cambodia, Laos, and Vietnam 1947–1964* (Berkeley: University of California Press, 1968), 90.

15. A. M. Malukhin (counsellor of Soviet embassy)-R. Melkhior (deputy secretary general of Polish delegation to the ICC), memorandum of conversation, January 31, 1955, AVP RF, f. 079, op. 10, p. 9, d. 5, l. 29.

16. Directives of the USSR delegation at the four-power conference at Geneva, draft version, July 13–15, 1955, AVP RF, f. 06, op. 14, p. 3, d. 43, ll. 82, 83–84.

17. *Documents relating to British Involvement,* extract from Eden's message to London, July 24, 1955, 90.

18. Anderson, *Trapped by Success,* 126.

19. Vyacheslav Molotov to the CPSU CC, memorandum, August 10, 1955, AVP RF, f. 06, op. 14, p. 12, d. 170, l. 16.

20. Cited in Combs, "The Path Not Taken," 52.

21. Arnold, *The First Domino,* 286.

22. Leonid Sokolov (chargé d'affaires)-Truong Chinh, memorandum of conversation, fall 1955, AVP RF, f. 079, op. 10, p. 9, d. 5, l. 133. Emphasis added.

23. Ibid., l. 134.

24. Combs, "The Path Not Taken," 53.

25. Ibid., 57.

26. SarDesai, *Indian Foreign Policy,* 96.

27. SarDesai, *Indian Foreign Policy,* 97.

28. Letter on Vietnam question received from Macmillan at Geneva, draft version, undated, AVP RF, f. 06, op. 11, p. 12, d. 170, l. 27.

29. *Documents relating to British Involvement,* 80.

30. Fall, *The Two Viet-Nams,* 152.

31. Vyacheslav Molotov to the CPSU CC, letter, November 23, 1955, AVP RF, f. 06, op. 14, p. 12, d. 170, l. 23.

32. SarDesai, *Indian Foreign Policy,* 98.

33. Ibid.

34. *Documents relating to British Involvement,* 119.

35. Vasilii V. Kuznetzov-Truong Chinh, memorandum of conversation, February, 28, 1956, AVP RF, f. 079, op. 11, p. 13, d. 2, ll. 3–4.

36. Ibid., l. 5.

37. *Vietnam and the Geneva Agreements. Documents concerning the discussion between Representatives of Her Majesty's Government and the Government of the Union of Soviet Socialist Republics held in London in April and May 1956,* Cmdn. 9763 (London: Her Majesty's Stationery Office, 1956), 7.

38. Cited in Fall, *The Two Viet-Nams,* 319.

39. SarDesai, *Indian Foreign Policy,* 98–99.

40. Fall, *The Two Viet-Nams,* 319.

41. Mikhail Zimyanin-Pham Hung, memorandum of conversation, March 23, 1956, AVP RF, f. 079, op. 11, p. 13, d. 5, ll. 39–40.

42. USSR embassy in the DRV, "Some Issues of the Implementation of the Geneva Agreements on Indochina," memorandum, top secret, April 2, 1956, AVP RF, f. 079, op. 11, p. 14, d. 16, l. 57–58.

43. Ibid., 61–62.

44. *Documents relating to British Involvement,* 23.

45. "In two fields, French influence has diminished very little: in the economic field, in which . . . Viet-Nam depends upon France more than ever before; and in educational field, in which France has made a considerable effort to maintain a toehold." Fall, *The Two Viet-Nams,* 321.

46. SarDesai, *Indian Foreign Policy,* 99.

47. Pavel Yudin-Zhang Wentien, attachment to memorandum of conversation, April 4, 1956, AVP RF, f. 0100, op. 49, p. 410, d. 9, l. 103.

48. Ang Cheng Guan, *Vietnamese Communists' Relations with China and the Second Indochina Conflict, 1956–1962* (Jefferson, N.C.: McFarland, 1997), 25; *Vietnam and the Geneva Agreements,* 10–12; *Documents relating to British Involvement,* 23.

49. SarDesai, *Indian Foreign Policy,* 101.

50. Smith, *An International History,* 32.

51. Ang, *Vietnamese Communists' Relations,* 27.

52. SarDesai, *Indian Foreign Policy,* 103.

53. The DRV repeated its plea for normal relations with the South later as well—for example, in Pham Van Dong's letters of July 20, 1957, March 7, 1958, and December 22, 1958. But the Saigon regime repeatedly rejected Hanoi's attempts "to make the division tolerable." Bernard Fall believed that it was this consistent rejection of normalization by Diem (along with the gradual disintegration of the Saigon regime) that impelled

the Communist leadership to resort to insurgency in its efforts to unify Vietnam. Fall, *The Two Viet-Nams,* 336–337.

54. Gabriel Kolko, *Anatomy of a War: Vietnam, the United States, and the Modern Historical Experience* (New York: Pantheon Books, 1985), 89.

55. Anderson, *Trapped by Success,* 132.

56. Kolko, *Anatomy of a War,* 85.

57. According to various estimates, five thousand to ten thousand cadres and soldiers were left in the South after the regrouping envisaged by the Geneva armistice was completed. Smith, *An International History,* 59.

58. Ang, *Vietnamese Communists' Relations,* 19.

59. Mikhail Zimyanin-Ho Chi Minh, memorandum of conversation, June 21, 1956, AVP RF, f. 079, op. 11, p. 13, d. 5, ll. 129–130.

60. Ibid., l. 131.

61. Ibid., l. 133.

62. SarDesai, *Indian Foreign Policy,* 110; Ang, *Vietnamese Communists' Relations,* 49.

63. B. Volkov (head of the Soviet Foreign Ministry's Southeast Asia Department) to N. S. Patolichev (deputy foreign minister), memorandum, January 30, 1957, AVP RF, f. 079, op. 12, p. 18, d. 18, l. 1.

64. Ang, *Vietnamese Communists' Relations,* 50.

65. SarDesai, *Indian Foreign Policy,* 110.

66. B. Volkov (head of the Soviet Foreign Ministry's Southeast Asia Department) to N. S. Patolichev (deputy foreign minister), memorandum, January 30, 1957, AVP RF, f. 079, op. 12, p. 18, d. 18, l. 1.

67. Mikhail Zimyanin-Ho Chi Minh, memorandum of conversation, January 30, 1957, AVP RF, f. 079, op. 12, p. 17, d. 5, l. 52.

68. Ibid.

69. B. Volkov (head of the Soviet Foreign Ministry's Southeast Asia Department) to N. S. Patolichev (deputy foreign minister), memorandum, January 30, 1957, AVP RF, f. 079, op. 12, p. 18, d. 18, l. 2.

70. Nikolai Fedorenko (deputy foreign minister) to Dmitri Shepilov (foreign minister), memorandum, February 14, 1957, Ibid., l. 7.

71. Ang, *Vietnamese Communists' Relations,* 50. It is noteworthy that neither China nor India supported a proposal to admit both parts of Vietnam to the United Nations. On India's position see SarDesai, *Indian Foreign Policy,* 110.

72. Mikhail Zimyanin-Li Zhimin (PRC chargé d'affaires in the DRV), memorandum of conversation, September 18, 1957, AVP RF, f. 079, op. 12, p. 17, d. 6, ll. 69–70.

73. Bruce D. Porter, *The USSR in Third World Conflicts: Soviet Arms and Diplomacy in Local Wars 1945–1980* (Cambridge: Cambridge University Press, 1984), 16.

74. John F. Copper and Daniel S. Papp, eds., *Communist Nations' Military Assistance* (Boulder, Colo.: Westview Press, 1983), 41.

75. Nikita S. Khrushchev, *Otchetnyi doklad Tsentral'nogo Komiteta Kommunisticheskoi Partii Sovetskogo Soyuza XX syezdu KPSS* (Report of the Central Committee of the Communist Party of the Soviet Union to the twentieth congress of the CPSU) (Moscow: Gospolitizdat, 1956), 21.

76. Roger E. Kanet, ed., *The Soviet Union and the Developing Nations* (Baltimore: Johns Hopkins University Press, 1974), 31.

77. Gaddis, *We Now Know,* 154.

78. Ang, *Vietnamese Communists' Relations,* 51.

79. SarDesai, *Indian Foreign Policy,* 105.

80. *Documents relating to British Involvement,* 23.

81. Southeast Asia Department of the USSR Foreign Ministry, "On the Situation with the Implementation of the Geneva Agreements on Indochina," memorandum, undated, AVP RF, f. 079, op. 12, p. 18, d. 17, l. 114.

82. Mikhail Zimyanin-Sziemanowski, memorandum of conversation, April 12, 1957, Ibid., d. 5, l. 138.

83. Mikhail Zimyanin-Pham Van Dong, memorandum of conversation, April 12, 1957, Ibid., l. 142.

84. Letter to CPSU CC, draft version, April, 1957, AVP RF, f. 079, op. 12, p. 18, d. 17, l. 24.

85. Ibid., ll. 30–31.

86. USSR Foreign Ministry to the CPSU CC, May 14, 1957, Ibid., ll. 46–47.

87. *Documents relating to British Involvement,* 23.

88. Southeast Asia Department of the USSR Foreign Ministry, "On the Situation with the Implementation of the Geneva Agreements on Indochina," l. 115.

89. USSR embassy in DRV, "Annual political report for 1957," April 3/7, 1958, RGANI, f. 5, op. 49, d. 45, l. 122.

90. USSR embassy in DRV, "Report on socialist countries' aid to DRV," April 28, 1960, AVP RF, f. 079, op. 15, p. 30, d. 18, ll. 35, 36, 37, 42.

91. Mikhail Zimyanin-Luo Guibo, memorandum of conversation, January 15, 1957, Ibid., op. 12, p. 17, d. 5, l. 7.

92. Mikhail Zimyanin-Ho Chi Minh-Truong Chinh-Nguyen Duy Trinh, memorandum of conversation, January 17, 1957, Ibid., l. 13.

93. For the effect of the twentieth CPSU congress see Gaddis, *We Now Know,* 208–218.

94. Khrushchev declared that "there is no fatal inevitability of war. Now there are powerful public and political forces who possess serious means for not allowing the imperialists to unleash the war. . . ." (Khrushchev, *Otchetnyi doklad Tsentral'nogo Komiteta,* 40). The Soviet leader's conviction was probably strengthened by information sent to him by various Soviet ministries, among them the Foreign Ministry's committee on information, which prepared a memorandum "On Changes in Placing and Correlation of Forces in the Bourgeois Circles of the Principal Capitalist Countries on the Questions of War and Peace," RGANI, f. 89, perechen' 70, doc. 3, l. 6. This memorandum includes the following passage:

> The influential bourgeois circles, especially in the West European countries, have come to the conclusion that the development of thermonuclear weapons, strategic aviation, and intercontinental ballistic missiles made hopeless the politics of reaching decisive predominance of the Western bloc over the countries of the socialist camp. This promoted neutralist and antimilitaristic tendencies in some bourgeois circles which respective governments could not fail but take into account.

95. Ang, *Vietnamese Communists' Relations,* 21.

96. Mikhail Zimyanin-Nguyen Duy Trinh, memorandum of conversation, April 27, 1956, AVP RF, f. 079, op. 11, p. 13, d. 5, l. 85.

97. Ibid., l. 90.

98. Fall, *The Two Viet-Nams,* 188. During a conversation with Soviet chargé d'affaires A. M. Popov, Ho Chi Minh himself assessed Stalin's actions as 70 percent positive. Ho believed the Soviet dictator's mistakes made up only 30 percent of his actions. See A. M. Popov-Ho Chi Minh, memorandum of conversation, January 3, 1957, AVP RF, f. 079, op. 12, p. 17, d. 5, l. 1.

99. Ibid., ll. 87–88. Vietnamese sources reported that during the agrarian reform 2,203 party members were imprisoned, 317 were executed by shooting, and 626 died in prison. Out of 95,934 farms that had been expropriated because they belonged to landlords, only 42,932 farms in fact belonged to landlords, while 53,002 belonged to rich peasants and peasants of average means. See P. Slyusarenko (counsellor)-Thai Diem (deputy chairman of provincial committee), memorandum of conversation, November 28, 1957, AVP RF, f. 079, op. 12, p. 17, d. 6, l. 162; USSR embassy in DRV, "Annual political report for 1957," RGANI, f. 5, op. 49, d. 45, l. 51.

100. The land reform in North Vietnam was patterned on the agrarian policy of China and was guided by Chinese advisers. In addition, in May 1956 China inaugurated a more relaxed ideology, which became known as the hundred-flowers policy. The Chinese communist leaders permitted free criticism and more freedom in literature and art. See Ang, *Vietnamese Communists' Relations,* 37; Fall, *The Two Viet-Nams,* 188.

101. Fall, *The Two Viet-Nams,* 188.

102. Ang, *Vietnamese Communists' Relations,* 36.

103. *Boyevoi avangard v'etnamskogo naroda. Istoriia Kommunisticheskoi partii V'etnama* (Militant vanguard of the Vietnamese people: History of the Communist party of Vietnam), trans. from the Vietnamese (Moscow: Politizdat, 1981), 114.

104. Cited in Ang, *Vietnamese Communists' Relations,* 26.

105. Khrushchev, *Otchetnyi doklad Tsentral'nogo Komiteta,* 43–44.

106. He Di, "The Most Respected Enemy: Mao Zedong's Perception of the United States," in *Toward a History of Chinese Communist Foreign Relations, 1920s–1960s: Personalities and Interpretive Approaches,* ed. Michael H. Hunt and Niu Jun (Washington, D.C.: Woodrow Wilson International Center for Scholars Asia Program, 1995), 40.

107. See *Boyevoi avangard v'etnamskogo naroda,* 107.

108. Anderson, *Trapped by Success,* 164.

109. Mikhail Zimyanin-Ho Chi Minh-Pham Van Dong-Vo Nguyen Giap, memorandum of conversation, March 17, 1956, AVP RF, f. 079, op. 11, p. 13, d. 5, l. 13.

110. USSR Foreign Ministry, "On Economic and Technical Aid Rendered by the Soviet Union to the DRV," memorandum, December, 31, 1955, Ibid., op. 10, p. 10, d. 15, ll. 61–62.

111. In his conversation with the Soviet ambassador, Ho Chi Minh mentioned that "Com. Mikoyan will be busy with the realization of the Soviet aid as well as perspectives of economic development of the country" during his visit to the DRV. Ibid., op. 11, p. 13, d. 5, l. 14.

112. Memorandum on the situation with the fulfillment of Soviet obligations within the agreement on Soviet aid in the restoration of DRV economy, undated, AVP RF, f. 079, op. 12, p. 18, d. 19, ll. 23–29.

113. Ang, *Vietnamese Communists' Relations,* 51–52.

114. Mikhail Zimyanin-Vo Nguyen Giap, memorandum of conversation, June 26, 1957, AVP RF, f. 079, op. 12, p. 17, d. 5, l. 241.

115. Vasilii Kuznetzov (deputy foreign minister)-V. D. Sokolovskii (chief of general

staff), memorandum, highly urgent, top secret, June 29, 1957, AVP RF, f. 079, op. 12, p. 18, d. 13, l. 13. This message informs the Soviet general staff about arrival of Ho Chi Minh to Moscow on an unofficial visit, during which "he is planning to discuss some political and economic questions as well as the question of army." The message requested the military to prepare materials "which could be required in the course of the negotiations and for the working out of proposals of the Soviet side."

116. Mikhail Zimyanin to Andrei Gromyko, memorandum, November 18, 1957, Ibid., l. 36.

117. See, for example, Ang, *Vietnamese Communists' Relations,* 62–65.

118. AVP RF, f. 079, op. 12, p. 18, d. 13, l. 36. The Soviet ambassador also confirmed to Gromyko Giap's sympathy toward the Soviet Union. He wrote that "Com. Vo Nguyen Giap is, after Ho Chi Minh, one of the closest to the Soviet Union, if not *the* closest party and state leader of Vietnam."

119. B. Volkov (head of Southeast Asia Department, USSR Foreign Ministry) to B. Podtserob (general secretary of the Foreign Ministry), memorandum, July 9, 1957, Ibid., l. 24.

120. N. S. Patolichev and Yu.V. Andropov to the CPSU CC, undated. Ibid., l. 33. Rumors about Ho's illness were justified; see Ang, *Vietnamese Communists' Relations,* 63.

Notes to Chapter 6

1. If the fractured world collapses, the fearless will be hit by the wreckage. Quintus Horatius Flaccus, *Carmina,* III, 3, 7.

2. *Cold War International History Project Bulletin,* 6–7 (Winter 1995/1996): 155.

3. On the Comintern's policy toward China and the CCP, see Brandt, *Stalin's Failure in China, 1924–1927.*

4. Chen Jian and Yang Kuisong, "Chinese Politics and the Collapse of the Sino-Soviet Alliance" in *Brothers in Arms: The Rise and Fall of the Sino-Soviet Alliance, 1945–1963,* ed. Odd Arne Westad (Stanford: Stanford University Press, 1998), 250.

5. François Fejtö, *Chine-URSS: La fin d'une hégémonie. Les origines du grand schisme communiste, 1950–1957* (Paris: Plon, 1964), 39.

6. Shu Guang Zhang, "Sino-Soviet Economic Cooperation," in *Brothers in Arms: The Rise and Fall of the Sino-Soviet Alliance, 1945–1963,* ed. Odd Arne Westad (Stanford: Stanford University Press, 1998), 195.

7. Khrushchev, *Vremia,* vol. 3, 23–24.

8. Kapitsa, *Na raznykh parallelyakh,* 67.

9. Khrushchev, *Vremia,* vol. 3, 21.

10. In *Chine-URSS,* on page 116, Fejtö writes, "[f]rom the formal point of view, there was no difference between Stalin's demand to Ràkosi to hang alleged Titoist Rajk and the pressure Khrushchev wanted to impose on the Hungarian and Bulgarian parties, in the name of the principles of the *Soviet* twentieth congress, to replace Stalinists Ràkosi and Chervenkov." Emphasis in original.

11. Ibid., 113.

12. Chen and Yang, "Chinese Politics," 260–261.

13. Fejtö, *Chine-URSS,* 87.

14. Chen and Yang, "Chinese Politics," 262.

15. Ibid., 260.

16. On the Polish and Hungarian crises and China's role in them see Chen and Yang, "Chinese Politics," 264; and *Sovietskii Soyuz i vengherskii krisis 1956 goda: Dokumenty* (The Soviet Union and the Hungarian 1956 crisis: Documents) (Moscow: ROSSPEN, 1998), 335, 457–462.

17. Chen and Yang, "Chinese Politics," 264.

18. Zhang, "Sino-Soviet Economic Cooperation," 207.

19. Khrushchev, *Vremia,* vol. 3, 57.

20. Chen and Yang, "Chinese Politics," 266.

21. Kapitsa, *Na raznykh parallelyakh,* 60.

22. Fejtö, *Chine-URSS,* 203.

23. Ang, *Vietnamese Communists' Relations,* 69.

24. Mao Zedong-Pavel Yudin, minutes of conversation, July 22, 1958, *Cold War International History Project Bulletin* 6–7 (Winter 1995/1996): 155.

25. For the contents of Khrushchev's negotiations with Mao in July–August, 1958, see "Peregovory N. S. Khrushcheva c Mao Tsedunom, 31 iulia–3 avgusta 1958 g. i 2 oktiabria 1959 g." (Negotiations of N. S. Khrushchev with Mao Zedong, 31 July–3 August, 1958, and 2 October 1959), *Novaiia i noveishaia istoriia* (Modern and contemporary history) (2001): 100–128.

26. USSR embassy in PRC, "1958 annual political report," March 30, 1959, noted: "While undertaking, in late August, a serious military-political action in the region of Taiwan, the Chinese friends, having based on the supposition that the resolution of the Taiwan question is but an internal business of China, did not inform the Soviet government well in advance about their plans." RGANI, f. 5, op. 49, d. 134, l. 84.

27. On other motives and considerations of the Chinese leadership, see Li Xiaobing, Chen Jian, and David L. Wilson, "Mao Zedong's Handling of the Taiwan Straits Crisis of 1958: Chinese Recollections and Documents" in *Cold War International History Project Bulletin* 6–7 (Winter 1995/1996): 208–227.

28. Although the timing of the turning point in the Sino-Soviet conflict is debatable and other scholars regard other events in 1957 or even 1956 as the watershed between cooperation and conflict in Soviet-Chinese relations, never before the summer of 1958 dared Mao openly accuse the Soviets of disregarding his claim to independence and equality. It is also worth noting that this open defiance followed the second session of the eighth CCP congress (May 2–23), which officially launched the Great Leap Forward, a "radical transformation of China's polity, economy, and society" (Chen and Yang, "Chinese Politics," 271). It was after this session that the Soviet embassy started to register a "more watchful approach toward the Soviet experience" on the part of Beijing. RGANI, f. 5, op. 49, d. 134, l. 90.

29. "My Observations on the Soviet Union," Zhou Enlai to Mao Zedong and the Central Leadership, January 24, 1957, *Cold War International History Project Bulletin* 6–7 (Winter 1995/1996): 154.

30. For details on the Sino-Indian border dispute, see *Cold War International History Project Bulletin* 8–9 (Winter 1996/1997): 251–269.

31. Mikhail Suslov to plenary session of CPSU CC, report, special dossier, December 22–26, 1959, RGANI, f. 2, op. 1, d. 415, ll. 28–29.

32. Ibid., l. 9; USSR embassy in PRC, "1958 annual political report," l. 91.

33. Suslov to CPSU CC, l. 13.

34. Cited in Zhang, "Sino-Soviet Economic Cooperation," 212.

35. Khrushchev, *Vremia,* vol. 3, 66–67.

36. USSR embassy in PRC, "1958 annual political report," l. 148.

37. USSR embassy in PRC, "The CCP's Attitude toward the National Liberation Movement," report, April 29, 1961, RGANI, f. 5, op. 49, d. 435, ll. 42–53.

38. Ibid., l. 56. See also USSR embassy in PRC, "Visits to China of Delegations from Latin American Countries in 1960: The Development of Relations between the PRC and Those Countries in the Second Half of 1960," report, January 11, 1961, RGANI, f. 5, op. 49, d. 435, ll. 1–6.

39. Mikhail Suslov, "On the Trip of the Soviet Party-Governmental Delegation to the People's Republic of China," draft of report prepared for the plenary session of the CPSU CC, December 22–26, 1959, RGANI, f. 2, op. 1, d. 415, ll. 34–35; see also "Peregovory N. S. Khrushcheva c Mao Tsedunom," 94–106.

40. "Peregovory N. S. Khrushcheva c Mao Tsedunom," 101.

41. "Nevertheless, [Khrushchev] said, the Chinese presented a special and delicate situation since they had their own way of looking on problems and the Soviets did not want to tell them how to run their country." See "Dispatch from the Embassy in the Soviet Union to the Department of State, June 26, 1959," U. S. Department of State, *Foreign Relations of the United States (FRUS), 1958–1960: Eastern Europe Region; Soviet Union; Cyprus,* vol. 10 (Washington, D.C.: U.S. Government Printing Office, 1993), part 1, 277.

42. U.S. Department of State, *FRUS, 1958–1960: China,* vol. 19 (Washington, D.C.: U.S. Government Printing Office, 1996), 593.

43. Ibid., 719–720.

44. See, for example, Partha S. Ghosh, *Sino-Soviet Relations: U.S. Perceptions and Policy Responses, 1949–1959* (New Delhi: Uppal Publishing House, 1981).

45. A. M. Popov (chargé d'affaires)-Ho Chi Minh, memorandum of conversation, January 3, 1957, AVP RF, f. 079, op. 12, p. 17, d. 5, l. 1.

46. See, for example, *Boyevoy avanguard v'etnamskogo naroda,* 114.

47. Ang, *Vietnamese Communists' Relations,* 68.

48. P. J. Honey, *Communism in North Vietnam: Its Role in the Sino-Soviet Dispute* (Westport, Conn.: Greenwood Press, 1973), 12.

49. Ibid., 62.

50. Ang, *Vietnamese Communists' Relations,* 74.

51. USSR embassy in PRC, "1958 annual political report," l. 154.

52. Ang, *Vietnamese Communists' Relations,* 102–103.

53. Southeast Asia Department, USSR Foreign Ministry, "On Vietnam-China Relations," memorandum, July 2, 1960, AVP RF, f. 079, op. 15, p. 30, d. 20, l. 49.

54. Ang, *Vietnamese Communists' Relations,* 77.

55. "On Vietnam-China Relations," l. 50.

56. Ibid.

57. USSR embassy in DRV, 1958 annual political report, February 19, 1959, RGANI, f. 5, op. 49, d. 139, ll. 78–79, 117. The embassy complained that almost all its proposals concerning the DRV remained unrealized (l. 117).

58. Radvanyi, *Delusion and Reality,* 26.

59. USSR embassy in DRV, "On Some Issues of the Struggle for the Fulfillment of

the Geneva Agreements on Indochina in 1959," political letter, May 28, 1959, RGANI, f. 5, op. 49, d. 253, ll. 3–5.

60. USSR embassy in DRV, 1958 annual political report, ll. 120–121. Emphasis added.

61. See A. M. Popov (chargé d'affaires)-Romanecki (head of Polish delegation in ICC), memorandum of conversation, October 1, 1958, AVP RF f. 079, op. 13, p. 20, d. 9, ll. 70–74; and Leonid Sokolov (Soviet ambassador)-S. S. Ansari (chairman of ICC in Vietnam), memorandum of conversation, December 8, 1958, RGANI, f. 5, op. 49, d. 252, l. 7.

62. The fact that the fifteenth plenum of the Lao Dong Party convened in December 1958 is mentioned in Southeast Asia Department, USSR Foreign Ministry, "The Situation in South Vietnam," memorandum, July 19, 1960, AVP RF, f. 079, op. 15, p. 30, d. 18, l. 113.

63. *Boyevoy avanguard v'etnamskogo naroda,* 117.

64. Ibid.

65. Cited in Ang, *Vietnamese Communists' Relations,* 98.

66. USSR embassy in DRV, 1959 annual political report, February 29, 1960, RGANI, f. 5, op. 49, d. 253, l. 31.

67. According to Ang in *Vietnamese Communists' Relations,* page 86, based on Chinese sources, during Ho Chi Minh's visit to China in the summer of 1958, the North Vietnamese leader discussed with Zhou Enlai and Deng Xiaoping how the Chinese could assist the Vietnamese Communists in their struggle in the South. Ho even gave the Chinese leaders a document regarding the North Vietnamese strategy in the struggle against the Americans in the South and asked for their opinion.

68. Leonid Sokolov-Pham Hung, memorandum of conversation, June 11, 1959, AVP RF, f. 079, op. 14, p. 23, d. 5, ll. 151, 152.

69. Ang, *Vietnamese Communists' Relations,* 131, 134.

70. Ibid., 116, 118.

71. Ibid., 123. Ang states that during a meeting with Zhou Enlai in August 1959, Ho Chi Minh informed the Chinese leader about North Vietnamese plans regarding the South. Zhou assured Ho of the readiness of China to provide the DRV with $500 million worth of weaponry, equipment, and funds to support the liberation struggle.

72. Information provided by Ung Van Khiem, DRV deputy foreign minister, to the heads of diplomatic missions of the socialist countries, April 15, 1960, RGANI, f. 5, op. 49, d. 347, ll. 107–108.

73. Ibid.

74. "Directives to the Representative of the Soviet Chairman of the Geneva Conference on Indochina at the Negotiations of the Two Chairmen on the Issue of the Further Financing of the International Commission on Supervision and Control in Indochina," April 14, 1960, AVP RF, f. 079, op. 15, p. 30, d. 15, l. 6.

75. With the Polish delegate dissenting, the ICC decided that Law 10/59 "does not contain any provision specifically designed to discriminate against, or subject to reprisals, persons or organizations on account of their activities during the hostilities, and therefore, Law 10/59 as such does not attract Article 14(c) or any other article of the Geneva Agreements." Regarding MAAG, the Indian and Canadian members of the ICC were of the view that the total number of foreign personnel could reach the level that the French had had at the time of the armistice. "This meant that the South Vietnam gov-

ernment could in fact invite more American military personnel than existed at the time, if the total number did not exceed 888 and if the entry and departure of the personnel were supervised by ICC teams." SarDesai, *Indian Foreign Policy,* 198, 200.

76. Vo Nguyen Giap (deputy prime minister and minister of defense)-Georgii Pushkin, meeting, May 16, 1960, AVP RF, f. 079, op. 15, p. 28, d. 4, ll. 10–11, 13.

77. Leonid Sokolov-Le Duan, memorandum of conversation, May 17, 1960, RGANI, f. 5, op. 49, d. 346, l. 122.

78. Ang, *Vietnamese Communists' Relations,* 149.

79. "Theses of the Political Report of the Central Committee to the Congress of the Workers' Party of Vietnam," undated, RGANI, f. 5, op. 49, d. 345, l. 27.

80. Ibid.

81. "Notes on the Two Sections of the Theses of the Report of the WPV CC to the Third Congress," June 1, 1960, AVP RF, f. 079, op. 15, p. 30, d. 18, l. 73.

82. Ibid.

83. Ibid., l. 74.

84. The Soviets were apparently relying on information provided by Deputy Foreign Minister Ung Van Khiem at a briefing in Hanoi. Khiem said that there was no need for Hanoi to dispatch arms to South Vietnam: "First, a significant amount of weaponry was left in the South during the regrouping [of Vietminh troops] and, second, reserves of weapons are constantly replenished in the course of the encounters with governmental troops." RGANI, f. 5, op. 49, d. 347, l. 108.

85. Ang, *Vietnamese Communists' Relations,* 147–148.

86. Leonid Sokolov-Pham Van Dong, memorandum of conversation, May 17, 1960, AVP RF, f. 079, op. 15, p. 28, d. 6, ll. 124, 126.

87. "On Vietnam-China Relations," ll. 47, 48.

88. Ibid., l. 48.

89. Far East Department, USSR Foreign Ministry, "The PRC's Relations with the KPDR, MPR, and DRV," memorandum, December 6, 1960, AVP RF, f. 0100, op. 53, p. 463, d. 82, ll. 22–32.

90. Frol Kozlov, "On the Results of the Conference of the Fraternal Parties in Bucharest and the Erroneous Position of the Leadership of the CCP CC on Some Issues of Principle of the Marxist-Leninist Theory and Contemporary International Relations," report at plenary session of CPSU CC, undated draft, RGANI, f. 2, op. 1, d. 458, l. 15.

91. Ibid., l. 74.

92. "Notes on the Two Sections of the Theses," l. 74.

93. A. M. Malukhin (counsellor)-Tran Chong Quat (DRV chargé d'affaires in China), memorandum of conversation, June 6, 1960, RGANI, f. 5, op. 49, d. 346, l. 161.

94. L. I. Arsenyev (representative of the Soviet news agency [Sovinformbureau] in the DRV)-Shi (official of the WPV CC propaganda department), memorandum of conversation, July 5, 1960, RGANI, f. 5, op. 49, d. 346, l. 162.

95. N. I. Godunov-Ung Van Khiem, memorandum of conversation, July 9, 1960, RGANI, f. 5, op. 49, d. 346, ll. 164–165.

96. Ibid., l. 165.

97. U.S. intelligence traced the visit of Ho Chi Minh as well as some other Communist leaders to the Soviet Union and connected it with "a forthcoming Sino-Soviet showdown." See "Memorandum Prepared in the State Department's Bureau of Intelligence and Research, August 26, 1960" *FRUS, 1958–1960,* vol. 19, 714.

98. Ang, *Vietnamese Communists' Relations,* 158. The author refers to the recollec-

tions of Hoang Van Hoan, a prominent Vietnamese official who later defected to China, who accompanied Ho Chi Minh on his trip to the Soviet Union.

99. N. I. Godunov-Ho Chi Minh, memorandum of conversation, June 17, 1960, AVP RF, f. 079, op. 15, p. 28, d. 6, l. 157.

100. Partiia trudiashchikhsia V'etnama, *III syezd Partii trudyashchikhsya V'etnama (Khanoi, 5–12 sentyabrya 1960 goda)* (The third congress of the Workers' Party of Vietnam, Hanoi, 5–12 September, 1960) (Moscow: Politizdat, 1961), 17.

101. "In order that North Vietnam can safely build up socialism, in order for peace in Indochina and in the whole world to be preserved, it is necessary to resolutely struggle against American imperialists and their lackeys in the South, to frustrate the realization of their policy of aggression and war and to overthrow their savage yoke. There is no other way for the population of South Vietnam." Ibid., 25.

102. Victor Likhachev (head of Southeast Asia Department, USSR Foreign Ministry) to Leonid Sokolov (ambassador to DRV), diplomatic communication, December 20, 1960, AVP RF, f. 079, op. 15, p. 28, d. 3, l. 39. The Foreign Ministry criticized the Soviet embassy for its failure to analyze properly the new tactics of the DRV leadership in the South and the Chinese influence in Hanoi.

103. Partiia trudiashchikhsia V'etnama, *III syezd Partii trudyashchikhsya V'etnama,* 123.

104. Honey, in *Communism in North Vietnam,* page 81, writes: "An analysis of all the Vietnamese speeches made before, during, and after the Hanoi Congress leaves no room for doubt that North Vietnam had shifted its previous position and moved closer to the Soviet Union."

105. I. K. Kiselyov-Willie Rumpf, memorandum of conversation, September, 12, 1960, RGANI, f. 5, op. 49, d. 345, ll. 120–121.

106. Honey, *Communism in North Vietnam,* 81.

107. Khrushchev, *Vremia,* vol. 3, 94.

108. Zhang, "Sino-Soviet Economic Cooperation," 214.

109. Kapitsa, *Na raznykh parallelyakh,* 71.

110. Mikhail Suslov, "On the Results of the Conference of Representatives of the Communist and Workers' Parties," report, December 16, 1960, RGANI, f. 2, op. 1, d. 495, l. 34.

111. Ibid., l. 36.

112. Ibid., ll. 47–49.

113. Ibid., l. 68.

114. Stenographic record of Suslov's report, January 18, 1961, RGANI, f. 2, op. 1, d. 510, l. 102.

115. Honey, *Communism in North Vietnam,* 87.

116. "Editorial Note," *FRUS, 1958–1960,* vol. 19, 742–743.

Notes to Chapter 7

1. "Peregovory N. S. Khrushcheva," 105.

2. Arthur J. Dommen, *Conflict in Laos: The Politics of Neutralization* (New York: Praeger, 1965), 104–105.

3. Ya. M. Lomakin (counsellor)-Nguyen Long Bang (DRV ambassador to USSR),

memorandum of conversation, January 5, 1954, AVP RF, f. 0100, op. 47, p. 379, d. 8, l. 43.

4. Point five of the final declaration demands that the governments of Cambodia and Laos not "join in any agreement with other States if this agreement includes the obligation to participate in a military alliance not in conformity with the principles of the Charter of the United Nations or, in the case of Laos, with the principles of the agreement on the cessation of hostilities in Laos or, so long as their security is not threatened, the obligation to establish bases on Cambodian or Lao territory for the military forces of foreign Powers." See *Documents relating to British Involvement,* 83–84.

5. AVP RF, f. 06, op. 14, p. 12, d. 171, l. 36.

6. See, for example, "Outline of General Smith's Remarks to the President and Bipartisan Congressional Group, June 23, 1954," *FRUS, 1952–1954,* vol. 13, part 2, 1732.

7. Ang, *Vietnamese Communists' Relations,* 23.

8. Vasilii Kuznetzov (deputy foreign minister)-Truong Chinh, memorandum of conversation, February 28, 1956, AVP RF, f. 079, op. 11, p. 13, d. 2, ll. 5–7.

9. Bernard Fall believed that the Soviets were at least partly responsible for the progress. See Bernard B. Fall, *Anatomy of a Crisis: The Laotian Crisis of 1960–1961* (Garden City: Doubleday, 1969), 71.

10. Ang, *Vietnamese Communists' Relations,* 34–35.

11. Ibid., 54–55.

12. Ibid.

13. Mikhail Zimyanin-Pham Van Dong, memorandum of conversation, January 18, 1957, AVP RF, f. 079, op. 12, p. 17, d. 5, l. 15.

14. Mikhail Zimyanin-Luo Guibo, memorandum of conversation, January 23, 1957, Ibid., l. 31.

15. Ibid., l. 32.

16. Mikhail Zimyanin-Luo Guibo, memorandum of conversation, March 8, 1957, Ibid., ll. 99–101.

17. Mikhail Zimyanin-Luo Guibo, memorandum of conversation, April 24, 1957, Ibid., l. 149.

18. Ang, *Vietnamese Communists' Relations,* 55.

19. Mikhail Zimyanin-Luo Guibo, memorandum of conversation, June 10, 1957, AVP RF, f. 079, op. 12, p. 17, d. 5, l. 209.

20. Mikhail Zimyanin-Thanh Son (chairman, WPV CC committee on Laos), memorandum of conversation, June 12, 1957, Ibid., ll. 211–219.

21. A. M. Popov (chargé d'affaires)-Thanh Son, memorandum of conversation, September 6, 1957, AVP RF, f. 079, op. 12, p. 17, d. 6, ll. 61, 64.

22. A. M. Popov (chargé d'affaires)-Li Zhiminh (PRC chargé d'affaires), memorandum of conversation, September 13, 1957, Ibid., ll. 52–54.

23. Ang, *Vietnamese Communists' Relations,* 60–61; Fall, *Anatomy of a Crisis,* 78.

24. A. M. Popov (chargé d'affaires)-Ung Van Khiem (DRV deputy foreign minister), memorandum of conversation, November 22, 1957, AVP RF, f. 079, op. 12, p. 17, d. 6, l. 149.

25. A. M. Popov-Ho Chi Minh, memorandum of conversation, January 28, 1958, AVP RF, f. 079, op. 13, p. 20, d. 8, l. 11.

26. A. M. Popov-He Wei, memorandum of conversation, February 3, 1958, Ibid., l. 25.

27. Fall, *Anatomy of a Crisis,* 86.

28. *Documents relating to British Involvement,* 25.

29. SarDesai, *Indian Foreign Policy,* 183.

30. *Documents relating to British Involvement,* 25.

31. Initially India opposed the Canadian proposal and suggested a compromise formula that envisaged a reduction in the commission's activities. But by the end of June it changed its stand, deciding to withdraw the commission from Laos. Among other reasons, "[i]t was persuaded by the RLG's inflexible attitude and therefore felt that there was no point in remaining in a country whose government did not want it." SarDesai, *Indian Foreign Policy,* 187.

32. Leonid I. Sokolov-heads of Polish delegations in Laos and Vietnam, memorandum of conversation, Sokolov diary, July 26, 1958, AVP RF, f. 079, op. 13, p. 20, d. 8, l. 180.

33. Fall, *Anatomy of a Crisis,* 88.

34. Leonid I. Sokolov-Ung Van Khiem, memorandum of conversation, November 3, 1958, AVP RF, f. 079, op. 13, p. 20, d. 8, l. 85.

35. Cited in Ang, *Vietnamese Communists' Relations,* 82.

36. A. M. Popov-Tiao Liung (head of USSR Department, DRV Foreign Ministry), memorandum of conversation, August 23, 1958, AVP RF, f. 079, op. 13, p. 20, d. 9, ll. 11–13.

37. A. M. Popov-Ung Van Khiem, memorandums of conversations, August 13 and 25, 1958, Ibid., ll. 6, 14.

38. "Resuming interparty contacts with our Laotian friends . . . we constantly remember that in this question we must be extremely careful in trying to provide no visible pretext to our enemies for accusing the Neo Lao Hak Xat of outside support, as well as us in political instigation and interference in the internal affairs of Laos." Ung Van Khiem to A. M. Popov, letter, August 25, 1958, AVP RF, f. 079, op. 13, p. 20, d. 9, l. 19.

39. V. I. Shvedov (Soviet attaché)-Van Phu (third secretary of PRC embassy in DRV), memorandum of conversation, November 26, 1958, RGANI, f. 5, op. 49, d. 252, ll. 1–5.

40. G. P. Popov (first secretary of USSR embassy in DRV)-Mo Yanzhun (counsellor of PRC embassy), memorandum of conversation, December 11, 1958, Ibid., ll. 11–13.

41. Ang, *Vietnamese Communists' Relations,* 95.

42. Dommen, *Conflict in Laos,* 115.

43. Fall, *Anatomy of a Crisis,* 97.

44. Leonid I. Sokolov-Ung Van Khiem, memorandum of conversation, February 28, 1959, RGANI, f. 5, op. 49, d. 252, ll. 180, 183.

45. Leonid I. Sokolov-Ung Van Khiem, memorandum of conversation, March 9, 1959, Ibid., ll. 176–179.

46. USSR embassy in DRV, "Political Situation in Laos after the Formation of the Government of Phoui Sananikone," report, May 28, 1959, Ibid., l. 134.

47. Ang, *Vietnamese Communists' Relations,* 107.

48. Dommen, *Conflict in Laos,* 117–118.

49. Leonid I. Sokolov-Pham Van Dong, memorandum of conversation, May 26, 1959, RGANI, f. 5, op. 49, d. 252, l. 238.

50. G. P. Popov-Le Loc (DRV foreign ministry), memorandum of conversation, June 12, 1959, Ibid., l. 251.

51. Dommen, *Conflict in Laos,* 118.

52. Ang, *Vietnamese Communists' Relations,* 119–120.

53. Pavel Yudin-Zhang Wentien, memorandum of conversation, May 25, 1959, RGANI, f. 5, op. 49, d. 252, l. 242.

54. G. P. Popov-Mo Yanzhun (PRC chargé d'affaires in DRV), memorandum of conversation, July 20, 1959, Ibid., l. 268.

55. G. P. Popov-Ung Van Khiem, memorandum of conversation, July 27, 1959, Ibid., l. 295.

56. Ang, *Vietnamese Communists' Relations,* 124.

57. G. P. Popov (chargé d'affaires)-Vo Nguyen Giap-Ung Van Khiem, memorandum of conversation, September 6, 1959, RGANI, f. 5, op. 49, d. 252, l. 156.

58. "Peregovory N. S. Khrushcheva," 105–106.

59. G. P. Popov-Ung Van Khiem, memorandum of conversation, September 5, 1959, RGANI, f. 5, op. 49, d. 252, l. 150.

60. Fall, *Anatomy of a Crisis,* 141.

61. S. F. Antonov (chargé d'affaires)-Pham Binh (DRV chargé d'affaires in PRC), memorandum of conversation, September 18, 1959; and Leonid I. Sokolov (USSR ambassador)-Nguyen Duc Duong (DRV deputy foreign minister), memorandum of conversation, September 23, 1959, RGANI, f. 5, op. 49, d. 252, ll. 316–320, 331–333.

62. N. I. Godunov (counsellor)-Mai Phang (member, WPV CC committee on Laos), memorandum of conversation, October 19, 1959, Ibid., l. 344.

63. Fall, *Anatomy of a Crisis,* 155.

64. Ibid., 143.

65. Dommen, *Conflict in Laos,* 121.

66. Fall, *Anatomy of a Crisis,* 165.

67. USSR embassy in DRV, "Aggravation of the Internal Political Situation in Laos in August–October 1959," report, November 26, 1959, RGANI, f. 5, op. 49, d. 252, l. 384.

68. Ang, *Vietnamese Communists' Relations,* 125.

69. 1959 annual political report of the Soviet embassy in the DRV, February 29, 1960, RGANI, f. 5, op. 49, d. 253, l. 90.

70. Fall, *Anatomy of a Crisis,* 176.

71. Soviet diplomats in the DRV provided a generally correct estimate of the events of late December 1959–early January 1960 in Laos; however, they credited the British and French, who did not want to see U.S. influence in the country, with initiating the démarche against Phoumi's coup. As to the United States, "it *had to* make certain concessions on this issue, *considering the international situation* and under the influence of Britain and France." RGANI, f. 5, op. 49, d.253, l. 93. Emphasis added.

72. Dommen, *Conflict in Laos,* 129.

73. Fall, *Anatomy of a Crisis,* 182.

74. Ibid., 183.

75. Ho Chi Minh confided to Soviet chargé N. I. Godunov that the North Vietnamese themselves tried to arrange the escape of the Pathet Lao leaders, but "this turned out to be a very difficult affair." See N. I. Godunov-Ho Chi Minh, memorandum of conversation, June 17, 1960, AVP RF, f. 079, op. 15, p. 28, d. 6, l. 158.

76. Dommen, *Conflict in Laos,* 138.

77. "We, said Khiem, are waiting for our esteemed friend, Prince Souphanouvong, with impatience. Nothing radical will be undertaken without him [in Laos]." See N. I. Godunov-Ung Van Khiem, memorandum of conversation, July 9, 1960, RGANI, f. 5, op. 49, d. 346, l. 167.

78. Fall, *Anatomy of a Crisis,* 184.

79. Ang, *Vietnamese Communists' Relations,* 156–157.

80. Ibid., 165.

81. Ibid.

82. Dommen, *Conflict in Laos,* 154–155.

83. Ibid., 158.

84. Ang, *Vietnamese Communists' Relations,* 166.

85. Fall, *Anatomy of a Crisis,* 194.

86. "Directives to the USSR Ambassador to Laos for Conversations with the Prime Minister of Laos and Other Laotian State and Political Officials," undated, AVP RF, f. 0570, op. 6, p. 3, d. 5, ll. 66–69. Abramov presented his credentials to the king of Laos on October 26, 1960.

87. Ang, *Vietnamese Communists' Relations,* 166.

88. Fall, *Anatomy of a Crisis,* 190.

89. Viktor Likhachev to Georgii Pushkin, diplomatic communication, November 19, 1960, AVP RF, f. 0570, op. 6, p. 3, d. 5, l. 62.

90. Ibid., ll. 62–63.

91. Ibid., ll. 63–64.

92. Ibid., l. 64.

93. Glenn H. Snyder and Paul Diesing, *Conflict among Nations: Bargaining, Decision Making, and System Structure in International Crises* (Princeton: Princeton University Press, 1977), 6.

94. Ang, *Vietnamese Communists' Relations,* 169. Of course, clandestine assistance to the Pathet Lao had been provided by the North Vietnamese for a long time.

95. Viktor Likhachev-Nguyen Van Kinh, memorandum of conversation, November 23, 1960, AVP RF, f. 079, op. 15, p. 28, d. 5, l. 48.

96. Yu. P. Kharkevich (third secretary of USSR embassy in DRV), report, December 22, 1960, RGANI, f. 5, op. 49, d. 446, ll. 12–13.

97. I. K. Kiselyov (counsellor)-Pham Van Dong, memorandum of conversation, December 4, 1960, RGANI, f. 5, op. 49, d. 445, l. 38.

98. N. G. Sudarikov (chargé d'affaires)-Chen Yi, memorandum of conversation, December 8, 1960, AVP RF, f. 0100, op. 53, p. 455, d. 13, ll. 30–34.

99. N. G. Sudarikov-Zhou Enlai, memorandum of conversation, December 9, 1960, Ibid., l. 36–37.

100. N. G. Sudarikov-Li Xian, memorandum of conversation, December 10, 1960, Ibid., l. 53.

101. Ang, *Vietnamese Communists' Relations,* 171.

102. N. G. Sudarikov-Tran Tu Binh (DRV ambassador to PRC), memorandum of conversation, December 13, 1960, AVP RF, f. 0100, op. 53, p. 455, d. 13, l. 58.

103. N. G. Sudarikov-Jien Yunqiuan, memorandum of conversation, December 14, 1960, AVP RF, f. 0100, op. 53, p. 455, d. 13, l. 62.

104. Ang, *Vietnamese Communists' Relations,* 172.

105. Fall, *Anatomy of a Crisis,* 203.

106. N. G. Sudarikov-Chen Yi, memorandum of conversation, December 18, 1960, AVP RF, f. 0100, op. 53, p. 455, d. 13, ll. 66–67.

107. SarDesai, *Indian Foreign Policy,* 227.

108. *Documents relating to British Involvement,* 26–27. For texts of the notes, see pages 154–155 (Nehru); 155–156 (the British); 156–158 (the Soviets).

109. Viktor Likhachev-Nguyen Van Kinh (DRV ambassador to USSR), memorandum of conversation, November 23, 1960, AVP RF, f. 079, op. 15, p. 28, d. 5, l. 49.

110. Pham Van Dong to Nikita S. Khrushchev, telegram, December 16, 1960, AVP RF, f. 079, op. 15, p. 14, d. 1, l. 81.

111. I. K. Kiselyov (Soviet chargé d'affaires)-Pham Van Dong, memorandum of conversation, November 23, 1960, RGANI, f. 5, op. 49, d. 445, ll. 18–22.

112. N. G. Sudarikov-Chen Yi, memorandum of conversation, December 8, 1960, AVP RF, f. 0100, op. 53, p. 454, d. 8, l. 33.

113. David K. E. Bruce, diary entry, January 5, 1961, U.S. Department of State, *FRUS, 1961–1963: Soviet Union,* vol. 5 (Washington, D.C.: U.S. Government Printing Office, 1998), 10.

114. SarDesai, *Indian Foreign Policy,* 227.

115. *Documents relating to British Involvement,* 163–165.

116. Vasilii V. Kuznetzov (USSR deputy foreign minister)-Frank Roberts (British ambassador to USSR), meeting, January 21, 1961, AVP RF, f. 0570, op. 7, p. 5, d. 14, l. 19.

117. N. G. Sudarikov-Zhou Enlai, memorandum of conversation, January 14, 1961, RGANI, f. 5, op. 49, d. 436, l. 37.

118. N. G. Sudarikov (minister-counsellor)-Zhang Hanfu, memorandum of conversation, February 6, 1961, Ibid., ll. 54–55.

119. Leonid I. Sokolov-Vo Nguyen Giap, memorandum of conversation, January 27, 1961, RGANI, f. 5, op. 49, d. 445, l. 59.

120. Ibid., l. 58.

121. Leonid I. Sokolov-Pham Van Dong, memorandum of conversation, February 2, 1961, Ibid., l. 61.

122. Ang, *Vietnamese Communists' Relations,* 175–176.

123. *Documents relating to British Involvement,* 166–168.

124. Kennedy came away with such a feeling from his meeting with the outgoing president on January 19, 1961; see U.S. Department of State, *FRUS, 1961–1963: Laos Crisis,* vol. 24 (Washington, D.C.: U.S. Government Printing Office, 1994), 20.

125. Arthur M. Schlesinger Jr. *A Thousand Days: John F. Kennedy in the White House* (Boston: Houghton Mifflin, 1965), 307.

126. William P. Bundy, unpublished manuscript, Lyndon B. Johnson Library (Johnson Library), papers of William P. Bundy, box 1.

127. "Laos," memorandum, undated, unsigned, top secret, Johnson Library, papers of L. B. Johnson, president, 1963–1969, Vice-Presidential Security File, box 4.

128. Bundy, unpublished manuscript, Johnson Library.

129. John F. Kennedy-Winthrop G. Brown (U.S. ambassador to Laos), memorandum of conversation, February 3, 1961, *FRUS, 1961–1963,* vol. 24, 46.

130. State Department to U.S. embassy in Laos, diplomatic cable, February 10, 1961, *FRUS, 1961–1963,* vol. 24, 51.

131. Fall, *Anatomy of a Crisis,* 212.

132. Diplomatic cable, *FRUS, 1961–1963,* vol. 24, 51.

133. Dean Rusk-Mikhail Menshikov, memorandum of conversation, February 20, 1961, Ibid., 56–58.

134. Mikhail Menshikov-Dean Rusk, memorandum of conversation, February 28, 1961, Ibid., 64–65.

135. Llewellyn Thompson to Department of State, diplomatic cable, March 10, 1961, Ibid., 80–81.

136. Ibid., 82.

137. Ibid., 100. In its message to Moscow on March 23, the British government reiterated its view that the first step in the settlement of the Laotian crisis should be the recall of the ICC to Laos and the arrangement of an armistice. These measures would be followed by an international conference. See *Documents relating to British Involvement,* 169–170.

138. Roger Warner, in *Shooting at the Moon. The Story of America's Clandestine War in Laos* (South Royalton, Vt.: Steerforth Press, 1996), wrote on page 47 that a true map "would have shown rough concentric circles, with the Plain of Jars red, then a blue-colored doughnut shape around it, and then more red outside the blue." The blue color indicated territory controlled by Phoumi Nosavan's forces.

139. Bundy, unpublished manuscript, Johnson Library.

140. John F. Kennedy to Dean Rusk, telegram, March 27, 1961, *FRUS, 1961–1963,* vol. 24, 105–106.

141. *Documents relating to British Involvement,* 27.

142. *FRUS, 1961–1963,* vol. 24, 135.

143. Ang, *Vietnamese Communists' Relations,* 189.

144. State Department to U.S. embassy in Laos, telegram, April 14, 1961, *FRUS, 1961–1963,* vol. 24, 130.

145. Dommen, *Conflict in Laos,* 196.

146. Walt Rostow (deputy special assistant for national security affairs) to John F. Kennedy, memorandum, April 13, 1961, *FRUS, 1961–1963,* vol. 24, 126.

147. Leonid I. Sokolov-Nguyen Chi Thanh, memorandum of conversation, March 25, 1961, RGANI, f. 5, op. 49, d. 445, l. 120.

148. Beijing to Moscow, telegram, March 31, 1961, AVP RF, f. 0570, op. 7, p. 5, d. 14, l. 32.

149. Nikita S. Khrushchev to John F. Kennedy (president-elect), letter, November 9, 1960, U.S. Department of State, *FRUS, 1961–1963: Kennedy-Khrushchev Exchanges,* vol. 6 (Washington, D.C.: U.S. Government Printing Office, 1996), 1.

150. USSR Foreign Ministry, "On Laos," memorandum, March 14, 1961, AVP RF, f. 0570, op. 7, p. 6, d. 19.

151. Ibid., l. 2.

152. Southeast Asia Department, "The Kingdom of Laos," survey, April 14, 1961, AVP RF, f. 0570, op. 7, p. 6, d. 19, l. 16.

153. Leonid I. Sokolov-Nguyen Chi Thanh, memorandum of conversation, March 25, 1961, RGANI, f. 5, op. 49, d. 445, l. 120.

154. Georgii Pushkin-Nguyen Duy Trinh, meeting, April 1, 1961, AVP RF, f. 0570, op. 7, p. 5, d. 14, l. 35.

155. Beijing to Moscow, telegram, April 12, 1961, Ibid., l. 46.

156. N. G. Sudarikov-Zhou Enlai, memorandum of conversation, April 19, 1961, RGANI, f. 5, op. 49, d. 436, ll. 106–107.

157. Beijing to Moscow, telegram, April 12, 1961, AVP RF, f. 0570, op. 7, p. 5, d. 14, l. 41.

158. N. I. Godunov (USSR chargé d'affaires in DRV)-Pham Van Dong, memorandum of conversation, April 27, 1961, RGANI, f. 5, op. 49, d. 445, l. 168.

159. Beijing to Moscow, telegram, April 12, 1961, AVP RF, f. 0570, op. 7, p. 5, d. 14, ll. 43–44.

160. Ang, *Vietnamese Communists' Relations,* 190; see also Souvanna Phouma, diary, April 18, 1961, Library of Congress, Manuscript Division, papers of Souvanna Phouma, box 1, for the prime minister's comment: "Was received by Premier Khrushchev in Sochi. Cordial conversation. Absolute Soviet support."

161. Marek Thee, *Notes of a Witness. Laos and the Second Indochinese War* (New York: Vintage Books, 1973), 18.

162. Ibid., 17.

163. *Documents relating to British Involvement,* 171–173.

164. N. I. Godunov (USSR chargé d'affaires)-Pham Van Dong, memorandum of conversation, April 27, 1961, RGANI, f. 5, op. 49, d. 445, l. 166.

165. Ang, *Vietnamese Communists' Relations,* 192.

166. N. I. Godunov-Pham Van Dong, memorandum of conversation, April 29, 1961, RGANI, f. 5, op. 49, d. 445, ll. 170–171.

167. Ang, *Vietnamese Communists' Relations,* 192.

168. Dommen, *Conflict in Laos,* 206.

169. Thee, *Notes of a Witness,* 53.

170. "Considerations toward Negotiations with the Delegations of the PRC, DRV, and PRP on the Question of a Common Line at the Conference on Laos in Geneva," memorandum, May 5, 1961, AVP RF, f. 0570, op. 7, p. 5, d. 14, ll. 89–92.

171. PRC government to USSR Foreign Ministry, aide-mémoire, delivered May 10, 1961, Ibid., ll. 100–101.

172. Ibid., l. 103.

173. Ibid., l. 104. The same idea had been put forward by the North Vietnamese, who claimed that Austria-like neutrality did not prevent a country from following imperialist powers in its foreign policy. See A. A. Skoryukov (first secretary of USSR embassy in DRV)-Nguyen (deputy head of Southeast Asia Department, DRV Foreign Ministry), memorandum of conversation, April 19, 1961, RGANI, f. 5, op. 49, d. 445, l. 146.

174. Thee, *Notes of a Witness,* 18.

175. Southeast Asia Department, USSR Foreign Ministry, "Toward the Aide-Mémoire of the PRC Government," report, May 12, 1961, AVP RF, f. 0570, op. 7, p. 5, d. 14, l. 108.

176. Southeast Asia Department, USSR Foreign Ministry to Vasilii Kuznetsov (deputy foreign minister), memorandum, May 12, 1961, Ibid., ll. 112–114.

177. "Directives to the Soviet delegation to the international conference on Laos," draft, April 12, 1961, Ibid., l. 63. It becomes clear from the context of other preparatory documents that this draft prepared by the Southeast Asia Department of the Soviet Foreign Ministry was accepted almost completely.

Notes to Chapter 8

1. USSR Foreign Ministry, "Directives to Soviet Delegation to Geneva Conference," draft, April 12, 1961, AVP RF, f. 0570, op. 7, p. 5, d. 14, l. 47.

2. "Taking into account that there is no unity among the U.S., France, and England, as well as among other countries adhered to this bloc, as concerns ways and methods of the

resolution of the Laotian question, it is necessary for the delegation to use this circumstance in the interest of a guarantee of the Conference's decisions acceptable for us." USSR Foreign Ministry, "Directives to Soviet Delegation to Geneva Conference," Ibid., l. 64.

3. N. N. Kryukov (acting head of Southeast Asia Department of the USSR Foreign Ministry)-Korolczyk (Polish counsellor), memorandum of conversation, May 13, 1961, Ibid., l. 115.

4. State Department to Secretary of State, diplomatic communication, May 9, 1961, *FRUS, 1961–1963,* vol. 24, 186.

5. Secretary of State to John F. Kennedy, memorandum, May 1, 1961, Ibid., 161.

6. Nikita S. Khrushchev-leaders of CC of Czechoslovak Communist Party, record of conversation near Bratislava, June 1, 1961, *Istochnik* 3 (1998): 90.

7. Editorial Note. *FRUS, 1961–1963,* vol. 24, 190.

8. Ibid., 192.

9. Heads of delegations of USSR, PRC, DRV and PPR, record of meeting, May 15, 1961, AVP RF, f. 0445, op. 1 p.1 d. 1, l. 11.

10. Chen Yi was handpicked by Mao Zedong during the Sino-Soviet negotiations in 1959 to mount an attack against Moscow's foreign policy. See Kapitsa, *Na raznykh parallelyakh,* 68–69.

11. Heads of delegations, record of meeting, Ibid., ll. 14–15.

12. Andrei Gromyko-Chen Yi, memorandum of conversation, May 14, 1961, AVP RF, f. 0445, op. 1, p. 1, d. 1, l. 2.

13. To justify China's retreat, Chen Yi put forward a suggestion that other countries also make similar proposals in order to deprive India of a unique role in this case. Ibid., l. 21.

14. Arthur Lall, *How Communist China Negotiates* (New York: Columbia University Press, 1968), 1.

15. Andrei Gromyko-Chen Yi, memorandum of conversation, May 14, 1961, AVP RF, f. 0445, op. 1, p. 1, d. 1, l. 6.

16. Qiang Zhai, *China and the Vietnam Wars, 1950–1975* (Chapel Hill: University of North Carolina Press, 2000), 93.

17. Georgii Pushkin-Zhang Hanfu (PRC deputy foreign minister), memorandum of conversation, May 16, 1961, AVP RF, f. 0445, op. 1, p. 1, d. 2, l. 17.

18. Ibid., l. 18.

19. Ibid., ll. 19–20.

20. Zhai, *China and the Vietnam Wars, 1950–1975,* 97, 98.

21. PRC government, aide-mémoire, May 10, 1961, AVP RF, f. 0570, op. 7, p. 5, d. 14, l. 103.

22. Lall, *How Communist China Negotiates,* 125.

23. Ibid., 51.

24. Ibid., 54.

25. U.S. delegation to the conference on Laos to Department of State, diplomatic communication, May 27, 1961, *FRUS, 1961–1963,* vol. 24, 209.

26. Lall, *How Communist China Negotiates,* 58.

27. Delegations of USSR, PRC, DRV, and PPR, record of meeting, May 23, 1961, AVP RF, f. 0445, op. 1, p. 1, d. 1, l. 32.

28. Ibid., l. 41.

29. A. A. Skoryukov (first secretary of USSR embassy in Laos)-Thau Tian, memorandum of conversation, June 4, 1961, RGANI, f. 5, op. 49, d. 445, l. 230.

30. John F. Kennedy to Nikita S. Khrushchev, letter, February 22, 1961, *FRUS, 1961–1963,* vol. 6, 6.

31. Ibid., 19.

32. Ibid., 20.

33. Khrushchev-leaders of CC of Czechoslovak Communist Party, record of conversation, June 1, 1961, 89–90.

34. Schlesinger, *Thousand Days,* 324–325.

35. David Mayers, *The Ambassadors and America's Soviet Policy* (Oxford: Oxford University Press, 1995), 202, 207.

36. U.S. embassy in USSR to Department of State, diplomatic cable, February, 1, 1961, *FRUS, 1961–1963,* vol. 5, 52.

37. Nikita S. Khrushchev-John F. Kennedy, memorandum of conversation, June 3, 1961, Ibid., 189.

38. Ibid., 184, 191–194.

39. Ibid., 191.

40. Nikita S. Khrushchev-John F. Kennedy, memorandum of conversation, June 4, 1961, Ibid., 211–224.

41. Schlesinger, *Thousand Days,* 349–350.

42. John F. Kennedy-Nikita S. Khrushchev, memorandum of conversation, June 4, 1961, *FRUS, 1961–1963,* vol. 5, 207–208, 210.

43. John F. Kennedy-Nikita S. Khrushchev, memorandum of conversation, June 3, 1961, Ibid., 195.

44. Ibid., 196.

45. U.S. delegation to the conference on Laos to the Department of State, diplomatic communication, June 7, 1961, *FRUS, 1961–1963,* vol. 24, 240.

46. Thee, *Notes of a Witness,* 64.

47. Nikolai Sudarikov (Soviet chargé d'affaires)-Chen Yi, memorandum of conversation, July 28, 1961, AVP RF, f. 0570, op. 7, p. 5, d. 14, l. 182.

48. A. A. Skoryukov-General Thong Di (DRV chief military adviser in Laos), memorandum of conversation, June 25–27, 1961, RGANI, f. 5, op. 49, d. 445, l. 247.

49. A. A. Skoryukov-General Man, memorandum of conversation, May 13, 1961, Ibid., l. 204.

50. Ibid., l. 248.

51. Vasilii Chivilyov (Soviet chargé d'affaires in Laos)-Marek Thee, memorandum of conversations, June 17 and 19, 1961, RGANI, f. 5, op. 49, d. 446, l. 166.

52. A. A. Skoryukov-Marek Thee, memorandum of conversation, June 13, 1961, Ibid., ll. 175–176. Emphasis added.

53. Vasilii Chivilyov (Soviet chargé d'affaires in Laos)-Marek Thee, memorandum of conversations, June 17 and 19, 1961, Ibid., ll. 167, 168, 170.

54. Thee, *Notes of a Witness,* 131.

55. Zhai, *China and the Vietnam Wars, 1950–1975,* 99.

56. "The Reaction in the PRC on the Summit between N. S. Khrushchev and Kennedy in Vienna," information report, June 30, 1961, RGANI, f. 5, op. 49, d. 435, ll. 95–96.

57. Ibid., l. 100.

58. Chen Yi went back to Beijing on July 4; he had remained in Geneva longer than

any other foreign minister of the great powers represented at the conference. Rusk had left Geneva in May, and Gromyko in June. Regarding Beijing's approval of Chen Yi's return to China, see Georgii Pushkin-Chen Yi, memorandum of conversation, June 30, 1961, AVP RF, f. 0445, op. 1, p. 1, d. 2, l. 100.

59. Nikolai Sudarikov (Soviet chargé d'affaires)-Chen Yi, memorandum of conversation, July 28, 1961, RGANI, f. 5, op. 49, d. 436, l. 173.

60. Ibid., l. 172.

61. Thee, *Notes of a Witness,* 120.

62. Marek Thee told the Soviet chargé in Laos that "Souphanouvong is in principle against the establishment of the coalition government in Laos. He was a member of such a government and remembers well what was the result. . . ." Vasilii Chivilyov-Marek Thee, memorandum of conversations, June 17 and 19, 1961, RGANI, f. 5, op. 49, d. 446, l. 173.

63. Thee, *Notes of a Witness,* 124.

64. Stepan Chervonenko (Soviet ambassador to China)-Souphanouvong-Zhou Enlai, memorandum of conversations, July 4 and 5, 1961, RGANI, f. 5, op. 49, d. 436, l. 143.

65. Vasilii Chivilyov-Souvanna Phouma, memorandum of conversation, May 10, 1961, RGANI, f. 5, op. 49, d. 446, l. 142.

66. Ibid., l. 147.

67. Vasilii Chivilyov (Soviet chargé d'affaires in Laos)-Khamsouk Keola (acting prime minister)-Sisoumang (state secretary on agriculture), memorandum of conversation, June 11, 1961, Ibid., l. 204.

68. Suren Tovmasyan (Soviet ambassador to DRV)- Czenek Herold (Czechoslovak ambassador to DRV), memorandum of conversation, November 17, 1961, RGANI, f. 5, op. 49, d. 445, l. 282.

69. Nikita S. Khrushchev-Ho Chi Minh, memorandum of conversation, August 19, 1961, Archive of the President of the Russian Federation, f. 3, op. 64, d. 560; published in *Istochnik* 2 (1998): 89.

70. The date of the CPSU CC memorandum on the Laotian problem was mentioned in a conversation between Ambassador Stepan Chervonenko and Chen Yi as being August 31, 1966. See RGANI, f. 5, op. 49, d. 436, l. 201. Marek Thee in his account of the memorandum and the ensuing discussion in Hanoi dated the memorandum to the beginning of September; see Thee, *Notes of a Witness,* 192.

71. Ibid., 192.

72. USSR embassy in DRV to Deputy Foreign Minister Nikolai Firyubin, diplomatic communication, November 14, 1961, AVP RF, f. 0570, op. 7, p. 5, d. 15, l. 76.

73. Suren A. Tovmasyan, presentation, September 23, 1961, Ibid., l. 125.

74. Georgii Pushkin-Zhang Hanfu, memorandum of conversation, July 5, 1961, AVP RF, f. 0445, op. 1, p. 1, d. 2, l. 107.

75. Ibid., l. 108.

76. W. Averell Harriman to the Department of State, diplomatic cable, July 12, 1961, *FRUS, 1961–1963,* vol. 24, 295.

77. W. Averell Harriman to Dean Rusk, diplomatic cable, July 18, 1961, Ibid., 303.

78. Lall, *How Communist China Negotiates,* 108–109.

79. Georgii Pushkin, "On the Activities of the Soviet Delegation at the International Conference on the Settlement of the Laotian Question," report for meeting of collegium of Foreign Ministry, December 27, 1961, AVP RF, f. 0570, op. 7, p. 5, d. 15, ll. 277–278.

80. W. Averell Harriman to Department of State, diplomatic cable, September 13, 1961, *FRUS, 1961–1963,* vol. 24, 411.

81. Memorandum of conversation, Pushkin-Harriman, September 12, 1961, AVP RF, f. 0445, op. 1, p. 1, d. 5, l. 10. The reconstruction of this conversation has been facilitated by the accessibility of both Harriman's (see the preceding note) and Pushkin's accounts, which differ between themselves on a number of points each of the participants wanted to draw their superiors' attention to.

82. See *FRUS, 1961–1963,* vol. 24, 417, 427–428.

83. Georgii Pushkin-W. Averell Harriman, memorandum of conversation, October 25, 1961, AVP RF, f. 0445, op. 1, p. 1, d. 5, l. 62.

84. W. Averell Harriman to Department of State, diplomatic cable, October 10, 1961, *FRUS, 1961–1963,* vol. 24, 460.

85. Another example of Moscow's eagerness can be found in a conversation between Soviet deputy foreign minister Vasilii Kuznetzov and British ambassador Frank Roberts about the Laotian problem. Kuznetzov "said with great emphasis that Soviet Union wanted to settle this problem and had no desire get involved in commitments in that part of world." See Llewellyn Thompson to the Department of State, November 8, 1961, Library of Congress, Manuscript Division, Papers of W. Averell Harriman (Harriman papers), Special Files: Public Service, Trips and Missions, box 529, folder Laos Conference: Chronological Files, Nov. 1961.

86. Zhai, *China and the Vietnam Wars, 1950–1975,* 106.

87. In his report to the collegium of the Soviet Foreign Ministry, Georgii Pushkin mentioned the following principal outcomes of the Geneva conference on Laos: "1. One of the most dangerous armed conflicts that threatened to grow from local into a large international conflict is liquidated. . . . 2. . . . The settlement of the Laotian problem opens the way for negotiations with the United States on other, more complicated international issues." Pushkin, "On the Activities of the Soviet Delegation," l. 278.

88. Meeting of the delegations of the USSR, PRC, DRV, and PPR, record of meeting, October 13, 1961, AVP RF, f. 0445, op. 1, p. 1, d. 6, l. 109.

89. Georgii Pushkin-Nguyen Co Thach, memorandum of conversation, October 10, 1961, AVP RF, f. 0445, op. 1, p. 1, d. 3, l. 40.

90. R. L. Khamidullin (Soviet attaché)-Khamphay Bufa (Laotian representative in DRV), memorandum of conversation, November 11, 1961, RGANI, f. 5, op. 49, d. 446, l. 254.

91. Suren Tovmasyan (Soviet ambassador)-members of the CC of the People's Party of Laos, memorandum of conversation, December 2, 1961, Ibid., l. 256.

92. AVP RF, f. 0570, op. 7, p. 5, d. 15, ll. 139–140.

93. See Zhai, *China and the Vietnam Wars, 1950–1975,* 111.

94. AVP RF, f. 0445, op. 1, p. 1, d. 6, l. 184.

95. Lall, *How Communist China Negotiates,* 178–179.

96. Harriman reported on a November 29 meeting with his Soviet and British counterparts: "We consider all agreements are tentative until we have united Lao delegation to speak for Lao Gov[ernmen]t, otherwise insult to Lao sovereignty." Harriman papers, Special Files: Public Service, Trips and Missions, box 529, Laos Conference: Chronological Files, Nov. 1961.

97. Pushkin, "On the Activities of the Soviet Delegation," l. 281.

98. Nikolai Sudarikov (Soviet chargé d'affaires)-Jie Penfei, memorandum of conversation, December 11, 1961, RGANI, f. 5, op. 49, d. 436, l. 245.

99. William Sullivan to W. Averell Harriman, memorandum, December 20, 1961, *FRUS, 1961–1963,* vol. 24, 543.

100. "Phoumi said he was too deeply shocked by defeatist policy of US to carry on. US was treating RLG like a small child, saying just give in here (concede Souvanna only Prime Minister-designate) and then a little more here (do Souvanna work for him to form a govt) and then final straw (Defense and Interior for Souvanna). US policy is completely downhill into communism." U.S. Embassy in Laos to Department of State, diplomatic cable, December 31, 1961, *FRUS, 1961–1963,* vol. 24, 551–552.

101. U.S. embassy in Laos to the Department of State, diplomatic cable, January 4, 1962, Ibid., 554–555.

102. Zhai, *China and the Vietnam Wars, 1950–1975,* 104.

103. Ang, *Vietnamese Communists' Relations,* 217.

104. Zhai, *China and the Vietnam Wars, 1950–1975,* 104.

105. Thee, *Notes of a Witness,* 240.

106. Ibid., 242.

107. Ibid.

108. Ang Cheng Guan referred to a report by the British ambassador in Laos about Soviet ambassador Abramov's "great efforts to persuade Souphanouvong to turn off the military pressure at Nam Tha" as proof of the Soviet general opposition to the military operation. However, it is unclear whether the British learned about these efforts from independent sources or from Abramov himself. If Abramov was the source, it is quite possible that the Soviets just wanted to put a brave face on a sorry business, trying to present themselves before the West as opponents of the violations of the cease-fire while tacitly approving the operation. Otherwise, the question arises of why, in its letter addressed directly to the DRV leadership, Moscow did not make efforts to dissuade Hanoi. See Ang, *Vietnamese Communists' Relations,* 218.

109. "The President wanted to be certain that Ambassador Brown had clear instructions to reiterate to Phoumi that what had happened at Nam Tha was exactly what we had told him to expect as a result of his intransigence in the negotiations." Winthrop Brown-John F. Kennedy, memorandum of conversation, May 8, 1962, *FRUS, 1961–1963,* vol. 24, 722.

110. Robert Kennedy (U.S. attorney general)-Anatolii Dobrynin (Soviet ambassador to the United States), memorandum of conversation, May 9, 1962, Ibid., 726.

111. For the text of the statement of the Laotian government incorporated into the Declaration on the Neutrality of Laos signed by the fourteen states participating in the conference, see *Documents relating to British Involvement,* 178–181.

112. W. Averell Harriman-Ung Van Khiem-James Barrington (under secretary for foreign affairs of Burma), memorandum of conversation, July 22, 1962, *FRUS, 1961–1963,* vol. 24, 867–868.

113. Ibid., 868.

114. Ibid., 869.

115. Ibid., 870.

116. Ibid.

117. "South Vietnam," review memorandum, May 19, 1962, AVP RF, f. 079, op. 17, p. 36, d. 18, ll. 35–36.

118. In his conversations with the U.S. ambassador, Llewellyn Thompson, in July 1962, Khrushchev "expressed great satisfaction at the settlement of the Laos problem and said both he and President Kennedy had honestly carried out their promises." See U.S. Embassy in the Soviet Union to the Department of State, diplomatic cable, July 26, 1962, *FRUS, 1961–1963,* vol. 5, 467.

119. During a conversation after the Laos conference, Soviet ambassador Anatolii Dobrynin, replying to Harriman's information "that President Kennedy had issued instructions to all concerned that we should adhere to the agreement in the spirit as well as the letter," assured his counterpart that "he knew Khrushchev felt the same way about it." See Anatolii Dobrynin-W. Averell Harriman, memorandum of conversation (draft), August 1, 1962, Harriman papers, Special Files: Public Service, Subject File: USSR, box 518, folder Memcons.

120. Thee, *Notes of a Witness,* 329. Not only the Chinese and North Vietnamese were disappointed with the policy the Soviet Union adopted with respect to Laos. Marek Thee, a Polish diplomat, did not conceal his disdain when he referred to it in his memoirs.

121. Heads of delegations of USSR, PRC, DRV and PPR, record of meeting, May 15, 1961, AVP RF, f. 0445, op. p. d. 1, l. 18.

122. Thee, *Notes of a Witness,* 285.

123. See, for example, Harriman's memorandum to Kennedy with a proposal to raise to Pushkin the possibility of discussing the issue of Vietnam within the framework of the Geneva conference on Laos in: U.S. Department of State, *FRUS, 1961–1963: Vietnam 1961,* vol. 1 (Washington, D.C.: U.S. Government Printing Office, 1988), 580–582.

124. Roger Warner, *Shooting at the Moon: The Story of America's Clandestine War in Laos* (South Royalton, Vt: Steerforth Press, 1996), 76.

Notes to Chapter 9

1. A book putting forth this thesis is John Newman's *JFK and Vietnam: Deception, Intrigue, and the Struggle for Power* (New York: Warner Books, 1992). See also David Kaiser, *American Tragedy* (Harvard: Harvard University Press, 2000), which develops Newman's theses. Another book that can be regarded as a continuation of the discussion is Harvey Neese and John O'Donnell, eds., *Prelude to Tragedy: Vietnam, 1960–1965* (Annapolis, Md.: Naval Institute Press, 2001). It is based on recollections of participants in the events, and on page 2 (emphasis added) it states:

> [I]f U.S. decision makers had sought and followed the advice of experts like General Lansdale and others who are represented by the contributing writers of this book, then the Buddhist crisis, the coup against President Diem, the subsequent disintegration of the Vietnamese government at all levels and the massive introduction of U.S. combat troops, beginning in 1965, might never have taken place. The real tragedy of the Vietnam War is that *it didn't have to happen.*

2. For the most recent example of the consistency-of-policy argument, see Fredrik Logevall, *Choosing War: The Lost Chance for Peace and the Escalation of War in Vietnam* (Berkeley: University of California Press, 1999).

3. Gary R. Hess, "Commitment in the Age of Counterinsurgency: Kennedy's Vietnam Options and Decisions, 1961–1963," in *Shadow on the White House: Presidents and the Vietnam War, 1945–1975,* ed. David L. Anderson (Lawrence: University Press of Kansas, 1993), 69.

4. Robert S. McNamara, *In Retrospect: The Tragedy and Lessons of Vietnam,* with Brian VanDeMark (New York: Times Books, 1995), 29.

5. Brian VanDeMark, "A Way of Thinking: The Kennedy Administration's Initial Assumptions about Vietnam and Their Consequences," in *Vietnam: The Early Decisions,* eds. Lloyd C. Gardner and Ted Gittinger (Austin: University of Texas Press, 1997), 26–27.

6. VanDeMark writes, "Kennedy chose to seek a neutralized Laos through negotiations . . . because of political and military difficulties. That decision and the Bay of Pigs fiasco in April 1961 made it seem imperative to stand firm elsewhere in Southeast Asia." Ibid., 27.

7. McNamara, *In Retrospect,* 32.

8. Paul W. Blackstock, *The Strategy of Subversion: Manipulating the Politics of Other Nations* (Chicago: Quadrangle Books, 1964), 38, 39.

9. Newman, *JFK and Vietnam,* 30–33.

10. Cited in William J. Rust, *Kennedy in Vietnam* (New York: Scribner, 1985), 70.

11. VanDeMark, "A Way of Thinking," 31.

12. Cited in Logevall, *Choosing War,* 73.

13. For details of these decisions, see Newman, *JFK and Vietnam,* 127–139; Rust, *Kennedy in Vietnam,* 52.

14. For the outcome of the strategic hamlet program, see Kolko, *Anatomy of War,* 132–133.

15. *FRUS, 1952–1954,* vol. 13, part 2, 1860.

16. Ang, *Vietnamese Communists' Relations,* 213.

17. McNamara, *In Retrospect,* 96. It is noteworthy that even the Soviet ambassador to the United States, Anatolii Dobrynin, who had a first-hand view of the developments in Washington in those crucial years, believed that Kennedy would have eventually disengaged from Vietnam. At least, he contrasts Kennedy, "who seemed to have been considering a withdrawal of his troops," with Johnson, "who became more deeply involved in the conflict and hoped to settle it from a position of strength." See Anatoly Dobrynin, *In Confidence: Moscow's Ambassador to America's Six Cold War Presidents (1962–1986)* (New York: Times Books, 1995), 119.

18. For the contents of Khrushchev's speech see *Communism—Peace and Happiness for the Peoples,* vol. 1, January–September 1961 (Moscow: Foreign Languages Publishing House, 1963), 37–45. The U.S. intelligence community, in its "Current Intelligence Weekly Review," drew the attention of U.S. policymakers to the fact that although a manifestation of a "more aggressive program in all 'colonial' areas," the speech "evaded the question—on which the Chinese have charged Khrushchev with timidity—of whether bloc support to 'liberation' forces will go so far as to risk military clashes with the West. Similarly, in distinguishing a fourth category of wars—'national uprisings' such as Castro's—and in stating his expectation of and favor for such uprisings, Khrushchev declared that such wars must not become wars between states. . . ." *FRUS, 1961–1963,* vol. 5, 40–41.

19. USSR embassy in DRV, "Aggravation of the Internal Political Situation in South

Vietnam," political letter, October 10, 1961, AVP RF, f. 079, op. 16, p. 31, d. 3, ll. 22, 23.

20. A Vietnam task force was set up on Kennedy's order in April 1961 for reviewing U.S. Vietnam policy and working out recommendations for the government; Sterling Cottrell of the State Department was its director. See Newman, *JFK and Vietnam,* 35, 60.

21. USSR embassy, "Aggravation of the Internal Political Situation," ll. 25–26.

22. Ibid., l. 32.

23. Ibid., l. 33.

24. Ibid., l. 34.

25. USSR Foreign Ministry to Suren A. Tovmasyan (Soviet ambassador to the DRV), diplomatic communication, top secret, December 7, 1961, AVP RF, f. 079, op. 16, p. 31, d. 3, ll. 59–60.

26. Ibid., l. 61.

27. Nikita S. Khrushchev to John F. Kennedy, letter, November 10, 1961, *FRUS, 1961–1963,* vol. 6, 60.

28. Maxwell Taylor to John F. Kennedy, letter, November 3, 1961, *FRUS, 1961–1963,* vol. 1, 532.

29. Robert S. McNamara to John F. Kennedy, draft memorandum, November 5, 1961, Ibid., 538. For the discussion of this recommendation by National Security Council, see Johnson Library, Papers of L. B. Johnson President, 1963–1969, Vice-Presidential Security File, box 4.

30. Hess, "Commitment in the Age of Counterinsurgency," 74.

31. Southeast Asia Department, USSR Foreign Ministry, "Toward the Situation in South Vietnam," memorandum, December 19, 1961, AVP RF, f. 079, op. 16, p. 33, d. 20, ll. 100–101.

32. According to British sources, economic aid from the Soviet Union and Eastern Europe for North Vietnam in 1961 was greater than that from China; see Ang, *Vietnamese Communists' Relations,* 183.

33. USSR embassy in DRV, "Some Issues of Activities of the WPV CC after the 1960 Moscow Conference of Communist and Workers' Parties," political letter, October 17, 1961, AVP RF, f. 079, op. 16, p. 31, d. 3, l. 37.

34. Ang, *Vietnamese Communists' Relations,* 193.

35. *Pravda,* June 28, 1961.

36. "'Ia veriu v velichie starshego brata.' Besedy N. S. Khrushcheva s Kho Shi Minom" ("'I believe in the greatness of the elder brother.' Conversations of N. S. Khrushchev with Ho Chi Minh"), *Istochnik* 2 (1998): 76–91.

37. USSR embassy, "Some Issues," l. 41.

38. USSR embassy, "Aggravation of the Internal Political Situation," l. 33.

39. "On the Issue of Soviet-Vietnamese Relations. (Brief Memorandum on the Activities of the Referentura on the DRV)," March 1962, AVP RF, f. 079, op. 17, p. 36, d. 19, l. 1.

40. National Intelligence Estimate, January 17, 1961, *FRUS, 1961–1963,* vol. 5, 17.

41. USSR embassy in PRC, "On the Combination of Internationalism and Nationalism in the CCP's Foreign Activities," memorandum, September 30, 1961, RGANI, f. 5, op. 49, d. 435, ll. 194, 210, 227.

42. Fejtö, *Chine-URSS,* 14–15.

43. USSR embassy, "Some Issues," ll. 42–44.

44. USSR embassy in DRV, "Some Aspects of Sino-Vietnamese Relations," memorandum, April 10, 1962, AVP RF, f. 079, op. 17, p. 36, d. 19, l. 15.

45. Ibid., l. 12.

46. Ang, *Vietnamese Communists' Relations,* 210–211.

47. Zhai, *China and the Vietnam Wars,* 113.

48. USSR embassy, "Some Aspects of Vietnamese-Chinese Relations," l. 10.

49. Nikita S. Khrushchev-Ho Chi Minh, memorandum of conversation, August 19, 1961, Archive of the President of the Russian Federation, f. 3, op. 64, d. 560, ll. 140–165; published in *Istochnik* 2 (1998): 88.

50. USSR embassy, "Some Aspects of the Vietnamese-Chinese Relations," l. 5.

51. Ibid., l. 23.

52. USSR embassy in DRV, "Some Issues," l. 48.

53. USSR embassy, "Some Aspects of Vietnamese-Chinese Relations," l. 9.

54. Honey, *Communism in North Vietnam,* 109.

55. For example, Ung Van Khiem and Duong Bac Mai during a visit to the DRV of a delegation of the Chinese parliament headed by Peng Zhen. See USSR embassy in DRV, "Visit to the DRV of the PRC Parliamentary Delegation," memorandum, November 23, 1962, AVP RF, f. 079, op. 17, p. 36, d. 19, l. 140.

56. Southeast Asia Department, USSR Foreign Ministry, "Soviet-Vietnamese Relations," memorandum, June 2, 1962, AVP RF, f. 079, op. 17, p. 35, d. 13, l. 41.

57. Nikita S. Khrushchev-Ho Chi Minh, memorandum of conversation, August 19, 1961, *Istochnik* 2 (1998): 90.

58. Cited in Logevall, *Choosing War,* 19.

59. Georgii Pushkin-Zhang Hanfu, memorandum of conversation, July 11, 1961, AVP RF, f. 0445, op. 1, p. 1, d. 2, ll. 113–114.

60. A. Ye. Nesterenko (counsellor of Soviet mission at UN)-Louis Dauge (French representative to UN), memorandum of conversation, December 25, 1960, AVP RF, f. 0570, op. 6, p. 3, d. 7, l. 199.

61. Logevall, *Choosing War,* 8.

62. Lall, *How Communist China Negotiates* (New York: Columbia University Press, 1968), 180.

63. Southeast Asia Department, USSR Foreign Ministry, "On the Perspective Questions of the SEAD," memorandum, January 6, 1962, AVP RF, f. 079, op. 17, p. 35, d. 13, l. 2.

64. Directives to USSR ambassador in DRV, draft, top secret, January 22, 1962, AVP RF, f. 079, op. 17, p. 35, d. 13, l. 14.

65. D. Chuvakhin (acting head of Southeast Asia Department) to Nikolai Firyubin (deputy foreign minister), memorandum, January 12, 1962, Ibid., l. 8.

66. Anatolii Chistyakov and Suren Tovmasyan to Georgii Pushkin, memorandum, August 1962, AVP RF, f. 079, op. 17, p. 35, d . 13, l. 68. Emphasis added.

67. Ibid., l. 70. Emphasis added.

68. For the fullest recent account of examples of Hanoi's activities as reported by Western diplomats see Logevall, *Choosing War,* 8–10. Western scholars, even "authorities" on Hanoi's strategy in the war among them, continue to be trapped by North Vietnamese propaganda in favor of negotiations in the early 1960s. On the basis of indirect evidence—for example, Le Duan's instructions to the southern Communist guerrillas to

avoid a major escalation of war against the Diem regime—these Western scholars have concluded that peaceful settlement of the Vietnam war was possible at that time. See William J. Duiker, *U.S. Containment Policy and the Conflict in Indochina* (Stanford: Stanford University Press, 1994), 287; Logevall, *Choosing War,* 8, 425n.

69. Anatolii Chistyakov, "Toward the Question of South Vietnam: Introductory Remarks," memorandum, December 25, 1962, AVP RF, f. 079, op. 17, p. 36, d. 18, l. 223.

70. S. A. Mkhitarian and T. T. Mkhitarian, *V'etnamskaya revolutziia: voprosy teorii i praktiki* (The Vietnamese revolution: Questions of theory and practice) (Moscow: Nauka, 1986), 218.

71. Ibid. On the basis of Ho Chi Minh's letter, the Southeast Asia Department of the USSR Foreign Ministry formulated the objectives that Hanoi pursued in its policy toward South Vietnam. The first objective was a general uprising that would lead to the establishment of Communist authority in the country. An alternative was a coalition government. A Geneva conference on Vietnam followed in third place.

72. Zhai, *China and the Vietnam Wars,* 116.

73. Directives to USSR ambassador in DRV.

74. SarDesai, *Indian Foreign Policy,* 206.

75. Honey, *Communism in North Vietnam,* 116.

76. USSR embassy in DRV, "Activities of the International Control Commission in Vietnam (March 1961–July 1962)," memorandum, August 30, 1962, AVP RF, f. 079, op. 17, p. 36, d. 19, ll. 84–85, 87.

77. USSR embassy, "Aggravation of the Internal Political Situation," ll. 28–29. On the establishment and immediate goals of the NLFSV, see Truong Nhu Tang, *A Vietcong Memoir,* writ. with David Chanoff and Doan Van Toai (New York: Vintage Books, 1986), 68, 73, 78.

78. "Proposals on the Further Development of Political, Economic, and Cultural Relations with the DRV and on the Settlement of International Problems," memorandum, September 5, 1962, AVP RF, f. 079, op. 17, p. 35, d. 13, l. 76.

79. USSR embassy in DRV, "The National Liberation Front of South Vietnam and its Struggle against the Diem Regime and American Involvement in 1962," report, December 14, 1962, AVP RF, f. 079, op. 17, p. 36, d. 18, ll. 140–146.

80. Report of the Soviet Afro-Asian Solidarity Committee on the visit to the Soviet Union of the NLFSV delegation, August 16, 1962, AVP RF, f. 079, op. 17, p. 36, d. 20, l. 51.

81. Ibid., l. 52.

82. USSR embassy in DRV, "The Visits of the Delegation of the National Liberation Front of South Vietnam to the DRV," report, November 4, 1962, AVP RF, f. 079, op. 17, p. 36, d. 19, l. 115.

83. There exists an impressive Western literature on the Cuban missile crisis. For a recent account of the events of the crisis and their impact on Soviet decision making afterward based on documents from Russian archives, see Aleksandr Fursenko and Timothy Naftali, *One Hell of a Gamble: Khrushchev, Castro, and Kennedy, 1958–1964* (New York: Norton, 1997).

84. Symptoms of the discontent among party members were noticed by U.S. diplomats in Moscow, who reported on them to the State Department. On the basis of their reports, former ambassador to the Soviet Union Llewellyn Thompson wrote to Dean Rusk: "I think there is indeed some possibility that Khrushchev is in some trouble at home. I think

it unlikely that this could be serious enough to lead to his removal, although this cannot be excluded, but it is probably serious enough to mean that he will have to be circumspect in his actions during the next few months." See memorandum from Ambassador-at-Large Llewellyn Thompson to Secretary of State Dean Rusk, March 2, 1963, *FRUS, 1961–1963*, vol. 5, 639.

85. Southeast Asia Department, "Toward the Events in South Vietnam," memorandum, April 14, 1962, AVP RF, f. 079, op. 17, p. 36, d. 18, ll. 13–14.

86. Zhai, *China and the Vietnam Wars*, 117.

87. Cited in Honey, *Communism in North Vietnam*, 155–156.

88. Ibid., 155.

89. Zhai, *China and the Vietnam Wars*, 124–125.

90. Logevall, *Choosing War*, 6.

91. "Memorandum of conversation, August 30, 1963," in U.S. Department of State, *FRUS, 1961–1963: Vietnam, August–December 1963*, vol. 4 (Washington, D.C.: U.S. Government Printing Office, 1991), 55.

92. Logevall, *Choosing War*, 14–15. The diplomat's surname was probably misspelled in Logevall's book as Laloulette. According to the CIA, Lalouette was even acting as a channel between Ngo Dinh Nhu and Pham Van Dong; see *FRUS, 1961–1963*, vol. 4, 89.

93. CIA station in Saigon to Washington, cable, September, 6, 1963, *FRUS, 1961–1963*, vol. 4, 125.

94. Mieczyslaw Maneli, *War of the Vanquished* (New York: Harper and Row, 1971), 126–129.

95. Memorandum prepared for the Director of Central Intelligence, September 26, 1963, *FRUS, 1961–1963*, vol. 4, 296.

96. Logevall, *Choosing War*, 7.

97. Anatolii Chistyakov (head of Southeast Asia Department, USSR Foreign Ministry), "Toward the Question of South Vietnam. Introductory Notes," memorandum, December 25, 1962, AVP RF, f. 079, op. 17, p. 36, d. 18, l. 223.

98. See Newman, *JFK and Vietnam*, 345–351.

99. Maneli, *War of the Vanquished*, 126–129.

100. Logevall, *Choosing War*, 17.

101. Ibid., 72–73.

102. McNamara, *In Retrospect*, 83–84. Kennedy did not want Diem's murder. The U.S. objective was only his removal from power. McNamara wrote about Kennedy's reaction to the news about the coup: "When President Kennedy received the news, he literally blanched. I had never seen him so moved." Other Kennedy associates confirmed this. See, for example, Schlesinger, *Thousand Days*, 909–910.

103. Mkhitarian and Mkhitarian, *Vietnamskaiia revolutsiia*, 220.

104. Zhai, *China and the Vietnam Wars*, 125.

105. Main Intelligence Directorate of USSR Ministry of Defense (GRU) to the CPSU CC, report, April 7, 1967, RGANI, f. 5, op. 59, d. 327, p. 152.

106. Maneli, *War of the Vanquished*, 174–175. The Polish commissioner's barely concealed gloating that is evident in this description is somewhat off the point. The situations were different. Unlike in Warsaw, Prague, and Budapest, Moscow was not very much alarmed at the time by its decreasing influence in Vietnam. Moreover, Moscow's loss of influence was to a considerable degree preordained owing to the lack of Soviet

interest in Southeast Asia, a region less strategically important to the Kremlin than Eastern Europe.

107. Xiaoming Zhang, "Communist Powers Divided: China, the Soviet Union, and the Vietnam War" in *International Perspectives on Vietnam,* eds. Lloyd C. Gardner and Ted Gittinger (College Station: Texas A&M University Press, 2000), 83–84.

108. Moscow to the Soviet ambassador in Paris, telegram, March 14, 1964, RGANI, f. 4, op. 18, d. 252, St-95/462g. For details of the visit of the DRV party delegation to Moscow, see Ilya V. Gaiduk, *The Soviet Union and the Vietnam War* (Chicago: Ivan R. Dee, 1996), 6–9.

Notes to Conclusion

1. McNamara, *In Retrospect,* 113.

2. Logevall, *Choosing War,* 78–79.

3. Cited in Lloyd C. Gardner, *Pay Any Price: Lyndon Johnson and the Wars for Vietnam* (Chicago: Ivan Dee, 1995), 87.

4. For a recent account of U.S. covert operations against North Vietnam, see Kenneth Conboy and Dale Andradé, *Spies and Commandos: How America Lost the Secret War in North Vietnam* (Lawrence: University Press of Kansas, 2000).

5. Henry Cabot Lodge Jr. (U.S. ambassador in South Vietnam) complained that OPLAN 34A did not even bother the North Vietnamese enough to make them protest openly. Edwin E. Moïse, *Tonkin Gulf and the Escalation of the Vietnam War* (Chapel Hill: University of North Carolina Press, 1996), 22.

6. McNamara, *In Retrospect,* 114.

7. For the fullest account to date of the events in the Gulf of Tonkin and their consequences, see Moïse, *Tonkin Gulf.*

8. See U.S. Department of State, *FRUS, 1964–1968, Vietnam 1964,* vol. 1 (Washington, D.C.: U.S. Government Printing Office, 1992), 637.

9. Douglas Pike, *Vietnam and the Soviet Union: Anatomy of an Alliance* (Boulder: Westview Press, 1987), 45.

10. Llewellyn Thompson, U.S. ambassador to Moscow, reported on his February 1967 conversation with Kosygin to the State Department: "I believe this is not the first time Kosygin has mentioned that we started bombing North Vietnam without consulting him when he was in Hanoi. He brought this up in context of importance of mutual confidence. Implication is however that had we consulted him, Soviet Union would at that time have been willing to do something about North Vietnamese intervention in South." See U.S. embassy in Moscow to Secretary of State, February 23, 1967, Johnson Library, National Security File, Country File, Vietnam, box 255.

11. The principles of such an approach were fully explained in Foreign Minister Andrei Gromyko's memorandum of January 13, 1967, which was approved by the Soviet Politburo. For excerpts from this memorandum, see Dobrynin, *In Confidence,* 649–651. Dobrynin also wrote on page 144 of his memoirs that Soviet leaders

> all agreed that Vietnam and its effect on our relations with the United States were among principal issues of our foreign policy. Yet our leadership unanimously recognized that our relations with the United States were a priority, while Vietnam was not that vital to our national interests.

Index

Note: Page numbers followed by "n" indicate endnote numbers.